Socializing Capital

Socializing Capital

THE RISE OF THE LARGE
INDUSTRIAL CORPORATION
IN AMERICA

WILLIAM G. ROY

PRINCETON UNIVERSITY PRESS

PRINCETON, NEW JERSEY

Library of Congress Cataloging-in-Publication Data

Roy, William G., 1946–
Socializing capital : the rise of the large industrial
corporation in America / William G. Roy
p. cm.
Includes bibliographical references (p.) and index.
ISBN 0-691-04353-1 (alk. paper)
1. Big business—United States—History. 2. Corporations—United States—
Finance—History. 3. Industrial policy—United States—History.
4. Capitalism—United States—History. 5. Social structure—United States—
History. 6. Rich people—United States—History. 7. Power
(Social sciences—United States—History. I. Title.
HD2785.R598   1996
338.6'44'0973—dc20   96-8672 CIP

This book has been composed in Sabon

Princeton University Press books are printed on acid-free paper and meet the guidelines for
permanence and durability of the Committee on Production Guidelines for Book
Longevity of the Council on Library Resources

Printed in the United States of America by Princeton Academic Press

1 2 3 4 5 6 7 8 9 10

FOR MY PARENTS

JAMES AND NONA ROY

WHO TAUGHT ME TO BE CURIOUS

ABOUT THE WORLD AND TO CARE

ABOUT THE PEOPLE IN IT

CONTENTS

FIGURES

TABLES

HISTORICAL SOCIOLOGY seeks to understand how the world we live in was constructed. Just as we cannot intimately know a person until we know his or her childhood, it is difficult to understand a society until we know its history. Few features of contemporary American society are more far-reaching or awesome than its large industrial corporations, the largest of which command more resources than the majority of nations in the world, employ more people than live in many cities, and shape our daily life more thoroughly than previously dominant institutions such as religion. This book asks why large American industrial corporations arose when they did, how they did, and where they did. Scholars in many disciplines have addressed this question, and their answers reflect some of the fundamental debates across and within sociology, history, economics, political science, and geography. The prevailing answer, which I characterize as efficiency theory, holds that large industrial corporations arose because they were more efficient than competing forms, an explanation that assumes that rational decision making, market processes of exchange, and technological development underlie economic activity. In contrast to efficiency as the fundamental determinant, I focus on power, not as a motivation for action—I am not trying to revive the debate over whether the first generation of corporate officials were robber barons or captains of industry—but as an explanatory concept for social relations. The two master concepts start with different questions. An efficiency theory asks why an organizational form like the corporation is more efficient than the partnerships and proprietorships that it replaced. A power theory begins with the question of who acted to transform one property regime into another and investigates how capital was reconfigured from the individual to the social level. I am not saying that efficiency theory is absolutely wrong or that there is nothing to learn from the scholars that have adopted its framework. Rather, the conditions under which efficiency might explain why one organizational form replaces another are (a) rare, and (b) did not exist in late nineteenth-century America. My argument is fundamentally historical: markets, selective processes of organizational change, and technological development, along with predatory monopolies, economic domination, and waste, wax and wane historically, and require historical explanation.

I began this study by focusing on the period around the turn of the century, hoping to understand the kind of institutional earthquake that transformed a society in 1890 with fewer than ten large publicly owned manufacturing corporations into one that by 1905 was dominated by many of the corporate giants that continue to reign. Most earlier authors aimed to explain the decision to adopt the corporate form, an approach that led them to focus on the corporation's advantageous features such as limited liability or perpetual existence. But this begs the question of why the corporate form was there to adopt and why it had the characteristics it did. Answering that pushed my analysis back further. As others have emphasized, the corporation was not created in the form that was adopted during the corporate revolution; it began as a quasi-public agency created by states to perform public services such as building turnpikes or canals, for which states vested it with special privileges such as limited liability. So the first historical puzzle is how the corporation was transformed from an extension of state power into the quintessence of private property, a sanctuary from government authority. It became clear that the explanation is not merely economic, but that the history of the corporation requires us to understand how the modern boundaries between the political and the economic were constituted. I focus on the political processes that created the corporate institution commonly known as "Wall Street." Its development presents a second historical puzzle. Although by the 1870s the corporate institution, including investment banks, brokerage houses, business press, and other components, existed much as it does today, it remained confined to transportation and communication until the turn of the century. Why did manufacturing remain institutionally separate from the corporate system for so long? And why was the corporate revolution so explosive when it finally occurred?

My analysis touches other currents in sociology. The social constructionists ask how taken-for-granted categories, structures, and assumptions have been historically developed; they reject the notion that such things as race, gender, markets, or the nature of time and space are fixed in nature and insist that their very constitution must be explained. The "new economic sociology" and the "new institutionalism" in organizations have brought the social constructionist approach to the study of the corporation per se. I align myself with the general spirit of those perspectives, tempered with a healthy dose of political sociology's emphasis on power. Indeed, if I must characterize my perspective in these terms, I would call this work a political sociology of the corporation.

But most fundamentally, my perspective is sociological. Although one recent line of thought has brought utilitarian assumptions, deductive logic, and evolutionary functionalism from economics into other social sciences, sociologists have in the last decade or so more forcefully asserted that political and economic life can be analyzed with the same fundamental concepts—interaction, power, cooperation, organization, division of labor, and so on—as the rest of social life. In other words, the boundaries between the social sciences are becoming less a matter of the topic examined than a matter of the conceptual tools and logical reasoning employed. This book aims to offer a more vitally sociological explanation of how the American corporate institution developed.

Until one writes a book, the litany of people typically acknowledged in books cannot be fully comprehended. When one does, it becomes patently clear how social the authorship of a book is. The community of scholars does more than exchange finished products. The finished products are the fruits that we collectively harvest. I have the privilege of claiming one tree as mine, but it was planted and nurtured by a broad group of indispensable and talented individuals. The National Science Foundation generously funded the collection of the quantitative data in Chapter 2 (SES 86 17679). Research assistants on various phases have included Jody Borrelli, Leslie Dwyer, Gail Livings, Rachel Parker-Gwin, Blake Rummel, and Teri Shumate. Nabil-El Ghourney volunteered his time as part of UCLA's Student Research Project and Cathrine Y. Lee worked in the Summer Minority Research Program. Although Rachel Parker-Gwin was employed as a research assistant, her contribution far transcends the label. From initial formulation to tidying up grammar and everything in between, she was a true colleague, improving every facet of the project. The staff of UCLA's Inter-Library Loan program spent many patient hours tracking down and procuring obscure historical sources, while the staff of the Social Science Computing facility made the data analysis easier. My greatest intellectual debts are to my generous and gifted colleagues who read part or all of the manuscript. Peter Carstensen, William Forbath, Patricia Harrington, and Frank Munger offered their expert opinions on the legal chapter. Craig Calhoun allowed me to work out some of my early ideas in an article published in his *Comparative Social Research* annual reader. The Macrosociology Research Seminar at UCLA over the years has provided a level of feedback far beyond what one would normally expect. Peter Dougherty, my editor at Princeton University Press, has enthusiastically supported the project from its conception. Good editors make for better books, and I have been lucky to have one of the best. Elizabeth Gretz's copyediting improved readability. Frank Dobbin, Neil Fligstein, Mark Mizruchi, Karen O'Neill, Charles Perrow, Michael Schwartz, and anonymous reviewers gave the best of feedback—minutely detailed, unflinchingly tough, impressively insightful, and consistently constructive. The book is much better for their effort. The careful reader will see the imprint of two scholars in particular. Maurice Zeitlin, my colleague at UCLA, has been a prodder, supporter, inspiration, critic, and friend. Chuck Tilly, my dissertation adviser at the University of Michigan, has continued to offer his wisdom, brilliance, and example to this project. And although even careful readers could not detect it, every page manifests the congenial and collegial shadow of my wife Alice, not the long-suffering supporter that sometimes appears in acknowledgments, but the scholar and partner that authors should hope for. Any errors or omission that the reader may find are no doubt due to my stubbornness or ignorance, not the careful work of all these distinguished colleagues and friends.

Socializing Capital

CHAPTER ONE

Introduction

IN THE FIRST YEAR of this century, a group of bankers led by the venerable J. P. Morgan and a group of steel men created the U.S. Steel Corporation, America's first billion-dollar corporation. Built around the core of the former Carnegie Steel Company, U.S. Steel merged nearly all major producers of iron, steel, and coke. Public opinion at the time focused on its mammoth size and its potential monopoly power. Looking back, we recognize it as a symbol of a broader movement that we now metaphorically but appropriately call the "corporate revolution." As in political revolutions, the economic changes that came to a head in these years were cataclysmic and far reaching. Like the transformations in France, Russia, or China, the corporate revolution had been brewing from slower, evolutionary changes, but was triggered by a set of events unanticipated by most of the participants. The nature of this revolution, its causes and consequences, have been energetically debated in both academic and popular circles, often with thinly veiled ideological overtones. But all agree that the corporate revolution was a major watershed in American history. The period at the turn of the twentieth century marked the transformation from one way of life to another, from a society based on rural, agrarian, local, small-scale, individual relations to one based on urban, industrial, national, large-scale, and organizational relations. At the heart of this was the rise of the large industrial corporation, which has continued to cast its shadow over all society ever since.

Americans recognized U.S. Steel as a milestone even if they did not realize all its historical ramifications. Only twenty years earlier, an entity like U.S. Steel would have been implausible. Although the institutional structure of corporate capitalism, including the stock market, investment banks, brokerage houses, and the financial press had been operating for decades, it was confined almost entirely to government bonds, transportation, and communication. The large, publicly traded *manufacturing* corporation was rare.

The large manufacturing corporation, unusual before 1890, became the dominant mode of business organization in two major steps. The first was the creation of the large private business corporate institution itself, its origins as a quasi-government agency and its metamorphosis into private property. The historical question is how an organizational form constituted as an extension of state power to accomplish publicly useful projects was transformed into a sanctuary from state power as the institutional basis of private accumulation. This was achieved in the 1870s. But until the century's end, the corporate institutional structure was confined to those arenas of economic life that Western governments have generally claimed special jurisdiction over, namely, infrastructural sectors of transportation, communication, and finance.

The second step was the extension of the corporate institutional structure into manufacturing. As late as 1890, fewer than ten manufacturing securities were traded on the major stock exchanges, and most of those, like Pullman's Palace Car Company were closely associated with the railroad (*Manual of Statistics* 1890). The world of manufacturing and the world of finance capital were institutionally distinct. Investors considered manufacturing companies too risky and industrialists resisted surrendering control to outsiders (Navin and Sears 1955; Carosso 1970). To be sure, there were large corporations. The hundred-million-dollar Pennsylvania Railroad was the largest company in the world. And there were large manufacturing companies. Carnegie Steel Company, an unincorporated limited partnership, was the largest manufacturing operation in the world (Wall 1989). The institutional structures of those two giants, however, were distinct from each other. Industrialists created firms through personal funds, reinvested mercantile capital, and internal growth. Andrew Carnegie started his steel company from personal profits amassed speculating in railroads and built it by selling steel to railroad and locomotive companies. He had close personal relations with railroad leaders, but few institutional relations outside of market transactions (Wall 1989). As in most industrial firms, ownership was personal and confined to one or a few individuals.

Wall Street, in contrast, operated as a distinct institutional structure, following the dynamics of a speculative securities market, only indirectly related to the world of manufacturing. The stocks and bonds traded there financed railroads, telegraph, municipalities, and governments. The railroad companies which laced the country with steel rails were considered virtual money machines for local elites, who were convinced that their city would become the next St. Louis, the archetypical boom town; for the deep-pocketed foreign investors, who hoped to capture their profits from America's Manifest Destiny; and for the investment bankers and stock brokers, who enjoyed commissions from others' investments as well as reaping the profits of their own.

In the years around the turn of the century, these two institutions, the industrial world of manufacturing and the financial world of stocks and bonds, merged together in what we now call the corporate revolution, a remarkably abrupt proliferation of large manufacturing corporations from virtually nothing to economic domination. Starting from 1890, the aggregate amount of capital in publicly traded manufacturing companies crept up until 1893, when the depression stalled economic expansion, then jumped from $33 million in 1890 to $260 million the following year (see Figure 1.1). But these figures were small compared with the multibillion-dollar totals after the turn of the century. In 1901 the food industry alone totaled $210 million in common stocks (*Manual of Statistics* 1901). The

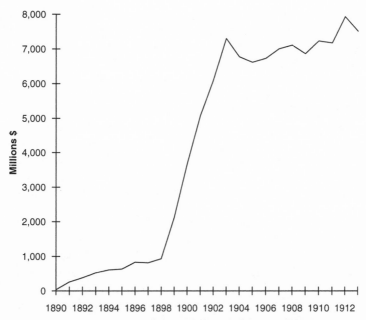

Figure 1.1. Aggregate Value of Stocks and Bonds of Corporations Listed on Major Stock Exchanges, 1890–1913. (Source: Data drawn from *Manual of Statistics*.)

major expansion began after 1897, and in 1898 almost reached a billion dollars. It doubled in 1899 to over two billion, and doubled again over the subsequent two years, and hit over seven billion dollars in 1903. It then fluctuated around the six- to seven-billion-dollar mark until the outbreak of World War I. These figures from the years 1898 to 1903 trace a major change from one economic system to another, a new corporate order in manufacturing. The total par value of manufacturing stocks and bonds listed on the major exchanges in 1904 was $6.8 billion, more than half the $11.6 billion book value of all manufacturing capital enumerated in the 1904 census (U.S. Bureau of the Census 1975, 684).[1]

The Significance of the Corporation

All agree that the events around the turn of the century were transformative and profoundly changed the nature of American society. But the nature of those changes has been vigorously debated, not only in terms of what explains the transformation, but also in terms of what is to be explained. Managerialists have described these changes as the rise of the modern business enterprise and have emphasized the internal organization of managerial structures (Chandler 1969, 1977, 1990). Historians of technology have described the inventions and practices that created the system of mass production (Piore and Sabel 1984; Hounshell 1984). Some business historians have focused on the process by which large corporations were formed through mergers (Nelson 1959; Lamoreaux 1985). Sociologists as well as historians have set the new large firms within the context of an organizational revolution in all major social institutions (Galambos 1970; Boulding 1953; Lash and Urry 1987; Perrow 1991). Organizational sociologists have emphasized the conception and structure of control over the enterprise (Fligstein 1990; Perrow 1986; Zald 1978). Marxists have analyzed the relationships between the classes within the productive process (Edwards 1979; Gordon, Edwards, and Reich 1982; Braverman 1974). All of these different perspectives identify important and consequential changes in the social dynamics of how our society creates and distributes material resources. Despite the different emphases, they address the same agenda in two ways: first, they all agree that the appearance of U.S. Steel, General Electric, American Tobacco, and similar entities marked a major transformation in the American social structure. Second, they have all participated in a major underlying debate over the extent to which the economy operates according to an economic logic based on efficiency or operates according to a social logic based on institutional arrangements, including power.

This book makes two simple claims. First, I argue that one of the most fundamental and dynamic facets of the transformation underlying the rise of entities like U.S. Steel was a shift in the form and organization of property, as constituted in major political and economic institutions. The large publicly traded corporation transformed the organization of ownership so that economic entities were each owned by many individuals rather than a few, and many individuals owned pieces of many units. This transformation socialized property, altering the basic relationships among owners, workers, managers, suppliers, and consumers. That is not to say that managerial structures, technologies, mergers, or systems of control were unimportant. Each of them had major autonomous effects, but their effects were refracted through the institutional relations of property. Second, I will argue that efficiency theory, the prevailing explanation of change in the organization of the economy, is inadequate to explain the rise of the large publicly traded industrial corporation. This chapter discusses some of the logical problems of efficiency theory; Chapter 2 demonstrates that it cannot explain variation among industries in the extent of incorporation, which its proponents assert it should be able to do. In contrast to efficiency theory, I argue that the concept of power provides a theoretically sounder and empirically more accurate foundation for understanding such economic processes as the rise of the large corporation.

The main body of this book will be a historical account of the rise of the large-scale industrial corporation in America. The discussion is based on the concepts of power, property, and institutions. From a quasi-public device used by governments to create and administer public services such as turnpikes and canals, the corporation germinated within a system of stock markets, brokerage houses, and investment banks. With railroads it shed its public accountability, then redefined its legal underpinning to redefine the nature of property, and then only when fully mature, flowered at the turn of this century into the realm of manufacturing, when many of the same giants that still dominate the American landscape were created. But before the story is told, it is necessary to clarify basic concepts.

EFFICIENCY THEORY

Although Weber's (1978) discussion of rationalization first raised the issue of the relationship between efficiency and the rise of large-scale economic enterprise early in this century, business historians and economists have developed the most influential efficiency explanations of the rise of large socially capitalized corporations in particular. Efficiency theory includes several variations that share the assumption that there is a selection process that ensures that more efficient economic forms will prevail over less efficient forms. Classical and neoclassical economics, focusing on the invisible hand of the market, describe how the independent decisions of individual buyers and sellers collectively determine what products will be produced, what technologies will be adopted, and what kinds of firms will thrive or wither. Institutional economists argue that transaction costs or institutional incentive structures (Williamson 1981; North 1981) select among competing organizational forms; they hypothesize the conditions under which firms will compete with one another in the market or join forces to create managerial hierarchies. The economic historian offering the most influential, best-known, and most formidable efficiency account of the corporate revolution is Alfred D. Chandler (1977, 1990).[2] Briefly stated, his argument is that technological changes created economies of scale, encouraging larger productive units, while vastly improved transportation and communication systems stimulated national and international markets, making it necessary to rationalize and integrate the stages of production and build extensive distribution organizations under the control of managerially administered bureaucratic hierarchies. The "visible hand" of management replaced the "invisible hand" of the market in coordinating and administering the economy. Rather than a process by which the aggregation of many actions to buy or sell products determines which products will be produced by which technologies—Adam Smith's "invisible hand"—the "visible hand" of managers makes these decisions within administrative hierarchies. Chandler summarizes the rise of "modern business enterprise":

> This institution appeared when managerial hierarchies were able to monitor and coordinate the activities of a number of business units more efficiently than did market mechanisms. It continued to grow so that these hierarchies of increasingly

professional managers might remain fully employed. It emerged and spread, however, only in those industries and sectors whose technology and markets permitted administrative coordination to be more profitable than market coordination. Because these areas were at the center of the American economy and because professional managers replaced families, financiers, or their representatives as decision makers in these areas, modern American capitalism became managerial capitalism. (1977, 11)

Chandler argues that when technological innovation increased the velocity of throughput (the speed at which raw materials move through the production process and are manufactured into finished products), firms could reduce the cost of production per unit and increase the output per worker, producing economies of scale that rendered administrative coordination more efficient than market coordination—the "visible hand" of hierarchy replacing the "invisible hand" of the market. The modern corporation was a rational innovation that performed productive tasks better than proprietorships and partnerships. This book offers an alternative analysis of the institutionalization of the large publicly traded manufacturing corporation in America.

The "new economic sociology" in the past decade, despite many variations, has been united on one basic point—a fundamental critique of efficiency theory (Granovetter 1985; Etzioni 1988; Powell and DiMaggio 1991; Friedland and Robertson 1990; Roy 1990; Fligstein 1990; Perrow 1990; Campbell, Hollingsworth, and Lindberg 1991; Jacoby 1990; Berk 1990, 1994). I would describe efficiency theory in terms that would be consistent with most who write from this perspective: according to efficiency theory, the actors that produce and distribute goods and services compete over scarce resources so that only the efficient survive. Whether efficiency is created by the adoption of productive technologies, rational organization, the ability to choose what products customers are willing to buy, or simple competency, the economic system is shaped by the structural selection of efficient actors. Thus if a product, technology, practice, or relationship arises and thrives, it must be because it is more efficient than its alternatives. Railroads arose because they were more efficient modes of transportation, factories arose because they were more efficient means of producing commodities, large factories arose because economies of scale made them more efficient than small factories, and the corporation arose because it was a more efficient organization than partnerships.

At its most basic, it is difficult to quarrel with the general formula. Ceteris paribus, when individual or organizational actors compete over scarce resources, the more efficient is most likely to prevail. I do not deny that efficiency dynamics are ever relevant or even that they might play a role in most economic processes. But the caveat, ceteris paribus, is the theory's Achilles' heel; things are almost never equal. In fact, things are often so unequal that they overwhelm efficiency considerations. Efficiency does not operate apart from other social processes like power. This problem is manifested in several ways.

1. Efficiency theory assumes a singular decision-making entity, that is, it assumes one actor assessing the advantages and disadvantages of a choice before making a decision. It interprets the creation of corporations like American Tobacco or U.S. Steel as a decision to take advantage of economies of scale and managerial hierarchies. But who is it that decides to take advantage of economies of scale? Large corporations were created by many decisions, often from many motivations. Sometimes many owners merged; often investors and promoters participated; sometimes managers were involved; and in some cases, customers, suppliers, or workers played a role. What needs to be explained is the social process by which various actors came together to negotiate their mutual and conflicting interests. Power is one of the most significant dimensions of social interaction in this process (Perrow 1981).

2. Efficiency theory only explains why actors might have been motivated to form large corporations, not why they were able to. Forming a large corporation required far greater resources than most companies could themselves mobilize, resources that were very unevenly distributed across the economy. If large corporations had been rational for manufacturing firms in 1850, they still would not have been created because those who controlled necessary resources would not have been willing to invest in them. When such corporations were formed at the turn of the century, power influenced the distribution of resources to industries where corporations were formed. Efficiency theory treats uneven availability as a flaw, an imperfect capital market that operated as an impersonal structure. I argue that power was basic to the system, highly institutionalized, and controlled by key decision makers, not a free capital market.

3. Insofar as actors do act to maximize their utilities, an explanation of change must also explain why available choices exist and why the effects of each choice follow. If an industrialist is faced with the choice of bankruptcy or merger and chooses merger, an explanation should not merely cite his rationality, but should explain why those choices and only those choices were available to him, including the actions of other businessmen that created a situation in which there was a "rational" choice to be made. The ability to determine the consequences of other people's actions is a form of power, as elaborated below.

4. Efficiency theory fits a functional logic, which implies an evolutionary process of change. Such theories are logically problematic because they explain change in terms of consequences: it is not an explanation to say that major corporations arose because they fulfilled certain functions better than other forms and that the corporation became common because it had the consequence of greater efficiency, effectiveness, and productivity. Insofar as

corporations make more efficient use of new technologies, stabilize costs in the face of high fixed costs, or increase profits, such consequences can be used as causes only under certain circumstances which do not apply here (Roy 1990). According to census figures, some industries, like glucose, became more efficient after the corporate revolution; others, like agricultural machinery or iron and steel, became less efficient.[3]

PROPERTY, POWER, AND INSTITUTIONS

While others have framed the rise of the large corporation in terms of managerial hierarchies, technological developments, mergers of smaller firms, the general growth of large organizations, the conception of internal control, and the conflict between classes, I examine major corporations as a form of property set within a broader institutional structure shaped by the dynamics of power at least as much as by efficiency. The major, publicly traded large-scale corporation constituted a new type of property, socialized property (Zeitlin 1989). Socialized property means that instead of each firm being owned by one or a few individuals, each firm became owned by many individuals, and individual owners in turn typically owned pieces of many firms.[4] In the process the social nature of property itself was transformed. The consideration of property implies a degree of inequality, that the social processes determining the shape of the economy are explainable by power, not just efficiency. Moreover, the social relations of property and the underlying dynamics of power are set within the interorganizational frameworks we know as institutions. This section sketches how the concepts of property, power, and institution shape the analysis of the corporate revolution and concludes that they intersect at the concept of social class.

Property

Property can be defined as the set of politically enforced rights, entitlements, and obligations that people have in relationship to objects and in relationship to other individuals (owners and nonowners). Rights include such things as authority to make decisions about what products to produce or whom to hire as labor, and how to dispose of a completed product. The conventional conception of property rights emphasizes that property rights limit government intrusion in the same sense that the right of free speech or religion limits the government's powers over individuals (Ryan 1987). Entitlements involve matters such as profits from the use of objects. Capitalism makes no distinction between the entitlement of using objects for oneself and regulating how others may use objects that one owns. A factory or leased land are legally equivalent to one's clothes or residence. Obligations are a matter of accountability concerning objects, especially liability for injuries suffered while using objects or debts incurred while using them. Although courts, especially in this century, have tightened the liability that owners have concerning injury related to their property, the corporation's limited liability has shielded owners from any risk greater than their invested capital. I want to emphasize three points about this definition: the fact that the specific rights, entitlements, and obligations are variable rather than fixed; the social nature of property relations; and the active role of the state in enforcing property rights.

First, the specific rights, entitlements, and obligations are quite variable. Contrary to classic liberalism, there are no inherent or natural "property rights." The conception of inalienable or natural property rights existing prior to society or history may have been an effective ideology for creating capitalism, but it has clouded the historical analysis of what specific rights, entitlements, and obligations govern economic relations. Rather, the content of property relations is historically constructed and must be explained, not taken for granted. The rise of the corporation fundamentally changed the nature of the rights, entitlements, and obligations bundled with ownership of productive enterprise (Berle and Means 1932; Horwitz 1977; Sklar 1988; Creighton 1990; Lindberg and Campbell 1991). The nominal owners effectively lost many of their rights, entitlements, and obligations. Whereas previously the right to determine what products to produce or whom to hire and the entitlement to profits and the obligation to pay debts had been bundled together with ownership, the corporation separated them.[5] Courts and legislatures increasingly treated the corporation as an entity in itself, legally distinct from the individuals who owned it, and increasingly treated management, not stockholders, as its representative. For example, prior to the 1880s, when a railroad entered receivership, judges ordinarily appointed a committee of owners, bondholders, and debtors to reorganize it. But the practice changed abruptly when judges began to appoint managers. Given that receivership was one of the primary means of altering the distribution of entitlements, stockholders were substantially disenfranchised (Berk 1994).

The second point to emphasize about this definition is that property is a social relationship; it involves rights, entitlements, and obligations not only in relation to an object itself but also in relationship to other individuals (Hurst 1978; Horwitz 1977; Renner 1949). The owner of a factory not only has the right to decide what to use his or her factory for, a relationship of the owner to the object, but also the right of authority over others participating in using the factory, the right to distribute the value created in the factory (an entitlement), and obligations to pay debts incurred in production. The social relationship among owners, managers, suppliers, workers, and customers was radically altered by the corporation. No particular owner retained any authority over any particular worker, but all authority was mediated through the board of directors and management. Rather than freeing those who run enterprise to become "soulful," manag-

ers are constrained to maximize profits for those to whom they are ultimately accountable.

Third, this definition of property emphasizes that property is a relationship enforced by the state (Sklar 1988; Weber 1978; Zald 1978; Fligstein
1990; Lindberg and Campbell 1991; Campbell and Lindberg 1991;
Scheiber 1975). Although the American state has developed a relatively
small apparatus to regulate markets and oversee production, even at its
most laissez-faire, it defined and enforced the rights, entitlements, and obligations of property. Even the freest of markets requires specific government
actions and policies to enforce contracts, punish cheaters, regulate money,
and ensure stability. There is no such thing as nonintervention (Polanyi
1957). The corporation is a creation of the law, a "legal fiction." Natural
individuals are automatically recognized by the law and have a basic right
to own property, sign contracts with others concerning that property, and
sell that property without explicit recognition by the state. But a corporation exists only when chartered by the state. A group of natural individuals
can constitute themselves as an organization, and can sign individual contracts defining their economic relationship to one another and the rights and
obligations they have to the organization, but the organization itself cannot
exercise property rights, sign enforceable contracts, or sell property unless
it is explicitly granted that right by the state. Thus explaining the rise of the
large industrial corporation requires analysis of the legal changes underlying corporate property. Although most treatments of the American state
have focused on the federal government, it was the individual states that
were constitutionally and practically responsible for defining and enforcing
property rights. There was considerable variation among the states in the
particular rights, entitlements, and obligations that came with incorporation, and these differences affected the form and location of corporations.
At the one extreme, by the end of the century New Jersey allowed corporations to own other corporations, making it the overwhelming choice of
huge mergers, while at the other, Ohio continued to uphold double liability,
by which owners were liable not only for their invested capital but for an
additional amount equal to it.

I will argue that corporate rights and entitlements and the new social
relations enforced by the state did not dissolve the class nature of property
as much as they changed it by socializing it throughout the class and by
creating an organizational mediation among the classes and class segments
(Zeitlin 1980, 1989).[6] By mediation, I mean that the underlying class relationship became redefined in terms of not just one's relationship to legal
ownership but one's social relationship to corporate property. The relationships that class describes, such as hiring people to labor, exercising authority over decisions about what to produce or what technologies to adopt,
determining how products are sold, are now mediated by the corporation.
One is no longer hired by individuals, but hired by a corporation; one can
no longer sue owners, but only the corporation. In contemporary America,

one's relationship to corporations is now the most important determinant of wealth. Whether one works for a corporation, manages a corporation, owns stock in a corporation, or lends money to a corporation differentiates the wealthy from the rest. To assert that the large corporation did not dissolve the capitalist class does not mean that I claim that class dynamics by themselves explain the rise of the corporation, nor does it indicate that the capitalist class acted as an organized, coherent, or conscious group throughout these events. The extent to which class interests are at stake, that is, the extent to which people objectively gain or lose from historical events, the extent to which people with common class interests act in concert, and the extent to which they are aware that they share interests with others are empirical questions, not articles of faith. But such issues of class do belong on the agenda for explaining how economic relationships change. When class interests (or the interests of class segments) are at stake, such as when manufacturers were resisting corporate takeover, the outcome will be determined in large part by the extent to which people with common class interests act in common. For example, the antitrust legal actions corroded class solidarity among small and medium-sized manufacturers, making it easier for corporate capitalists, who were knitted together by shared ownership and common investment institutions, to prevail both economically and legally.

Power

The conventional sociological definition of power is taken from Weber (1978): the ability of one actor to impose his or her will on another despite resistance. I broaden that to define power as the extent to which the behavior of one person is explained in terms of the behavior of another. Like Weber's, this definition characterizes a relationship rather than a single person. It incorporates Weber's definition as one dimension of power, "behavioral power," which refers to the visible overt behavior of the power wielder in the form of a command, request, or suggestion. But Weber's definition does not go far enough to cover all the ways that behavior is affected by others. There is a second dimension of power, "structural power," the ability to determine the context within which decisions are made by affecting the consequences of one alternative over another. For example, an employer that hires sociology majors rather than economics majors structures the consequences of choosing a major and is exercising power over students deciding on a major.[7]

This second dimension of power, structural power, allows us to include rational action within a theory of power. The concept of structural power permits a variety of motives for behavior, including rationality. The fact that an actor rationally decides to maximize his or her utility does not mean that power is irrelevant to an explanation of behavior; power operates in setting up the choices the actor faces and the consequences of any particular

action. For example, most of the new manufacturing corporations formed
at the turn of the century were mergers of many entrepreneurially owned
companies. Many proud, hardworking manufacturers sold their family legacy for stock certificates and a demotion from owner to manager. Why?
Efficiency theory posits that economies of scale and productive technologies led to ruinous competition and the necessary amalgamation into
managerial hierarchies. Such accounts are devoid of actors except for the
rationalizing managers creating a more efficient division of labor. But we
also need to know what alternatives the owners of merged firms faced and
who determined the consequences of their choices. If an owner had to
choose between competing against a corporation selling products below
cost or joining a merger and enjoying continuing profits, it is understand-
able that he or she chose the latter. The choices the manufacturers faced in
1899 were radically different from those of just a decade earlier, and to
understand why manufacturers incorporated we must also understand how
financiers, government officials, and other industrialists affected the consequences of reorganizing enterprise within the corporate system, in other
words, the institutional structure.

    In this perspective rationality becomes an empirical question, not an a
priori assumption. Compared with efficiency theory, power theory thus
proposes a very different agenda for research: Who made the decisions that
created large industrial corporations? What were the alternative choices
they faced? To what extent did rationality, social influence, or other decision-making logics shape their decisions? Who set the alternative choices
and the consequences of each alternative they faced? How did their choices
shape the alternatives and payoffs for other actors? One of the reasons these
questions are often difficult to answer is that the alternative choices and the
payoffs are embedded within institutions whose genesis has been forgotten
or obscured.

Institutions

As a system of property relations shaped by the dynamics of power, corporations operated within and helped constitute a social institution (Meyer
and Rowan 1977; DiMaggio and Powell 1983; Zucker 1988; Powell and
DiMaggio 1991). To understand how the corporation operates requires
more than knowing how it works internally, the people who operate it,
its goals and strategies, or its division of labor and hierarchy. By social institution I mean the matrix of organizations, taken-for-granted categories,
and the agreed-upon modes of relationship among those organizations
that administer a major social task. The concept includes three analytically
distinct aspects: (1) Institutions use a set of categories and practices that are
understood to be the "way things are done" (Meyer and Rowan 1977).
Corporations develop a standard division of authority among the owners,
directors, managers, and workers; particular accounting practices to mea-

sure performance and validate strategies; customary separation of white-collar and blue-collar occupations; and characteristic bureaucratic structures that codify procedures. Institutional practices include such practices as issuing stock, speculation, hiring and promotion of workers and managers, and measurement of success in terms of balance sheets. (2) Institutions include a matrix of organizations, or an organizational field, that in the aggregate constitutes a recognized area of institutional life (DiMaggio and Powell 1983). Just as the medical institution includes hospitals as well as laboratories or medical schools, the institution of corporate capitalism includes factories and railroads as well as the stock markets, investment banks, brokerage houses, and news organizations. Thus when I speak of major public corporations I mean much more than those companies that happen to be incorporated. I mean companies that are legally incorporated and that operate within the institutional structures of corporate capitalism by publicly offering their securities to the securities market, raising capital through investment banks, recruiting directors from the community of corporate directors, and socializing ownership through widespread ownership. It was the transformation of manufacturing enterprise into this institutional structure that exploded at the end of the nineteenth century in the corporate revolution. (3) Institutions describe cultural categories, a sense of reality, a "thing" (Zucker 1977, 1983). All members of society recognize that medicine, education, politics, and mass media are institutions. They are "real." The institutionalization of the entities that do things is more than just a codification of existing practices; the process selects from among competing alternative forms by designating one form as "real" or "established" while marginalizing other forms as "experimental," "fledgling," "novel," "alternative," or "artificial." This process was very important in the institutionalization of the corporation in the late nineteenth century, when writers from a variety of ideological perspectives, speaking to many different types of audiences, declared that good or bad, the corporation was here to stay. Although in retrospect it may appear that things could have been different, the nearly universal feeling that large corporations were inevitable was an important part of their institutionalization, a cause as well as a result of how large corporations became the standard way of doing business.

What is the relationship among property, power, and institutions? All three are interwoven together throughout this analysis, but three propositions succinctly capture their relationship.

Power institutionalizes property. The specific rights, entitlements, and obligations that the state enforces relative to objects is determined by the operation of power and embedded within institutions. Corporate lawyers were able to persuade the New Jersey legislature to change its corporate law to allow corporations to own stock in other corporations, a right that had been previously denied to both partnerships and corporations and that, once granted, created the legal basis for the corporate revolution at the end of the century. The New Jersey legislature was more compliant than other states because that state had long enjoyed a profitable relationship with railroad corporations. The choices it faced and the relative payoff of each differed from the situation faced by other states. The relationship among power, institution, and property was very reflexive and historical: early exercise of power institutionalized a set of property relationships that became the context within which power was exercised to embed new property relations within the institutional relations of corporate capital.

Property institutionalizes power. The specific rights, entitlements, and obligations that are embedded within institutions shape the context within which people make decisions. Those who want to benefit from how a system operates do not need to constantly impose their will, but institutions reproduce power relationships. Berle and Means (1932) describe how in the late nineteenth and early twentieth centuries, such new legal features of the corporations as proxy voting and no par stock[8] disenfranchised stockholders. New property relations were the means by which small stockholders lost power.

Power and property shape institutions. Just as Starr (1982) describes how physicians prevailed to shape modern medicine or Logan and Molotch (1988) demonstrate how property relations shape modern urban relations, a major theme of this book is how power and property, more than efficiency, shaped the corporate institution.

The Story

When applied to the rise of the American industrial corporation these analytical concepts yield a story very different from that found in efficiency studies. Instead of rational managers making pragmatic organizational innovations adapting to new technologies and growing markets, the story depicts a series of political and financial developments redistributing power into new institutional structures and eventually resulting in a new property regime. The lead players in the story are the state; the corporate institutional structure, including investment banks, stock exchanges, brokers, and others; newly privatized railroads; and finally manufacturers themselves. It is the larger structures that best explain why the corporation became the dominant form. These actors and the roles they played are summarized in Table 1.1.

The story spans three eras. In the late eighteenth and early 19th centuries, business corporations were only one type of corporation created by governments to perform public functions like education, urban services, churches, charities, and infrastructure. Because they were performing a task considered critical for the public, they were given such privileges as monopoly rights, eminent domain, and an exemption on liability. Because they were quasi-government agencies they were financed by institutional structures we

TABLE 1.1
Historical Account of the Rise of the Large Corporation

	Era and Role of Corporation		
Actors	Early 19th Century: Corporation as quasi-government agency	Mid-19th Century: Corporation private but separate from manufacturing	Late 19th– Early 20th Century: Merger of corporate institution with manufacturing
State	· Actively forms corporations · Mobilizes resources · Holds corporations publicly accountable	· Passes general incorporation laws · Defines new rights, entitlements, and obligations · Treats corporation as legal individual	· Prohibits industry governance · Enforces relations of corporate property
Corporate Institutional Structure	· Arises to administer public finance · Spreads to private corporations · Remained distinct from manufacturing	· Develops into modern structure · Excludes manufacturing	· Brings manufacturing in
Railroads	· Arise as semipublic agency	· Privatize · Grow to unprecedented size · Amass corporate wealth for reinvestment	· Experience declining profitability · Merge with manufacturing capital
Manufacturing Capital	· Exists apart from corporate capital · Governs itself by local and regional suprafirm relations	· Develops national markets · Destabilizes suprafirm relations	· Merge with corporate capital

now call Wall Street, which then functioned mainly to circulate government securities. In the middle of the nineteenth century, they fully privatized within the mature corporate infrastructure but remained separate from manufacturing. By allowing incorporation through the simple acts of filing papers and paying a fee rather than requiring a legislative act, states made incorporation a right accessible to all rather than a privilege. Railroad corporations grew to unprecedented size and scope; the institutions of Wall Street congealed into their present form, but still remained distinct from manufacturing. Finally the corporate revolution at the turn of the century absorbed manufacturing and fully established the corporate system as we have it today. The corporate revolution was precipitated by government actions that prevented manufacturing industries from governing themselves except through merger, by the saturation and financial collapse of the railroad system, and by an ideological acceptance that the large socially capitalized manufacturing corporation was inevitable.

By 1890 the corporate revolution in manufacturing was probably inevitable in some form, although exactly what form was not entirely clear. The resources concentrated in the corporate institutions were vast and the opportunities to profit from railroad and related sectors diminishing, so investors were looking for new outlets. The legal foundation, insofar as it was based on the railroad as a profit-making company rather than a common carrier accountable to the public, could easily be borrowed by manufacturing. And manufacturers' opposition to corporate takeover was already weakened by the frequent declaration that big business was inevitable, by the temptations of monopolistic profits, and by the trauma inflicted by the Great Depression of 1893. Belief in the corporate revolution's inevitability has led to its treatment as fairly unproblematic in most conventional accounts, which tell how in the 1880s industrialists like John D. Rockefeller in oil and Henry O. Havemeyer in sugar, after failing to control competition through pools, formed trusts, whereby each constituent firm incorporated for the purpose of exchanging corporate stock for trust certificates, allowing a central board to control entire industries. After the trusts were declared illegal, industries reorganized in holding companies like Standard Oil or the American Sugar Refining Company. At the end of the 1890s hundreds of such corporations were founded primarily through mergers by financiers like J. P. Morgan, who organized General Electric, International Harvester, and U.S. Steel. But such accounts too often neglect how the nature and definition of property, the organization and distribution of wealth, and the institutional practices and definitions were all socially constructed and far from inevitable. My account focuses on explaining these broader factors, emphasizing that they were determined less by the exigencies of economic efficiency or managerial rationality than by the very political dynamics of power.

PREVIEW

This chapter sets the conceptual stage for the story that follows. Chapter 2 puts efficiency theory to an empirical test and finds it wanting, validating the need for an alternative account. The next three chapters describe how the corporate system was historically constructed, growing into the basic forms it continues to have today but remaining rigidly confined to a few sectors of the economy. Chapter 3 reviews the early business corporation in America, emphasizing the active role of government in creating corporations whose political purposes explain what were later labeled inherent features, features that purportedly made corporations more efficient. I also describe how the line between public and private power was historically constructed and not a matter of natural division of labor. Chapter 4 focuses on the transition from the publicly accountable corporation to the corporation as a form of private property, especially in large railroad corporations. Chapter 5 shows how the institutional structure of investment banks, brokerage houses, stock exchanges, and other organizations arose around government and public corporations, remaining apart from manufacturing even when well developed. The final four chapters address the corporate revolution itself. Chapter 6 discusses the legal definition of corporate property, the specific rights, entitlements, and obligations that structured the relationships that constituted economic interaction, and how it created a distinctly new form of property that varied among the individual American states. Chapter 7 describes the interaction of manufacturers and the state over the way in which manufacturers would govern themselves, leading to the first generation of large-scale socially capitalized firms like the American Cotton Oil Company and the American Sugar Refining Company. Chapter 8 presents the climax of the story, with the leading actors in manufacturing and banking in simultaneous conflict and cooperation, transforming manufacturing in the corporate revolution. The Conclusion explores implications for both social theory and contemporary change. Along the way I focus on three states, since most of the action, especially concerning the role of government, took place on the state rather than the national level.[9] New Jersey was known as the "home of the trusts" because its permissive corporate laws made it possible to organize capital into very large holding companies, precipitating the corporate revolution. Ohio occupied the other end of the spectrum, a state whose rigorous laws demanded more public accountability than most large corporations were willing to tolerate. Pennsylvania took a middle course, perhaps the most typical but the least fascinating. The three of them together offer a representative view of how large corporations arose and changed.

CONCLUSION

If the concepts of property, power, and institution are intimately connected, theoretical perspectives conventionally considered rivals can be synthesized. Insofar as class relations become embedded within institutions, class theory and neo-institutionalization theory can both explain the outcome. I will emphasize the important role that investment banks, stock markets, and brokerage houses played in the rise and spread of large corporations. Moreover, to the extent that institutions are shaped by the actions of some groups exerting power over others, political sociology and neo-institutionalization theory must speak to each other. Recent advocates of neo-institutionalization theory have criticized earlier renditions for neglecting power (DiMaggio and Powell 1991). I will argue that one of the primary ideological factors underlying the corporate revolution at the end of the century was the widespread assumption that large corporations were not only inevitable but an established fact, that is, the form was already institutionalized before its full blossoming. Such an accomplishment reflected the power of business and government leaders to define the situation, a critical feature of the institutionalization process. To be sure, some of the specific hypotheses offered by particular representatives of these theories contradict one another. But I hope to demonstrate by the detailed analysis herein that the basic orientations of these theories can be synthesized. In the final analysis my argument owes more to the logic of political sociology than to economic sociology. By this I mean that my argument operates according to processes of power, not just rational decision making or efficiency.

The socialization of capital does not exist in a social vacuum but within a new corporate institutional structure including the stock market, banks (both commercial and investment), brokerage houses, the investing public, and later, government agencies like the Securities and Exchange Commission. These institutions structure the relationship among the corporations, intervening in the mobilization and distribution of capital. Before the end of the nineteenth century, manufacturing companies formed a different world from these institutions. Finance capital revolved around first government finance and, later, public improvement corporations, especially the railroad. But what set the late nineteenth century apart was the reorganization of the institutional structure within which business firms relate to one another. Finance capital and manufacturing capital merged. This was the big merger in the merger movement—not just the combination of individual firms into major corporations, but the fusion of two formerly distinct class segments. The corporations that became linked together through these institutions constituted a distinctive and new class segment characterized by qualities we normally associate with "big business."[10]

CHAPTER TWO

A Quantitative Test of Efficiency Theory

THE EFFICIENCY THEORY discussed in Chapter 1 holds that the corporation offered a more efficient organizational structure for increasingly large-scale, capital-intensive manufacturing activity than did traditional entrepreneurial firms. My criticisms focused on logical and conceptual issues—the unrealistic assumptions about rational decision making, the functional logic that confuses causes and consequences, the lack of historical logic, and the inattention to power. But social science seeks to assess well-developed theories with empirical tests. This chapter first examines how well efficiency theory, especially Chandler's version, explains the temporal patterns characterizing the formation of large, socially capitalized corporations from 1880 to 1913. The results challenge theories based on evolutionary adaption to the development of technology or the growth of markets and the underlying efficiency theories that cite them. Then in a more specific examination of efficiency theory, I test whether it can explain why large-scale publicly traded corporations—corporations tied into the corporate institutional structure—were founded in some industries rather than others. The results fail to support hypotheses derived from the theory. Finally, I test Chandler's contention that the reasons for the initial formation of large corporations were less important in determining the long-term distribution of large corporations among industries than the selective process by which large corporations survived where the technology and market conditions were appropriate and withered where they were not. I conclude that efficiency theory does not adequately explain the rise of large socially capitalized corporations at the turn of this century. Subsequent chapters provide an alternative account to explain why the large socially capitalized corporation developed as it did.

WHAT IS TO BE EXPLAINED

The focus of this book is the large, socially capitalized industrial corporation. Throughout, except when explicit reference is made to small corporations or all corporations, this is the topic. The social processes that explain the rise of the small corporation and the large socially capitalized corporation are not the same. Incorporation spread to small, generally privately held corporations through a process of diffusion. Individual owners were able to consciously consider the advantages and disadvantages of filing corporation papers to change the legal status of their firms within the context of a relatively institutionalized system. The act rarely had dramatic effects on day-to-day operations. The large publicly traded industrial corporation, in contrast, arose abruptly through novel and contested economic processes. Decision makers, including promoters, owners of existing firms, and investors were facing a new institutional, economic, and political environment, acutely aware that they were reshaping not only the way goods and services were produced and distributed but the social landscape of the nation. As described in Chapter 1 and depicted in Figure 1.1, there was not a gradual trend toward large corporations, but a circumscribed period during which large corporations took hold. The graph represents what this book seeks to explain, the sudden development of the large socially capitalized corporation at the turn of the century and the long-term genesis of the institutional structure which made it possible. Its dramatic growth is clearly different from the diffusion of the corporate form into small business.

No single explanation applies equally to all types of corporations. Feature-based explanations that focus on the positive advantages of corporations over entrepreneurships or partnerships apply more to small firms than to large firms. Such models assume that someone, having reached the point of conceiving an idea and mobilizing the capital, with everything set in place except the choice of whether to incorporate or not, then makes a decision. As in most conventional economic thinking, the implied decision maker is homo economicus embarking on his entrepreneurial venture, rationally weighing the pros and cons of incorporation. Such a model is appropriate when an unproblematic innovation diffuses through a stable population or after patterns of organizational operation have become institutionalized. The virtual explosion of incorporation in the four or five years around the turn of the century cannot be explained by diffusion theories. The events were discontinuous rather than evolutionary, a revolution not a trend.

The shape of the temporal pattern by which events occur has important theoretical implications. Social and economic theories not only suggest which factors explain a phenomenon, but also implicitly assume patterns of development over time (Abbott 1990; Aminzade 1992). Three conditions could logically create the explosive activity represented by Figure 1.1, when suddenly hundreds of very large corporations appeared within a few short years. The first condition is that the acting units are independent from one another, but some sudden common change affects many of them similarly— something like a war, revolution, or sweeping legal change. Second, the acting units could be independent from one another, but a coincidence of exogenous factors or some link among exogenous factors each affects one unit at a time. For example, if technology changed quickly in many industries, each industry with a technological change might see large corporations arising about the same time. Third, the units may not be independent from one another, but the fact that one unit changes induces others to change, creating a contagion effect. None of these fits efficiency theory. Technological changes and the growth of large national markets are said to have created new conditions to which manufacturing firms had to adapt. Adaption is the dynamic causal force. Chandler explains the timing in one of his central propositions: "[M]odern business enterprise appeared for the first time in history when the volume of economic activities reached a level that made administrative coordination more efficient and more profitable than market coordination" (Chandler 1977, 8). He specifies the most important factors: "Modern business enterprise was thus the institutional response to the rapid pace of technological innovation and increasing consumer demand in the United States during the second half of the nineteenth century" (1977, 12). This account does not conform to any of the conditions that might stimulate rapid change among many organizations. It does not fit the first condition of a single quick cause: the volume of economic activities that might make administrative coordination more efficient and more profitable than market coordination will be reached at different times for different industries. This is not a single event. Nor does it fit the second condition of a simultaneous but separate cause: the volume of economic activities grows slowly and different industries grow at different rates. Technologies could plausibly have affected one another so that many industries would face similar technological innovation, just as computerization may be provoking flexible specialization in many industries today, but Chandler does not make any such case. His particular examples tell of technological changes at many points in time, the sugar industry in the 1850s, Bessemer steel in the 1870s, the Bonsack cigarette machine in the 1880s, and the rise of the assembly line after the turn of the century. Efficiency theory does not conform to the third condition of nonindependent entities influencing one another because it assumes that each unit is independent: change comes when managers autonomously respond to exogenous conditions. Although managers imitate particular adaptations—Chandler stresses the innovations developed by railroad managers—the adoption of new techniques or organizational forms by any particular firm is always explained in terms of the situation that particular firm faces. As Meyer and Rowan (1977) emphasize, however, the pattern by which firms adapt to changing conditions—even rapid changes—occurs through a gradual evolutionary process. While Chandler acknowledges that the rise of large corporations was compacted into a short period of time, he treats this as of mere descriptive importance, with no implications for the underlying causal process. He sees nothing anomalous about the precipitous growth of corporations and his reliance on adaptive causal mechanisms.

A similar trajectory fits one variation of institutionalization theory—when an innovator sparks a quickly spreading mimetic process in an organizational field. The difference between the adaptive process of diffusion and the mimetic process of diffusion is that in the adaptive model, rational actors monitor the environment and choose to adopt the innovation when the conditions ripen; in the mimetic process, there is no assumption that the innovation is rational, only that it becomes defined within a particular organizational field in which it is institutionally appropriate (Stinchcombe 1965; DiMaggio and Powell 1983; Meyer and Rowan 1977). The adaptive process mirrors, perhaps with some lag, change in the environment. In the mimetic process, environmental conditions, especially at the institutional level, pose necessary but far from sufficient conditions. As elaborated later in the book, the development of large publicly traded corporations is more consistent with the mimetic than with the adaptive mechanism of change.

While the foregoing addressed the timing of the corporate revolution, explanations must also address the locus of incorporation. Not only was the growth of large publicly traded corporations discontinuous over time, but its distribution across industries was extremely skewed. At one extreme, industries became virtually dominated by one giant monopoly. By 1905, corporations in petroleum, steel, and tobacco controlled over 90 percent of their industries. At the other extreme, and more typically, industries continued to be characterized by proprietorships, partnerships, and privately held corporations. As late as 1905, 63 percent of the census-defined industries listed no firms on the stock exchange. Thus a majority of industries did not participate in the first wave of the corporate revolution. Theories that explain the rise of the modern industrial corporation should be able to distinguish those industries with major manufacturing corporations from those without them.

Instead of the tired debate about whether business leaders were "robber barons" or "industrial statesmen," Chandler reoriented academic and popular attention to the more intellectually challenging question of why some industries but not others adopted the new organizational, managerial, and legal forms. Moreover, he distinguished between the processes of forming corporations and the factors that explain their persistence. Especially during the height of the corporate revolution, when hundreds of very large corporations were being cobbled together by promoters as well as by industrialists, many corporations were founded for nonefficiency reasons. But Chandler maintains that they persisted and succeeded only in those industries with fertile economic and technological conditions and only where the managers adopted the strategies and structures of modern business enterprise. This chapter will thus test whether his propositions about the rise and durability of large corporations stand up to systematic scrutiny.

UNEVENNESS OF INCORPORATION

Half of all manufacturing capital listed in the 1905 *Manual of Statistics* was accounted for by six industries: iron and steel, with the billion-dollar U.S. Steel, alone accounted for a third of all common stock, followed by tobacco, railroad cars, leather, chemicals, and foundry and machine shop products. The fifteen industries with at least one hundred million dollars in authorized capital accounted for two-thirds of all corporate capital. Thus there was not only the well-known concentration within industries, but also a remarkable concentration of corporate capital among industries.

The fact that corporations were clustered in so few industries was a fundamental, not just an incidental, facet of the corporate revolution. First, incorporation required several scarce commodities, which were unevenly distributed across the economy. Finance capital increasingly turned to manufacturing as investors abandoned their earlier faith in railroad securities and their distrust of industrial securities (Navin and Sears 1955), but they favored some industries over others. Industrialists themselves could merge and create securities, some from their assets and some from "promotional securities." In this instance, the newly created securities were controlled by owners of constituent companies and promoters. Both financially promoted incorporations and mergers among industrialists depended on a finite supply of institutional facilities like brokers, investment banks, and promoters.

The second and perhaps more important reason why the unevenness of incorporation was important is that large-scale incorporation altered the relationships among industries, bifurcating the economy between "big business" and "small business." The restriction of large-scale incorporation to so few industries is a major feature of the division. Increasingly, large corporations have defined one another as their major organizational field, using one another rather than small firms in their own industry as the appropriate organizational model (Fligstein 1990).

The use of industry as the unit of analysis conforms more closely to efficiency theory's orientation to technology and markets than to my orientation to power and social relations. Industries are fundamentally technological and market categories. What the firms of an industry have in common is that they make the same product, purchase from the same suppliers, and sell to the same customers. Insofar as technology and markets explain the rise of large corporations, industry is an appropriate unit of analysis. Creating a large publicly financed corporation required relationships with a variety of organizations, only some of which were homogeneous within industries. The personal and economic relationships forged by leaders of particular firms strongly influenced whether corporations were founded independently of the other firms in the industry. For example, J. P. Morgan, who presided over the creation of more major industrial corporations than any other individual, emphasized the importance of personal relations when he testified at a congressional hearing that "character" was a more important criterion for extending credit than assets (Allen 1965). Economic relationships—especially with finance—were also important. Unless there was a perfect capital market—a dubious proposition—it can be assumed that the nature of past ties with finance explains why major corporations were founded in some industries rather than others. Railroad rebates and kickbacks facilitated the growth of particular firms in industries like petroleum, sugar refining, and whiskey, often at the expense of independent firms. Interaction with railroad companies influenced major suppliers such as the steel, leather, lumber, and locomotive manufacturers to reorganize as part of the corporate institution. All these factors are ignored in perspectives that focus on industries rather than firms. Nonetheless efficiency theory's emphasis on technology and markets makes the industry an appropriate unit with which to test the theory, to which we now turn.[1]

EFFICIENCY THEORY

Efficiency theory holds that corporations offer certain technological and functional advantages over other organizational forms. The advantages usually cited include limited liability, continuity of existence beyond the life of founders, easy transfer of ownership shares, ability to raise capital, and sometimes legal privileges such as franchise, monopoly and even rights of eminent domain (for example, see Seager and Gulick 1929; Porter 1973; Ransom 1981). The key concepts in this theory are technological development and rational, functional adaptation.

Chandler makes two major points about the structural properties explaining variation among industries: (1) The economic structure underlying large firms arose between 1880 and 1920 and has been stable since then. The distribution of the leading two hundred firms among industries in 1917 was virtually identical to that of 1973. This implies that the inherent characteristics of industries underlie the development of giant firms. (2) Nearly all industries tried to create giant firms, but only some succeeded, so differences were a matter not of motivation, but of structure. McCraw describes it: "Try as they might, businessmen in peripheral industries simply could not make their combinations work, precisely because of the nature of those industries" (1981, 22). He cites failures such as United States Leather, American Cattle, Standard Rope and Twine, and National Cordage. The failed trusts tended to have a high ratio of variable to fixed costs, were labor intensive, lacked any important scale economics in either production or marketing, and were thus easily overtaken by new entrants. Chandler summarized his argument: "Therefore modern business enterprise first appeared, grew, and continued to flourish in those sectors and industries characterized by new and advancing technology and expanding markets" (Chandler 1977, 8; see also his chap. 8). He reasoned that when technological innovation increased the velocity of throughput, firms could reduce the cost of production per unit and increase the output per worker, producing economies of scale that rendered administrative coordination more efficient than market coordination—the "visible hand" of hierarchy replacing the "invisible hand" of the market. The crucial issue is whether this line of reasoning holds up to empirical test.

DEPENDENT VARIABLE

The dependent variable is the extent to which industries incorporated in major corporations regardless of whether they were formed by merger or other means, in 1901–1904, the peak years of the corporate revolution.[2] Two aspects are distinguished. One is whether any firms in an industry took the form of a major corporation. The other is the extent to which those industries with any major corporations were organized by corporate capital. As detailed in Appendix 2.1, this concept has several facets. The data were taken from the *Manual of Statistics*, an annual compilation of information on all firms listed on the major stock exchanges, a precursor to the more well known volumes like *Standard and Poor's* or *Moody's Manual*. The first dependent variable is a dummy variable (a binary yes/no variable) indicating whether the industry had any major corporations, that is, any corporations with at least $1,000,000 total capital, listed in the *Manual of Statistics* in the years 1901–1904.[3] Of the 278 industries, only 104 had major companies listed on the stock exchanges, while 174 did not.[4]

The facet of the dependent variable is the extent to which industries with any major corporations were organized by corporate capital, which is operationalized as the *average aggregated value of authorized stocks and bonds for the years 1901 to 1904* (logged to reduce skewness in its distribution). In order to minimize the effect of different industry boundaries, the number of establishments (logged) is used as a control variable.[5]

INDEPENDENT VARIABLES

These data were taken from the Census of Manufacturing, which recorded the number of establishments, average number of wage earners, primary horsepower, capital, wages, cost of materials, value of products, and value added by manufacture (value of products minus cost of materials). All the independent variables were measured prior to the dependent variable. Thus reciprocal causation from cross-sectional analysis is not a problem.[6] Operationalizations of these independent variables are given in Appendix 2.1.

1. GROWTH. Chandler treats modern enterprise as a response to changes in the economic structure. The industries that were growing most quickly would have the greatest need for the administrative management of a large corporation. Stagnant or declining industries would have no need for new organizational forms. Industries where technology increased output would be especially prone to create large corporations. Thus growth would be hypothesized to explain variation in the formation of large corporations.

2. WORKER PRODUCTIVITY. This is one of the central factors in efficiency theory: large corporations with managerial hierarchies succeeded because they increased the output per worker. Because they were more efficient, they

captured the market from smaller, less productive firms. Chandler states in one of his major propositions: "[M]odern multiunit business enterprise replaced small traditional enterprise when administrative coordination permitted greater productivity, lower costs, and higher profits than coordination by market mechanisms" (1977, 6). Productivity has also been used as an indirect measure of technological development (Robinson and Briggs 1990). The reasoning is that if workers are producing more, it is due to either enhanced technology or enhanced management. In either case, greater productivity would stimulate the creation of large corporations.

3. CAPITAL INTENSITY. Chandler has argued that "[t]he changing ratio of capital to labor and of managers to labor thus helped to create pressures to integrate within a single industrial enterprise the processes of mass distribution with those of mass production. By 1900 in many main production industries the factory, works, or plant had become part of much larger enterprise" (1977, 282). Although he emphasizes that most manufacturing growth relied on internal profits, when firms needed external financing, the corporate form facilitated raising capital. So capital intensity created an incentive for incorporation. Thus both the relationship of capital intensity to technology and the need for outside capital underlie the hypothesis that high capital-intense industries would be more likely to incorporate than low capital-intense industries.

4. SIZE OF FIRM. According to Weber, bureaucracies are more efficient than other forms of administration. The need for monitoring, coordinating, recording, and planning is best served in bureaucratic organizations. Moreover, managerialism (Berle and Means 1932) holds that rational bureaucratic organization is more likely to be found where ownership and management are separated, where expert managers can develop administrative structures of control and coordination, that is, in a corporation. However, Chandler (1977) argues that size of firm per se was less important than the benefits of increased scale of production and administrative coordination. It was not scale that led to large corporations, but the economics that scale made possible. This reasoning would hypothesize that any zero-order relationship would disappear when other factors are held constant.

RESULTS

The results show that efficiency theory has little empirical support. Of the variables tested, only size and capital intensity consistently explain variation in the extent to which major corporations arose in different industries. Surprisingly, growth, productivity, and change in productivity—variables widely cited as major factors stimulating the rise of corporations—explained virtually no variation. The results challenge the conventional wisdom in general and the logic of efficiency theory in particular that major corporations arose in industries that were unusually efficient, technologically advanced, or had the greatest functional need for high technology.

TABLE 2.1
Comparison of Industries with Major Corporations and Those without

Variable	Mean (W/o corp.) (With corp.)	Standard Error	t (Equal Variances)[a]	p
Growth	0.14	0.02	−1.68	.09
	0.20	0.03		
Productivity (logged)	6.98	0.04	−1.71	.09
	7.08	0.04		
Change in Productivity	0.99	0.02	2.21	.03
(logged)	1.06	0.03		
Capital Intensity	1.53	0.04	−5.70	.07
(logged)	1.89	0.06		
Average Size of Firm	3.10	0.08	−4.50	.0001
(logged)	3.70	0.11		
Establishments (logged)	4.60	0.11	−3.36	.0009
	5.26	0.18		

[a] On some variables, the variances were significantly different, but the results of the t-tests were the same whether the variables were assumed to be equal or unequal.
N = 104 Industries with major corporations, 174 without.

As the quotations cited in the hypotheses indicate, Chandler did not explicitly state any ceteris paribus caveats, but only that industries that were more productive, had higher capital, and were growing more quickly would be more likely to give rise to large corporations. Thus a simple difference of means test is used to see if industries with large corporations differed from those without any on those variables. I then use multivariate logistic regression to see which factors explain the difference between industries with and without large corporations, holding other factors constant. Finally, for those industries that had any large corporations I report which factors explain why some were more highly incorporated than others.

Distinguishing between Industries with and without Major Corporations

Comparing the industries with and without major corporations by using a difference of means test (t-test) in Table 2.1 indicates that all the independent variables had a significant or nearly significant effect. Size had an especially strong effect. The geometric mean of the size (the anti-log of the mean in Table 2.1) was 1,259 workers per establishment in those industries without major corporations compared with 5,011 workers per establishment in industries with major corporations. Compared with industries that had no major corporations, industries with corporations grew slightly more; they were more capital intensive; they tended to be slightly more productive; and their firms tended to be larger. On the face of it, efficiency theory is modestly supported. Further analysis, however, reveals that this conclusion is not unambiguous.

Although the differences between industries with major corporations and those without were generally statistically significant, they were surprisingly substantively modest. Case-by-case examination of industries reveals why. The industries that have the highest scores on these independent variables are quite different from what might be expected. For example, the most capital-intensive industries included malt, linseed oil, varnishes, and bone, carbon, and lamp black. These are not the heavy industries typically associated with capital intensity. The industries commonly thought of as heavy capital-intensive industries were distributed throughout the ranking of the 278 industries: petroleum, 15th; chemicals, 81st; iron and steel, steelworks and rolling mills, 121st; locomotives, 163rd; and glass, 248th. But Chandler is correct on one score: most of the capital-intensive industries were processing industries, in which products were manufactured by continuous output rather than by assembling materials (like bicycles), or by batch processing (like Bessemer steel). Chandler is also correct that many of the early large corporations were found in highly capital-intensive processing industries. But if one examines all processing industries, it becomes clear that the technological mode of production (processing) is far from a sufficient cause of incorporation. Indeed, Chandler's greatest methodological weakness may be his reasoning backward from examining the common characteristics of what he considers successful companies rather than systematically comparing successful companies or industries with a control group. In other words, even though his theory addresses the momentous issue of variation among industries—why major corporations were found in some industries rather than others—his case-study-oriented method does not.

Close examination of the growth patterns is also revealing. Those industries with corporations grew slightly more rapidly than those without. As with capital intensity, the fast-growing industries differed from those conventionally considered ripe for large corporations. Even the most rapidly growing industries that did have major corporations (enameling, motorcycles, bicycles and parts,[7] and ground and refined graphite) did not foster corporate giants. Some fast-growing industries did spawn major corporations. The electrical machinery industry, which grew nearly as rapidly as those just mentioned, included General Electric. But others did not. Electrical machinery did not grow as rapidly as five industries that had no major corporations: lapidary works, wood preserving, drug grinding, grindstones, and hammocks. Like capital intensity, the most rapidly growing industries tended to be processing industries, though somewhat less so. The most rapidly growing industries also included electrical machinery and bicycles that were assembled rather than produced in continuous processing.

Looking at the industries highest on these independent variables thus helps explain why the differences between industries with and without major corporations are so modest. It highlights the importance of comparative analysis of all cases both with and without whatever feature is being studied, in contrast to searching for commonalities among cases that share a value on the dependent variable. Case studies are a valuable tool for developing theories and for the elaboration of solidly validated theories, but any conclusions from them should be subjected to systematic analysis across variation in the dependent variables if they are to be considered as established truth.

Further analysis addressed the separate effects of each independent variable, holding the others constant. Table 2.2 shows the results of logistic regression analysis distinguishing between industries with major corporations and those without. Instead of merely examining each variable in isolation, this analysis allows entire models to be tested.

Efficiency theory poorly distinguishes industries with any major corporations from those with none, as seen in Model 1 of Table 2.2. Only one hypothesized variable, capital intensity, had a significant regression coefficient in the predicted direction. Net of other variables, high capital-intensive industries were more likely to have at least one major corporation than low capital-intensive industries. The positive effect of productivity disappeared and in fact changed its sign. Net of other variables, highly productive industries were significantly less inclined to spawn major corporations. At the same time, Chandler's contention that not size per se, but the economies of scale, gave rise to large corporations, is not sustained. As shown in Model 2 of Table 2.2, when average size of establishment (measured in number of workers) is added to the logistic regression model, it and capital intensity become the only substantive variables to have a significant effect on whether or not an industry had a large corporation. Given that productivity was negatively associated with incorporation, we can surmise that scale, not economies of scale, accounted for the creation of corporations. Any economies of scale, at least as indicated by productivity, had little influence. Separate analysis fails to support any positive relationship between average establishment size and productivity: the simple correlation between size and productivity is −.45, but this is at least partially artifactual: the denominator of the productivity variable is the numerator of the size variable. Nonetheless, the results clearly indicate that not productivity but size per se was a critical precondition (and no doubt, later a consequence) of incorporation.

Explaining Variation in the Extent of Incorporation among Industries with Any Major Corporations

For those industries with large corporations, the results explaining the amount of corporate capital were similar to those explaining the mere existence of large corporations. Reasoning that the independent variables should explain variation in the dependent variable net of the effect of number of establishments, I first computed the amount of variation explained by

TABLE 2.2
Estimated Logistic Regression on Whether an Industry Had Major Corporations:
Analysis of Maximum Likelihood Estimates

Model 1: Variables Predicted by Efficiency Model

Variable	Parameter Estimate	Standard Error	Wald χ^2	$Pr > \chi^2$
Intercept	0.38	2.37	0.03	.87
Establishments	0.38	0.09	18.53	.0001
Growth	0.70	0.53	1.77	.18
Productivity	−0.92	0.39	5.59	.02
Capital Intensity	2.09	0.38	29.60	.0001
N		278		
Concordant		73%		
Discordant		26%		
Somers' D_{yx}		.48		
−2 log L.R.: Intercept and Covariates		312		
χ^2 for Covariates		56		
p of χ^2 with 3 d.f.		.0001		

Model 2: Variables Predicted by Efficiency Model plus Average Size of Establishment

Variable	Parameter Estimate	Standard Error	Wald χ^2	$Pr > \chi^2$
Intercept	14.56	3.70	15.48	.0001
Establishments	0.63	0.11	33.59	.0001
Growth	0.31	0.58	0.28	.60
Productivity	0.59	0.49	1.49	.22
Capital Intensity	1.72	0.41	17.50	.0001
Size	1.10	0.20	31.10	.0001
N		278		
Concordant		82%		
Discordant		18%		
Somers' D_{yx}		.65		
−2 log L.R.: Intercept and Covariates		274		
χ^2 for Covariates		94		
p of χ^2 with 3 d.f.		.0001		

the number of establishments to correct for differences in how finely or broadly industry boundaries were drawn. Compared with the amount of variance that the number of establishments explained, the variables in the efficiency theory collectively increased explained variance a substantial 18 percent. However, as seen in Table 2.3, like the model predicting whether or not an industry had any large corporations, only capital intensity had a

TABLE 2.3

Estimated Regression Coefficients on Aggregate Corporate Capital in Industries with any Major Corporations, 1900–1904

Model 1: Variables Predicted by Efficiency Model

Variable	Parameter Estimate	Standard Error	t for H_0 Parameter = 0	$Pr > |T|$
Intercept	19.11	2.15	8.88	.0001
Establishments	0.31	0.07	4.60	.0001
Growth	0.44	0.44	1.01	.32
Productivity	−0.94	0.34	−2.77	.01
Capital Intensity	1.30	0.27	4.85	.0001
N	104			
R^2	.29			
Adjusted R^2	.26			
F	10.1			
Pr > F	.0001			

Model 2: Variables Predicted by Efficiency Model plus Average Size of Establishment

Variable	Parameter Estimate	Standard Error	t for H_0 Parameter = 0	$Pr > |T|$
Intercept	9.51	2.58	3.69	.0004
Establishments	0.50	0.07	7.31	.0001
Growth	0.28	0.39	0.73	.47
Productivity	−0.07	0.34	−0.20	.84
Capital Intensity	1.22	0.24	5.15	.0001
Size	0.71	0.13	5.48	.0001
N	104			
R^2	.45			
Adjusted R^2	.42			
F	16.45			
Pr > F	.0001			

significant regression coefficient in the predicted direction. Growth had virtually no effect. Productivity had negative effect. The more productive industries had less corporate capital. Surprisingly, among industries with any corporations, industries that were rapidly growing, and that were highly productive, garnered no advantage in mobilizing corporate capital. Only capital-intensive industries were able to do so. Within the efficiency theory, at least, the same factor—capital intensity—that accounted for whether an industry had a major corporation explained the most about how much corporate capital the industry had. Productivity again had an effect the opposite of that predicted by efficiency theory. The results show that productive industries were less likely to foster extensive incorporation. The size variable had similar effects, as in the analysis of whether industries had any large corporations at all. Size and capital intensity alone among substantive variables significantly predicted the amount of capital in industries with large corporations.

DISCUSSION

The major result on how incorporating industries differed from nonincorporating industries is in one sense pedestrian and in another startling. The firms in incorporating industries were larger and more capital intensive than those in nonincorporating industries. This is pedestrian in the sense that it would be quite surprising to find otherwise. Indeed if all the variables operated as hypothesized, the findings would not have been at all remarkable. On the basis of the conventional wisdom, one would expect to find that industries with corporations and extensive corporate capital grew more quickly and were more productive. Such results would have validated the image in the efficiency theory in general and Chandler in particular that American industry in the last quarter of the nineteenth century headed into the second industrial revolution by increasing productivity and efficiency, thereby creating new economies of scale and stimulating the need for modern organization, which unproblematically induced the flow of capital where needed. The surprise is that size and capital intensity were the only hypothesized variables to matter, results which challenge the conventional wisdom. Although American industry was becoming more efficient, such progress was just as likely in industries that did not incorporate as those that did.

In order to advance beyond the negative results on the factors that did not explain the extent of incorporation, we must interpret the finding that size and capital intensity were such important factors in explaining the presence of corporations in an industry. Size of firm is interpreted by most analysts to represent a proxy for some other more "basic" variable. Chandler is quite explicit about this:

> It was not the size of a manufacturing establishment in terms of number of workers and the amount and value of productive equipment but the velocity of throughput and the resulting increase in the volume that permitted economies that lowered costs and increased output per worker and per machine. . . . In industries where the processes of production had the potential for such technological innovation—and this was not the case in many industries—a manufacturing establishment that exploited such a potential was able to produce a greater output at lower cost than could a larger plant or works that had not adopted similar improvements. In such mass production industries, organizational and technological innovators acquired a powerful competitive advantage. (1977, 244)

In his most recent book (1990), which includes the word "scale" in its title, Chandler explains that the critical factor is not assets, market value of shares, or size of work force, but the number of units, and he proposes using a measure of assets as a proxy. Thus he is more accurately theorizing about complexity than about size. But the results here show that when size is held constant, growth and productivity do not determine whether an industry incorporated.

Although size can be interpreted in many ways,[8] the concept has an affinity equally as close to the logic of power as to the logic of efficiency (Duboff and Herman 1980; Perrow 1981). While large firms were not necessarily more efficient, they were more powerful. Competition, overproduction, and falling profits without the presence of large firms in an industry would only create hard times, not institutional change. The difference between an efficiency logic and a power logic would lie in the reasons why large establishments fostered large corporations. Chandler's argument distinguishing between size per se and the economies of scale that he assumes come with size lucidly illustrates the logic of efficiency. It is efficiency that gives large firms their advantage and creates the objective need for managerial coordination and integration of different productive processes under an integrated organizational umbrella. But if what size gives you is the power to control markets and dominate others, a logic of power may be more appropriate than a logic of efficiency.

Just as size has often been used as a proxy for other variables, so has capital intensity. It is sometimes used to indicate increasing technology and greater efficiency, for which this study has more direct measures, none of which accounts for incorporation. Because incorporation was not explained by such related factors, it is difficult to say that these industries had an objective need for more capital. We can only know that they had a greater appetite, not whether that appetite was technologically determined or socially created. Plausibly, normative and institutional processes could have made some industries more inclined to invest heavily than others or could have inclined investors to seek out some industries rather than others.

CORPORATE SURVIVAL

Since Chandler acknowledges that corporations could have been established for many reasons, including capricious ones, but that they persisted only in those industries with the appropriate objective conditions, it is necessary to follow the fate of the first generation of corporations to see which survived and which failed. He examines 156 mergers formed between 1888 and 1906 for which Livermore coded the degree of success or failure, based on earning power on capitalization. Chandler specifies two kinds of factors that influenced the chances of success. Internal factors included whether or not corporations consolidated production, centralized management, and

TABLE 2.4
Estimation of Tobit Model for Average Authorized Capital, 1912: Analysis of
Maximum Likelihood Estimates

Model 1: Variables Predicted by Efficiency Model

Variable	Parameter Estimate	Standard Error	χ^2	$Pr > \chi^2$
Intercept	−13.83	5.84	5.60	.08
Average Capital, 1904	4.42	0.36	20.73	.0001
Growth, 1905–1909	5.19	2.66	3.84	.05
Productivity, 1905	2.92	2.08	1.97	.16
Capital Intensity	−0.52	1.16	0.20	.65
Scale	4.62	0.36		
Noncensored Values			90	
Left Censored Values			8	
Log Likelihood for Normal Scale Parameter			−278.50	

Model 2: Variables Predicted by Efficiency Model plus Average Size of Establishment

Variable	Parameter Estimate	Standard Error	χ^2	$Pr > \chi^2$
Intercept	−14.67	6.06	5.87	.02
Average Capital, 1904	1.59	0.36	19.88	.0001
Growth, 1905–1909	5.49	2.72	4.08	.04
Productivity, 1905	3.25	2.17	2.23	.04
Capital Intensity	−0.52	1.16	0.21	.65
Size of Establishment	0.22	0.43	0.27	.61
Scale	4.61	0.36		
Noncensored Values			90	
Left Censored Values			8	
Log Likelihood for Normal Scale Parameter			−278.37	

built their own marketing and purchasing organizations (1977, 336), conditions that I cannot test here. He also cited external factors related to the
industry of the merger. "[Successful mergers] operated in industries where
technology and markets permitted such integration to increase the speed
and lower the cost of materials through the processes of production and
distribution. For these reasons the long-lived mergers came to cluster in the
same industries in which the large integrated enterprise appeared in the
1880s" (1977, 336). Thus another test of efficiency theory is the systematic
examination of the success or failure of the first generation of large industrial corporations by looking to see how they fared in 1912, a decade after
most of them were formed. Rather than using return on capital, I use the
amount of authorized capital as given in the *Manual of Statistics* and
Moody's Manual of Railroad and Corporation Securities[9] to ascertain
whether the industry was unable to support any large corporations (zero

capital), sustain itself at constant levels, or attract more capital. The logic is to ascertain what factors of industries in 1904 explained the aggregate amount of capital in 1912, net of capital in 1904.[10]

As seen in Table 2.4, the main determinant of authorized book capital for industries in 1912 is their level of capital in 1904. Thus Chandler's hypothesis that the original cause for the creation of large corporations is less important than the factors that explain their persistence is not supported. I interpret the effect of capital in 1904 as an indication of the power and resources that large corporations attained at their formation. The capital concentrated in large corporations gave them an advantage that could help them persist.

Of the factors that efficiency theory would hypothesize as having positive effects on capital in 1912, only growth has a significant effect. Net of capital in 1904, quickly growing industries are more likely to have high capital in 1912 than slowly growing industries. Thus major corporations were generally able to prosper from growth in output. This is not completely tautological. One could imagine that the capital invested to 1904 paid off in output between 1904 and 1912, but that there was not necessarily greater investment during that period or that increased output was achieved by firms other than major corporations. This result is a change from 1904, as reported above, when growth had virtually no effect on the first generation of large corporations. Yet capital intensity, which had such a strong effect in 1904, had virtually no effect in 1912. This is especially troubling for efficiency theory's hypothesis that continuity in the distribution of modern business enterprise is a function of stable technological and market forces. However, the reduced effect of capital intensity is consistent with institutionalization theory, which suggests that structural factors have a stronger effect on the adoption of organizational forms when they are first introduced than after they become institutionalized, when new organizations adopt the innovation regardless of structural conditions (Tolbert and Zucker 1983). Similarly the effect of average size of establishment, which was hypothesized by power theory rather than efficiency theory, shows no significant effect. This can also be seen as the result of institutionalization, in which persistence results from contextual factors more than specific characteristics that create the initial adoption of the innovative organizational feature. Altogether, the analysis of capital in 1912 shows that only the level of capital in 1904 and the rate of growth are significant factors. Contrary to efficiency theory, the initial causes of variation in the creation of large corporations are highly consequential and seem to become increasingly so since new large firms have tended to become organized as large-scale socially capitalized corporations as a matter of routine. The results are consistent with the argument that firms with initial advantages use those advantages to reproduce their prominence. To understand why large firms are organized in large corporations today, a historical perspective that explains why the corporate revolution happened at all is necessary.

CONCLUSION

This chapter has posed a major challenge to the conventional wisdom about the rise of modern economic forms in general and the large corporation in particular. Efficiency theory has advanced our understanding of economic processes by addressing the issue of why a major institutional change like the large corporation was distributed so unevenly across the industrial landscape. Its answer is that large corporations were more rational in some industries than others. During the critical period known as the corporate revolution, when large-scale industrial corporations came to dominate the American economy, corporations should have arisen in industries with high capital intensity, high productivity, and rapid growth. This chapter's most important finding is that these widely cited factors did not stimulate incorporation. Only the average size of the firm and capital intensity accounted for the rate of incorporation.

In a systematic test, efficiency theory thus fails to explain why major corporations arose in the industries they did. This "negative finding" is a point of departure for the rest of this book. The results of this empirical statistical analysis set the stage for a more historical and institutional analysis that is less amenable to model quantitatively.

Subsequent chapters will develop an alternative account of the rise of the American industrial corporation. I explore the historical process that explains why the corporate institutional structure was there to adopt at the end of the century, why it remained distinct from manufacturing, and how the corporate institution and manufacturing finally fused. Unlike the efficiency model, with its emphasis on markets and technology, I focus on the role of the state, especially law, and the dynamics of institutional power.

APPENDIX 2.1: DETAILS OF VARIABLES

The data for the dependent variables were taken from the *Manual of Statistics*, an annual compilation of information on all firms listed on the major stock exchanges. Each annual issue was read by a coder, who recorded data on every manufacturing corporation. Data included the name, founding information, and the authorized amount of common stock, preferred stock, and bonds. The amount of authorized common stock and bonds does not indicate true monetary value of the firm or its assets. The period is notorious for nearly worthless "watered" stock. Rather, the variable indicates the firm's stature within the corporate sector. Highly capitalized firms could successfully market their securities. The extent to which capital listed on stock exchanges represented the money value of their capital assets varied substantially. Thus I will distinguish an industry's *corporate* "capital" represented by stocks and bonds from *manufacturing* "capital" reported to the census representing the value of physical assets.

As noted, the first dependent variable is a dummy variable indicating whether the industry had any major corporations, that is any corporations that totaled at least $1,000,000 capital, listed in the *Manual of Statistics* in the years 1901–1904. The effects of the independent variables could have been estimated in one operation rather than two using Tobit analysis.[11] Tobit is not used here because I do not assume that the same factors that determine whether or not an industry had any corporate capital also determine how much capital an industry had if there were corporations.[12]

The second dependent variable is the *extent* to which industries with any major corporations were organized by corporate capital. Several options exist for operationalizing this: (1) One could measure the number of corporations. But concentrated industries had few corporations. (2) One could assess the amount of capital in corporations, either the total corporate activity or the amount of new corporate activity. If one measures all corporate capital, one cannot establish the causal direction between independent and dependent variables, because much of that capital might have been incorporated before the time point when the independent variables were measured. If one measures only new incorporation, industries that had been previously fully incorporated would be erroneously measured as unincorporated. (3) Finally, one could use the size of the largest corporation in an industry. Insofar as the degree of incorporation is explained in terms of such factors as economies of scale that treat the corporation as an indication of scale, the largest corporation in the industry is appropriate. Moreover, it has the computational advantage that it is not relative to the way that the boundaries of the industry are drawn. The size of the largest firm, however, indicates more about the degree of concentration than the total level of incorporation.

These four variables are highly correlated, with all intercorrelations in the .8 and .9 range. Thus the results using any of these four dependent variables approximates the results with the other three. It is pointless to present the results using all four dependent variables, even though there are conceptual nuances in what is being measured. All four indicate the extent of incorporation for the industry.

Total capital rather than new capital is used for two reasons. New capital might be used to eliminate reciprocal effects between dependent and independent variables by requiring that the measurement of the dependent variable temporally follow that of the independent variable. However, virtually all corporations listed on the stock exchanges were created between 1898 and 1904. It is unlikely that characteristics of industries measured in the 1900 census, which is based on data collected in 1899, would be materially affected by corporations formed in the previous year. The results using total capital as the dependent variable are stronger than using new capital. Since the substantive conclusions emphasize the weakness of some results, it is methodologically conservative to choose the methods that tend to yield the strongest results. Thus I use the *average aggregated value of authorized stocks and bonds averaged for the years 1901 to 1904* (logged to reduce skewness in its distribution). In order to minimize the effect of different industry boundaries, the number of establishments (logged) is used as a control variable.

Independent Variables

These data were taken from the Census of Manufacturing. All the independent variables were measured prior to the dependent variable. Thus reciprocal causation from cross-sectional analysis is not a problem.

A. GROWTH: (aggregate value of production in 1900 – value of production in 1890)/(value of production 1890 + value of production in 1900).

B. WORKER PRODUCTIVITY: (value added in manufacturing)/(number of workers).

C. CAPITAL INTENSITY: (capital costs)/(labor costs).

D. SIZE OF FIRM: (number of workers)/(number of establishments).

The following variables were logged to reduce skewness: PRODUCTIVITY, CAPITAL INTENSITY, and SIZE.

CHAPTER THREE

The Corporation as Public and Private Enterprise

IN THE TWENTIETH CENTURY the corporation has been the preeminent institutional form of the system of private enterprise that we call capitalism. When we think of who wields private power, such corporations as Exxon, AT&T, General Electric, or USX (U.S. Steel) quickly come to mind. Even though capitalist states have, until the last decade or so, regularly intensified their intervention into the economy, the very language we use to describe this process assumes a fundamental distinction between public and private spheres. Most U.S. observers assume that production and distribution are naturally private, best administered by the enlightened self-interest of owners and managers, with government protecting the public from business excesses. The corporation's most fundamental deterrents against government interference have been its right to privacy and the belief of policymakers that as many functions as possible should be left to private rather than public decisions.

The corporation, however, has not always been a private institution. Corporations were originally chartered by governments to accomplish public tasks, to build roads, construct canals, explore and settle new lands, conduct banking, and other tasks governments felt could not or should not be conducted privately. Contrary to the notion that corporations autonomously developed because they competed more efficiently or effectively in the market, governments created the corporate form to do things that rational businessmen would not do because they were too risky, too expensive, too unprofitable, or too public, that is, to perform tasks that would not have gotten done if left to the efficient operation of markets. Corporations were developed to undertake jobs that were not rational or not appropriate from the perspective of the individual businessman.

This chapter will describe how the large corporation shifted from a quasi-public agency—in principle accountable to all, embedded within an institutional structure that served the public sector—into a private agency, protected from government accountability by individual rights and legally accountable to no one but its owners. My goal is to demonstrate that the corporation grew into its modern form less by efficiently adapting to the demands of technological development and the growth of markets, than politically, by the exercise of power. The state not only defined what the corporation was and the particular rights, entitlements, and responsibilities that owners, managers, workers, consumers, and citizens could legally exercise relative to the corporation, it actively established and capitalized corporations.

   The implicit causal model underlying my analysis manifests a tension between path dependence and contingency. Path dependence is a model of
change and continuity. Historians of technology have observed that certain
innovations established practices that were very difficult to change when
new conditions made them maladapted. The archetypical case is the so-
called QWERTY typewriter keyboard, which was designed to prevent typists
from typing so fast they would jam the keys. Very common letters like
the vowels were placed so that the typist's fingers would have to reach or
use a weak finger. But once typewriters improved so that keys did not jam
so readily, the difficulty of retraining typists prevented the adoption of
more efficient keyboards (David 1975, 1986). McGuire, Granovetter, and
Schwartz (forthcoming) have broadened the concept to institutional innovations. Material and intellectual resources are invested in institutions
which exact a very high cost of change. However, they add an additional
dimension to the model: consistent with the logic of power, they pay careful
attention to whose cost is being considered. They emphasize conflict over
which choices are made in the construction of an institution as well as
whose costs are at stake in perpetuating the initial structures. Examining the
formation of the American electrical power industry, they analyze how the
interaction of inventors like Thomas Edison, financiers like J. P. Morgan,
electric company executives like Samuel Insull, and government officials determined not only the technological form of electricity in central power stations rather than home generators or AC rather than DC, but also the very
boundaries of the industry itself, for example, in whether the generation of
power and the manufacture of generators would be included in the same
industry. These outcomes then framed the "paths" which subsequently
structured the vested interests of providers, consumers, and regulators of
electricity and electrical equipment. The concept of path dependency assumes that contingency is historically variable. If we are looking retrospec-
tively from the maturation of a social institution, methodologically, we
must identify those points at which options became remote when paths
were crystallized. Analysis then requires that we specify what options are
relatively closed and what issues remain to be contested.
   For the history of the large corporation in America, this chapter will examine how corporate form became privatized, closing off reasonable prospects for continued public accountability. I will review the experience of
three states, Pennsylvania, Ohio, New Jersey, to show how their experience
with corporations in the first half of the nineteenth century created legacies,
or paths, that help explain their different stances toward corporations in the
late nineteenth century. The early experience did not determine the later
policies, but did set the context within which later actors had to contend,
the "circumstances not of their own choosing" under which, as Marx told
us, people make their own history. By the decades around the Civil War, the
modern large corporation was protected by law as a form of private property, embedded in financial institutions that had once been dedicated to

public finance, but confined to transportation and communication industries. This chapter describes how government became involved in creating corporations, especially in canals and turnpikes, and what sort of experiences led to its retreat, emphasizing that neither the initial role of government nor its retreat was inevitable. Retreat occurred not because of the inherent inefficiency of government, but because particular events became issues in particular conflicts, whose outcome was determined at least as much by political power as by the efficient operation of the market. And insofar as industrialists and financiers were creating corporations to take advantage of economies of scale in the late nineteenth century, the institutional forms they had to choose from were built along the paths set by the contingent, political outcomes in the first half of the century. The next chapter describes how the modern private corporation as we know it arose around the railroad. But many issues remained contingent, especially the particular rights, entitlements, and responsibilities that states would allow, as discussed in Chapter 6, and most important, whether large corporations would remain confined to industries like railroad and communication or spread into manufacturing, as discussed in Chapters 7 and 8.

THE MEANING OF PUBLIC AND PRIVATE ARENAS

What are the implications of the pervasive assumption that economic activities are naturally economic, that is, that imagining, inventing, producing, distributing, and consuming for human needs "naturally" occurs autonomously from state structures? Except for explaining how the unnatural fetters of traditionalism had to be removed in order for the market economy to reach its immanent potential, analysts of this perspective are relieved of having to explain the divergence or interdependence between state and economy. Only active government involvement is treated as something requiring explanation. Like an egg without a chicken, only the shell that impedes the chick from pecking its way out is problematized. The chick itself is taken as a given, a creature destined to mature when its protective shell is tossed aside. The economic nature of property, commerce, and material infrastructure is taken as a given, needing no explanation; only their political nature becomes the object of historical inquiry. For example, in discussing why large American land companies in the late eighteenth and early nineteenth centuries did not acquire charters, Livermore writes, "A charter was needed only for some exclusive privilege which included the right to govern an area (for example, the proprietary colonies) or the right to engage in a business otherwise closed to private enterprise for reasons of public policy (as banking, turnpike roads). . . . Purely private organization there held the field, and experimentation in form and operation, unhampered by legislative restriction, was the rule" (Livermore 1939, 215). He assumes that what some might see as a "natural" government activity—distributing virgin public land—is a naturally private activity that was best "unhampered by legislative restriction." His analysis anachronistically assumes that such activities as banking or building roads were normally private business activities, a notion that would have surprised eighteenth-century observers, who viewed money and roads as public concerns. He leaves unexplained how these activities (at least some of them, like highways, are still public) became privatized, and how the legal form became used by private businesses. Whether or not the public policy was appropriate, Livermore problematizes only the deviation from "the rule." Had the large land companies operated privately, he presumably would have found no need for explanation. My perspective is that we must explain not only why any particular activity is public or private, but why and how the distinction is historically constructed and altered.

The division of power between public and private sectors is important because it frames the structure of authority, accountability, and power (Horwitz 1977). In the public arena all citizens theoretically have a right to make claims and be taken into account when important decisions are contemplated. Organizations can be held accountable to the collective interest of citizens. In the private sphere, people have a right to influence activities only to the extent that they have vested rights. Vested rights can take the form of membership in voluntary organizations or economic resources in market-based organizations. Marx and Weber both recognized that the most powerful vested rights are those constituted in property. These lines of accountability determine for whose benefit activity is conducted. Is a canal, turnpike, or railroad built to serve the interests of the public at large, or is it built to serve the interests of the stockholders? This is the fundamental difference between public and private property. Public property, of course, does not guarantee that activity is conducted in the public interest, but merely places it in a structure with potential lines of accountability to the public. Private property does not mean there can be no benefit to the public, but only that those making decisions are free to weigh their own interests however they choose.

The division between public and private is itself a historical construct. Economic and political categories are not natural and inevitable, nor is the division of labor between them. What the state does and what others do is historically constructed, constituted in the way that states and other institutions develop. Many of the activities that states routinely conduct have been—and some continue to be—handled privately. Private groups have built roads, supplied water, adjudicated disputes, protected people from enemies, disposed of sewage, educated children, and issued currency. States have in contrast performed such "private" tasks as producing consumer goods, trading commodities, speculating in land, and investing in enterprise. The boundaries that separate modern polities and economies could have been very different. The corporation could have continued as a kind of state agency, an organizational means of mobilizing private resources to serve collective or state interests. For example, the financial market institutions developed in tandem with the federal treasury (Ardent 1975). Rather than sell securities through private brokers, the state could have sold, and at times attempted to sell, securities directly. These boundaries must be explicitly explained, not simply taken as natural.

Thus the private sphere is not the natural home for corporations, which arose after public and private spheres had been not only constructed, but radically redefined and the distinction between them deepened. The organizational features, the social relations constituted among directors, owners, managers, workers, and customers, were all socially constructed. When corporations were public, they were accountable to the government and, in principle, to the people, so profit was only one organizational goal. In order to have the privilege of limited liability, gain access to the bountiful supply of Wall Street capital, and achieve the right to act as legal individuals, the incorporating individuals had to pledge fealty to the state. They had to be accomplishing something for the public good, at least as legislators defined it. Those who pursued private profits for personal gain were on their own. They had to risk their own assets, as business norms dictated responsible individuals should. Even when they supplemented their own resources with those of other similarly liable individuals, the law treated them as their own natural person without the shield of a corporate entity. But they owed nothing to any larger authority or broader public. Profit could be pursued for the sake of profit—private enterprise for private ends.

To say that states and other institutional structures are built, not discovered, is not to say that historical development is entirely accidental or that there are no general principles that help explain the particular structures that did develop. This chapter will show that the corporation arose as a quasi-state activity and became privatized as the result of concrete political conflicts over the nature of the state. The debate was not about whether corporations should be located in preexisting public and private sectors. Rather, the conflict over the corporation coincided with a broader movement for a new definition of appropriate state powers, one that would construct a private sphere that was eventually understood as though it were separate. Within this broad process of socially constructing the boundaries between state and economy, my focus is on the large corporation and the political movements and conflicts that shaped it.

THE CORPORATION AS A PUBLIC INSTITUTION

In 1772, George Washington led a movement in the Virginia legislature to create a company to make the Potomac River navigable. After the American Revolution and some interstate squabbles delayed the project, the Potomac Company was created in 1785, with Washington as president and Thomas Jefferson as one of the directors. By 1801, despite numerous problems and setbacks, 338 miles of river were open for navigation at a total cost of about half a million dollars. Maryland and Virginia had supplied over half the capital, and foreign (Dutch) investors were also involved (Davis 1917; Littlefield 1984). What made this project unusual was its interstate nature and the prominence of its organizers. For Washington, an owner of considerable Virginia land, private interest conveniently coincided with public interest, another common feature of early corporations. Ultimately it was a financial disappointment and technical failure. One historian concludes that "indeed its significance lies primarily in its demonstration that joint-stock companies were poorly equipped to carry out major internal improvements without massive and reliable government aid, especially during the first few decades after independence" (Littlefield 1984, 565).[1]

Before the liberal revolutions of the eighteenth and nineteenth centuries, European governments extended sovereignlike legal status to many corporate bodies (Sewell 1992). Guilds, municipalities, associations, and corporations were granted particular rights and the authority to enforce their own law. Each individual was subject to the law of the corporate bodies to which he or she belonged, often without recourse to adjudication to a higher authority. It was against this system that the founders of liberalism professed that all men are created equal, meaning that all men should be under the sovereignty of a single authority, that some should not be privileged with special rights or responsibilities. The corporation, that most "modern" of economic organizations, thus is the continuation of a premodern system. Its legally binding by-laws are a delegation of state sovereignty, a vestige of its public origins. Why the business corporation (along with municipalities, churches, and universities) was able to escape the sword of liberalizing egalitarianism is something that needs to be explained. The taint of privilege and monopoly continued to be the basis of considerable anticorporate mobilization, as we shall see below. Corporations were opposed both by those who advocated the elimination of corporate rights and privileges because they usurped legitimate public power and by those who wanted to extend corporate rights to all. The latter group won; the government extended the rights and entitlements of collective ownership to all who could afford it, and retreated from demanding the responsibilities it once had. The corporation survived, but as a private rather than as a public organization.

As it turned out, the corporation came to be legally constituted in a way that conformed to the liberal doctrine of equal rights for all while maintaining many of the rights and privileges that made corporate property different from individual property. The key to the meaning of privatization is that corporate property could be legally created by the state while being protected from the state by constitutional rights; it could be legally democratic and private. Privatization was achieved by a sociologically naive legal redefinition: treating the corporation as though it were an individual legally separate from the individuals who participated in it. This feature conflicts with a basic tenet of the common law of property: it clouds the distinction between personal rights (in personem) and rights in property (in rem)

(Creighton 1990). Traditionally, to redress an injustice or a debt, one could sue not property, but only people. Ownership carried the privileges of profiting from property but also the liability of being responsible for it, a responsibility that extended beyond the value of the property itself to the other assets of the owner. If a horse throws you because the owner failed to shoe him properly, you may sue for more than the value of the horse itself. The owner's possessions can also be taken. In contrast, the corporation embodies a legal entity between the property and the owners. It owns the corporate property and the stockholders own pieces of it. Because of the common law distinction between in personem and in rem, private individuals lack the prerogative to create a property-owning corporate entity, but can hold property only as individuals. However, the state can create a new legal entity, an extension of itself and its powers. It is only as a delegation of state powers that states would allow corporations to exist independently of the individuals they comprised. As it turned out historically, states defined the relationship between the groups and their members as a relationship of property, thereby undermining accountability to the public and framing political discourse over the corporation within the language of privacy rights versus state interference. But it need not have been so. Considering all the rights, entitlements, and responsibilities of property, it is curious that states defined the members as owners. States could have created commissions with citizens who served as directors. Such organizations could have raised capital through financial instruments, like bonds, or the powers of taxation, like municipal corporations. Mayors and city council members do not own the city but exercise binding authority within it. Business corporations, however, typically required financial resources from a small number of wealthy individuals who demanded control. Since organizations are inclined to use existing institutionalized forms rather than create entirely new relations, states defined the relations between members and the new organizations as property rights, but transformed the meaning of property by legally divorcing the rights in personem and the rights in rem. The "owners" originally had the rights of ownership but not all the responsibilities. At first this new definition of property was negotiated, because the state had to depend on external resources. And it was for the convenience of the state that such entities were created. Thus the earliest forms of corporations in this country were those that had the clearest public purpose—churches, schools, and cities. Over time, the institution was used for public needs with clear economic benefits—canals, banks, bridges, and turnpikes. It was last used for explicitly private enterprise in manufacturing and later retail activities.

The boundaries between the personhood of rulers, the state apparatus, and the citizenry have always been fluid and contested. Modern states have created many instruments other than official government agencies to perform tasks. Armies have been composed primarily of mercenaries hired by contracting with professional soldier/entrepreneurs with their own militia.

Venality and tax farming were used to allocate jobs and raise funds; justices of the peace and parliaments did so elsewhere. States have created academies of science to develop and certify technical expertise needed for economic and political power. In this country between 1800 and 1860, especially at the state level, governments extensively built penitentiaries, reformatories, and institutions for the aged, mentally unfit, and disabled. They gave aid to schools and colleges and subsidized county and state agricultural societies (Scheiber 1975; Studenski and Krooss 1963). They financed and regulated banks, insurance companies, and transportation. As will be detailed later, internal improvements were among the most ambitious and most consequential projects they undertook.

Among the various alternatives that American governments had with which to accomplish tasks, it was the corporation they turned to for projects that required more resources than they could raise from taxes. While fledgling American governments were limited by both the low level of commercialization and the strong antitax sentiment that had helped fuel rebellion against colonial rule, the corporate form gave them access to the resources of the world of finance capitalism, especially from abroad. As public entities, corporations were created by what is now known as a special charter, an act of a legislature (or monarch, in some nations) to create a corporation. By the time general incorporation replaced special incorporation, most legislatures were acting pro forma, routinely passing charters without debate. But in the eighteenth century, when corporations were considered public entities, legislatures would conscientiously consider requests for incorporation in committee, hold hearings, and openly debate the merits of each charter. New England towns often collectively supported or opposed proposed water or highway companies (Davis 1917). Failure to serve a public need was sufficient grounds for denying a charter. For example, in 1833 the Pennsylvania legislature vigorously debated a coal company charter, the opposition maintaining that the industry had become sufficiently developed that it could attract private capital and had no need for a charter (Hartz 1968). Both sides assumed that charters were appropriate only for public needs. In New Jersey and Pennsylvania until well into the nineteenth century, legislatures allowed highway companies to be created according to specified procedures, but the corporate charter would be granted only by the governor after the company proved itself. As public entities, corporations had both privileges and responsibilities. Seavoy (1982) explains that the device of the charter "assumed that corporations were legally privileged organizations that had to be closely scrutinized by the legislature because their purposes had to be made consistent with public welfare" (5). By the end of the eighteenth century many states had general incorporation laws for religions, academies, and libraries, but not business corporations. By early in the nineteenth century states were developing laws to regulate all corporations of a particular type, such as canals, turnpikes, banks, or manufacturing.

A charter would be created granting a monopoly over some function if individuals would share in the financing and operation of the new organization. Whether initiated by citizens or officials, the corporate form was used for tasks that served the public, but which neither the government nor the citizens were willing to do on their own—universities (like America's oldest corporation, chartered in 1688, Harvard University), banks, churches, canals, municipalities, and roads.

Business corporations before the late eighteenth century were rare, with only six nonbank business corporations prior to 1789 (Bosland 1949):

The New York Company for Settling a Fishery in These Parts (1675)

The Free Society of Traders in Pennsylvania (1682)

The New London Society United for Trade and Commerce in Connecticut (1732)

The Union Wharf Company of New Haven (1760)

The Philadelphia Contributorship for Insuring of Houses from Loss by Fire (1768)

The Proprietors of Boston Pier or Long Wharf, in the Town of Boston in New England (1772)

The Bank of North America was the first wholly American corporation, being chartered by the Continental Congress in 1781. The Society for Establishing Useful Manufactures of New Jersey, chartered in 1791, was the first postconstitutional corporation, an outgrowth of Alexander Hamilton's policy of aggressive industrial development (Davis 1961). In 1795 North Carolina passed the first general enabling act for canal companies to incorporate. Four years later, Massachusetts gave water supply companies the same option. "By the end of the eighteenth century the corporation was a familiar figure in the economic life of the larger American cities; and it was rapidly ceasing to be an object of awe in the smaller towns and country districts" (Davis 1917, 291). By 1800 there were 335 business corporations in the country, of which nearly two-thirds were in New England.[2] Highway companies (including inland navigation, toll bridge, and turnpike) were the most common, with 219 companies (65 percent), with banking second at 67 companies (20 percent) (although the capital invested in banks and insurance exceeded that of bridges and turnpikes). Local public service companies (primarily water supply) made up about 11 percent of the total. But manufacturing and merchant corporations (not public utilities, insurance, or banks) constituted only 4 percent of the total (thirteen charters) (Davis 1917, 26). All of these were struggling at the turn of the nineteenth century. None had paid dividends, several had suspended operations or dissolved. None was profitable. No sensible person would have predicted that at the end of the new century, corporations not only would be distinct from government but would also dominate the manufacturing sector.

From the end of the eighteenth century forward, states readily incorporated businesses relating to infrastructures, especially canals, turnpikes, water supply, and wharf companies. New York led the way with the famous Erie Canal, linking the Hudson River with Lake Erie and intended to stimulate territorial development in the West. Its financial success—it paid for itself in ten years—was a powerful weapon for growth coalitions in other states. Between 1825 and 1833, Ohio built the Ohio Canal, costing more than $3 million, providing another route to the West. Maryland gave or loaned $15 million for the Chesapeake and Ohio, Baltimore and Ohio, and Baltimore and Susquehanna railroads. Pennsylvania built almost a thousand miles of canals and incurred a nearly $17 million debt (Studenski and Krooss 1963). We can metaphorically say that transportation paved the road for the modern business corporation.

The early infrastructure projects not only constructed canals, turnpikes, and railroads; they were among the more formidable American state-building activities of the first half of the nineteenth century. That is, they not only developed the "private" sector, but also helped build the government apparatus itself. Despite the mid-century retreat from direct investment, the job of planning and financing infrastructure compelled governments to build bureaucracies for administration as taxation. For example in 1838, the last year before a depression which severely curtailed government activity, the federal government spent over $1 million on rivers and harbors out of budget that spent just under $15 million for nonmilitary expenditures (U.S. Bureau of the Census 1975, 675, 1115).

The constitutional convention considered and rejected a motion to vest the power of incorporation in Congress. Davis (1917) cites discussions indicating that the delegates assumed that the Congress would have power to charter corporations engaged in interstate commerce. In the debates surrounding the Constitution, five states, fearing monopoly, passed resolutions to ban Congress from chartering corporations. After the Constitution was ratified, Alexander Hamilton, despite considerable opposition, convinced Congress and the President to charter the Bank of the United States, but controversy continued when it was rechartered in 1811–12. The question was finally put to the Supreme Court in 1819, when Chief Justice Marshall upheld the charter in the historic *McCulloch v. Maryland*. The bank, however, could not withstand Andrew Jackson's attacks a decade later. Although the Court affirmed the constitutionality of congressional charters, the intense political conflict mitigated against routine use of the power. Davis (1917) summarizes, "Interstate communications of various sorts, at least, might well have been set afoot under congressional charter, but the fear of sinister influence at Philadelphia, the jealousy of the dignity of the state legislatures, the wish to have the ultimate decisions made locally in matters not of universal scope—these shut off at the outset any tendency which might have arisen in favor of numerous federal acts of incorporation" (15–16). When the Bureau of Corporations, with the active support of many corporate leaders, attempted to pass a general federal incorporation law a century later, these same objections were successfully raised again.

GOVERNMENTS AND ECONOMIC GROWTH

In addition to protecting life and property while providing for the common defense, modern governments have been dedicated to the common wealth. Modern capitalist states have overwhelmingly committed themselves to economic development. Whether legitimized by mercantilist, laissez-faire, or Keynesian ideologies, they have vigorously promoted economic development. In the early decades of the nineteenth century, Pennsylvania had a policy of making direct loans to manufacturers who could not raise enough capital. For example, in 1809 William M'Dermott of Bedford County received a loan to expand his steelworks on the justification that "works of public importance deserve public encouragement" (Hartz 1968, 56). Hartz argues that such a policy was rarely explicitly justified because its legitimacy of government economic activism was taken for granted. Throughout the first third of the nineteenth century, judicial decisions took for granted the public nature of corporations supplying infrastructural needs. Chancellor Kent of New York crystallized legal opinion in 1823, writing, "Turnpike roads are, in point of fact, the most public roads or highways that are known to exist, and, in point of law, they are made entirely for public use, and the community have [sic] a deep interest in their construction and preservation. They are under legislative regulations, and the gates are subject to be thrown open, and the company indicted and fined, if the road is not made and kept easy and safe for the public use" (quoted in Dodd 1954, 44). That virtually all early road and canal corporations were given the power of eminent domain also attests to their public nature. It was not until mid-century, when laissez-faire ideologies became thinkable, that explicit justifications for state intervention were articulated. Chief Justice Black in the 1853 *Sharpless* case over the legality of Philadelphia's investing in a branch of the Pennsylvania Railroad, illustrates the new defensiveness: "It is a grave error to suppose that the duty of a state stops with the establishment of those institutions which are necessary to the existence of government: such as those for the administration of justice, the preservation of the peace, and the protection of the country from foreign enemies. . . . To aid, encourage, and stimulate commerce, domestic and foreign, is a duty of the sovereign, as plain and as universally recognized as any other" (quoted in Hartz 1968, 122).

OPPOSITION TO CORPORATIONS

The public nature of the corporation was not only a justification for corporations but also a basis for opposition to business corporations. For much of the antebellum period the public arena provided the discourse for both sides of the debate over corporations. Hurst (1970) has called this the responsibility principle, by which issues were framed in terms of the reasonable use of government power to achieve public responsibilities.[3] When corporations unequivocally provided public functions, opposition tended to be sporadic and ad hoc. Support for infrastructure improvement was widespread and enthusiastic, with frequent appeals for people to invest in canals and railroads. One railroad president scolded stockholders demanding higher dividends for acting "as if they had invested as capitalists" (quoted in Goodrich 1960, 4). Corporations created for primarily private business purposes provoked criticism. John Taylor, a militant republican, arguing that corporations were a legal device to surrender public responsibility and public benefits to private parties, in 1792 warned that "corporations are only deeds of gift, or of bargain and sale, for portions of valuable common rights; and *parts* may be disposed of, until the whole is distributed among a few individuals" (quoted in Davis 1917, 305). In other words, corporations were not public enough because they parcellized and sold public responsibilities.

But the most enduring basis of opposition to corporations has been the charge of monopoly and privilege. Many early corporations were given monopoly rights as an incentive for investment. People were less likely to invest in a turnpike, bridge, or canal if they faced the prospect that their project could run into competition. There was nothing anomalous about this if the corporation was seen as an extension of the state, for which the essence of sovereignty is monopoly over authority. Sovereignty means that the state claims sole jurisdiction and the discretion to determine to whom it will delegate authority as it performs its historically determined tasks, including the authority to build roads, operate prisons, supply water, or enforce laws. When a state delegates authority to perform public tasks, it reserves for the delegatee some of its rights, entitlements, and responsibilities, which thereby constitute "privileges," or authority that others lack. When the delegatee is clearly performing a public task, we more often use the language of "duty" than "privilege." Municipal corporations are said to have a "duty" to enforce traffic laws; it would be unusual to hear of a policeman's "privilege" to carry a firearm or make arrests. It is only after the appearance of a private sphere, separate from government, in which individuals are presumed to have the same rights, that the concepts of monopoly or privilege gain potency. Both terms are used to criticize situations where the state extends its authority inappropriately into the private sphere. The business corporation was, in fact, a form of privilege. When granted to private interests, it extended economic rights not available to all. Turnpikes, canals, and especially banks were opposed because they allegedly squandered the common good to private individuals. Thus the charge of monopoly and privilege did not originally imply a desire for a free market. It could just as easily have been a demand for greater government accountability, enjoining the state from peddling or squandering its legitimate authority.

This anticharter philosophy crystallized in the first half of the century to become "one of the most powerful, repetitious, and exaggerated themes in popular literature" (Hartz 1968, 69). Corporations were characterized as "monopolies" and "aristocracies" and violated the "social contract." As Hartz analyzed it, the anticharter philosophy had several specific points: (1) It criticized organizational immortality as a form of inheritance that perpetuated wealth. (2) It pitted the individual against corporate rights. Limited liability, today universally hailed as a fundamental benefit of incorporation, was criticized because it undermined the right of the creditor and worker to just compensation. Eminent domain, which was often conferred on transportation companies, assaulted the rights of property owners. Because of this conflict between the organization's collective rights and individual rights, corporations were (ironically, in retrospect) labeled "communist." (3) In a constitutional attack on the corporation, it was claimed that the state was making invidious distinctions among individuals, affirming some people's property but not others'. (4) Presaging twentieth-century critiques, some argued that corporations would rule the state, gain political power, control the press, and dominate the electorate. Pennsylvania's governor, James Porter, argued at the state's Constitutional Convention of 1837, "In this country, sovereignty is vested in the people themselves, and whatever power is granted to corporations, is so much abstracted from the people themselves" (quoted in Hartz 1968, 75).

Finally, another Pennsylvania chief executive, Governor Shunk, arguing that corporations were monarchical impositions against popular sovereignty, offered the most ironic critique: "They are behind the times, they belong to an age that is past" (quoted in Hartz 1968, 75).

The solution to the other points implies more direct government involvement in performing the tasks than even the critics of corporations approved of. Preventing the corporation from perpetuating wealth, protecting individual rights from corporate intrusion, and protecting the state from inordinate corporate power would have been most effectively achieved by the state's reserving corporate prerogatives to itself. But as we shall see, when the state itself became vulnerable to a charge that it could not effectively and honestly ensure economic growth, the charge that corporations created privileges for some but not others became the focus of the anticorporate movement, solved by making incorporation a general right rather than a special privilege.

The anticorporate philosophy was embraced by both business and workers' movements. Workers' periodicals and pamphlets, drawing on republican ideology, identified laborers as the "people," the universal class. Labor legislation to uphold workers' rights was thus not class legislation but represented the public interest. Hartz explains, "As markets expanded and the factory system appeared, workers failed persistently to grasp the legitimacy of the functions that the new merchant, banking, and entrepreneurial groups were performing. Their thinking was wedded to an older period governed by a simple master-workman relation in which both employer and employee performed pretty much the same type of labor" (1968, 196).

Proponents of corporations rebutted the criticisms by invoking the same responsibility discourse, arguing that charters ensured public responsibility. Because charters were legislative enactments, the public interest was protected by restrictive clauses and the threat of having a charter revoked. Charters to business corporations in the eighteenth century routinely prohibited trading. Although few charters granted complete monopoly, charters often included clauses to prevent the concentration of power. For example, charters often specified a minimum number of subscribers to prevent any one individual from seizing control. Regular meetings of shareholders were required, as was election of directors. In some charters, rotation of directors was required, although this practice seems to have ceased by the end of the century. Interlocking directorates were sometimes prohibited. In the second decade of the nineteenth century, legislatures routinely placed a time limit and other restrictions specifying the conditions under which the charter would be revoked. For example, transportation companies were required to complete the project by a certain date, to use profits to redeem stock so that the facility would become free to the public, and to allow the state to purchase the facility after a given time. Later charters often carried a provision that the legislature had the power "to revoke, alter, or annul the charter hereby granted, at any time they may think proper" (quoted in Hartz 1968, 239). In Pennsylvania, an 1849 General Manufacturing Act set a twenty-year limit on manufacturing corporations. Throughout the first half of the century, regulative clauses were increasingly inserted in charters, specifying the number of directors, how they were chosen, and their powers and responsibilities. Manufacturing charters were especially restrictive. They limited the type of business that could be conducted and specified minimum levels of production, which if not met would lead to the revocation of the charter (Creighton 1990). For example, the Pennsylvania Coke and Iron Company chartered in 1831–32 was compelled to manufacture within three years five hundred tons of iron using only bituminous coal or anthracite in the process. Ordinarily authorization to borrow money or issue bonds was not given in the original charter, but required supplementary legislation. It was clear that ordinary manufacturing rarely merited the special privileges that corporations extended to those serving the public in general.

Over the nineteenth century the terms of the debate shifted from public to individualistic and utilitarian ideology. The new terms of the debate both reflected and helped constitute the deepening boundary between state and society. The "individual" was increasingly seen to reside outside of the state. While the conceptual boundaries solidified around the state, market and society were becoming ideologically blurred together in "civil society."[4] The abstract individual became situated within the market/society, where his needs were to be met. Liberalism's marriage of individualism and utilitarianism thus became the ideological linchpin of the privatization of the corporation. Rather than being an extension of government power to perform tasks on behalf of the public, it became a legal individual, legitimized by its alleged ability to maximize utility in the market. For example, both sides of a debate over selling the Pennsylvania canal system in the 1850s used the "individual enterprise" symbol. The anticharter partisans, who wanted the state to keep the canal, claimed that private corporations would hurt individual enterprise; the advocates of the sale maintained that transportation should be left to individual enterprise. Opponents drew on the anticorporate philosophy, charging corporations with centralized power, corruption, and lack of accountability to people. But proponents were able to draw on the novel but widespread sentiment that private firms were more effective and efficient, even though the spotty record of private corporations hardly warranted this. "Clearly something was happening here to the great 'individual enterprise' symbol. . . . The corporate system was simply beginning to appropriate for its own purposes the rich individualism of the anticharter theory" (Hartz 1968, 173–74). This was the last serious principled defense of state enterprise, fading in the face of rising laissez-faire.

THE ORIGINS OF LEGACIES: PENNSYLVANIA, NEW JERSEY, AND OHIO

The foregoing has discussed the ideological framework within which the corporation was privatized, but is not intended to provide a causal analysis. A fuller explanation involves specifying the groups who were acting and the constraints they were facing, who determined the constraints they were facing, and the interests at stake. My narrative focuses on several groups: urban merchants, finance capitalists, state officials, and farmers. The privatization of the corporation was not inevitable, not the result of inexorable historical impulses, but forged out of contingent concrete events. The construction of the transportation infrastructure by the various American states was the locus of most action, especially the development of canals, primarily through state-initiated corporations, followed more fully by railroads. The bad timing of the canal system, just as railroad technology was making canals virtually obsolete, the unfortunate occurrence of the depression of the late 1830s, and the way it was interpreted were all contingent events without which the modern corporation would have developed very differently. As the next chapter will elaborate, the development and privatization of railroad corporations were virtually synonymous. This chapter will describe the experience of three major bordering states that had very different outcomes and created very different legacies.

In 1812 the state of New York unsuccessfully asked Congress to support its plan to build a canal linking the Great Lakes with the Atlantic. Although the project undisputedly offered national benefits, the feeble national government left it to the states to construct the material infrastructure. New York proceeded on its own and built the Erie Canal, the most successful public works project of the nineteenth century, setting off an imitative wave throughout the country. However, few others were as successful. Had they been, the government's relationship to the economy might be very different today.

The public nature of the corporation, the states' commitment to economic growth, the anticorporate movement, and the eventual retreat from direct government investment were nationwide phenomena, occurring on the state level. There were important differences among the states, differences which established enduring legacies which molded states' relationship with corporations. As I will discuss more fully later, the marked difference among states' legal environments toward corporations helped shape what the corporation was to become and its ability to develop into the overwhelmingly dominant form for major economic activity. These differences were not the result of local conditions in the later part of the century, but emerged from paths taken generations earlier. Thus the explanation of differences among states that were so important in the late nineteenth and twentieth centuries is a historical explanation. I have selected the three major states, Pennsylvania, New Jersey, and Ohio, for examination. Although they share a single region, they differ remarkably in their policies toward corporations. New Jersey is well known as the "home of the trusts," where nearly all the large socially capitalized corporations at the turn of the century were chartered. Ohio throughout the nineteenth and into the twentieth century was one of the most rigorous states, not even fully limiting liability until this century. Pennsylvania fell into the middle, a heavy industrial state neither as permissive as New Jersey nor as restrictive as Ohio. Pennsylvania's investment in infrastructure was undertaken at the behest of Philadelphia merchants who subsequently decided the private Pennsylvania Railroad offered both the sinews of trade and private profit. Although Pennsylvania developed one of the longest and most physically impressive canal systems in the country, it was soon overshadowed by the railroad. Pennsylvania continued to closely regulate manufacturing corporations and maintain a suspicious attitude toward foreign (out-of-state) corporations. New Jersey, the headquarters of the corporation revolution at the end of the century, had an unusually positive experience with corporations in the first half of the century. It invested—and therefore lost—very little of its own funds. On the contrary, it had a uniquely symbiotic relationship with a single corporation, the Camden and Amboy Railway, which it endowed with monopoly rights in exchange for sufficient income to afford its citizens the luxury of a very low tax rate. Ohio's direct investment in corporations shared success and failure, the failure a result of the success. It initially created and supported an effective canal system that greatly facilitated the state's economic growth without fiscal stress. But its success, in the context of a strong democratic ethos, spurred a movement to extend its benefits to all regions of the state, whether or not they could support it. Ohio overextended itself building canals that could not pay for themselves, swamping the state in debt. The enduring legacy was a widespread apprehension of corporations and a desire for close state regulation. All three states were committed to facilitating economic growth; leaders in all three ambitiously pitted themselves in competition against other states. But the legacies of their experiences in using the corporation as a form of state building and economic development led them down very different paths, resulting in quite different corporate policies.

Pennsylvania

Pennsylvania is perhaps the most typical of the three states examined here. It had two major cities, a financial-commercial center in Philadelphia and a budding industrial giant in Pittsburgh; but, as in the nation as a whole, the majority of the people worked in agrarian pursuits. Pennsylvania's party system was well developed and consistently competitive, with neither party able to take incumbency for granted. The state government, like most in antebellum America, took an active interest in economic development and both sponsored and invested in the development of infrastructure, which was facilitated by its balance of agrarian and urban economies and the competitiveness of its political parties. Finally it was typical in the timing of events that included competition over western trade, investment in corporations, economic depression, the coming of the railroad, and the rise of laissez-faire ideology that undermined the publicly accountable corporation.

As in so many areas of early American economic development, Pennsylvania was a leader in the development of what would today be called the mixed corporation. Pennsylvania was extensively involved in creating and supporting corporations from 1793, when it chartered the Bank of Pennsylvania and subscribed to 2,500 shares at a value of $1 million, until it ceased such direct investment in 1857, when a constitutional convention forbade state investment in business corporations. Between 1790 and 1860, the state chartered 2,333 corporations for business purposes, of which 64 percent were in transportation, 11 percent insurance, 7 percent banks, and 8 percent manufacturing (Hartz 1968). Altogether it invested more than $6 million in 150 mixed corporations (Lively 1968; Bruchey 1990). While much of this investment was intended to stimulate economic growth, it was also seen as a source of revenue alternative to taxes. Hartz argues that the state invested in banking for the profit, since there was no shortage of capital for banks. In the 1820s the state's first and principal source of revenue was banks, semipublic institutions presumed to operate for the benefit of the public and not just bankers. The state frequently appointed directors to the corporations in which they had a financial stake. Yet other corporations were intended primarily for economic growth, not revenue. After 1806 the state began to assist turnpike companies by contributing capital, eventually investing over $2 million. In contrast to the rationale for supporting the banks, political leaders, when justifying state support of infrastructure, cited the high risk and difficulty in attracting private capital. Since no private company had ever returned as much as 5 percent on investment, the free market would not have developed the transportation facilities that nurtured development. If one assumes that modern economic development was inevitable, these corporations could be characterized as stop-gap measures to compensate for imperfections in the market. But such a teleological conception would anachronistically assume the bifurcation of public and private economic arenas. Building turnpikes, then, as now, was just something government did. And the corporation was merely the organizational device it used to do it. The ideological assumption that the state was responsible for economic development and the territorially based competition among the merchants of the large eastern seaboard cities reinforced each other to forge a compelling political logic.

Immediately after the Revolution, governments had taken total responsibility for turnpikes, but this had waned thereafter. Yet even in the 1820s debate centered on practical considerations, not the principle of public ownership. Hurst (1970) describes the ideological legitimation of corporations in this period as a "responsibility ethic." Debates concerned the ends for which the corporation was used, but not the states' right to own any public facility, either to promote development or to earn a profit. The "utility ethic," according to which corporations would be legitimated by their greater efficiency, had not yet arisen. The success of the Erie Canal would have undercut any attacks questioning the corporation on the basis of its efficiency. By the mid-twenties "[a] movement developed in behalf of state ownership which had the passion of a religious campaign" (Hartz 1968, 131). Led by the Pennsylvania Society for the Promotion of Internal Improvements in the Commonwealth, formed in Philadelphia in 1824, leaders included Chief Justice William Tilghman of the Supreme Court, the banker Nicholas Biddle, and the publisher Mathew Carey. Highly mobilized from the elite state level to local chapters, these advocates persuaded the legislature in 1826 to construct two canals, one from the western end of the Union Canal to the Susquehanna River, another from Pittsburgh to the Kiskeminitas River (Rubin 1961). By 1828, 5,000 workers were engaged in canal construction on contracts totaling $2 million (Bogart 1924). Although the prospects of a state-built canal system were vigorously debated, the terms of the debate took the legitimacy of public involvement for granted. The cleavage of the debate followed a political logic of class and sectionalism—the rural farmers against the urban merchants—not the utilitarian (and equally class-based) logic of efficiency. Rural criticism, that the canals would benefit only Philadelphia, was rebutted with the promise of development: everyone would prosper from the canal regardless of region. Supporters also optimistically envisioned enough public profit to provide other services and reduce taxes. "The older reliance on the private profit motive in the transportation field gave way to enthusiastic visions of public profit, free public services, and reduced taxation" (Hartz 1968, 138). Nonetheless, the arguments for public activism went beyond utility and pragmatism. Some advocated state ownership on the basis of anticorporate sentiment. Corporations would concentrate economic power and would be motivated by private gain rather than public service. What stands out about the debate is that both sides argued on behalf of public benefit and against private enrichment. No one argued that a private corporation would be a more efficient means of providing transportation. As long as the original conception of public accountability prevailed, the venture's problems would have been manageable. The project was designed to stimulate economic growth, not necessarily pay for itself, just as our highways are today. But when the ethic changed, its inability to compete with the unforeseen railroads undermined support not only for canals but for public enterprise in general.

The work was directed by a public canal commission. When it was created in 1824, its members were appointed by the governor, but antiexecutive sentiment in the thirties put the authority in the hands of the legislature. Public opinion turned against this system and in 1844, in the context of strong democratic sentiment, appointment to the board was changed to election by the public. "One of the knottiest administrative problems in the state was thus thrown into the lap of the people, and the prevailing democratic ideology was completely satisfied. Yet the measure was clearly unsuited to the immense administrative tasks involved in the works program" (Hartz 1968, 151). Because of fear of centralized power, the board was given little power. Most measures had to be approved by the legislature. Moreover, there was no precedent for this type of agency, which was not entirely legislative, executive, or judicial, and the leadership did little to establish an identity for itself or to establish consistent and appropriate relations with other branches and the public. The system's legitimacy was further damaged when a number of engineers and contractors were caught defrauding the public.

Sectional interests and logrolling fragmented the program and prevented a coherent system to meet the overall goal of linking Pittsburgh and Philadelphia. Each locality near the route wanted the canal to pass through or wanted a spur for access to the main line. The state was too weak a structure with too little autonomy from particular interests to rationally plan the system. As more legislators withheld approval unless their region was served, the price rose, reaching the enormous sum of $101,611,234. Without any state bureaucracy, financing and spending were not carefully planned or administered. By 1835 a Main Line of railroad and canal segments totaling 359 miles had been completed at a cost of $12,000,000, half of which was spent on branches so that communities other than those along the route could benefit (Goodrich 1960; Shaw 1990). The state debt was $24,589,743, most of which was for public works. In that year income from the tolls was only $684,557 compared with interest payments of $1,169,455 (Hartz 1968). Nonetheless, the accomplishment was quite impressive: a direct link from Philadelphia to Pittsburgh, transversing a major mountain range. The inclined plane railroad was the first double-track rail in the country, even though it was a stationary engine, and operated more steam engines (thirty-four in 1836) than any other line nationwide. It entered Pittsburgh over a 1,140-foot aqueduct resting on seven piers, completed in 1829, later replaced by a suspension bridge aqueduct, the first such structure in America. It connected the Monongahela through an 810-foot tunnel with four locks, completed in 1831. One 1835 account described part of the line east of Pittsburgh: "We passed over a beautiful stone aqueduct with leads into the mouth of a large tunnel eight hundred feet long which perforates the mountain and cuts off a circuit of four miles. The tunnel is cut through limestone rock for four hundred feet, and the rest is arched with solid masonry, as are both the entrances" (quoted in Shaw 1990, 69–70). The Erie Canal claims the honor of being the first and, because of its more fortunate timing, the most successful major canal. But the Pennsylvania Main Line was a more impressive engineering achievement. If the unforeseen development of the railroad had not rendered it obsolete within a decade or so of its completion, it would surely rank among the nation's most historic public works.

By the 1830s it was generally agreed that both the "mixed" corporation and the supplementary policy of public investment were not successfully meeting transportation needs, and full-fledged public ownership began to be debated. The vision of the proponents would have been difficult to achieve under any circumstances. But given the continuation of sectional and local demands on where to locate the canal, the ups and downs of the business cycle, and the lack of state administrative structures, the system's weaknesses made ready fodder for those who were increasingly applying the new utilitarian logic, using a bottom-line criterion to question the basic legitimacy of state enterprise.

In the early 1840s the movement to sell public works had picked up steam. Proponents of privatization contrasted state incompetence with the profitability of private railroads. The legislature was unwilling to supplement the revenues with taxation, especially during the depression when so many other states were becoming insolvent. As the discomfort of debt became the embarrassment of threatened insolvency, the state acted to change the system. By 1842, when the state failed to meet its interest payments, a debt of $33 million had been incurred for the public works (Goodrich 1960). Pennsylvania began disposing of its canal system in 1843. The Main Line from Philadelphia to Pittsburgh was offered for $20 million, too high a price to attract any bidders. In 1844 a public referendum asked whether the state should sell the Main Line. The most frequently cited justification of privatization was the state's need for money. Debate over the sale continued into the fifties, when a select committee of the Senate considering the sale in 1854 advocated a novel sentiment: "The separation of politics and trade would do much to restore our government to its original purity, and would be hailed by every virtuous citizen as the dawn of a brighter day. . . . Governments should be restricted to purely political powers necessary to the existence of society" (quoted in Hartz 1968, 166–167). The "original purity" was no more real than the Garden of Eden; the state had never been uninvolved in enterprise. The "separation of politics and trade" was a new idea. Its corollary, that the state should not compete with private enterprise, had only recently become a pragmatically plausible doctrine. Before 1825, only the fanciful would have imagined that private enterprise and state could have competed at the same level. No private enterprise could have managed the tasks. Not until the Pennsylvania Railroad was chartered and demonstrated its success would it have been conceivable to sell the Main Line to private interests. So how can we explain the fact that in 1857, the Pennsylvania Railroad bought it for only $10 million, with a provision for permanent tax exemption?

The anticorporate forces and the leaders of the Pennsylvania Railroad itself, as we shall see in the next chapter, wanted the government to retreat from direct enterprise. Both interpreted the fiscal crisis of the late thirties and forties in terms of the failure of public ventures, not the dangers of concentrated private power. The Pennsylvania Railroad became the world's largest corporation and helped the state achieve what the Main Line canal system had been intended for, linking the east and the west and helping the state compete against its neighbors. It is easy to look back and anachronistically condemn the canal system for its inefficiency, administrative frailty, and lack of foresight. However, by the goals set for it, it was relatively successful. It provided transportation for a generation of merchants and farmers in a relatively egalitarian fashion. Many political projects are not expected to make money for the state or even pay their own way, from the Department of Defense to the national parks. It is flawed history for those in the twentieth century to accept the novel arguments of the canal's opponents as the appropriate interpretation of events long past. In any case, the debates did not cease. The anticorporate legacy never died. Pennsylvania continued to monitor its corporations and was especially suspicious of out-of-state corporations, for example, prohibiting them from owning real estate. It eventually became a state of modest regulation, neither a home of the trusts like New Jersey nor a trust buster like Ohio.

Ohio

Although Ohio did not participate in the merchant-led competition among major cities that Pennsylvania did, it did develop an extensive canal system. But its government was even more generous with even less oversight, resulting in greater financial embarrassment. The legacy was stricter corporate law and a stronger antitrust tradition.

Ohio's first state constitution in 1802 had no provision for any corporation other than publicly owned corporations. By the time of its next constitution in 1852, it chartered an average of forty-five corporations per year, all of them public, in transportation, communication, banks, academies, churches, and literary societies (Bennett 1901). In one of the first acts after its admission to the union, Ohio, in 1803, created a saltworks to sell salt to its citizens. By the 1820s, overtly emulating New York's promising experience with the Erie Canal, it began its own canal project.

As Bogart (1924) tells the story, in 1822 the legislature passed a bill appointing an engineer and seven commissioners to survey and compare four possible routes to link the Ohio River with the Great Lakes. Led by James Geddes, who had worked on the Erie Canal, over the next two years they studied and planned, deciding on a route and estimating it would need $2 million in financing, which they felt was practical to raise. An 1825 referendum approved public funds for schools and canals, the latter to be planned by a commission with the power to borrow money against anticipated revenues. Typical of the privileges granted to corporations, it was given the right of eminent domain, and employees were exempt from military service or arrest in civil cases. Since taxes could not have raised sufficient revenues, an initial funding of $400,000, the state's first debt, was secured from the money markets in New York, Baltimore, Boston, and Philadelphia. The event illustrates how the construction of institutional structures in government and finance reciprocally shaped each other: Nathaniel Prime, John Jacob Astor, John Robins, and John Bone, four of the leading figures on Wall Street, created Wall Street's first lending syndicate to meet with delegates from the state and hammer out an agreement, setting conditions which the legislature then agreed to. Weak powers of taxation and a sprouting financial system underlay the institutional structure available for mobilizing resources for this kind of project. Other strategies to raise funds proved inadequate. For example, in 1826 towns and individuals with land on the route were asked to contribute land and donations, but the state received only $25,000.

The state was more than a passive investor. The administration of the canal and the finances were divided between the Board of Canal Commissioners and the Board of Canal Fund Commissioners. Learning from the New York experience of extensive overruns, Ohio required that contractors fulfill their contracts at the specified price. The actual construction was handled by private contractors, but the surveys, measurement of work and materials, laying out of the line of the canal, and general superintendence were done by state employees.

On July 4, 1827, amid boisterous patriotic and civic celebration over the accomplishment, the northern section, the most difficult part, was opened to traffic, linking Akron with Lake Erie and Cleveland. The following year, 5000 workers were constructing Ohio canals in contracts totaling $2 million. The branch from Cincinnati to Dayton opened in 1831, a length of 67 miles, and two years later so did the 333-mile link to Portsmouth on the Ohio River. The state had assumed a debt of $4,500,000 against expenses of $5,144,539. Although the debt was heavy, Ohio joined New York as a builder of effective, reasonably priced, and profitable canals. One authoritative history concludes, "The figures certainly indicate careful, economical, and honest administration of the work of construction" (Bogart 1924, 29; see also Goodrich 1960).

In 1846, when the projects were finished, the state had 731 miles of canal fully operating, 91 miles of slackwater navigation, and 31 miles of turnpike, all built for less than $16 million (Goodrich 1960). Thereafter the responsibility for public works fell on local governments. An 1852 report to Congress on colonial and lake trade by J. D. Andrews stated, "The rapidity of her progress has been the marvel of the country. In a very few years she rose from obscurity to the first rank among her sister states—The canals were the great cause of her unexampled prosperity, as they supplied a cheap route to market" (quoted in Bogart 1924, 79–80).

In the early years, the canals paid their own way, at least as far as operations were concerned. Receipts from the sale of land, levies, and other income exceeded expenses every year until 1856. But receipts did not pay the interest on the loans, so Ohio, like other states, used a variety of fiscal measures to meet its immediate obligations. To avoid using tax revenues, it "borrowed" funds from the state school fund, which included money raised by selling land given to the state for schools, and in some years, used surplus federal funds returned to the state. These ad hoc measures, which were not atypical of states in that era, enabled it to pay the interest on its loans. It tried every alternative to taxes it could think of, including drawing from the sinking fund (a fund to accumulate money in anticipation of a debt's due date). As a result the sinking fund did not accrue as needed to pay off the principal on the $16 million due in 1850. The existence of the sinking fund—even though inadequate—enhanced the state's credit rating, so that many of the loans in the late twenties and early thirties were sold at a premium, with one, the loan of 1832, reaching 24 percent above face value. As a consequence Ohio had a strategic canal system underlying the state's commercial development and a fiscal time bomb waiting to go off.

The success of the canals induced others to invest in transportation, both canals and railroads. As in Pennsylvania, the democratic ethos legitimized the demands of areas without canals that they be included in the system. Investors saw an opportunity for a safe investment. Democratic values of equality joined with private self-interest and state entrepreneurship in a flurry of infrastructure corporations. "In fact, it seemed as though the major part of the business of the legislature consisted of grants of articles of incorporation" (Bogart 1924, 47). The governor, in his 1834 message to the legislature, stated, "Statesmen of liberal minds cannot look with indifference upon any description of improvement that is calculated to better the condition and add to the comforts of the people in any part of the state" (quoted in Bogart 1924, 47). In 1837 the state passed a law that in retrospect seems like the height of folly, but in the context of the times was one of several experiments states were adopting in order to foster development. Ohio passed a general law assisting corporations in internal improvement, according to which any railroad, turnpike, canal, and slackwater navigation company that had two-thirds of its capital stock subscribed was entitled to a government loan for the additional third in the form of negotiable scrip or certificates of stock of the state. The assets of the company were to be the collateral. Turnpike companies had to raise only half of the stock themselves. Although the system did not meet modern standards of security, it did not entirely lack safeguards. Each loan had to be approved by the Board of Public Works, which had to establish that the company was financially sound and that its construction would not compete with any other company. No company could receive more than $300,000 a year. But it essentially put the credit of the state at the companies' disposal. The law, variously known as the "Loan Law," "General Improvement Law," and the "Plunder Law" was in effect for only three years, but was seized upon by the opponents of state activity as an example of government irresponsibility, risking public funds on poorly planned and at times corrupt private ventures.

The state also entered into "an extravagant policy of expansion of the public works" (Bogart 1924, 54). The governor, pushed to extend public works to all the counties not included in previous programs, built more in response to public opinion than any objective need, including six canals that cost a total in excess of $8.5 million. This and the loan law put a burden on the state that the depression made disastrous. By 1839 the state debt was $12 million, of which almost $2.5 million was for the loan law, generating increasing difficulties in placing loans on the capital market. In response to the growing state debt, the governor proposed to repeal the loan law, which the legislature did. By 1840 the situation had reached crisis proportions. The cost of unfinished public works overran general expectations, but the state lacked the means to pay for them. Its ability to borrow more had become severely circumscribed, but the cost of abandoning the projects would have been unthinkable. The desperate commissioners circulated a letter to local Ohio banks asking for loans, which secured $500,000 and got them through the year. At the end of the year, when the governor reported to the legislature that the debt was $14,809,477 and that nearly $2.5 million was needed to complete the public works, the state loaned the commission as much as it could. The New York market offered no viable terms, so Ohio again turned to state banks to get through the year. In March 1842, authorities suspended work on all projects except the Wabash and Erie Canal, ended further subscriptions to the stock of turnpike and canal companies, and discontinued the loan of state credit to railroad companies. This was the turning point. From then on the state abandoned its policy of active government economic action, adopting a purely defensive strategy, attempting to meet existing obligations but hastening resolutely toward a laissez-faire state.

The increasing burden of taxes, the growth of state debt, and repeated underestimates for unfinished public works were seized upon by the laissez-faire advocates, as were considerable incompetence, corruption, and loose oversight. Many modern interpretations (for example, Bogart 1924) see the attack on state activism as a natural and inevitable reaction. However, a case could have also been made, as it was very effectively made in France (Dobbin 1994), that what was needed was more government involvement, not less. One could have argued that the state system was primitive, but not inherently inept or corrupt. In other words, it was the interpretation given to events that made their consequence seem inevitable, not the events themselves. These states were charting unknown organizational/institutional territory and could have cleared a path in many other directions. For example, the structure of the canal fund commission changed four times in the late 1830s and early 1840s. The methods of accounting, organizational monitoring, planning, and administration were crude and simple. Little was institutionalized. Instead of using these circumstances to make a case for greater government involvement, politicians and journalists labeled government failure as inevitable and corporations necessary. In seeking to eliminate special corporate privileges, the anticorporate movement settled for democratizing corporate rights, or at least democratizing them for those able to own corporate property.

What might have been a swing of the pendulum of political ideology became cemented into law at a constitutional convention in 1851, dominated by antistate partisans. They included a provision that state debt, except for defense, could never exceed $750,000, prohibited the state or any agency or any locality from subscribing to private stock, and forbade the state from contracting any debt for internal improvement. The legislative session of 1852–53, following the constitutional convention, began to sell the canal system. A new public works committee proposed to sell the system for $4 million, but the legislature took no action until the next session, when some pieces were sold off. Opponents to state ownership pressed forward, citing the declining revenues, arguing that partisan politics had led to inefficient decisions and appointments. Ownership advocates charged that the real force advocating that the state abandon the canals was the railroads, who wanted to reduce competition. A very expensive 1860 flood, though not much worse than earlier floods, became another rallying point against state ownership, influencing the legislature the following year to lease the state's public works to the highest bidder for ten years. Only two bids, obviously in collusion, were received. The canals remained in private hands for sixteen years until the company failed, when they were returned to state management, where they stayed for good. For the entire period of private control, they paid only $332,238 in rental fees (Bogart 1924).

Although the canals were essential to Ohio's economic development and although they could have been completed in no other way, the state's legacy was a lingering anticorporate sentiment. Goodrich (1960) states,

"Ohio had been one of the major improvement states, with public investment amounting to some $27,000,000, and its early public works had made a substantial contribution to development. By the end of the period, however, with its program of public construction long since ended and with mixed enterprise prohibited, it stood as one of the chief examples of the revulsion of feeling against governmental promotion of internal improvements" (138). But the feeling was not just against government involvement. In the loan program, private corporations had taken advantage of the state. The state suffered not only because the canals lost the competition to the railroads, not only because it overextended its debt, and not only because it responded to a widespread democratic demand for equal access. The state also lost money to private corporations who took advantage of the state's largesse in the loan program. Even into this century, it was more restrictive of corporations and less permissive of their powers, vigorously resisting the chartermongering competition of other states at the end of the century.

Thus what began as a very promising proactive strategy of semipublic ownership and active government promotion of development-oriented corporations resulted in a strict constitutional prohibition on government participation in corporations and a legacy of rigorous suspicion of corporate power. It is the interaction of particular historical events such as the timing of the antebellum depressions, the mobilization of distinctive political groups advocating laissez-faire, and the specific definitions by which the latter were able to characterize the former that explains the relationship of the state to the corporation in Ohio.

New Jersey

In 1791 New Jersey incorporated America's first postrevolutionary manufacturing corporation, Alexander Hamilton's Society for Establishing Useful Manufactures.[5] A century later apologists for New Jersey's permissive corporation laws would cite this to show that New Jersey had always welcomed out-of-state business (Keasbey 1898). The society's advertisement solicited subscriptions on the grounds that New Jersey had fewer opponents of manufacturing than states with more extensive external trade or cultivatable land. Although the company may have been a harbinger of things to come, it was neither cause nor active precedent. After three years the company failed. Looking back, we can see that it was the first private manufacturing corporation, but it did not blaze any trails. The Society for Establishing Useful Manufactures' failure tells us more about its context than its projection to the future. Even in New Jersey, the "home of the trusts," the eventual route to the modern industrial corporation was via the public corporation. But the latter-day apologists for New Jersey were correct about its long legacy of corporate permissiveness. New Jersey did have an experience with corporations vastly different from that of Ohio or Pennsylvania. The state government invested much less capital in corporations and received much more, resulting in an unusually congenial relationship. To understand why New Jersey opened the legal door to the giant socially capitalized corporation, precipitating the corporate revolution at the end of the century, one must understand how its experience with corporations differed from that of states like Pennsylvania or Ohio.

New Jersey, more than other states, was inclined to favor private development for infrastructural development. It first encouraged private individuals to build canals, bridges, and turnpikes, before reluctantly using the power of the charter to grant the incentive of special privilege. The state's two bridge companies were entirely private, but the success of the third, a chartered corporation, set a precedent followed by all later companies (Cadman 1949). Turnpike corporations were even slower to develop. The only money New Jersey ever appropriated for a corporation was to the never completed Newark Turnpike Company in 1804, a sum of only $12,500, making up half its stock (Goodrich 1960). By 1801 there were seventy-two turnpike corporations in other states, but none in New Jersey, where Democrats charged that turnpikes were "subversive of the liberties of the people, closing old roads and making the proprietors rich at the expense of the people's rights, and in general a direct tendency to subvert our Republican Institutions" (Cadman 1949, 47). In 1811 the legislature rejected an application for a charter to build a railroad across the state, declaring it to be impractical. More than an ironic footnote to history, this indicates that the legislature exercised independent judgment about the economic feasibility of proposed corporations. It would not have occurred to the legislators to leave such judgment to the "discipline of the market." The legislature did pass another railroad charter three years later, but declined to risk public funds in support, instead granting the company the privilege of creating a lottery to raise its capital funds. In 1816 a Democratic governor expressed an opinion that foreshadowed later policy: "By enhancing the value of taxable property, they have increased the means of filling the state treasury, while they have taken nothing from it. No further legislative aid has been necessary, than to give a proper direction to the enterprise of our wealthy citizens" (Cadman 1949, 47).

Following the success of New York's Erie Canal, New Jersey, like Pennsylvania, Ohio, and many other states, decided to follow suit, but unlike many other states, avoided investing public funds. Instead it granted potential companies liberal provisions to help them raise the kinds of private capital that would have been attractive to ordinary companies. For an 1820 canal company hoping to link the Delaware and Raritan rivers, the trade-off between financial support and liberal provisions was explicit, "it being certain, if accomplished, the people of this state, will be abundantly remunerated now and in all future time for the liberality of the terms of incorporation" (quoted in Cadman 1949, 49). When the inducements were not sufficient to attract financial support, many in the state advocated that it follow New York's example with public funding. A second attempt to charter the Delaware and Raritan project pledged a quarter of the capital funding from the state, but a conflict with Pennsylvania, which borders the Delaware River, killed the project. So those unwilling to risk state funds prevailed. In 1824 the Morris Canal and Banking Company was chartered to connect the Delaware and Passaic rivers. The provisions were acknowledged as liberal, especially the company's right to perform banking functions, a privilege tightly tied to public accountability in most other states.

In the late twenties the public debate continued over whether transportation should be built with public or private sponsorship and over whether it should be railroad or canal. In 1830 the state granted charters to both the Delaware and Raritan Canal Company and the Camden and Amboy Rail Road and Transportation Company, which were later merged into what is known as the Joint Companies. The state pledged funds to neither, but their charters specified that a quarter of the capital stock was to be reserved for the state's option. At the same time, the state was to receive a duty on passengers and freight. The most consequential provision was the company's proposal for a grant of monopoly rights for the route between New York and Philadelphia in exchange for a thousand shares of fully paid-in stock. After a spirited debate throughout the state, in which many newspapers forcefully opposed the agreement, it passed, but only after the company had offered the state an additional thousand shares and pledged to pay no dividends until the state had received at least $30,000 a year in duties. New Jersey was in the transportation business, not as an investor but as a franchiser, not with public responsibility for general welfare but with a vested interest in a single company. The Joint Companies actively entered politics, effectively controlling the Democratic Party and, through it, the state government, leading to such monikers for New Jersey as the "State of Camden and Amboy." Cadman (1949) comments, "Thus New Jersey was willing to surrender a large part of its freedom of action in return for revenue that promised to reduce state taxes to the vanishing point" (56). Revenues exceeded expectations, giving the state one of the lowest tax rates in the country and freeing it from the fiscal crises faced by so many other states in the depressions of 1837 and 1857. In fact from 1848 until the Civil War years, no direct taxes were levied.

The government's lucrative relationship with the railroad monopoly did not exempt the state from an anticorporate movement, but it did shape the form that the opposition took, the resolution achieved, and the state's legacy of permissive corporate law. Jacksonian democracy in the 1830s made corporations an issue of the relationship between the state and the people. Unlike in Pennsylvania and Ohio, where critics continued to press for public accountability, in New Jersey primary criticisms targeted corporate privilege and monopoly. Whereas the demand for public accountability implies a solution of stronger, more active government, the condemnation of privilege and monopoly implies a solution of less government. The problem with privilege, the critics charged, was that charters and the corporate rights granted in them gave an unfair advantage to corporations in competition against other businesses. Democratic governor Peter D. Vroom told the legislature, "Hence corporations, of any description, should be sparingly created. If they are to compete with private and individual enterprise, they should be discountenanced. Powers and privileges are necessarily conferred by them, which individuals do not possess and cannot exercise. The contest between the two is an unequal contest, and the result is always in favor of the corporation" (quoted in Cadman 1949, 78). A Trenton newspaper was just as pointed: "To have the land scattered over with incorporated companies, is to have a class of privileged, if not titled, nobility—a nobility that will ever be reaching forward to higher emoluments, at the hazard of more deeply involving the rights of the public" (Cadman 1949, 77, quoted from the Trenton *Emporium and True American*, a Democratic newspaper). The antimonopoly theme is found in a passage from the same newspaper: "All Bank charters, all laws conferring special privileges, with all acts of incorporations, for purposes of private gain, are monopolies, inasmuch as they are calculated to enhance the power of wealth, produce inequalities among the people, and to subvert liberty" (quoted in Cadman 1949, 75). The New Jersey anticorporation movement was nationally prominent for three or four years, spearheaded by the Locofoco or Equal Rights wing of the Democratic party. Several Democratic governors joined the criticism. Some agreed that corporations could serve a useful purpose in new fields, where they did not compete with already established businesses and where charters could be temporary. Some Democratic papers charged the Whigs with being the "corporation party."

In 1837 the legislature passed a limited partnership act, hoping to make some of the privileges of incorporation available to all while reducing the number of charters that the legislature had to consider. Some Democratic newspapers opposed the bill because it would create organizations too similar to corporations. However, the law was little used; clearly businessmen did not see it as a substitute for corporations, which implies that the prospect of limited liability by itself was an insufficient incentive to change their legal format.

By the end of the thirties, the anticorporate movement was losing steam. Cadman explains that the anticorporation advocates conceded that corporation was inevitable and turned their attention to curing the worst abuses rather than eliminating the form itself. Altogether the movement, though vocal, had little actual influence on granting charters. In fact more charters were granted in the years when the Democrats were in power than when other parties ruled. The movement's remnant did have influence in the years following 1844 in advocating general incorporation laws, in stiffening state regulation, and in ensuring protection of creditors. But the movement for general incorporation still lagged behind some of the other states, in part because its advocates continued to be associated with the extremes—the anticorporate perspective on the one hand, and on the other the Camden and Amboy Railroad, who feared that any extensions to the general incorporation of railroads would threaten its monopoly. The movement succeeded in passing a general incorporation act in 1858, but not in prohibiting special incorporation. Moreover, since both Pennsylvania and New York prohibited special incorporation, New Jersey saw an opportunity to draw companies from those two neighboring states. Because of the relatively restrictive nature of the general incorporation provisions, special incorporation continued to be the preferred option.

When the Camden and Amboy Railroad was sold to the Pennsylvania Railroad in 1871, the sale ended its grip on New Jersey politics.[6] At the same time, the burden of special incorporation acts on the legislature's time and energy seemed to be offering relatively little return. Meanwhile New Jersey, unlike at the end of the century, was a laggard in the institutionalization process. The fact that most other states had abandoned special incorporation put pressure on the state to do so.[7] A constitutional convention in 1875 became the forum for revising the corporation laws. Corporations were thenceforth to be established only by the general incorporation law. It prohibited the state from exempting corporations from taxation. Neither the state nor any municipality could offer any form of financial assistance or investment to corporations. However, the legislature was given unusual discretion to decide the provisions general incorporation charters would specify. In most other states, constitutional provisions restricted the powers that legislatures could grant to corporations and dictated more of the content of those charters, specifying such policies as the type and degree of limited liability, the powers of boards of directors, and the circumstances under which corporations could own stock in other corporations. New Jersey's constitutional blank check on corporate powers created the potential for radically different corporate powers with unprecedented rights, responsibilities, and entitlements that eventually gave a new meaning to corporate property.

New Jersey's corporate legacy turned the state down a path that eventually transformed modern America. The forces for accountability lost to the forces of accommodation. The critique of corporate privilege was overshadowed by the sanctity of private property, even while fundamentally redefining the nature of property. The state that had once enjoyed the largesse of a franchised railroad monopoly had no qualms about enjoying the windfall of franchise fees of corporations that would have been illegal anywhere else in the country. If New Jersey had had a different history, we might have experienced a different present.

EROSION OF THE PUBLIC CORPORATION

These three cases illustrate how different experiences with early infrastructure corporations created different legacies and different corporate policies at the end of the century. New Jersey's distinctiveness in particular needs to be explained. Nonetheless, the similarities among the states are also striking, especially the erection of the solid boundary between public and private enterprise and the general privatization of the corporation. Some of these similarities are due to similar endogenous processes of change, but more important are the ways in which what happened in one state affected other states. Not only did legal changes in any one state set a precedent for decisions in other cases, but states closely monitored one another and used other states as points of reference. Few ideological appeals were as effective in persuading legislators as the charge that other states were "ahead" or that a state lagged "behind" on some policy. Of course states could also act as negative referents, when legislators could "prove" the folly of proposed policies by pointing to other states. The legacies of Pennsylvania, Ohio, and New Jersey, for example, were often articulated in reference to other states. Thus methodologically, states can only tenuously be considered independent cases in examining changing policy. This section will analyze some of the similarities in how the corporation became privatized and will focus on the conflict over state-sponsored corporations and the nature of public accountability and private rights.

Privatization of the corporation is often treated as inevitable or natural, taking the government shackles off free enterprise. True, there was a deep-seated antistatist impulse in American political culture. And some observers have assumed that private companies would take charge of canals and railroads as soon as the private sector was strong enough to mobilize the capital and the organizational capacity to purchase and operate public improvements. But from the perspective of the early nineteenth century, private ownership and control of corporations were not viewed as inevitable. The nation's largest bank was federal. Most infrastructure was mixed ownership. In fact, the most common type of corporations—road and water transportation—have become almost entirely public. How many private turnpikes or canals operate today? Only the late entrant, the railroad, which waited until the 1830s to begin, became privately owned. The erosion of the public corporation is therefore something that needs to be explained, not merely assumed to have been inevitable. More important, it was forged in political institutions and must be explained in political terms. It cannot be assumed that the privately controlled corporation was the rational adaptation to a natural relationship between economy and polity, because those very boundaries were historically constructed by such processes as the privatization of the corporation. The private corporation did not "need" to arise as it did. It was a socially and politically constructed, historically situated institution.

Two contingent factors helped close the door on public ownership of corporations. The first was that the anticorporation political movement was split into two irreconcilable factions, one favoring greater public accountability and the other advocating a radical separation of public and private power and the reduction of state power. The antistatist ideology then became a self-fulfilling prophecy by "proving" the futility of government investment in and supervision of corporations. The second was the timing of the depression of 1837. The failing state enterprises were effectively used by the opponents of public accountability not only to legislatively limit state investment and supervision, but also to permanently seal the public sector off from private corporations by constitutional amendments.

Although there were important variations among the states, we can identify general stages of state policies toward public ownership: (1) Immediately after the Revolution individual states took responsibility. Corporations were founded for churches, schools, municipalities, and the economic infrastructure, including some of Alexander Hamilton's Society for Establishing Useful Manufactures, to stimulate industrial development. (2) Between 1791 and 1825 states relied on private, public, and mixed corporations to stimulate economic growth, especially by building infrastructures. Some, like the federally incorporated Potomac Company, failed, but failure was interpreted as demonstrating the need for more active government involvement, especially to supply capital (Littlefield 1984). Others, like New York's widely emulated Erie Canal, were interpreted as demonstrating the enormous potential of public/private partnerships. (3) States then developed extensive public works systems. Citizens argued that state involvement was necessary to foster economic development in competition with other states. Even basically rural states like Texas and Minnesota became active. The public overwhelmingly approved public ownership as desirable and practical (Goodrich 1960). (4) After 1830 anticorporate movements challenged state ownership, raising principled objections that state ownership was wrong and violated deep principles, that it was antidemocratic and unnatural. (5) After the depression of 1837 the movement against corporate privileges used the failure of state-supported corporations to create constitutionally binding prohibitions on state investment in and support of public works corporations. Business corporations became entirely distinct from other corporations and fully privatized through general incorporation laws that virtually eliminated the accountability of corporations to ongoing supervision.

The outcome might have been different if the anticorporate movement had been different, both in terms of its particular program and in terms of its division into two factions with conflicting attitudes toward government. A general anticharter movement advocated public accountability for large-scale capital projects like turnpikes and canals. This pro-government movement feared that the creation of private power would overwhelm government, that the corporation would erode sovereignty. Corporations were seen as aristocracies and monopolies that violated the social contract. In particular, this movement attacked the special corporate privileges that it felt were inherent functions and should not be delegated except to serve the public, privileges like limited liability, immortal life, and eminent domain. If the government delegated these powers without accountability, it could be overwhelmed (Hartz 1968). At the same time, a coalition advocating Jacksonian democracy attacked all large-scale power, public or private. The government was seen as the enemy of popular sovereignty, not its protector. Callender (1902) cited an 1820 work on political economy: "[Corporations] are, and ought to be, considered as artificial engines of power, contrived by the rich for the purpose of increasing their already too great ascendancy and calculated to destroy that natural equality among men which no government ought to lend it power in destroying" (quoted on 156). Jackson himself in a presidential address attacked "the multitudes of corporations with exclusive privileges which they have succeeded in obtaining in different States" (quoted in Bruchey 1968, 145). Like the pro-government anticorporation movement, the antigovernment branch of the anticorporation movement focused on the privileges that corporations enjoyed, but its solution was not more accountability to the government, but less. Democracy was equated with universalism. This movement was a major factor in the rise of general incorporation laws. If the state legislatures no longer had control over who could enjoy corporate privileges, but only over the general nature of corporations, the corporation would no longer be a form of privilege (Seavoy 1982).

The primary force to privatize corporations was not the corporations themselves. In fact, corporate leaders did not always favor a more laissez-faire government, especially where they benefited from the privileges and powers that corporate status bestowed. For example, when New York was considering a general incorporation law in 1847, the legislature addressed the issue of whether railroad companies should be considered a public highway, as canals were. At a time when the issue of which corporate powers were "inherent" and which were discretionary had not been fully institutionalized, railroad companies were reluctant to surrender such privileges as the right of eminent domain and protection from competition. Although they were not given the protection of public utility status, an 1850 law did grant them the right of eminent domain and a generous grant of state lands (Seavoy 1982).

The antistatist ideology was effective, in part, because it created a self-fulfilling prophecy. As Ohio best illustrates, suspicion of autonomous bureaucracies prevented rational organization and operation. A project's failure could then "prove" that public operation was inferior to private. The irony is that a democratic ideology that opposed rational bureaucracy in the name of the people, demanding that public planning be controlled by popular representatives, created a structure that could later be interpreted as evidence of the folly of public accountability. But the ideology was effective at interpreting events that were beyond anyone's control. The canal system in particular was probably doomed to eventual failure. Investing in canals in the 1830s was like investing in buggies at the beginning of this century or typewriters in the 1980s. It's not that these decisions were necessarily irrational at the time. Just as the technical viability of nuclear fusion as a source of energy is debated today, the future viability of canals and railroads was still ambiguous. The lessons drawn from these experiences were perhaps the critical juncture in privatizing the corporation. Other lessons could have been drawn, as did the French, who—facing the same setbacks, corruption, and mixed record of success—drew the opposite conclusion, that the problem was not too much government supervision but rather too little. They made their railroad companies more accountable to the national state, which planned the routes, set the fares, and subsidized their capitalization. Even after the Civil War, when America was at its most laissez-faire, some railroad men advocated a more European system. The railroad executive Charles Francis Adams wrote, "In any other country, [an undertaking like the Union Pacific] would have been built by the Government as a military road" (quoted in Goodrich 1960, 201). In this century, the French have nationalized the railways and now have a modern, well-functioning, widely used system, in stark contrast to America's "lemon socialism."

What sealed the doom of the public corporation was how effectively the advocates of laissez-faire used the depression and stock market crashes of 1837 and 1857 to make a case against government economic activity. Seavoy (1982) calls the depression of 1837 a "watershed in the development of the modern American business corporation" (180), because thereafter nearly all state constitutional conventions erected formidable barriers between the government and the corporation. Governments that had invested heavily in canals, bridges, turnpikes, and railroads suffered major losses. Ohio by 1839 had accumulated a debt of $12 million, which the state auditor declared a debt "of a startling character, and certainly a most miserable financial operation" (quoted in Bogart 1924, 170). But it was one of the few midwestern states to avoid defaulting on loans. Illinois, for example, picked the inopportune year of 1837 to create a major internal improvement project, authorizing the sale of $8 million in bonds to finance seven railroads and a navigable river. The depression killed the project and the state defaulted on the bonds. Altogether at least five states[8] defaulted on interest and one on principal, leading to a "wave of revulsion" against public investments (Bruchey 1990). As a result, major European investors avoided American securities for years thereafter. But the critical factor was the widespread definition of the problem. Despite the fact that panic arose in the private sector from business practices on Wall Street, despite the fact that many of the failing companies were weak from mismanagement (and sometimes corruption) by private managers, and despite the fact that many of these projects were created to serve a general public service rather than make a profit, the government was blamed. The lesson drawn was not the need for better management, less corruption, or greater regulation. Instead, there was a general revulsion against state investment.

Moreover, as Hurst (1970) argues, the attack on public corporations after 1840 articulated a new rationale. Instead of the former responsibility ethic, which legitimized corporations on the basis of what they did for the public and criticized them for serving only private interests, an efficiency ethic legitimized corporations for how effectively they could serve private interests while criticizing public corporations for how ineffectively they served the public. States quickly began to sell off their corporate securities at any price they could get, often incurring millions in losses. More important, in addition to the cathartic outburst that often follows the discovery of a scapegoat in a crisis, states made it impossible to reverse their course by enacting legislation and, in many cases, constitutional provisions against government investment in corporations. What might have been a temporary setback was irreversibly set into law. New York, for example, in 1846 adopted a "People's Resolution" prohibiting the use of state credit to any individual or corporation under any circumstances, and permitting borrowing only to suppress an insurrection or for public improvements only after a general referendum. Ohio in 1851 forbade the state to take on a debt for any public improvement (Studenski and Krooss, 1963). This does not mean that states were shrinking from any activities. From 1840 to 1860, state debts increased from $190 million to $257 million, four times the size of the national debt (Studenski and Krooss, 1963). It was in the investment in corporations, especially in public improvements, where the retreat was greatest. The role of the state was redefined as the enforcer of contracts and property rights in general and the protection of the market in particular. Its authority continued to permit or prohibit the social forms of economic activity, but the content of economic activity would be left to the newly constituted private sector.

CONCLUSION

This account of the early rise of the large corporation differs from efficiency theory in three major respects: the role of the state, the consideration of power, and the duration of the explanatory framework. Efficiency theory assumes that private enterprise, disciplined by the unforgiving market, is inherently more efficient than government decision making. The conventional division of labor in social science among economics, political science, and sociology assumes three very different logics of causation in economy, politics, and society. Recent work in all three disciplines has chipped away at the conceptual wall dividing them. Economists have increasingly attempted to extend utilitarian logic to understand political and social life and have seen a Nobel Prize awarded to one of their members, Gary Becker, who has extended this approach the furthest. Political scientists have widely embraced rational choice theories based on economic logic, drawing the two disciplines much closer together. Although some sociologists, including a recent president of the American Sociological Association (Coleman 1990), have advocated utilitarian models, their impact has been less pervasive in their discipline than in political science. Economic sociologists have not only offered the most fundamental critiques of utilitarian models in general, but have increasingly questioned their ability to explain important facets of economic life (Block 1990; Zukin and DiMaggio 1990; Fligstein 1990; Friedland and Robertson 1990; Campbell, Hollingsworth, and Lindberg 1991). My analysis falls in this last camp. This chapter has shown how that most private of our economic structures, the large business corporation, arose as quasi-government agency. Some of its particular features, such as limited liability, perpetual life, and parcellized ownership, were established not so much because they were efficient but to compensate for the inefficient tasks corporations were assigned, like building canals, turnpikes, and bridges, where markets would not support them. Other particular features, including the enumeration of powers in a charter, the creation of boards of directors, and the election of officers, were established to embody the accountability of the corporation to the public. The corporation was after all a delegation of sovereign powers to serve the public interest. Thus the corporation did not grow by an evolutionary process by which an organizational form was perfected to its maximum efficiency.

While some representatives of efficiency theory recognize that the corporate form was a creation of government, they generally attribute the corporation's privatization to the general inefficiency of government ownership, the inevitable failures that plague enterprise not disciplined by the market. The account here interprets the problems of canal companies as the result of such contingent events as heavy investment when virtually no one could have foreseen how quickly railroads would render canals uncompetitive, the first depression of international finance, and the political ascendancy of Jacksonian democracy with its antistate brand of anticorporatism. I have emphasized these contingent events, which suggest an explanatory logic of power rather than efficiency. In this perspective, actors' actions are explained in terms of their relationships with other social actors. The various alternatives they have to choose from and the costs and benefits resulting from the alternatives are determined by some social actors much more than others. Whether or not the resulting structures tend to increase efficiency is thus very contingent and not at all built into the system.

This chapter also illustrates what I mean by a logic of power rather than a logic of efficiency. Whereas efficiency theory was challenged in the previous chapter on empirical grounds, here I offer an alternative formulation. Efficiency theory identifies a pattern or structure such as the modern corporation and seeks to identify ways in which the pattern or structure more efficiently fulfilled important functions. Chandler (1977, 1990), for example, argues that modern business enterprise increased throughput of production and more effectively got products to the customer through extensive sales facilities. Power theory, in contrast, asks who was contending or cooperating to develop a pattern or structure and how the winners were able to prevail. This chapter shows how some actors were able to define unprofitable state ventures in canal building as proof of the folly of government involvement. When decisions are made, the efficiency model asks what the consequences of each alternative are and how the best choice is made to maximize consensually agreed-upon goals. Industrialists at the end of the century are described as facing a choice between the anarchy of ruinous competition or the stability of mergers. A power logic asks how the choices that people face are set by the actions of others. Power does not necessarily involve one actor giving commands, but more typically takes the form of determining the consequences for choices another actor might take. State governments under pressure from merchants to build infrastructures so that trade could more easily flow between cities and frontiers had the "choice" of raising taxes or issuing bonds to finance corporations. Rather than focusing on why the decision to sell bonds was more rational than raising taxes, a power perspective asks why the opponents of taxes and the marketers of bonds prevailed over those who feared that government-financed corporations would compromise government autonomy. Thus with a logic of power, there is greater emphasis on who is involved and why some actors win while others lose.

Efficiency theory is problematic not only because it neglects the dynamics of power, but also because it attends only to short-term change. By focusing on the events at the end of the nineteenth century, the immediate unfolding of the corporate revolution, it is easy to miss the critical role that government played in the corporation's long-term development. Later chapters will focus more on government's later role, but this chapter has emphasized that a long-term perspective is necessary. The context in which decisions were made at the end of the century was very much structured by the events early in the century. The fact that the corporation arose in the form that it did, the particular powers and features that it embodied, the nature of the class that controlled it, and perhaps most important, the institutional structures in which it was embedded and through which capital became socialized were all shaped by its development as a quasi-government agency. When American manufacturing wedded the corporate infrastructure at the end of the century, it must be remembered that the latter never would have been there if only efficiency had shaped the economy.

CHAPTER FOUR

Railroads: The Corporation's Institutional Wellspring

NO ECONOMIC SECTOR was as important to the rise of large American business corporations as the railroads. Indeed until the end of the nineteenth century, railroad companies and large corporations were synonymous. For decades, nearly all the corporate securities traded on the stock market were railroad securities. Corporate law was primarily railroad law. The corporate elite were primarily railroad leaders. In short, by the last third of the century, the corporate institutional structure *was* the railroad institutional structure.

The importance of the railroad is unparalleled and undisputed. Virtually all accounts agree that the railroad was the dominant factor in the development of the nineteenth-century American economy (Davis 1961; Goodrich 1960; Jenks 1944; Cochran 1955; Chandler 1965; Fishlow 1966; McClelland 1968; Lightner 1983). The railroad is to American imagery in the last half of the nineteenth century what the Church was to European imagery in the Middle Ages. The soul of the nation was captured in John Henry, who laid the tracks, Casey Jones, who drove the iron horse, the anonymous cowboy who drove livestock to a terminal shipping point, Jay Gould, whose rapacious stock maneuvers destroyed railroads, and J. P. Morgan, whose indomitable leadership forged railroads into giant systems. To the extent that one can identify a symbol of an era, the railroad represented all that was good and all that was bad of America's coming to economic maturity.

This chapter will describe how railroads constructed the foundation of the American corporate institution. First, it was railroad companies that changed the meaning of incorporation from a semipublic agency to a private business with all the accompanying freedoms and autonomy. Although the railroad was created to meet a felt need to stimulate economic growth by lowering the costs of transportation, that "need" does not explain why the railroad arose in the form that it did. If the railroad had developed earlier or later, it probably would have been, and perhaps remained, more of a government enterprise. But beginning as the railroads did, immediately following the construction of canal companies, precluded greater government state investment and involvement. Efficiency theory overestimates the extent to which the private sector was the natural home of the private corporations which arose to build and operate railroads. Second, by socializing capital in a new type of property, by centralizing capital in a form that became readily available for large-scale enterprise in other sectors, and by breeding a new segment of the capitalist class that mobilized and acted on behalf of its interests, the railroad created the institutions of corporate capitalism and the corporate class segment. At first the new segment was confined to transportation and communication but then radiated outward into other sectors. It became distinguished from other sectors less by its sectoral location—railroad capital—than by its institutional basis—corporate capital. Finally, as frequently described, by lowering the cost of transportation, by purchasing huge quantities of goods and services, by expanding the geographical scope of markets, and by instituting new organizational forms that others could imitate, the railroad changed the context in which others made economic decisions—individual decisions which, when aggregated together, fueled economic growth.

The railroad was the foundation on which corporate capitalism was built. If the railroad had not developed in the form it did, modern enterprise would not have taken the institutional forms we know as corporate capitalism. Enterprise probably would not have remained in the small entrepreneurial firms of the early nineteenth century, but it is impossible to know all the roads not taken. Thus the rise of the large American business corporation cannot be explained in terms of manufacturing itself or even the private sector itself. The large corporation as a form of private property emerged out of the institutional structure of publicly supported business corporations and the institutional structures that arose to mediate the relationship between government finance and private wealth. This chapter focuses on the railroads as the first fully private, large-scale, socially capitalized business corporations. The analytical model employed here draws from institutionalization theory the insight that social relationships become codified and reified into taken-for-granted categories and relationships, from class theory the notion that people who have a common relationship to production seek to serve those interests by organizing themselves into coherent collective actors, and from political sociology the assumption that actors' behavior must take into account the influence of their relationships with identifiable others. From specific variations of all three comes the tenet that the state's claim to sovereignty makes it a unique social force. In their explanations for the rise of institutions like the railroad, these perspectives all minimize the role of efficiency as a causal force. The next chapter focuses on the institutional structure within which these corporations were set—the stock market, investment banks, brokerage houses, and auxiliary organizations. Together they set the stage for the corporate revolution in manufacturing at the end of the nineteenth century.

CHANDLER ON THE RAILROAD

Chandler is often cited for acclaiming the railroad as "America's first big business" (Williamson 1981; Hamilton and Biggart 1988; Porter 1992). His description of how the railroad companies made innovations in modern managerial, organizational, and accounting practices convincingly demonstrates that label is indeed appropriate. The railroad unequivocally served as the template for how modern large businesses operate today, and Chandler has vividly portrayed the internal operations of innovating firms. He has focused on what has happened inside of large railroad organizations, in contrast to my more institutional perspective, but there are also three more specific points on which my account differs from his: (1) In contrast to his view that increasing scale unproblematically and functionally shaped the organizational form that railroads took, I suggest that political and economic power were used to make railroads large and hierarchical. (2) Further, other businesses emulated railroad financial and organizational structures less because the railroads had resolved endemic problems of large-scale organization than in order to conform to an institutional structure that imposed itself on particular businesses. (3) Thus financial institutions played a major role in the development of railroads, not just a role overshadowed by the functional needs of the railroad for more capital. Even though Chandler acknowledges that finance institutions influenced railroad organizations more than they did manufacturing, he still understates their importance.

Chandler takes the scale of railroad operation for granted and assumes that the functional requirements of scale explain the form that railroads took. "[S]afe, regular, reliable movement of goods and passengers, as well as the continuing maintenance and repair of locomotives, rolling stock, and track, roadbed, stations, roundhouses, and other equipment, required the creation of a sizable administrative organization. . . . Hence, the operational requirements of the railroads demanded the creation of the first administrative hierarchies in American business" (1977, 87). This passage not only shows a functionalist orientation, but also demonstrates how unproblematic change is assumed to be: simply because locomotives and other equipment "required" the creation of sizable administrative structures, they arose. Managers automatically had not only the insight to see the need but the foresight to delegate some of their authority to middle managers. They faced no resistance from workers who would come under the authority of standardized, regimented bureaucratic policy. The companies had no problem finding managers who were not only competent but willing to act on behalf of management without the benefits of property. It is ironic that Chandler, like other historians working out of a functionalist framework, seems so impressed by the utter novelty, profound originality, and deep transformation of modern forms while depicting change as unfolding so effortlessly. As he tells the story, the raw material of history is plastic enough to be molded without serious challenge. It takes acumen, not power, to shape history.

In Chandler's formulation, scale also explains the separation of ownership and control. The railroads were too large for any person or family to own or manage, leading to the separation of ownership and control. The managers, who lacked sufficient resources to own controlling interests in the companies, gained control of normal operation, and the role of owners receded. "Only in the raising and allocating of capital, in the setting of financial policies, and in the selection of top managers did the owners or their representatives have a real say in railroad management" (Chandler 1977, 87). Thus the rights, entitlements, and responsibilities of ownership were determined by the functional needs of operation, not the institutional level of power and the law. Owners "only" had to raise capital, set financial policies, and select top management. This discussion, however, locates change in the structures of property external to the corporation, not internal to it, and sees change as shaped by the dynamics of power, not the objective needs of efficient operation. That is not to say that the internal dynamics are irrelevant or that managers did not make important and consequential innovations in the pursuit of more efficient operation, but that the managers had to act within the context of larger structures which themselves must be explained. Moreover, the powers that owners did retain, though delegating daily operation to management, remained fundamental, especially in terms of allocating the overall distribution of resources in society and creating the structures through which wealth is created.

While there is no disputing that the railroad was the nation's first big business, the means by which its innovations spread to other industries raise important theoretical issues about the functionalist logic of explanation. For Chandler, the railroad served as a model for other industries to follow when objective need dictated adaptation. In speaking of the railroad and telegraph, he wrote, "They were the first to require a large number of full-time managers to coordinate, control, and evaluate the activities of a number of widely scattered operating units. For this reason, they provided the most relevant administrative models for enterprises in the production and distribution of goods and services when such enterprises began to build, on the basis of the new transportation and communication network, their own geographically extended, multiunit business empires" (1977, 79). Serving as a model is an important part of the institutionalization process, and there is no doubt that when organizational leaders define a problem they turn first to solutions adopted by others (Meyer and Rowan 1977; Scott 1983; Lindberg and Campbell 1991). DiMaggio and Powell (1983) invoke the concept of mimetic isomorphism to explain why so many organizations share structures and practices. It is not, they emphasize, that organizations face the same problem and have devised the same solution, but that they mimic one another whether or not they have the same problems and whether or not the structures and practices solve the problems they do have. From this perspective one cannot use the adoption of an innovation as evidence of the nature of the problem the innovation is supposed to solve. There are many reasons for adopting an innovation besides the objective need to solve a problem. For Chandler the fact that railroad companies emulated one another seems to be evidence that they faced common problems. The goal of the analyst is to discover what common problems motivated the common solutions that firms borrowed from one another. If large-scale organization functions to coordinate activities and if railroad companies adopted large-scale organizations, it must have been that they had a problem of coordination and that the innovation solved the problem. One does not need to look for the source of change at the institutional level because the development of large-scale firms is found within the firm itself and the problems it was attempting to solve.

When Chandler does deal with the institutional level of the railroad, he modifies the functionalist logic of need to some extent but consistently maintains that institutional structures were built to facilitate the operational aspects of railroads, not financial gain. This is evident in several of his points. First, he argues that the centralization of the American capital market in the 1850s was due to the railroads' demand for more capital (1977, chap. 3).[1] He offers little more evidence than the fact that the largest railroad companies were becoming very large. Second, he argues that the attempts to manage competition by forming pools and cartels were the actions of managers to facilitate the smooth operation of the transportation system: "The new class of middle and top managers had the responsibility for defining the new types of interfirm relationships. The part-time members of the board of directors had neither the time, the training, nor the technical understanding and competence needed to decide complex questions of cooperation and competition" (1977, 123). He explains that the pools did not succeed because the needs for coordination outstripped the industry's organizational capacity.[2] When the pools and cartels failed railroad managers turned to system building, creating large communities of interest in which many companies were tied together by common ownership and interlocking directorates. However, in the process they lost some of their autonomy to financiers and speculators, causing redundancy, overconstruction, and more competition. "The railroad systems thus became and remained the private business enterprises that most closely exemplified financial capitalism in the United States. . . . In few other types of American business enterprise did investment bankers and other financiers have such influence" (1977, 187). But the power of finance was negative: "Except in the promoting of communities of interest, bankers rarely defined strategic plans and were even less involved in operating matters. Financiers may have had some say in the organization and management of American railroads, but full-time, salaried, career managers had a great deal more. The American railroad enterprise might more properly be considered a variation of managerial capitalism than an unalloyed expression of financial capitalism" (1977, 187). Even at the institutional level, it is the operation of the railroad functioning as a transportation system that explains the configuration of power and the distribution of resources. Chandler concludes: "The operational requirements of the new technology in communication and transportation thus brought, indeed demanded, the creation of modern managerially operated business enterprises" (1977, 189). In contrast, this chapter will show

how the railroads were shaped by forces other than functional need, especially the actions of the government and the financial community, and then show how the railroad served not only as a model of innovative organization but, more important, as the foundation of an institutional structure and form of property, in a word a structure of power, that eventually enveloped industry whether it needed it or not.

THE RAILROAD AND THE STATE

Although the railroads have profoundly affected the scope and structure of the economy, they have been shaped by political dynamics at least as much as by economic processes. Government provided much early impetus for railroads, a critical portion of the original capital, a protective legal environment that shielded them from the consequences of poor judgment and corruption, and various other sorts of resources that made the difference between solvency and failure (Cochran 1955; Goodrich 1960; Hartz 1968; Scheiber 1978; Myers 1970; Hurst 1956; Berk 1990). It is difficult to imagine that the railroad companies could have been built as extensively or as quickly without vast government support.[3] The railroads' public origins were critical in shaping their organization and structure, which in turn determined the modern corporate institution. Thus examining the history of the railroad is essential to understanding that the corporation arose for reasons other than economic efficiency.

One of the most important contributions that the railroad made to the rise of the modern corporation was spearheading the privatization of the corporation, as discussed in the previous chapter. Until the railroad industry matured, corporations were universally seen as quasi-public entities created by governments to serve a public good (Scheiber 1978; Handlin and Handlin 1945; Seavoy 1982; Hartz 1968; Berk 1990). While canals, turnpikes, and bridges remained primarily public, by the last third of the nineteenth century the railroad had redefined the corporation into a form of private property, retaining many privileges that states had granted corporations for serving a public function, but shedding their accountability. Even though popular thought and the law held the railroad to be a public interest, its institutional and legal form, the corporation, was increasingly emancipated from that accountability. To understand how the business corporation became a fully private entity requires examining the history of railroad corporations.[4]

In the conventional view, which can be characterized as a national evolution perspective, railroad corporations naturally evolved into private entities because of the functional failures of public accountability (Scheiber 1975). For example, Ward (1975) describes how the Pennsylvania Railroad was created by the legislature in 1847 as a miniature republic in order to preserve public accountability. The "citizen" stockholders elected a representative body, the board of directors, who elected a president. The annual meeting was a quasi–town meeting of all voting stockholder "citizens." To further limit the corporation's powers, its charter was limited to twenty years, its capital stock was capped, the public was given access to the records, and the legislature reserved the right to repeal the charter. All these provisions secured the corporation's accountability to the public in stark contrast to the ordinary companies, whose property rights guaranteed a wall of privacy. In Ward's rendition, this structure only created an internal power vacuum. The functional necessities of coordination dictated that power would become centralized in management, specifically the chief engineer, J. Edgar Thomson, who rose to the company's presidency and became one of the legendary figures of American railroad history. A board of directors, even meeting weekly, could not effectively operate one of the world's largest corporations and eventually became a rubber stamp body, asserting itself only sporadically and ineffectively. During the Civil War, Thomson assumed more discretion, deciding how many locomotives to purchase, recruiting skilled labor in Europe, buying and selling company-owned stock, and making financial arrangements to purchase the Philadelphia and Erie Railroad. But by that point, the system of checks and balances created by the legislature had disappeared. "[P]aramount executive authority had emerged despite organizational restrictions, the directors had receded to the role of pliant acceders, and the shareholders had been reduced to virtual impotency" (Ward 1975, 58).

While Seavoy's (1982) variant of the natural evolution perspective examines privatization from the perspective of government rather than the internal dynamics of the firm, he also treats it as inevitable. Discussing the retreat of state governments from active economic participation during the 1840s, he writes, "The rigid fiscal limitations it imposed left the state with no alternative but to adopt a laissez faire economic policy that radically separated business enterprises from state participation in almost the same way that the 1784 general incorporation statute for religious congregations had excluded the state from interfering in religious matters" (Seavoy 1982, 200). The underlying story is similar to Ward's. The public corporation was inherently inefficient. For Ward, managerial efficiency required private autonomy from the state; for Seavoy, the need for fiscal flexibility dictated the same results.

Both accounts note that privatization was accepted at the time because there was "no viable alternative" that could effectively meet the need for efficient coordination or fiscal flexibility. As is often the case in political conflict, "no viable alternative" was a rhetorical device articulated by the advocates of one of the alternatives. Alternatives are selected from within a world view. To propose a new alternative, it is often rhetorically effective to declare the existing alternatives unfeasible, to argue that there is no choice.[5] Dobbin (1994) describes how the same problems of economic depression, the loss of government investment in railroads, and extensive political corruption in railroad affairs provoked entirely different reactions in the United States and France. While American governments reacted by withdrawing from active investment, ownership, and oversight, the French interpreted these events as evidence of too loose supervision and increased the government's role, eventually nationalizing the railroads. In both countries, political leaders argued that they had no alternative. Historical explanation must specify the features of the U.S. context that made privatization seem inevitable. In the abstract, nationalization of the railroads would have been equally plausible. The states held equity in the bankrupt properties and could have taken control. Dobbin's explanation rests on political culture and enduring policy styles. Jacksonian ideologies, with their emphasis on equality and limited government, prevailed, while the political structures that placed sovereignty in the legislature rather than the executive hindered the growth of administrative bureaucracies. The prevailing federal legal tendencies favored competition and private development (see also Horwitz 1977). And the railroad companies themselves lobbied energetically for autonomy.[6]

Treating privatization as a natural, inevitable process propelled by organizational need ignores the legal and institutional factors that made the change possible. It assumes what must be explained, that railroad companies were unfettered autonomous profit maximizers accountable only to their stockholders. It does this by presuming that managers were the uncontested shapers of corporate action with an unproblematic capacity to act within an unchanging institutional setting. As uncontested shapers they were able to control the railroad companies with little accountability to government policies, public pressures, or competing interests of investors, shippers, and suppliers. With an unproblematic capacity to act, they possessed the resources, legitimacy, knowledge, and legal sanction to act autonomously in the pursuit of efficient operation and respectable profits. The depiction of an unchanging institutional environment assumes the relationship of government and economy as we conceive of it today. To assume that railroad managers were uncontested shapers of action with unproblematic capacity to act in an unchanging environment assumes away knotty issues of power: who were the actors that privatized the corporation, why were they able to succeed, and how did privatization help construct the subsequent relationship of government to economy? The natural evolution perspective assumes that the functional requisites of efficient operation compelled privatization. The presence of other actors, constraints on the mobilization of resources, and the preexisting institutional structure were irrelevant to the preordained outcome. In contrast, understanding the plausible alternative courses the railroad might have followed requires attention to the actors involved, the resources necessary for action, and the institutional transformations taking place.

Before the second half of the nineteenth century, economic growth was a partnership between government authority and private resources. Taxation was but one means of extracting resources from the population (Tilly 1975). Manpower for war was mobilized by conscription. Land for projects was obtained by eminent domain. State enterprise sometimes provided goods and services for governments and sometimes was profitable enough to provide the state with funds. As discussed in Chapter 3, corporations were a means of organizing and mobilizing resources from both the government and the private sector for public needs. The more the government depended on private resources, the greater the concessions it had to grant. Even when corporations were initiated at the behest of private citizens, government was actively involved in granting them powers and privileges.

The mercantilist commitment to economic activism underlay a policy to develop transportation and communication infrastructure (Hartz 1968; Scheiber 1969, 1975; Horwitz 1977; Hovenkamp 1991).[7] But in an accident of historical timing, an initial investment in the more proven technologies of turnpikes and canals discouraged state involvement in railroads, forcing private interests to take an unprecedented role in major public projects. Although there was variation in how actively state governments invested in and planned early railroad companies, private interests generally played a stronger role in the coalition creating railroads than that which had developed canals and turnpikes. State government typically compensated for the lack of financial support by granting charters with liberal provisions and special privileges. When governments retreated from economic activism in the 1840s and 1850s, these railroad companies, now becoming major economic forces, retained many of their special privileges but were freed of their earlier accountability. As discussed in Chapter 3, the political forces which held an egalitarian ethos were not strong enough to roll back those privileges but were effective enough to make them available to all corporations. What had been privileges became the frequently cited advantages of corporate organization, including limited liability, perpetual existence, and separation of ownership and control.

Ohio's experience aptly illustrates how contingent political forces and their untimely commitment to canal construction helped privatize railroads.[8] As in most states, a growth coalition led by urban merchants mobilized a movement advocating transportation as the key to prosperity. As noted in Chapter 3, the state responded by building one of the most extensive canal systems in the country. Although canals were considered the ideal medium of mobility (Frey 1985), many places could not be easily integrated into the system, so the state allowed private companies to build railroads. But the private sector lacked the institutional structure to capitalize them.[9] Merchants in small towns cited the promise of commercial success and the threat of isolation to induce local governments to generously invest land and capital in the many small railroads that patched the state together into a mosaic of rails (Goodrich 1960; Scheiber 1969). Kirkland (1961) describes the typical scene: "The necessary prelude to local aid was consequently a revivalistic campaign with damnation or salvation present on the platform. The local press, the best citizens, and assorted spellbinders united to mesmerize the electorate. But, those sufficiently jaundiced about public moods or outside the area of excitement were sure that good sense was likely to be the victim" (66–67). Within this context, chartering the railroads was a political process that was more responsive to group mobilization than to efficiency. For example, the leaders of Sandusky, disappointed that the canal was routed to Cleveland rather than their city, unsuccessfully asked the legislature to support a railroad. Consequently, in 1831, the backers decided to privately construct the Mad River and Lake Erie Railroad. The legislature agreed to grant a charter only if it would meander through towns represented by influential politicians, crossing the Sandusky River no less than four times. By 1838 it had constructed only fifteen miles, but can be remembered as the answer to a trivia question: the first steam railroad in the west (Scheiber 1969).

The Mad River's slow start illustrates how risky the railroad business was during that period. In the 1830s Ohio chartered twenty-four companies but only one railroad was built; in the following decade only eight of twenty-three were built. The state boldly experimented with financing, for example, giving companies the right to borrow money when only 10 percent of their stock had been paid in, or giving corporations banking rights. One of them, the Ohio Railroad Company, chartered in 1836, used its powers to issue $300,000 in currency, all of which proved to be worthless. MacGill (1948) explains that these schemes were tolerated because of the widespread feeling that transportation was critical to development, but difficult to raise financing for. To compensate for the lack of efficiency, states decided to create new rights, entitlements, and obligations, that is, new forms of property that determined who benefited the most, who directed the process of economic growth, and to whom those in charge were accountable.

The early charters reveal Ohio's antebellum railroad policy.[10] Most charters were very permissive, conforming more to investor desires than to commonwealth values. The most important privilege was limited liability, reflecting the prevailing doctrine that the corporation served a public purpose. States could attract capital for the general good by using state power to absolve investors of the risk they would face in the private economy.[11] This, of course, did not eliminate risk, but transferred some of it from investors to creditors. Another privilege, found in all charters before 1851, was the right of eminent domain for land, stone, and timber companies. Many corporations were given tax exemptions. When these were legally challenged, judges validated the railroads' public purpose. One judge pronounced, "It is our duty to foster and promote such enterprises. We cannot and ought not to be indifferent to the imperative demand made by the rapid progress of the age" (quoted in Scheiber 1969, 279).

Despite growing support for transportation and the added incentive of seductively liberal corporate charters, railroad companies did not thrive.

Left to an inhospitable free economy without the protective help of government, their development would have been much slower and probably in a very different form. Before the forties they lacked adequate financing and few of the companies chartered ever operated, even when subsidized by public funds. In the late forties, when sentiment against state investment was festering, railroad promoters convinced the legislature to authorize local governments to invest in railroads. Railroad companies could play towns against one another by offering to place their routes where they got the most support, frequently sparking intense political conflict (Bogart 1924). One group of organizers argued that railroads "are not selfish and soulless corporations, to be controlled by a few capitalists for their benefit alone, but are rather the 'people's lines' to be owned and managed by and in behalf of the various counties which take a majority of the stock" (quoted in Scheiber 1969, 285–286). This sentiment was prevalent enough that local governments contributed nearly half of the estimated $12.8 million invested in Ohio railroads up to 1850.

While Ohio was busy chartering private railroad companies, farmers who felt that railroads benefited mostly merchants, cities that had lost their investments, and the general anticorporate movement were gaining more and more influence. In the constitutional convention of 1850 a coalition of conservatives opposed to any extension of public debt and anticorporate radicals secured a provision outlawing any government investment in corporations.[12] The 1850s was a decade of extensive railroad building in Ohio, expanding between 1852 and 1855 from 1,000 to 2,500 miles and tapering off thereafter. By 1860 there were 3,000 miles, more than any other state. Thus Ohio privatized the railroads by granting the companies liberal corporate provisions as an alternative to state support, while allowing railroads to essentially blackmail localities into underwriting construction. When the risk was high, local governments paid and generally lost. Although economic growth was promised to all, the direct beneficiaries of early railroads were few in number. When the system was secure enough to reasonably promise profits, eastern and European finance capital stepped in and took over.

What difference did it make whether the public financing of railroads was city or state? Public financing was necessary whether it came from state or local governments. While the heavy involvement of government, whether state or local, challenges any explanation based on the efficiency of private markets, there is a crucial and historically consequential difference in its effect on privatization. As entities created by the state, both chartered and owned in large part by the state, corporations were much more accountable to the state. The corporation's public nature is thoroughly embedded in the structures of control. However, when a railroad corporation is chartered by a state government and financed largely through local governments, the relationship of the corporation to both state and local government becomes very much like that of a private corporation. The fact that some stockholders are cities (municipal corporations) is virtually irrelevant to the chartering state. For example, the Pennsylvania legislature granted the charter for the Pennsylvania Railroad to the Philadelphia merchants who applied for it and treated it as a competitor to its own Main Line. Equally private was the relationship of the corporation to equity-owning cities, who had no more power than their voting power. Local governments had no regulatory powers, no ability to define corporate powers, no power to define the nature of corporate property, and little capacity to prevent other cities from offering sweeter deals. They could only work within the structure set by the state. As minority owners, they were as powerless as private minority owners. When they controlled a majority, they could, if they chose, vote their stock in the public interest, as the public directors of the Baltimore and Ohio (B&O) often did (Stover 1987). Whereas state governments, as the chartering agencies, had a structural capacity to hold corporations accountable to the public, local governments were more likely to behave like private owners. Like private owners, they had a vested interest in following a logic of profit maximization to protect their equity. Thus where local governments were major investors in railroads, local public support was a necessary cause for the development of railroad corporations, but an ineffective barrier to privatizing those corporations.

Private funding did not necessarily mean raising money to pay for construction or expansion, but the use of many devices states created for corporations to mobilize resources with a minimum of money. Many early railroads sold very little of their capital stock for cash, some fewer than 5 percent. Instead they exchanged stock for land, the work of contractors, and supplies. The land was often appropriated involuntarily under powers of eminent domain given to the companies, with courts approving railroads' common practice of estimating the increased value to the owner's other land as part of the compensation for seized land. The received land could then be mortgaged to raise whatever cash they needed for construction (Cleveland and Powell 1909). Thus the particular rights defining corporate property were an important factor in the growth of railroad corporations.

Once railroad companies became relatively large, they became formidable organizational entities that exerted an autonomous force on the process of privatization. The larger railroad companies often surpassed states in the resources they could mobilize, the organizational power they could wield, and the level of knowledge they could draw on. The Pennsylvania Railroad and the United Companies of New Jersey each privatized in a way that challenged the sovereignty of the states who chartered them.

Whereas Ohio, swept by contending political forces fighting over the nature of the corporation, floundered into privatization, Pennsylvania abdicated its public authority by spawning a single force so formidable that the government became its subject rather than its master. But the Pennsylvania Railroad was a powerful private corporation not only because "natural" market forces constructed a powerful contender who dominated the game,

but also because the mercantile elites in the state's two large cities, Philadelphia and Pittsburgh, persuaded it to help map the playing field and the rules
of the game, giving private corporations like the Pennsylvania Railroad a
marked advantage.

As in Ohio, Pennsylvania's bountiful investment in the canal-based Main
Line severely limited both its resources and its willingness to invest in railroads. The state directly invested more than $6 million in 150 mixed corpo-
rations and spent more than $100 million on the Main Line canal and rail-
road systems (Lively 1968). Early infrastructure corporations were a way of
mobilizing resources to complete public tasks with a mixture of public and
private resources. However, the particular devices governments granted
corporations to construct their facilities engendered a set of interests contrary to the common weal and gave them a power base to pursue those
interests. Among the powers granted were the right to issue quasi-governmental financial instruments to raise funds. At first railroad companies issued primarily stock, until governments offered to support companies by
guaranteeing bonds. Bonds, a device used primarily for government finance,
were considered a sounder investment and were more easily marketed. By
the end of the century, bonds were the primary instrument for financing
construction (Cleveland and Powell 1909). The Pennsylvania Railroad paid
for its original construction as it went along, using funds mobilized from
the sale of stock to cities and paying as often as possible with stock. But
construction was slowed when some contractors refused to take payment in
that form and the city of Philadelphia was unable to sell bonds in London
for cash to buy the company's stock (Ward 1980).

Unlike Ohio, where the canal commission concentrated on canals and
left the railroad to private interests, in Pennsylvania, the canal commission
had jurisdiction over railroads from the beginning. The merchant-led Pennsylvania Society for the Promotion of Internal Improvements in the Commonwealth published technical papers, disseminated knowledge, and set up
local chapters throughout the state, spawning a movement for state ownership of transportation "which had the passion of a religious campaign"
(Hartz 1968, 131). The relative merits and disadvantages of canals versus
railroads were widely debated, with Mathew Carey's argument that railroads were unproved in the rugged mountain terrain convincing a majority
of the legislature (Rubin 1961; Hartz 1968; Shaw 1990). Their 1828 plan
for the Main Line reaching from Philadelphia called for a forty-mile stretch
of railroad from Philadelphia to Columbia. Pennsylvania's decision to build
railroads was no more visionary or daring than those of other states. The
railroad was initially a secondary link, filling the gap where the more practical canals were impossible (Cummings 1950; Shaw 1990). Because private
plans up to that point had failed, private capital would not support the un-
proven and unpromising technology. Colonel John Stevens, one of the early
railroad enthusiasts, had won approval for a Pennsylvania Rail Road Company in 1823, but had not been able to raise the $5,000 necessary to begin

operation (Frey 1985). Cleveland and Powell describe the investment climate of this period: "Capitalists were as a rule averse to putting money into early railroad ventures, and they met the plans of promoters not only with ridicule, but with outright opposition" (Cleveland and Powell 1909, 76).

The canal-based state-owned Main Line included the Philadelphia and Columbia Railroad, canals to the mountains, and a "Portage Railroad," which was a series of stationary engines that pulled cars up inclined planes with a cable, and then another canal to Pittsburgh. When the system was operating, travelers could speed from Philadelphia to Pittsburgh in as little as four days (Burgess and Kennedy 1949). The system did not work well, however, primarily because the mixed system of canals and rails required so many changes. The weakest link in this chain was the railroad. When the company began to use locomotives, it had so little faith in the technology that it often sent a car of horses in the event the engineers needed more reliable horsepower. When the weather was not good, they did not try to use locomotives at all (Cleveland and Powell 1909). It was not unusual for passengers to be asked to help push the train.

The technical deficiencies of the Main Line were especially distressing to the merchants of Philadelphia, who saw the west as the key to their future prosperity. Their attempts to convince the legislature to create a railroad across the state could not overcome the resistance created by the prospect of losing revenues the Main Line needed to pay for itself, the conflict among the different state regions, and the anticorporate ideologies. Just as the rivalry with New York following the success of the Erie Canal had spurred earlier development, commercial rivalry between Philadelphia and Baltimore induced Pennsylvania to support railroad development. When the Baltimore and Ohio Railroad sought access to Pittsburgh, Pennsylvanians joined forces for a new railroad. A group of Philadelphia businessmen in 1845 organized to mobilize for a railroad and petitioned the legislature that "we do respectfully, but earnestly, exhort and entreat the representatives of the whole people to guard and protect the *general interest*, and not to permit the same to be sacrificed or placed in great jeopardy by the rival schemes and projects of other states, or the citizens thereof, designed for their aggrandizement by our impoverishment, and enabling them to reap private advantages whilst they bear no portion of the public burden" (quoted in Burgess and Kennedy 1949, 37, emphasis in the original).

The legislature responded by chartering the Pennsylvania Railroad. Its original directors were a cross-section of the Philadelphia elite: six merchants, four manufacturers, two bankers, and one merchant/manufacturer. None had any experience in railroad construction or operation. Samuel V. Merrick, a local fire engine magnate, was elected president (Ward 1975). The creation of the Pennsylvania Railroad was highly politicized by intense conflict among the various regions over whether the state should permit the B&O to extend to Pittsburgh, and whether there should be a new company within the state. On a very close vote, the legislature decided to deny the

B&O access if the Pennsylvania Railroad could subscribe $3 million in stock, of which 10 percent was to be paid in, and if construction began within a year. The state reserved the right to purchase the railroad at the end of twenty years. Initially, the city of Philadelphia declined to subscribe to any stock, but an election, in which the railroad was a major issue, changed the composition of the city council. It then authorized a bond of $2.5 million to purchase railroad securities. Up to that time, the company had procured less than a million dollars in subscriptions. Still, it took a six-month campaign to raise the legislated minimum to begin construction. Despite merchant leadership, most purchases were small, with the average subscriber taking only 11.6 shares. In 1848 Allegheny County, where Pittsburgh is located, subscribed to a million dollars. The public investments and many of the small investments reflected broad public support for the endeavor. The statewide campaign to raise funds emphasized the contribution to the state's economic development. Investors no doubt hoped to make a profit, but the appeal was one of more public than private benefit (Schotter 1927). Nonetheless, between March 1847 and the end of 1851, only $827,500 in new funds were subscribed. Up until this time, most of the financing had come from towns to be served by the railroad, but in 1852, the state constitution was amended to forbid such practice (Frey 1985). Thus it was less the impersonal play of market forces that institutionalized privatization than the overt action of the prevailing political forces at the time of the convention. Privatization was rigidly institutionalized into the state constitution. The Pennsylvania Railroad was still well short of the funds needed to complete authorized construction, so it reluctantly, after much debate, decided to issue bonds. As late as 1856, of roughly $12.4 million in stock, almost $6.8 million was owned by government bodies (Burgess and Kennedy 1949). When the line was declared complete in 1855, it extended east from Pittsburgh to Lancaster where it connected with the state-owned Philadelphia and Columbia, then to the west bank of the Schuylkill River and from there over city-owned tracks to the port. The last two segments were poorly maintained and difficult to traverse. Although nominally a private corporation, it could not have been built without public investment by the cities along the route.

The transformation of the Pennsylvania Railroad and other major corporations in Pennsylvania from public to private accountability can be explained by three reinforcing but analytically separate factors: (1) The construction of these corporations within the institutions of public finance made it possible for them to mobilize enough resources to become formidable contenders with their own power base, strong enough to challenge the government for control of transportation within the state. (2) Unintended consequences of early promises for infrastructure corporations and of Jacksonian democracy created the opportunity for the new corporate powers to declare their independence. (3) The growing movement for laissez-faire, especially acting through the legal system, neutralized the anticorporate movement by successfully defining privatization as practical, principled, and predestined. These are, respectively, economic, political, and ideological factors. It is unlikely that any one of them acting in isolation would have had the same effect, but their conjuncture and reinforcement were critical for transforming the corporation from government agency to private property.

By the 1850s the Pennsylvania Railroad was large enough to thwart government attempts to control the transportation system, even though it was still nominally owned in part by many government bodies. One of the first demonstrations of its formidable independence occurred in 1857, when, after heated debate, the legislature decided to eliminate the tonnage tax, exempt the company from all taxation, and relinquish the state's right to purchase the line. The canal commission sued, and the courts decided that the state could not relinquish the tonnage tax or exempt the company from taxation. The railroad company then successfully sued in the federal courts for the state's right to eliminate the tax. After one legislature repealed the tax, the following session negated the decision, but the agreement had been signed as a contract between the state and company and was therefore inviolable (Schotter 1927; Hartz 1968; Ward 1980). Goodrich (1960) argues that after the Civil War, railroad companies were themselves major financial powers with resources greater than some states and territorial governments. This changed the nature of bargaining between railroad companies and governments, especially local governments. Earlier the state had been a senior partner in public/private joint projects. But thereafter, it was quite junior. The corporation superseded its begetter by using its quasi-public status, the powers that came with that status, and the resources mobilized through institutions of public finance.

Hartz (1968) finds the debate over the taxation of the Pennsylvania Railroad especially important because it departed from previous debates over the role of corporations, in which both sides assumed public accountability. In this debate he found unprecedented sentiment against any government involvement, based on arguments that there was a "natural" separation between government and the private economy that benefited both. Opponents of the tonnage tax argued that it was an "artificial political intervention" (quoted on p. 272). This laissez-faire doctrine was strongly rooted in individualism, but unlike some of the earlier uses of individualism which criticized the corporation's collectivism and its special privileges, the new individualism condemned government action against "individuals" like the Pennsylvania Railroad. This moral argument was buttressed with an efficiency argument that the private sector could more effectively ensure prosperity and progress than government. Rather than bearing responsibility for economic growth, government activity came to be seen as an impediment to it (Goodrich 1960; Hurst 1970). In the conflict over the tonnage tax, the Pennsylvania Railroad continued to emphasize its benefit to the public, arguing that the onerous tax was handicapping its competition with New

York's Erie Canal and the Baltimore and Ohio Railroad. The people of Pennsylvania were to be best served by setting their railroad free and relieving it of the burden of public accountability and taxation, not by positive government activity (Schotter 1927).

The new individualist laissez-faire provided one—and as it turned out, a very effective and consequential—interpretation of events that stemmed from two unintended consequences of previous events. One was that the promise made by advocates of public corporations for both economic development and profitable operation was starkly unfulfilled. The other was the success of Jacksonian democrats to shift state power to the administratively feeble legislative branch.

As we have seen, most of the early infrastructural developments were intended to stimulate development where there was none, not to respond to existing market demand for transportation. Unfortunately most of the early ventures were canal companies that could not have anticipated that they would be eclipsed by the railroad within a few short decades. So it is no surprise that they were not especially profitable, especially during the depression of the late thirties. In 1839, the net operating revenue of the Main Line was less than a quarter of interest payments. By 1842, when the state failed to meet its interest payments, a debt of $33 million had been incurred for public works. The critical turning point was the panic of 1857, when many governments, including Allegheny County, who had sold bonds to finance the railroad, repudiated their debt, which "brought to a head a statewide movement of opposition to mixed enterprise" (Goodrich 1960, 71). After a constitutional convention forbade state aid to corporations, either by loans or by subscriptions, and prohibited local authorities from making loans or gifts, the new amendments were approved by a nine-to-one vote in a popular referendum. Goodrich (1960) notes that the Pennsylvania Railroad played a major role in this movement. Ward describes the company president J. Edgar Thomson's attitude: "[G]overnments had the authority to aid private internal improvement projects everywhere, but not the power to interfere with domestic social relations anywhere" (1980, 65).

The charge that government enterprise was inherently inefficient gained further plausibility with decisions to shift political authority from the executive to the legislative branch. The tendency of American legislative branches to dominate the executive branches at both national and state levels was reinforced by the Jacksonian movement, which held legislatures to be more democratic and closer to the people than the executive. The original planning and construction of the Pennsylvania system was directed by the canal commission. When created in 1824, it was appointed by the governor, but anti-executive sentiment in the thirties put the authority in the hands of the legislature. Public opinion also turned against this system, and in 1844, in the context of strong democratic sentiment, the board was changed to election by the public.

It was in this context that J. Edgar Thomson built the administrative system described by Chandler (1977) and Ward (1980). It was not so much that railroads grew naturally from the fertile sustenance of a free market to only then require administrative coordination, as much as that the railroads were created as public agencies without the administrative means to perform the tasks for which they were created. The administrative structures were not adaptations to naturally large-scale enterprise, but were necessary to operate the organizations created outside of market forces. The problem faced by people like Thomson was not so much that they lacked efficient coordination but that they had to build some administrative structure, efficient or not. While many aspects of the structures they developed were genuinely innovative, they also borrowed liberally from existing models of organization, which at this time meant government, particularly the military, borrowing such forms as the line and staff organization.[13]

Pennsylvania thus relieved corporations from the obligation of public accountability and allowed privatization to spawn organizations that overshadowed government itself. The explanation has involved the mobilization and actions of political movements, including the efforts of the corporations themselves; it includes the interaction of social institutions, especially corporations and the local governments that financed them without effective instruments of accountability; it entails political movements' articulation of ideologies to interpret historical events, preventing alternative solutions to real problems; and it requires recognition of some of the accidents of history, such as the massive investment of government funds, the largest nonmilitary commitment in the nation's first century, in a technology that was doomed to become obsolete before the investments could pay off, or the poor timing of the depressions of the 1830s and 1850s that coincided with the wave of democratic sentiment.

In privatizing the railroad corporation, the organizations were not just adapting to the functional needs for more efficient operation. They were redefining property and thus whose interests were served. They were not just retreating from a preexisting public sphere into a preexisting private sphere. They were actively constructing the categories of public and private. The railroad was widely hailed as the engine of economic growth, the locomotive that pulled American manufacturing, trade, and commercial agriculture into the modern era. When the locomotive started the journey, a team of horses pulling a few boxes on wheels over wooden tracks, or in a few cases an undependable kettle with pipes, governments assumed active responsibility for building the economy. By the time the locomotive reached full speed, now a powerful engine pulling scores of full-size freight cars, tank cars, and sleek passenger cars, the roles of government and private capital had been redefined, the government enforcing the rights and obligations enjoyed by owners and managers. The manifest form was private but the public roots remained.

Privatization did not mean that the railroad would thenceforth operate according to purely market forces or that the government receded to the role of exogenous regulator. The federal government in particular became much more active in shaping the development of the railroad and the institutional form it took. During and after the Civil War, when state governments had almost universally ceased active proprietary involvement in railroads, the federal government heavily subsidized railroads. The wartime administration recognized the strategic military value of railroads, took over the operation of some of them, and began investing in others. After the war, it renewed its commitment to creating what had been a national dream since the time of Lewis and Clark, a transcontinental thoroughfare. In addition to loans, tax breaks, and legal exemptions, federal, state, and local governments ceded nearly a tenth of the continental United States to the railroads, a spread of land equal to the state of Texas (Mercer 1982). This land included not only the rights of way but alternating ten- or twenty-mile blocks, land that could be resold at the high prices trackside land could demand.

From an institutional point of view, these contributions were less important in creating a new organizational form than in expanding the scale of operation and the potential for power. The concentrated control of resources, the size of the organizational structures, and the dense network of personal relationships among the leaders who controlled the railroads meant that the institution of corporate capitalism grew to overshadow all other institutions with the possible exception of government. By the end of the Civil War, railroad companies were wholly private in ownership and control. They were generally financed in the national and international capital market and operated by professional managers. In the next few decades, at least in part because of government subsidies, railroads were merged into corporate *systems*, groups of railroads tied together by common ownership, leasing arrangements, shared directors, and operational interdependencies. Corporations of a size at one time unfathomable became common. Their size, the amount of resources at their disposal, the number of people dependent on their prosperity from income, sales, profits, and taxes increased to the point that society as a whole became beholden. By the end of the century the state and the corporation stood as a class by themselves in the field of organized power, with institutions like religion, education, media, and medicine subordinate to them.

Thus government, in creating, nurturing, and setting free the railroad, actively and decisively created, nurtured, and set free corporate capitalism. The railroads were not just the harbingers of the modern corporation; until the very end of the century, they *were* corporate capitalism. The modern corporation arose not out of the objective functional needs of the economy through the actions of rational businessmen operating in a market, but by the proactive, contingent, and historically consequential actions of government and businessmen. In fact it was only after the corporation became privatized that the government and the corporation were even fully distinguishable. The result was not only the creation of a new set of organizations, the specific corporations that built and operated the railroads, but a new type of property, and with it a new segment of the capitalist class, to which we now turn.

A NEW FORM OF PROPERTY

The new form of property was socialized property. The new class segment was the corporate class segment, a historically specific set of people tied together through specific institutional structures and possessing a particular historically constituted sense of themselves and their relation to society. Although the particular relationship to production was specific to the railroad by virtue of the fact that it transported rather than produced goods, its corporate form along with the capacity for speculative property was generalizable to other sectors.

Depicting the railroad as America's "first big business" can mean many things to many people. The characterization can refer to size, management structure, organizational form, institutional structure, or form of property. All these dimensions are descriptively appropriate. The industry, in terms of both individual companies and aggregated as a whole, was gargantuan. In the 1850s the largest industrial firm, the Pepperell Mills, operated for about $300,000 a year, while the Pennsylvania Railroad spent nearly $5 million (Robertson 1985, 124). By 1889 the railroad industry's (admittedly watered) volume of stock and bond book value, $8.56 billion (U.S. Interstate Commerce Commission 1905, 57), surpassed the concurrent book value of the nation's total manufacturing capital, $5.7 billion (U.S. Department of Commerce 1975, 684). As the railroads grew, they made innovations in modern managerial practices to handle unprecedented volumes of business, as Chandler has portrayed. Louis McLane and Benjamin Latrobe of the B&O created the first functional form, with departments divided on the basis of the role in the operation, lifting bureaucratic organization to new levels of complexity and coordination, creating a division of labor theretofore unknown (Robertson 1985). As already noted, the line and staff structure was brought from the military into economic life. Cost accounting and strategic planning helped administer huge organizational empires (Chandler 1965, 1977). While the railroad's contribution to aggregate economic growth, especially by enabling wider and cheaper marketing, has been widely treated (Davis 1961; Goodrich 1960; Jenks 1944; Cochran 1955; Chandler 1965; Fishlow 1966; McClelland 1968; Lightner 1983), I emphasize the railroad's distinctive form of property. Chapter 6 will address the legal aspects of corporate property, the rights, entitlements, and responsibilities enforced by the state. Here I want to analyze the institutional aspects of the social relationships among important economic actors. To understand the historical role that the railroad played in the rise of major industrial corporations, it is necessary to explore its earlier relationship to industry, focusing on how railroads and industry operated in two distinct institutional environments and the kinds of relationships that connected them to each other.

Railroad property was institutionalized as corporate capital. Its growth, dynamics, and internal relationships were structured through the institutions of corporate capitalism. The class who owned it was the corporate class segment. I use these terms rather than finance capitalism and finance class segment because the financial dynamics were only one aspect of its operation. To be sure, the ability to issue corporate securities, mobilize resources from finance capital markets, expand through securities manipulation, and control enterprise by financial power all structured corporate growth. But the financial system was but one component of the corporate system which, as I have stressed, was a system of property. The definition of the class segment thus is based on the entire system of property, not just the institutions that administered the flow of capital.[14]

Although the financial dynamics were only one facet of the system of corporate capitalism, the institutions of finance were a critical component distinguishing corporate capital from other parts of the economy. Corporate capital separated the paper representation of capital from the physical objects of capital and thereby redefined the meaning of ownership. Ownership became more fungible and alienable. Ownership could be parcellized and sold without directly affecting management and operation, creating a form of profit distinct from company revenue and expenses. Although in entrepreneurial capitalism the paper deed was literally separate from the objects producing commodities, ownership of the deed, except for silent partners, granted the right to control production. Transferring the deed meant transferring control of the plant. So there was a singular system of property, with the physical plants and the ownership papers constituting the same social relationships. Finance capital is essentially a mercantile system in which securities—stocks and bonds—are traded like barrels of barley, pecks of peppers, or sacks of sugar. The marketing and trading of securities take on a life of their own that is only loosely coupled to the daily operation of the physical facilities which the security-holders nominally "own." As a consequence, firms capitalized as publicly traded corporations could operate somewhat independently of revenue and could easily grow and combine with relatively little cash capital.

Although the institutions of finance made it possible to create wealth somewhat independently of the underlying real property, that independence was only relative. The operation of the broader economy set limits on corporate capital. Ultimately the railroad system depended on manufacturing, farming, and merchandizing. This section will describe how the railroads, organized as large corporations, both operated within the context of financial institutions and were connected to the more basic means of production, organizationally distinct from industry, commerce, and farming but dependent on them. When the continent was saturated with tracks and when the depression of 1893 ended construction and speculation, the corporate class segment merged with the growing industrial class segment.

As discussed above, early railroads, before the system of finance capital was fully institutionalized, financed their construction from a variety of sources that hoped to benefit from the availability of transportation. State and local governments (and later the federal government), merchants, farmers, and tradesmen contributed liberally to the early railroads, which, because they were quasi-government organizations, were financed in the institutions that administered government debts—the stock exchanges, investment banks, and brokerage houses in New York and other large cities. For example, the Pennsylvania Railroad was initially financed primarily by the city of Philadelphia in a six-month campaign to sell stock. This was at a time when stocks could be subscribed for as little as 10 percent paid in. The city financed its purchase by selling (with some difficulty) its own bonds on the London markets. Few large investors became involved with railroads until its technical superiority was proved in the late 1840s (Seavoy 1982). One of the first railroads built without any public support was the Cincinnati, Hamilton & Dayton, a harbinger of later financing patterns, selling one-fifth of its $800,000 stock in New York and securing the rest of its capital from residents of Cincinnati and the contractors who built it (Scheiber 1969). But for the most part, only after the Civil War were railroads primarily financed by the wealthy investors who dominated the national and international financial system.

The role that finance capital played in the rise of the railroads could have been very different. The fact that investment banks and the stock market were involved at all stemmed from the status of early corporations as quasi-government agencies. Since publicly marketed securities were used for government finance, it was not only easy but also defined as appropriate for railroad securities—like canal securities—to be administered through the institutions of finance capital. One factor which enhanced supply was the rapid repayment of debt from the War of 1812, which augmented capital available for reinvestment. Between 1815 and 1830, over $123 million was repaid to bondholders (Callender 1902). Similarly foreign capital first became involved in canal and railroad finance as an offshoot of investment in government securities. By the 1830s fifty to sixty state and state bank securities were listed on the London Stock Exchange when the first railroad stock, that of Camden and Amboy, New Jersey's franchised monopoly, became listed. Most government issues disappeared after the 1837 depression, to be generally replaced by railroad securities. But these receded into the background during the British railroad boom of the forties. Later some railroad securities reached the London market via English iron masters who accepted them as payment (Duguid 1901). The eventual relationship of railroads to finance capital could also have been different if railroad corpora-

tions—like many canal companies—had remained quasi-government agencies. Or the relationship could have been different if the practice of giving railroad corporations banking powers had not been opposed by both bankers and the antimonopoly movement. The fact that some of the early railroad banks were corrupt did not help matters, although it is not clear whether they were any more corrupt than other means of finance.

Finance Capital and the Railroad

Increasingly, as railroads became more dependent on the institutions of finance capital to become established and develop, fewer railroads were begun without the involvement of major investors, especially foreign investors. From the 1850s on, the investment banks that railroads depended on to issue new securities for construction, expansion, and (too frequently) for operation were those with affiliates or branches in European centers. Many feeder lines were initiated by local interests in the towns off of the trunk lines, but often these were brought into the orbit of the major systems by financial transactions administered by investment institutions.

The more railroads became embedded in the institutions of finance capitalism, the more the dynamics of growth and development operated according to its practices, practices that eventually became standard for large corporations, creating opportunities denied to enterprise outside the corporate system. These practices included profiting from speculation, a short-run autonomy from dependence on revenue when new securities could be sold, but a long-run instability leading to periodic depressions, and finally the easy merger and building of large economic empires through the manipulation of financial instruments.

Until the 1890s, the enormous railroad profits came at least as much from constructing and merging railroads as from operating them. Once the capital was invested and the construction completed, it became necessary to mobilize revenues to continue operation and secure dividends on stock. If this could not be done by receipts on traffic, the railroad companies could return to the capital market and issue additional stocks or, more typically, mortgage bonds with a fixed interest rate and due date. Thus one of the distinctive features of corporate capital is that the relationship between revenues and solvency is quite indirect, especially at the level of any particular company. Credit is, of course, one of the essential characteristics of capitalism, one that makes it possible for firms to weather the inevitable storms of depression and disaster. But the rise of the corporate institution fundamentally changed institutional practices, loosening the link between revenues and survival and, more important, changing who survives or fails. Insofar as the efficiency of the system depends on selective market mechanisms to winnow out inefficient enterprises, loosening the link between revenues and survival can undermine system efficiency.

In the long run, revenues were necessary if the investments were to return a profit, but specific railroads could remain profitable without adequate receipts from traffic, at least in the short run. The link between revenue and capital was severed by socializing capital within the class. Since ownership was not held by any specific individual but distributed throughout the class, any failure to realize a profit through the market could be compensated for by further investment from the class. Just as an individual entrepreneur can use personal funds to sustain an ailing firm, the socialization of investment capital made it possible for railroads to exist without short-term viability. The difference is that when capital is socialized through a class, the ability to sustain a firm depends not on the resources or credit of the individual owner or family, but on the resources of the class. Moreover, we cannot assume that the class has perfect knowledge. Definitions of success, fashions of some types of business, reputations of leaders, interpersonal affiliations and loyalties, and taken-for-granted assumptions of business practices and standards all color investment decisions that transcend economic "rationality." Investors' collective reluctance to abandon feeble railroad securities, followed by their contagious rush to industrial mergers in the 1890s (Navin and Sears 1955), amply documents these institutional processes.

Inefficient firms were able to survive because the relationship between revenues and profits became mediated by financial institutions. A weak railroad could continue operation by issuing bonds or other securities. When these became due, new bonds could be issued to cover the older ones as long as the dominant financiers gave their blessing. In the inevitable absence of perfect information, interpersonal influence substituted for rational investment decisions in the flow of socialized capital among corporations. Many railroads were, by the early 1850s, carrying first, second, and third mortgage bonds, common and preferred stock, and miscellaneous forms of indebtedness. As long as investment bankers were willing to sustain this "pyramid game" by marketing the securities (and recommending them to customers who could buy them with money borrowed on other securities), the railroads could remain solvent. As a result, railroad companies were often extraordinarily overburdened with debt. Revenues then had to be split between operations and interest payments.

The socialization of capital and the separation from physical objects of capital made it much easier to merge firms and build large empires, often with little or no "real" money. If one entrepreneurial firm wanted to buy another, an owner would typically have to offer money, although this could sometimes be gained by credit. But a railroad could offer pieces of paper, which if recognized by the seller and the larger community of socialized capital, could act as a currency of exchanging property. One railroad could take over another by "buying" it with new stocks or bonds that represented the assets of the selling company. A railroad could also gain control of other companies by leasing property, guaranteeing bonds, and other means. With all these devices corporations could construct organizations and secure dominance through transactions that involved only the partial use of money. In many cases no real money had to change hands at all. Such transactions were confined not only to corporations but more precisely to corporations that were part of the larger system of corporate finance. The "currency" that bought and sold the tracks, locomotives, cars, and other assets was socially constructed and made "real" by the institution. The point is not that corporate currency or property is any less inherently real or any more socially constructed than other forms of property. Real money or cash is only as real as the participants in a transaction agree and as certain as organizations of enforcement will back it up. But the stocks, bonds, and other instruments of capitalization were socially constructed and enforced by a set of organizations and had a set of relationships to physical assets different from that of entrepreneurial capitalism.

Thus the system of finance capital was inherently unstable, giving rise to periodic blood-letting depressions. It is no coincidence that the most severe depressions in the history of capitalism occurred during the height of finance capitalism between the 1870s and the 1930s. Capitalism before that was moderated by small locally controlled markets and government investment. Capitalism since then has been moderated by nationally administered markets and government regulation.

The Pennsylvania Railroad illustrates the way in which these devices were used to create the world's largest company. It was initially financially a very conservative company, run by Philadelphia merchants to secure the city's commercial success by tapping the rich resources of the expanding west. Unlike later corporations financed mainly by fixed interest bonds, it was financed entirely by stock, minimizing the vulnerability of newness by leaving it free of mandatory dividend payments. J. Edgar Thomson began to build its great empire in 1852, after he was elected president in part because of a conflict over financial policy (Ward 1980). Shortly after he took office, the state legislature granted the corporation two important, new, and at that time unusual, property rights: the right to buy securities in out-of-state corporations and the right to issue bonds in an amount up to the value of their paid-in stock. Although the company's directors had declined to invest in the new Ohio and Pennsylvania Railroad in 1851, once Thomson had become president, they agreed to issue $5 million in bonds to purchase a controlling interest, linking Pittsburgh with the west (Schotter 1927). A few years later the Pennsylvania Railroad guaranteed bonds of the Pittsburgh, Ft. Wayne, and Chicago, enabling it to merge with the Ohio and Pennsylvania, completing a thorough connection between the Keystone State and the Windy City.

Over the next decades the Pennsylvania Railroad expanded throughout the eastern half of the country. For example, the Marietta and Cincinnati, one of hundreds of small railroads it affiliated with, was a modest-sized railroad which provided a strategic link between Pittsburgh and Cincinnati, one of the Midwest's major industrial centers. The Pennsylvania Railroad bought $750,000 of the M&C's capital stock, to be paid in either Pennsylvania Railroad stock or cash, with the provision that the subsidiary company would pay the interest on the Pennsylvania Railroad stock and not sell it for less than par. Some of the M&C stock that the Pennsylvania Railroad bought was later exchanged for stock in the Maysville & Big Sandy Railroad Company, intended to give it a link to Lexington, Kentucky, but the investment came to nothing (Schotter 1927; Burgess and Kennedy 1949). Although not large by railroad standards, these typical transactions in the hundreds of thousands of dollars dwarfed the amounts that were being spent to capitalize industrial concerns. When multiplied over hundreds of transactions, these railroad purchases show how economic empires could be constructed by manipulating securities, rather than by creating new productive value—arrangements made possible only by the institutional structure that validated and facilitated them. Through many other transactions like this, the company grew enormously over Thomson's tenure. When he died in 1873, the Pennsylvania itself owned 1,574 miles of track and controlled companies with more than 6,000 miles (Schotter 1927).

The issue here is not whether this mode of building an economic empire is corrupt or extravagant. The Pennsylvania Railroad was unusually fiscally conservative. In contrast to the many corporations bloated with watered stock, it probably was undercapitalized. Because it generally financed construction with stocks rather than bonds, it freed itself from obligatory dividends in hard times. It paid construction contracts in cash. As a result, it consistently paid dividends. The point here is that this was a very different mode of organizing property from that of industrial capital.

So what was the relationship of railroad corporations to industry? The system that was built through the institutions of corporate capital, though drawing investment and revenue from manufacturing, remained separated from it. Very little wealth created by corporate capital (only the minute proportion of securities owned by individual manufacturers) was invested in industrial production. Industry interacted with railroads almost entirely through market transactions, the shipping of goods. Ownership remained separate as long as railroad investors avoided industrial securities as too risky and industrialists preferred to maintain control rather than seek greater wealth by going public.

As the country's largest sector, the railroads powerfully shaped the flow of material resources and the distribution of wealth throughout society. They not only funneled resources into the basic industries such as iron and steel, leather, lumber, and coal that supplied their needs, but also drew resources out of the agrarian, mercantile, and industrial economies into the system of finance capital. Figure 4.1 shows the aggregate gross revenues of American railroads from 1851 to 1890. The rate of growth was, by any standard, spectacular and, by the scale of industry at that time, unfathomable.

The railroad's impact was felt in not only the amount of wealth mobilized but also the institutional form and distribution. Its institutional form

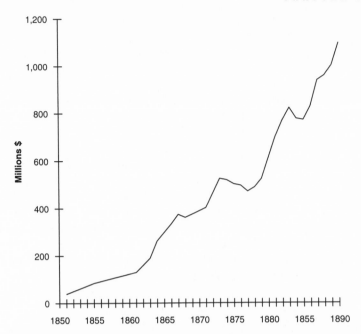

Figure 4.1. Total Traffic Earnings of U.S. Railroads, 1851–1890.
(Source: Data drawn from U.S. Bureau of the Census 1975, 734.)

structured who could control its use and thus the purposes for which it was used. One of the most far-reaching institutional changes in the second half of the nineteenth century was the centralization of capital into the capital markets of the major cities, especially New York. Wealth flowing through small rural banks or merchants' bills of lading creates a different industrial system than does wealth circulating as corporate stocks and bonds. The creation of a General Electric, U.S. Steel, or International Harvester cannot happen without the mobilization through specific institutions of millions of—and for U.S. Steel a billion—dollars of capital. The aggregate sum of wealth throughout the economy does not help spawn large firms unless there are means to funnel it into single entities. One of the pivotal preconditions for the corporate revolution at the end of the century was the centralization of wealth into a form accessible to publicly traded corporations. The railroad system mobilized and centralized the expanding quantities of wealth.

The biggest factor in concentrating corporate capital was the centralization of the institutions of finance capital in eastern cities, especially New York, as will be discussed in Chapter 5. Whether railroad corporations were spectacular successes or abysmal failures, wealth flowed into the metropolitan investment institutions. Although many small investors, especially in towns served by railroads, contributed what for them were substantial amounts, by the time of the Civil War no railroad of any consequence could be built without Philadelphia, Boston, or New York financiers to raise the necessary funds. To build or expand a railroad, the services of an investment bank were necessary, usually a private bank like Prime, Ward & King in the early days, or J. P. Morgan & Company at the turn of the century. The investment bank would make a study of the properties and individuals involved, draw up a contract for selling securities, agreeing to either take the securities on commission, underwrite them (guarantee their sale), or purchase them outright. If the issue was very large, the bank might organize a syndicate of other banks and individuals to spread the risk. It would then offer to sell the securities to major investors, including commercial banks, insurance companies, and wealthy capitalists, and, for a few banks, small investors (Carosso 1970). British and European customers were normally essential for any major offering. Railroads could thus raise funds in large amounts relatively quickly. Once sold by investment bankers, the securities could migrate to the stock market for speculative profits.

The revenues from passengers and freight far surpassed the scope of business in any other sector. While the revenues, of course, paid for the construction bonds and operation of the railroads, there were also huge, though wildly fluctuating, profits. In the early nineties American railroads as important as the Union Pacific allocated more than half their gross revenues to interest payments (Campbell 1938).[15] Half of every dollar a farmer or merchant paid to ship a bushel of wheat or a barrel of nails was forwarded directly to Wall Street. Agrarian and merchant capital was thus expropriated into corporate capital and reorganized into larger parcels. Instead of millions of farmers and merchants making the decisions that determined how the wealth would be appropriated, a few hundred railroad executives and financiers decided. Typically, the wealth so mobilized was reinvested into the railroads to buy more securities (along with mansions and yachts). In the last third of the century, the railroad companies and the supporting institutional structure amassed huge quantities of wealth, creating huge organizational and financial structures.

Because control of railroad capital was concentrated, wealth flowed into a central pool. By 1871 the top twenty-five railroad companies, capitalized at a total of nearly $1.2 billion, accounted for 44 percent of all railroad capital. These twenty-five companies had only 453 directorships, and with interlocks, fewer individuals, controlling over a billion dollars in wealth (Bunting 1979) when the gross national product was under $7 billion (U.S. Bureau of the Census 1975). Even considering the inflated value of railroad securities, this level of concentration is striking, especially since these figures predate the decades of the end of the century conventionally described as the period of increasing concentration.

The more dependent railroads became on investment banks, the more active control banks could exercise. Until the last two decades of the century, most investment bankers confined their influence to fiscal issues rather than operational policies or the appointment of managers. However, insofar as they set the criteria by which firms would be evaluated as worthy of capitalization, they exercised power. J. P. Morgan created a new role for investment bankers when in 1879 William H. Vanderbilt solicited his assistance to sell $30 million of his New York Central stock to English investors.[16] Morgan sold the shares discreetly to avoid a rush on the securities, and as holder of the proxies for the English purchasers, gained a seat on the company's board. As the strategic link between European capital and American railroads, Morgan grew into the archetypical active investment banker who not only vouched for the soundness of the companies whose stock he marketed, but amassed the power to solidify these companies (Allen 1965). If the railroad was desperate enough, it might have to surrender control for relatively small amounts. The Atchison, Topeka and Santa Fe, the country's longest railway, in 1888 had to agree to these conditions just to get a three-year loan of $7 million dollars from Kidder, Peabody & Company: George C. Maguon, one of Kidder's partners, was appointed to the railroad's finance committee; the investment bank also named an accountant who was to institute the Pennsylvania Railroad bookkeeping system; any expenditure beyond $25,000 had to be approved by the finance committee. The following year Kidder, Peabody & Company called for proxies and gained active control by appointing six new directors, two of whom were partners. Maguon became chairman of the board (Carosso 1970).

The relationship of banks to railroads is a classic case of power and dependence. Especially after government agencies stopped financing the railroads, banks controlled the resource that railroads needed most to grow. Conversely, railroad investment was a major source of profit for banks; major banks were dominant because of their close connection to railroads. But what shaped the railroad corporations at the institutional level was less the influence that bankers may have had on particular railroad decisions than the definition of success that both managers and investors adopted. Instead of a managerial definition of success based on the efficient delivery of goods and people, success was defined as the appreciation of securities on the stock and bond markets. While appreciation of investment was in no way contrary to efficient service and could be created by it, what determined the fate of railroad corporations was in the final analysis their performance in securities markets. As a consequence, the centralization of investment institutions in New York meant the centralization of power over the corporate system.

Investment banks were strategic nodes and gatekeepers in the financial network. Railroad corporations and investors both depended on them. Corporations needed access to the investors and investors depended on the bankers to select and monitor reliable investment opportunities. Corporations often welcomed a stable relationship with a bank and were willing to conform to bank influence because investors trusted the bank's advice (Carosso 1970). Moreover, and probably more important, investment banking defined the form that capital took. The stocks and bonds represented more than physical capital, fundamentally constructing the social reality of securities. A charter gave a corporation the right to issue stocks and bonds legally on its own. Whether anyone else would accord them any value was socially determined. A company could issue securities and sell them to members of the owners' social circle. Family or friends could subscribe, paying in any currency the corporation accepted.[17] It all depended on an owner's connections. Large railroad corporations were part of a social circle comprising investment institutions and capitalists. Investment banks had the power to socially define which corporate securities for which corporations had value. Of course, this was not entirely at their discretion. Railroads they promoted often failed. But no corporation could raise finance capital without playing by the rules that investment bankers enforced. When investment banks retreated from active control, the fundamental operation of the corporate capital system was not fundamentally altered. Nonetheless, in the latter part of the nineteenth century the investment banks were more than passive conduits between railroad and investor. They played a critical role in the larger institutional framework.

The form of capital that the institutions of finance created thus concentrated wealth in the large eastern cities. Most railroad property was capitalized by a combination of common stocks, preferred stocks, and bonds. From the 1850s on, construction was financed primarily by bonds (loans used for construction [Kirkland 1961] or acquisition, mortgaged on that property). They were typically issued for a set period with a fixed rate of interest, for example, twenty years at 6 percent interest. When they matured the corporation had to pay back the principal, although this was typically accomplished by converting them to stock or issuing new bonds. Preferred stock had the advantage of a nominally guaranteed rate of return along with title to the property. Preferred stock was frequently used to pay for the construction or acquisition of subsidiaries. Common stock was the riskiest form of investment. It represented title to the property, the right to control through the board of directors, and the possibility of potentially unlimited profits. But dividends were paid only after the obligations of bonds and preferred stock were met. Most railroads carried a combination of all three.

Railroads further concentrated wealth not only when they succeeded but also when they failed, which, considering the enormous wealth they controlled, was surprisingly frequent. The corporate system of railroads, despite the rise of managerial systems that rationalized operation, was efficient only in its ability to create large systems, not in its ability to effectively use resources and return reliable profits. Throughout the 1890s, including the banner years at the end of the century when they were paying over $4 billion in dividends, over half the country's railroad companies paid no dividends at all (Campbell 1938). The corporate system effectively raised capital and built systems, but the result was investment far beyond what the system "needed" or could support (Berk 1990). Its large scale created as many diseconomies as economies. The widespread failures, however, further concentrated control, until investors sought alternative outlets for their capital. The process of overcapitalization, failure, reorganization, and merger was an important part of the process of concentrating capital; it eventually fueled the creation of large industrial corporations.

From 1875 to 1897, seven hundred railroad companies representing 100,000 miles of track (more than half the country's rails) went bankrupt (Berk 1990). When railroads failed, the reorganization process created a new company, often with the same name as the old, which would purchase the securities of the old company at a discount and reduce or change the funded debt. Since the discount differed on various stock issues—common, first, second, and higher preferred—and bonds, and since stockholders could be assessed, such plans could effectively redistribute large amounts of wealth. Campbell (1938) describes how seven large railroad systems in the 1890s levied assessments of more than $80 million on their stockholders, for which they generally issued new securities. In addition, they sold new stocks and bonds for about $50 million. "The combined total of about $130,000,000 represents the expenses which past mistakes and the ensuing receiverships and reorganizations cost these companies" (322). But all these new obligations meant that common stocks, which paid dividends only after other obligations were met, plummeted in market value. The net effect of such reorganizations often further centralized wealth in the New York financial markets.

These receivership cases helped redefine the nature of corporate property by altering the rights and obligations of different participants, thereby redefining the relationship of owners and managers to the operation. On May 28, 1884, Jay Gould, president of Wabash, St. Louis and Pacific Railway, requested that the federal district court in St. Louis appoint his representatives as receivers, even though the company was still solvent. There had been no precedent for receivers to be appointed to a railroad not in default or for managers to be appointed receivers. The prevailing doctrine gave control to creditors and held managers responsible for bankruptcy, so as a rule, outside impartial receivers were appointed to balance the interests of stockholders, creditors, workers, and the public. Creditors could decide either to refund debt or to auction assets and distribute the income to unpaid bondholders. When the railroad company survived, as was typical, the same capital structure remained in place. The *Wabash* decision set a precedent by which creditors were stripped of many rights in receivership. The courts gave management the right to reorganize the bankrupt corporation under the doctrine that the corporation itself was an entity to be preserved. Berk (1990) aptly describes how receivership decisions beginning with *Wabash* treated the managers as the representatives of the corporate entity and the owners as just another interest group, rendering a reallocation of resources within a new set of rights, entitlements, and obligations. Judges gradually abandoned the contract theory of the corporation, which conceived of it as a contract among investors (Horwitz 1992), and adopted a natural entity theory, treating corporations as collective bodies best directed by managers rather than owners. By defining the relationship among owners, creditors, workers, and the public as mediated by the entity itself, which itself had a legal life, property became more fundamentally socialized. The rights of individual owners and creditors were drastically weakened so that the resources under corporate title were more thoroughly controlled by a limited number of officers and directors.

J. P. Morgan "virtually institutionalized Gould's financial and legal principles of reorganization" (Berk 1990, 146). When reorganizing railroad officials anticipated that they would have to go to investment bankers in the future, they often elicited the bankers' participation during receivership. Moreover, many judges evaluated a bankrupt railroad's long-term viability from the attitude of investment bankers on whom the company would be dependent. It is thus not surprising that investment bankers increasingly took on reorganization as one of their services. For example, Morgan agreed to serve as reorganization manager for the Southern Railroad only if a majority of stockholders put voting rights in trust not only during reorganization, but for some time afterward. He used his power to gain "enormous concessions" from bondholders: debt was cut by about a third and participating railroad companies were consolidated in one large holding company. The same principles were used in other reorganizations, which also put bondholders at a disadvantage (Berk 1990).

Concentration of control was further enhanced by the geographical convergence of finance in the eastern part of the country, especially in New York City. While Boston and Philadelphia continued to administer many financial functions, by the 1850s New York was the gateway to large-scale financing, the undisputed center of finance capital. As railroads developed and required more capital to become established and expand, the dependence on eastern money, especially from New York, increased. Beginning in 1846, John Murray Forbes was one of the leaders channeling eastern money into western railroads (Cochran 1953). The eastern cities of Boston, New York, and Philadelphia sprouted as centers of financial power because they served as strategic nodes for two types of resources—merchandise and capital. While the production and sale of merchandise, of course, flourished throughout America, merchant capital played a critical role when commercial transactions crossed boundaries, especially political boundaries. As the ports through which most international commerce passed, these cities were the sites of many of the larger merchant banking houses and thus became financial centers as well. The large banking houses also mediated the international flow of capital. Many of the early prominent investment banks such as John E. Thayer and Brother of Boston, E. W. Clark and Company of Philadelphia, or Winslow, Lanier and Company began as merchant banks and, because of their access to European capital, evolved into full-fledged investment banks capitalizing American infrastructure corporations

(Carosso 1970). Once the eastern cities became dominant, their dominance attracted more capital.

The centralization of finance capital in New York in particular was associated with two closely related factors. First, bonds were increasingly the device used to capitalize construction and expansion, in part because they were more easily marketed abroad (Cleveland and Powell 1909; Myers 1970). Over the course of the nineteenth century, Europeans, especially the British, invested over $2 billion in American railroads (Campbell 1938; Adler 1970). Second, as with much of corporate development, government played a role. It was initially as a center of trading government securities that New York established its financial importance. Since government financing and infrastructure development were so closely intertwined, New York became the center of railroad financing. Moreover, when states guaranteed the bonds of canals or railroads, they not only induced railroads to finance with bonds rather than stocks, but also persuaded customers, especially foreign buyers, to invest in the new untried technology. By 1856 railroad securities listed in the New York financial press surpassed government securities (Myers 1970). While a few major investment banks like Kidder, Peabody & Company were headquartered in other cities, from mid-century, nearly all the investment bankers—companies synonymous with high finance like Jay Cooke, Jay Gould, and J. P. Morgan, all of whom were deeply involved with railroads—were based in New York City.

Wealth was also centralized into corporations through local banking. The 1863 banking act made it easier for local banks to deposit funds in regional banks, which typically deposited funds in New York banks (Berk 1990; Myers 1970; James 1978). As elaborated in the next chapter, these deposited funds provided much of the collateral for loans that New York banks made to investors in the stock market (Stedman and Easton 1969; Carosso 1970).

Thus the railroad industry was built around state-fostered institutions and based on a legal form of property that enabled it to free itself from short-term market dynamics and siphon off great wealth from the atomized merchants and farmers. But because railroad capital was structurally distinct from merchant, agrarian, and industrial capital, the mobilized wealth was not systematically reinvested extensively across the whole economy.

Changing the Rational Calculus

The new form of property, the new institutions of corporate capitalism, and the new class structure not only provided a form—the corporation—that manufacturing enterprise could adopt, but also made it rational to do so. This change in the rational calculus of decision making is the aspect that most economists and historians have emphasized in discussing the railroad's awesome impact (Jenks 1944; Chandler 1965, 1977; Fishlow 1966; McClelland 1968). Although the conventional accounts are incomplete, there is no doubt that the contribution of the railroad to the growth of the national market was enormous and that the mechanisms of growth identified by economic historians who have studied railroads were critical.[18] In this perspective, economic growth results when enough individuals make decisions to invest, loan, borrow, buy, and sell. Changes that alter the relative payoffs from various decisions by lowering costs, increasing profits, or making transactions easier thereby contribute to economic growth. The primary role through which the railroad changed the rational calculus of decision making was as a form of transportation. Extralocal commerce had increasingly to take the railroad into account in deciding where to trade and sometimes whom to trade with. Especially in large-volume products like petroleum or sugar, transportation was a relatively large proportion of total costs (U.S. Bureau of Corporations 1906; Eichner 1969). But the impact was felt in other ways. For many large industries, the railroad was a major customer. By 1860 the railroad purchased 40 percent of all rolled iron, and until 1880 it consumed 80 percent of all Bessemer steel (Bruchey 1990). It was also important for industries like leather, which was used in seats; lumber, used in freight cars; and paper, used in the expanding new bureaucracies (Chandler 1977). Far larger than any other industry, the railroad was a potential customer of all general business products. Finally, and most important, the railroad changed the calculus of decision making by creating a national market. It opened access to areas that had been previously unreachable while enhancing the speed, flexibility, and adaptability of transportation (Jenks 1944).

In the conventional accounts, it is noted that the impact was asymmetric—railroads had much greater influence on farmers, merchants, small towns, and consumers than vice versa. But this is rarely theorized in terms of power for at least three reasons. First, the motivations imputed to the actors are economic or organizational rather than dominance oriented. Railroad leaders are treated as ordinary entrepreneurs engaged in business to earn a livelihood (Cochran 1955) or as managers attempting to adapt to the exigencies of increased scale and complexity (Chandler 1965, 1977). However, the issue of whether power is being exercised should be distinct from the question of motivation. Even if actors are motivated by economic or organizational rationality, they can still exercise power. Second, the people dealing with the railroads are assumed to have been free to make decisions as they saw fit, with no external constraint. Yet just as benign motivation versus power is a false dichotomy, so is freedom versus power. The fact that people are making choices without overt constraint does not necessarily mean that no power is exercised. When power is exercised by determining the consequences of alternative choices—resource control power—the object of power is still free, in the way that term is typically understood. The town leaders who had a choice between investing in a railroad that would be selecting where stations would be located were free to not invest. But if the consequence of not investing was that the station was located elsewhere, power was certainly being exercised. Finally, the issue of power is often conflated with the issue of legitimate or legal power. Some accounts pose the question of whether the railroads were acting within the parameters of conventional business ethics or legal operation (Kirkland 1961). They do not consider how power might operate within the boundaries of ethical and legal propriety.

Nonetheless, power operated. I stress this not to condemn what happened, but to explain it. The dynamics of power affect the system within which the rational calculation of interests is made in at least three ways. First, the parties calculating their interests are affecting one another by more than just the mere exchange of resources, more than just neutral buying and selling. The extent to which firms must conform to the others' organizational structure, mode of operation, and at times form of property is quite uneven. Organizational sociologists call this pressure for conformity "structural isomorphism" (DiMaggio and Powell 1983). Shippers, suppliers, and small investors had to conform to the railroad much more than the railroad to them. More important, firms which interacted extensively with the railroads had to adapt to the railroads' needs. The giant railroads used a small number of suppliers to reduce transaction costs, so there was a tendency for suppliers of steel like the Carnegie Company, of freight cars like Pressed Steel Car Company or of locomotives like the Baldwin Locomotive works[19] to grow to become some of the largest manufacturing companies in the country. Large organizations, however, do not always prefer to deal with large suppliers. Some large organizations prefer to keep those on whom they are dependent small in scale and disorganized, to give themselves bargaining advantages by taking advantage of their monopsony power. If market dynamics were the only determinant of interaction, large firms would be expected to balance the gains they would make by monopsony power against the transaction costs they would pay when buying from many suppliers. However, when the transactions are embedded in tight social ties such as those that Carnegie or Baldwin had or interlocking directorates and common ownership such as those that the Pullman Company had, market dynamics cannot explain the outcome. For many industries, dealing with the railroad hardly constituted operating in a free market. Whether as shipper or customer the railroad was a formidable negotiating adversary. Rates and prices were set at least as much by bargaining power, personal deals, and inside information as by the operation of a free market. Andrew Carnegie used his personal acquaintance with his former colleagues in the Pennsylvania Railroad, including his patronage relationship with the company's president Thomas Scott (as well as espionage in his competitors' offices), to consistently gain a competitive edge in shipping rates and the price paid for steel rails (Wall 1989).

Similar economies of scale favored large shippers. Railroad companies rationally though at times illegally offered lower rates to large shippers, often in the form of kickbacks and rebates. John D. Rockefeller used an initial edge in volume to win rebates with several major roads. At one point he even negotiated a kickback on shipments by his competitors, although it never took effect (U.S. Bureau of Corporations 1906, 1907). Railroad rebates have been widely discussed, but much of the literature fails to identify their long-term consequences. Earlier discussions, especially during the Progressive era, focused on their legality. More recent economic historians have argued that even though illegal, they were rational because of the economies of scale involved in large shipments (Chandler 1990). However, the most consequential effect was the tendency toward concentration in industry. A disproportionate number of industries that concentrated in the 1870s and 1880s had high transportation costs, and their dominating companies enjoyed rebates or other special relationships with the railroad. Standard Oil is the best-known example but the same pattern was found in sugar, meat packing and others.[20] Rebates and similar practices were an exercise in power—it was the industrial firms who were doing the conforming and the railroads who had the greater impact on the environment in which decisions were made.

One might argue that even if the relationships were shaped by the dynamics of power, the outcome would have been identical if the parties were negotiating from positions of equality because the relationship was not a zero-sum game. However, it is difficult to argue that all interests were equally served. True, the conflict of interests was not railroad against industry. The beneficiaries of railroad contracts like Andrew Carnegie or of railroad rebates like John D. Rockefeller hardly suffered from their relationship with the railroads. One might even argue—although the point is highly debatable—that overall, some farmers benefited from the development of markets. But the conflict of interests was within industries. Companies with special relationships with the railroad used their advantage to dominate their competitors and accelerate the process of industrial consolidation, which was very much an exercise in power and a conflicting set of interests.

The most fundamental flaw in conventional accounts of the way that the railroad changed the calculus of rational decision making is the assumption that the social result of individual decisions is greater efficiency in the system as a whole. Some versions emphasize the lower transportation costs and the creation of a broader market (Jenks 1944). Others focus on the benefits of managerial decision making (Chandler 1965, 1977). Most accounts that address the efficiencies engendered by the railroad assume rather than demonstrate those effects. They typically adopt a utilitarian logic that assumes that the automatic result of individuals' freely maximizing their own utilities is the greatest good for all. But this needs to be demonstrated rather than assumed.[21] This chapter has described some of the social costs that railroads exacted, and raises the question of the overall balance of costs and benefits. It has shown how railroad's rise and the far-reaching consequences it engendered cannot be explained in terms of the dynamics of efficiency.

SETTING THE STAGE FOR THE CORPORATE REVOLUTION

The railroad matured, privatizing the corporation and in the process becoming the centerpiece of an institutional structure of investment banks, brokerage houses, stock markets, and other auxiliaries, all structuring the socialization of capital. By the 1880s, the railroads and the institutions of finance capitalism were organized essentially as they are today. Changes since then have been elaborations on the system of that time. The government has increased its regulation, the instruments of investment, merger, and control have become more sophisticated, and the quantities of dollars involved have mushroomed beyond what Cornelius Vanderbilt or Jay Gould could have ever imagined. But Vanderbilt or Gould would be equally surprised at how universal the large corporation has become across the economy. When Vanderbilt died in 1877, there were no industrial giants. When Gould died in 1892, a few trusts had discovered the holding company, but few would have predicted that the industrial order would within a decade become the corporate order. The stage was set for the corporate revolution.

Auxiliary Institutions: The Stock Market, Investment Banking, and Brokers

THE EMERGENCE of the modern large corporation as a public institution and its subsequent privatization stemmed not just from the internal dynamics of managerial ascendancy or from the legal changes that redefined the nature of property. The corporation's institutional origins (in contrast to its technical or legal origins) lie within a framework of investment banks, brokerage houses, and stock markets that arose to serve the state. When these institutions developed as private auxiliaries to the public sector and redirected their activities toward the private sector, the corporation itself privatized.

Insofar as the large, socially capitalized corporation arose at the turn of the century because it solved problems of entrepreneurial firms such as the desire for greater capital resources, one must still explain why the corporation was able to solve those problems. If corporations were able to tap the fountain of copious capital, where did the flow come from and why did it gush so bountifully? Moreover, the large-scale corporation arose not only as a set of autonomous, self-contained organizations, but as part of a system of interacting parts. Understanding how corporations arise and thrive or wither requires an analysis of the economic institution of corporate capitalism.

In recent years both economists (Coase 1937; Williamson 1975, 1981, 1985; Hodgson 1988; Jacoby 1990; North 1981) and sociologists (DiMaggio and Powell 1983, 1991; Meyer and Rowan 1977; Tolbert and Zucker 1983; Zucker 1983, 1987; Campbell, Hollingsworth, and Lindberg 1991; Fligstein 1990) have vigorously debated the ways that institutions have structured economic life. Both disciplines have recognized a "new institutionalism" that has highlighted the limitations of conventional theories that focus on autonomous individuals. I adopt a sociological definition of "institution" as a set of ongoing social interactions characterized by:

1. *Mutually recognized customs and rules* (DiMaggio and Powell 1991; Meyer and Rowan 1977). While institutional economists treat customs and rules as consciously constructed to achieve greater efficiency, sociologists emphasize that the customs and rules arise from any number of reasons and persist by becoming taken for granted, often despite inefficiency (Meyer and Rowan 1977; Scott 1983).

2. *Categories and typifications* (DiMaggio and Powell 1991; Zucker 1977). Institutions structure not only a sense of "should" but also a sense

of what "is." They are a basic building block of the social construction of reality (Berger and Luckmann 1966) by which regular interactions become reified as things. Thus a territorially focused interaction in a bounded set of buildings in which people collectively create a product, render records of interactions on paper, recognize symbols of unity, and enact rituals of common purpose is given a name and recognized as a "real" organization. Institutions themselves, through the mutual recognition that there *is* an economy, a polity, an educational institution, a medical institution, and so on are reifications of complex sets of interaction. These categories and typifications would include the symbols, myths, and rituals that give it a sense of "realness." Symbols include an institution's name, constitution or by-laws, physical location and characteristic site (for example, an office building vis-à-vis a classroom building), and named roles (such as president, supervisor, or congressperson), and objects that embody its existence such as letterhead stationery, annual reports, and logos. Myths are stories that define its reality, including its origins, designations of heroes or villains, understandings about how roles are allocated, and routine gossip. Rituals include actions that embody its existence, such as meetings, annual awards dinners, and regular sessions of its basic activities.

3. *Logic and strategies.* Each institution has a socially constructed logic of operation, defined by Friedland and Alford (1991) as "a set of material practices and symbolic constructions . . . which constitutes its organizing principles and which is available to organizations and individuals to elaborate" (248), that helps define strategies for its characteristic activity (Fligstein 1990). These logics are not just the goals that are pursued, but social processes by which goals are related to action. For example, the economic institution in capitalist society is based on the goal of profit. In an entrepreneurial economy, a businessperson must mobilize resources to construct a business from a variety of sources in a more or less ad hoc manner, drawing capital from personal savings, family members, commercial banks, and perhaps friends. In corporate capitalism, the resources to build a business are drawn from a more regular (more institutionalized) set of sources such as investment bankers, government agencies, and individual investors (strangers) who learn about the project through the business press. The logic has changed from "entrepreneurial" to "corporate." But both entrepreneurial and corporate institutions are different from the logic of strategies in the political institution that has both a different set of goals (social order, legitimation, and so on) and a different set of strategies (both electoral and bureaucratic) from those of the economy. While the logics differ, it should be emphasized that these logics are neither inherent in the different functions that the institutions play nor inevitable from the process of institutional differentiation. The different logics in politics and economics (and other institutions) are historically constructed, perpetuated, and deconstructed.[1]

4. *Institutionalization is not a dichotomous quality, but a matter of degree.* Sets of interaction are more or less institutionalized, and we can

observe the process of institutionalization and deinstitutionalization. Even though institutionalization is not necessarily conscious—although it often is—it is always, by definition, observable, since it involves the mutual recognition of the "reality" of the emerging institution and is inscribed in the language, symbols, myths, and rituals constructed in the process.

This chapter will set the stage for the transformation of industrial capital into corporate capital at the end of the century. By 1880, the basic institutional structure of corporate capitalism existed more or less as it does today. The New York Stock Exchange was the center stage for the financial capital market, with investment banks and brokerage houses playing critical leading roles. The publicly traded corporation was well institutionalized, but confined primarily to the railroad and related industries. When manufacturers did incorporate before 1890, they did not form what we think of as a modern, socially capitalized, managerially administered, "big" corporation, but typically remained outside the corporate institutional structure and operated in a traditional entrepreneurial fashion. Manufacturing and corporate capital were organizationally and financially distinct.

This chapter will describe the early history of the stock market, investment banks, and related organizations, showing how their public origins contrasted with the later private operation. Before the Civil War, when they served primarily government and railroad financing, they were connected to the manufacturing economy primarily through the mechanisms of commercial capital, which mediated the world of merchants and that of manufacturers. The Civil War presented the occasion for transforming the institutions of finance capital into their modern form, when investment capital became socialized throughout the population, when the present New York Stock Exchange was founded, when the telegraph nationalized the stock market, and when the open board made it possible to transact an unprecedented volume of securities. The chapter will also show that the development of these institutions was by no means only a national phenomenon, but that investment capital has, from its origins, been an international system. Not only did European investment capital set the model that was adopted here, but the organizations which mediated national and international capital emerged as the builders of the American corporate system, another way by which power, not functional adaptation or innovation, explains its rise.

The role that these institutions played in the rise of the modern large industrial corporation aptly illustrates the differences between functional and historical causation. While both functional and historical models allow the cause of a social formation to differ from the reasons for its persistence, the assumed importance of origins differs. In functionalist logic, regardless of the reasons for a structure's genesis, it persists only if it serves essential functions better than available alternatives. For example, in evolutionary models, innovation may be as arbitrary as genetic mutation, but only changes that increase adaptation will survive and spread. In analogous fashion

Chandler maintained that even though some mergers at the turn of the century were created to control markets, they persisted only when they used their size to create economies of scale (1977, chap. 8). In a historical model, innovations create the conditions of their own reproduction.[2] They become the context in which subsequent decisions are made and define the consequences of various alternatives that subsequent actors face. In the metaphor of historians of technology, innovations create paths that close off other alternatives.[3] The degree to which new structures attain the ability to reproduce themselves is highly variable, depending on such factors as the quantity of scarce resources that flow to it, the relative power of those who develop a vested interest in its perpetuation, and the degree to which it is ideologically seen as an institutional reality. While Chandler acknowledges that investment banks, stock markets, and other institutions of corporate capital were founded for public finance, their origins are irrelevant to his analysis, because he assumes that they would persist only if they efficiently served the market. In my analysis, the institutions of finance capital wielded power as the only source of large-scale capital, a power which allowed them to persist whether they worked efficiently or not. If they had not arisen from their public origins, there is no guarantee that they would have arisen at all or in anything like the form they did. It was because they arose in the form that they did that large-scale enterprise developed as socialized capital in the property regime we still live with today. Such features as the use of bonds rather than stocks were adopted for reasons of power. That is, some individuals defined the consequences of choices made by railroad leaders: foreign investors, for example, who initially had far greater assets available for investment, wanted the greater security bonds offered. As an unintended consequence, American businessmen later discovered that they could use bonds for construction and expansion while maintaining a controlling ownership interest.

Other developments stemmed from government actions that had little direct connection to market dynamics. A national banking structure adopted to facilitate the wartime mobilization of wealth to purchase arms, blankets, and food for soldiers created a national currency system that reduced the high transaction costs of exchanging bank currencies in interstate commerce. In other words, the development of auxiliary institutions illustrates how causes may differ from its consequences and how, once formed, structures may control the resources and organizational capability to reproduce themselves. The institutions of corporate capitalism arose to trade government securities, that is, for public finance, but became central institutions for private capital. At the outset, no one intended that they become a source for capitalizing manufacturing corporations. But the modern corporation could not have developed without these institutions. Manufacturing capital could not have developed such institutions on its own. If one looks only at the immediate "needs" or intentions that fostered the development of the large corporation at the end of the century, one is likely to miss many of the deeper underlying historical developments. The stock market, investment banking, brokers, and the investing public did not arise to fulfill a functional need in production or distribution. They did not create more efficient technologies. They did not inherently enhance managerial rationality. Although they were part of the central institutional core of corporate capitalism, and although they were unquestionably necessary for the rise of corporate capitalism, they arose for quite different purposes.

A similar historical path can be seen in the fungible nature of corporate ownership. It was the mercantile character of the stock market, stemming from its origins as a secondary market of government securities, that explains why the entities sold were both fungible and alienated from their source. The fact that the securities were fungible set the stage for the socialization of capital. Ownership was divided into small parcels, each of which could be owned separately. As parcellized entities they could be alienated in both senses of the word—they could be sold and they could be separated from the responsibilities of ownership. Enumerating these qualities will be news to no one. But the point is that they must be explained not as a functional adaptation to a need but as a historical precedent that shaped corporate capital only because corporate capital grew out of these institutions. If one were creating a capitalist economic system out of whole cloth, it is quite likely one would design it differently.

The theoretical importance of institutions like the stock market, investment banks, and stock brokers is seen especially clearly in the difference between the way they are treated by the new institutional economists and the institutionalization perspective that sociologists have applied to organizations. New institutional economists like Chandler, Williamson, and North have treated institutions as any stable social arrangements which exist outside of markets, that is, they define institutions in terms of what they are *not*. The task is then to explain why and under what conditions economic arrangements are structured in institutions rather than markets (Coase 1937; Williamson 1975, 1981, 1985; Chandler 1977; Davis and North 1971; North 1981). As many economic sociologists have argued, it distorts history to take the market as the given, the natural way of being, without any need of explanation. Polanyi's (1957) account of how the states intentionally created the legal and institutional shell in which markets could operate opened the agenda of economic sociology to the historical roots of the market in social and political processes (Campbell and Lindberg 1991; Zukin and DiMaggio 1990; Friedland and Robertson 1990; Block 1990; Lie 1993). In contrast, the agenda of the new institutional economists problematizes only deviations from the market, not the market itself. Moreover, they still base their explanation on notions of efficiency, either the minimizing of transaction costs for Williamson or the maximization of throughput for Chandler. In each case the rise of stock markets, investment banks, brokerage houses, and other auxiliary institutions is seen as a functional adaptation to changes in the nature of the capital market, growth in the scope of product markets, and the technological requirements of production.

In contrast the institutionalization perspective in sociology sees institutions not so much as an alternative to the market, but as a general characteristic of organizational life, in which market entities are one type of institution, which can be just as fully institutionalized as a corporation. A market system is historically constructed and begs historical explanation no less than more socialized systems of production and distribution (Polanyi 1957). The goal is then to explain why the economy is organized in whatever institutional form it is, market or otherwise. Efficiency considerations may influence the ways that institutions are shaped, but more often institutions are shaped by the dynamics of social interaction in which efficiency is incidental. Once formed, organizations within an organizational field can wield considerable influence on other organizations to conform. Insofar as organizations within a field are similar, the cause is to be sought in the mutual effect of organizations on one another rather than in the similarity of their external environment. In the explanation of the rise of large socially capitalized corporations, this means that auxiliary institutions had at least as much effect on the form that these corporations took as the effect that corporations had on them. Most important, the effect that institutions had on corporations occurred as much through the dynamics of power as through the demands of efficiency.

Since the large corporation itself cannot exist apart from these institutions, an explanation of its rise must address its relationship to them. The stock market, investment bank, brokerage house, and other organizations are the fertile soil that nourish and form the foundation of the corporate forest. With a different institutional foundation, the modern business organization would be very different. Firms would probably not be as large, unless government had continued to capitalize them. Ownership would not be as socialized. Transactions between firms would probably be determined more by markets, at least where governments support markets. Relations among firms would probably not be as densely networked. Managers would not have to pay as much attention to the seemingly capricious dynamics of the capital market when making ordinary decisions. There is no way to know what would have developed, since there is no modern economy without these auxiliary institutions. They are thus profoundly implicated in the rise of the modern large corporation.

The corporate system was not designed fully formed but arose out of its roots in public finance. The history of the institutional framework is one more manifestation of the public origins of the modern corporation. Early corporations were capitalized from these institutions of public finance not just because that was where the capital was available, but also because corporations were created by governments and set up within the system of government finance. These institutions did not simply mediate between the corporations and their shareholders any more than soil simply mediates between trees and nutrients. Large corporations were quite firmly grounded in them.

The efficiency model would hold that the institutions of corporate capitalism developed to serve the objective needs of the economic system. They are seen as neutral conduits of capital to the places where it would be most profitable and most socially beneficial. Yet the historical record offers ample evidence to support doubts about whether the capital that flowed through these institutions gravitated to where it was most profitable or socially beneficial. The severe depressions that plagued society from the 1830s to the 1930s had their origins in the dynamics of Wall Street, precipitated by the failure of recipients of finance capital to meet their fiscal obligations. In the 1830s, it was the governments and their canal companies who were overextended. In 1857, 1873, and 1893, it was the railroads who overconstructed and were bloated with fixed debts. Thereafter it was industrial corporations who had absorbed more capital than they could repay. Given the nation's bountiful natural resources, its clean break from the feudal past, the benefits of its labor power, and talent from a flood of immigrants, it did not take great genius to achieve impressive economic growth. To say that the economic system that made this possible was therefore the most efficient possible (while ignoring the obvious failures) is a leap of faith. Finance capital flowed more to those parts of the economy that were the closest institutionally than to sectors that necessarily would have been the most productive. While capital was flowing freely to first the canals and later the railroads, the industrial sector was still relying on commercial banks and personal funds. Hounshell (1984) describes how the system of interchangeable parts and mass production was conceived in the early nineteenth century, but took nearly a century to perfect because market forces were not sufficient to mobilize the resources for the technological developments in precision tool parts that were needed. While the benefits of interchangeable parts and mass production were often celebrated, it was only in government-subsidized arms factories and industries with substantial international markets (such as sewing machines) that research and development was able to bring the promise to fruition. If investors had supported earlier research and development as generously as they did later in the century when inventors like Thomas Edison developed close relations with investors like J. P. Morgan, the course of industrial development could have been very different. What would have happened if the institutions of finance capital had been different is unknown, but we can examine how those institutions developed and funneled capital into the sectors that were institutionally proximate whether or not overall efficiency was maximized.

Origins

Since "Wall Street" is commonly regarded as the bastion of private enterprise, the conservative, antigovernment heart of laissez-faire sentiments, the relationship between Wall Street and the government is framed in terms of regulation, that is, the extent to which the government exercises its surveillance and policing powers to prevent pernicious economic practices. From this perspective, there is little sense of what the government can do for Wall Street except leave it alone, let it operate freely, and keep the money supply balanced between overheating and throttling the economy. News accounts or public officials occasionally mention the effect that government actions might have on a public agency's credit rating, but this is typically treated as an impersonal factor in the economic environment, not an exercise in power. However, historically the relationship between government and the institutions of corporate capitalism has been much closer. Wall Street essentially was created to handle the securities of governments and quasi-governmental corporations. Without the active role of government to issue securities and at times to purchase transportation and public utility securities, the institutions of Wall Street might never have developed or, if they had, would have taken very different forms.

Stock Market

Before 1800 the notion of buying a parcel of a manufacturing company merely for the purpose of selling it at a profit was virtually unknown. Such securities speculation that existed was primarily in government bonds or banks (Davis 1917; Werner and Smith 1991). In a few large cities individuals bought and sold securities frequently enough to constitute informal markets. On May 17, 1792, twenty-four New York brokers and merchants signed an agreement, known as the Buttonwood Agreement after the tree under which brokers often met, to give preference to one another in selling public securities and to sell at no less than a quarter of a percent commission. In the language of a century later, they agreed to restrain trade and fix prices. They had no place and no name, but met regularly on the north side of New York's Wall Street. By 1793 they had two hundred members when they moved into the nearby newly completed Tontine Coffee House. At that time, several major European cities had organized stock markets, including London's Royal Exchange, which met in the rotunda of the Bank of England, and the Change de Paris, predecessor to the Paris Bourse. In the second decade of the nineteenth century the modern system began to institutionalize, being recognized as a specific activity occurring within permanent organizations. In 1817, thirteen individuals and seven firms that had traded at the Tontine organized the New York Stock and Exchange Board, modeled after a similar Philadelphia board (Stedman and Easton 1969; Werner and Smith 1991). They met daily on the second floor of George Vaupell's property at 40 Wall Street, where part-time brokers auctioned securities one offering at a time among the members (Sobel 1965). By 1827, the exchange handled eight government securities, twelve bank stocks, nineteen marine or fire insurance companies, and a few miscellaneous companies (Stedman and Easton 1969).

The year the New York Stock Exchange and Board was founded was also the year New York's Erie Canal touched off a "canal mania," as we saw in Chapter 3, during which state and local governments aggressively built canals between nearly every two bodies of water within striking distance. New York, for example, between 1817 and 1825 issued $7 million in canal bonds which were sold by underwriters and bought by individuals and towns close to the canal, by banks, and by European investors. But once sold, they became a lively object of speculative resale at the Board and similar organizations in other cities. Just as "canal mania" dominated the fledgling stock market in the 1820s, "railroad mania" dominated the next half century. In 1830, the stock of the new Mohawk and Hudson Railroad became the first railroad security sold on the exchange. Railroad stocks soon became more common on Wall Street, even before the industry really took off. Between 1841 and 1848 railroads grew less than seven hundred miles per year. Then in 1849 alone, nearly fourteen hundred miles of rail were constructed. During the fifties both construction and speculation exploded. Between 1848 and 1856, total mileage grew from 1,996 miles to 22,016 miles and by 1860, on the verge of the Civil War, to 30,635 miles (Stedman and Easton 1969). As the railroad grew, so did the stock market. The relationship between railroad growth and stock market growth was not just one of mutual assistance among separate entities, but one in which the two outcomes were inextricably bound together as part of a single institutional complex (Werner and Smith 1991). Railroads could not possibly have grown as rapidly without the institutional structures that funneled capital to them. At the same time, the more the railroad came to dominate the stock market, the more it assumed its modern form.

The stock market withered with the rest of the economy following the depression of 1837, one of the first major depressions in which investment financing played a major role. By 1842 several states had defaulted on bonds, making it difficult to sell not only government securities but also rail and utility securities, which had prospered because of government support (Cochran 1955; Sobel 1965; Adler 1970). By 1844 even South American bonds were selling above American bonds on the London markets. During that decade telegraph securities provided a minor rally, but the lethargy continued until the California Gold Rush of 1849 fostered not only mining companies with great speculative potential, but also the romance of the West. New railroad companies, many with transcontinental pretensions, came on the market. In 1857 another depression hit, attributable, as never before, to the vicissitudes of finance capital. Foreign investment again withdrew from American securities, action that stiffened the resolve of state governments to discontinue direct economic investment.

By the onset of the Civil War, the New York stock market was still only a sprig of the present tree. Stocks were sold one at a time by auction. Most securities transactions were options to buy, stretching from ten to ninety days because each transaction had to be consummated separately. There was no clearing house to compute net credit or debts among members (Chamberlin 1969). There was no stock ticker to instantly communicate prices or volume of sales. Although it was true that many prominent features were already present—the sale of seats, the speculative dynamics of bull and bear markets, and the quick amassing and collapsing of fortunes on paper—the stock market was peripheral to the overall economy. The London stock market was probably more important for government securities and railroad corporations, but the American upstarts were rapidly gaining momentum.

Investment Banking

Early corporations could raise capital beyond the personal resources of the organizers by selling shares either directly to the public or indirectly, working through a banker, by such devices as lotteries or auctions. America's first manufacturing corporation was financed in part with a $100,000 lottery that the state of New Jersey organized for the purpose (Keasbey 1899a). By one estimate the value of lotteries to capitalize corporations sold in a single year, 1832, amounted to $53 million (Carosso 1970). Over time, some private banks began to specialize in the task of providing capital for governments and corporation securities and became known as investment banks. Up to the Civil War there were only a few investment banks, and they played a minor economic role, underwriting small stock issues, marketing government bonds, and acting as private banks for the rare corporations. They were relatively unimportant compared with various other means of capitalizing relatively large-scale projects such as factoring, brokerage, and lotteries (Sobel 1965; Carosso 1970). When selling directly to the public, corporations often sold for a fraction of the par value and called in funds as needed. The Utica Glass Company, for example, raised its capital with eighteen calls on its subscribers in 1812 (Myers 1970). But what began as only one of a variety of means to finance corporate establishment and expansion became the institutionalized device overshadowing the others.

Investment banking emerged as a specialized type of banking in the years around the Civil War, primarily to market railroad and government securities. Most early investment banks had their origins in merchant or commercial banking that engaged in investment banking as a sideline. S. M. Allen, one of the pioneering investment banks, in its early years specialized in selling lottery tickets to finance enterprise (Larson 1936). Levi P. Morton, founder of Morton, Bliss & Company and later Grover Cleveland's vice-president, began in rural retailing in the 1840s, moved to import-export trade and, during the Civil War, to international private banking (Greenberg 1980). Some, like Junius Morgan, had started as merchant bankers. James Stillman's first job was as a cotton merchandiser (Carosso 1987). Kidder, Peabody & Company also arose from mercantile origins. The Lehman Brothers, cotton bankers before the war, afterward became investment bankers. Some were originally brokers who shifted over to investment banking, including Jahnestock & Company, Charles D. Barney & Company, Fisk & Hatch, and Marquand & Dimock (Sobel 1965).

The origins of modern investment banking stemmed from financing America's war with England in 1812. Until then, the federal government had financed expensive projects by selling stocks and bonds primarily to foreign investors, banks, and municipal corporations. After failing to find subscribers for several issues of securities, as a temporary expedient, Secretary of the Treasury Albert Gallatin announced a new offering with the unprecedented provision that the government would accept proposals for taking the unsubscribed residue. Proposals were to specify the amount to be loaned, the species or stocks wanted, and the price the buyer would pay. The government required a minimum acceptance of $100,000 and would pay a quarter percent commission. "The Treasury thus initiated the public bidding system that was to characterize subsequent loans and simultaneously set the stage for the nation's first investment banking endeavor" (Adams 1978, 104). A syndicate led by David Parish, including Stephen Girard and John Jacob Astor, decided to subscribe the loan if peace were imminent, setting a precedent for an intermediary to subscribe to securities in anticipation of selling to others. Although most of the subscription was taken up by banks and insurance companies, some was bought by individuals, mostly merchants, but also including a boarding school operator, a clerk, a conveyancer, an attorney, a widow, a sea captain, a bookbinder, a brewer, a grocer, and a shoemaker. The old system of borrowing from banks was to a large extent replaced by a system in which institutions and individuals, including banks, bid for stocks. For the first time, bankers distinguished between the role of buying securities on their own and the more specialized activity of loan contracting (like investment banking). Adams (1978) concludes, "[T]he essence of the intermediary function known as investment banking was well established by the second decade of the 19th century" (115). Nonetheless not until the Civil War and Jay Cooke's campaigns did such ventures became prominent (Adams 1978; Carosso 1970).

By the 1830s chartered banks in several states were buying bonds and reselling them in smaller lots to subcontractors or directly to investors. Nicholas Biddle's United States Bank of Philadelphia was especially active. Biddle was also involved in the Morris Canal and Banking Company, an "improvement bank" to raise capital for state-sponsored internal improvements, and as noted in Chapter 3, the Pennsylvania Main Line. Brokerage houses, lotteries, and auctioneers, who sold securities in public auctions just like any other commodity, were also active. Brokerage houses attempted to bar auctioneers from stock exchanges, but the line between them was so vague that this was impossible. As exchanges became more regulated, several auctioneers became brokers. But over the thirties and forties and into the fifties, these other forms were giving way to an increasingly dominant form, the private banker. Although private bankers, lacking a charter, could not issue their own notes (paper money) as commercial banks could, they had no accountability to anyone other than their clients, whom they could promise an unparalleled degree of privacy. They differed from brokerage houses by accepting deposits, discounting loans, and trading extensively in foreign exchange. Most important, private investment banks could purchase and speculate in securities on their own, not just selling on commission (which they often did do) or linking buyers and sellers, but putting their own resources at risk.

Nathaniel Prime of New York was the first genuine private banker in this country. He began on Wall Street in the 1790s as a stock and commission broker, and in 1826 founded Prime, Ward & King. At first its main business was to buy state securities and sell them for a profit. States like Ohio that were building canals too ambitious to finance locally were able to sell securities through Prime, Ward & King, which used a close relationship with England's Baring Brothers to market them abroad (Larson 1936; Scheiber 1969; Myers 1970; Greenberg 1980). These foreign ties were critical in shaping the American financial system. Private investment banks were not invented simply to meet an existing and obvious need. They were patterned after their correspondent English private banks, for which they served virtually as franchises. Most major private investment banks had close working relationships with particular European banks and could probably not have survived without those ties. August Belmont epitomized this relationship. In 1837, N. M. Rothschild & Sons of London sent the twenty-one-year-old Belmont to America to investigate the financial conditions. Finding the U.S. correspondent bankrupt, he persuaded the Rothschilds to recognize his new firm, August Belmont & Company, as their agent in America. That same year an American, George Peabody, moved to London, where he sold Maryland bonds and in 1851 established his own banking house. Three years later, he took in Junius Spencer Morgan, a Boston dry goods merchant, as a partner. When Peabody retired in 1864, the company reorganized as J. S. Morgan & Company.

The prototype of the modern investment banker, though at the time just one of many styles of banking, was Winslow, Lanier and Company of New York, which more than anyone else offered most of the services investment banks did later in the century. It marketed new securities, acted as purchasing agent, registrar, transfer and fiscal agent, and was unusually active, especially for the antebellum period, in monitoring its clients' behavior, even placing its representatives on corporate boards. It specialized in railroads, especially western railroads, which until that time had been handled mostly by Boston bankers. Carosso (1970) gives Winslow, Lanier and Company credit for being the bank that contributed the most to making New York the center of railroad financing. It would later help finance the Cotton Oil Trust, one of the first major industrial trusts, discussed in Chapter 7.

As the system of corporate capital developed, its relationship to manufacturing remained almost entirely indirect. Manufacturing was not organized in corporations, and the capital that underwrote the transportation and communications corporations was organizationally distinct from manufacturing capital, keeping finance and manufacturing in two institutionally distinct worlds. Except for some New England textile factories begun by wealthy merchants, manufacturers would never have considered raising capital by selling stock on the stock market. The tendency for private bankers to capitalize canals and railroads rather than industry was not a conscious decision to invest in the most profitable or socially beneficial sector of the economy but stemmed from preexisting institutional relations. Discussing the Baring and Rothschild banks, Carosso explains: "The move from government to railroad finance raised few new problems, for some of the private bankers' earliest government loans were intended for transportation enterprises, either owned or guaranteed by the state. Since this generally was not true of manufacturing properties, London's merchant banks hesitated to finance industrial projects unless the business was closely tied to the interests of their trading clients. Sometimes one or more of a bank's partners might invest in an industrial promotion, but in such cases their participation was entirely on their own, not the firm's" (Carosso 1987, 11). Thus the industrial and financial sectors were related, though indirectly and tenuously.

Finance and Industrial Capital

To understand how corporate capital and manufacturing capital later coalesced, it is necessary to understand how manufacturing capital was institutionalized prior to the rise of the large-scale industrial corporation. The relationship between finance and manufacturing took several forms, most of which were mediated by commercial capital. The institutional system differed fundamentally from later forms, starting with the social structure of money itself. Money represented a very different set of social relationships than it now does, with the state playing a very different role. While the state played a more profound role in establishing and capitalizing corporations before the Civil War than after, it was less active in creating and regulating money before the war than after (James 1978). In the antebellum era, there was no national currency other than coin specie since currency was mostly bank notes drawn on state banks; commercial transactions were generally paid in bank notes, sometimes payable on presentation, but more often redeemable in thirty, sixty, or ninety days. Some of the larger merchants issued their own notes and acted as their own banks. A few of them, like Levi P. Morton or J. & W. Seligman, eventually dropped the mercantile end to become full-time bankers. The receiver of notes rarely redeemed them, but used them to make purchases or sold them at discount to a broker, who might sell them again. With the thousands of banks in the country, many of which were unchartered private banks, the currency was a complex mix of thousands of different kinds of commercial paper. Several of the money brokers who provided the indispensable function of arbitrating among all the participants in this dense web evolved into stock brokers. Buying and selling commercial paper was a central function of most private bankers, most of whom were still generalists performing a wide variety of monetary and financial tasks. Buying and selling commercial paper along with buying and selling government securities was all part of their role, providing an indirect link between commercial and financial capital (James 1978; Davis 1965; Myers 1970).

While Wall Street and industrial capital both drew on mercantile capital, they were embedded in very different institutional structures. The institutions of Wall Street developed around long-distance trade and government securities; industrialization was capitalized primarily from direct investment of merchant capitalists (Livesay and Porter 1971). Over the course of the first half of the century, as American manufacturing was evolving from the artisan's shop to the factory, mechanics often had the technical knowledge to run a factory, but lacked the capital needed for expansion and access to broad markets. Merchants supplied both. Banks would rarely make loans without collateral, but aspiring manufacturers had none until they became well established. Merchants not only had greater financial resources themselves, but greater access to banks, where they could often get credit on their signature alone. In many places the bankers *were* the merchants. Thus before the Civil War, most manufacturing firms that produced for more than a local market were partnerships of merchants and manufacturers (Livesay and Porter 1971; Hirsch 1980). For example, Francis Cabot Lowell was a merchant who saw the potential of textile manufacturing while visiting England. When the War of 1812 hampered foreign investments, he turned to manufacturing. Further south, David Reeves, a Philadelphia merchant, took the profits from importing British iron rails to create the Phoenix Iron Works (Livesay and Porter 1971). Noah Farewell Blanchard, after an apprenticeship in leather and a small unsuccessful leather operation in New England, then moved to Newark, New Jersey, in 1847 as an employee of T. P. Howell, eventually becoming superintendent. He joined the firm as a partner and in 1860 began his own business, a well-capitalized, mechanized leather firm, and thereafter broadened his business interests, helping to form the Prudential Insurance Company. Sometimes merchants would finance a factory by incorporating and selling stock to close personal acquaintances, but more typically the business took the form of a partnership between manufacturer and merchant.

When merchants capitalized manufacturing, the distinction between their role as capitalizer and their role as customer was also blurred. Merchants often paid for both capital goods and finished products in their own notes. The notes of prominent merchants were readily discounted and entered into circulation along with bank notes. Other merchants, especially those already acting as brokers, bought and sold these notes. For example, Nathan Trotter, a Philadelphia metal dealer, made a half-million dollars between 1833 and 1852 discounting paper. "Out of this symbiotic combination of old mercantile wealth and talents, and new manufacturing technologies, emerged two pillars of American industrial maturity—the factory system that produced the goods, and the specialized institutions that financed their production and distribution" (Livesay and Porter 1971, 87).

On the verge of the Civil War, Wall Street was thus a specialized institution primarily handling government, banking, and railroad securities with strong links to international mercantile capital. It directly touched a very small part of the population, although the depressions in 1837 and 1857 had shown that the indirect effects could be devastating. Industrial capital was distinct from that institutional framework, and the money system was tied more to commercial banks than to government.

THE CIVIL WAR: INVESTMENT BANKING GOES PUBLIC

The American Civil War was the precipitating event for the creation of the corporate infrastructure as we know it. War has historically stimulated profound economic change as much as any other kind of political event (Tilly 1975), so it is not surprising that America's most traumatic war had far-reaching economic as well as social consequences.[4] No American war has penetrated as far into routine social relations or demanded as much sacrifice of the citizenry. As has been true of other conflicts, the theretofore unthinkably radical changes adopted for the crisis situation were only partially rescinded afterward and became institutionalized into taken-for-granted practices. Necessity may be a mother of invention, but a historical logic of explanation emphasizes that the "need" for which inventions are intended is often quite different from the greater consequences. The war thus helped pave the road that eventually led to large-scale industrial corporations: it created a national currency and banking system. It stimulated the first truly large-scale securities market in the United States. It created the wholesale merchandising of securities, established Wall Street as the center of the securities market, strengthened and developed financial relations with Europe, and launched the careers of the first generation of national business leaders, including Jay Cooke, Joseph Seligman, and J. P. Morgan.

Broadening the Securities Market

War is expensive. The Union forces prevailed not only because of the North's greater financial, manufacturing, and manpower resources but because of its greater organizational capacity to mobilize those resources. Despite popular support for the war effort, businessmen rarely volunteered to provide guns, blankets, and food for the soldiers. The government had to find a way to pay for supplies, not out of its puny revenues but by borrowing as much as it could and inventing a national currency. At the beginning of the war, the federal government had little capacity or experience to mobilize the necessary resources. Because the economy was agrarian, with little industrial base, savings were small and not in any institutional form that the government could tap. There was no national bank that could act as a fiscal agent for the government. Each loan had to be approved by the Congress. Seven thousand different kinds of bank notes circulated, with more than half being spurious (Studenski and Krooss 1963). To borrow, the Union government had to further develop the existing system of finance, a system that incidentally had become used for corporations, and when more fully developed in the course of financing the war, could more effectively underwrite corporations.

Jay Cooke, as much as any one man, brought Wall Street into the modern era, developing techniques of mass marketing and syndicated underwriting, two innovations that deeply transformed the relationship of investment bankers to the public and to one another, innovations that radically socialized capital. While mass marketing democratized finance capital, syndication further centralized it. Cooke changed banking by pioneering proactive investment banking (Larson 1936). Departing from the conventional banking role of acting primarily as agents, waiting for customers to come to them to purchase securities, Cooke's bank began to actively market securities. He had begun before the war to offer securities to small investors by contracting with agents to visit small towns. When the national government was unable to market its war bonds, Secretary of Treasury Salmon P. Chase contacted Cooke, a former partner of E. W. Clark, Dodge & Company, one of the nation's preeminent private banks, to act as investment banker for the government. Cooke had just formed his company in 1861 as a general private banker to deal in bank notes, bills of exchange, and stock, to discount paper, and to receive deposits. Jay Cooke's brother, Henry D. Cooke, who represented the firm's interests in Washington, had become a political friend of Chase when Chase had been governor of Ohio. In April 1861 Jay Cooke & Company was allotted $200,000 of Treasury notes, which it quickly sold, quite a respectable transaction for a firm only four months old. Rather than follow the ordinary strategy of selling notes and bonds to investors who evaluated them in terms of their profitability, Cooke saw an opportunity to market them widely on the basis of patriotic appeal. In 1862, the government wanted to issue an unprecedented half-billion dollar issue of 6 percent bonds, more than the total amount of currency at the beginning of the war. After August Belmont, representing the Rothschilds, informed him that Europeans would be unreceptive to such an issue, Chase appointed Cooke as a special agent to sell them. The issue was too large for one bank to handle so Cooke, copying the French *syndicate*, created an investment syndicate by which four banks collectively subscribed to the bonds. Copying the practice of Napoleon III to finance the Crimean War by mass market sales, Cooke created a large organization of 2,500 agents and subagents who took the securities across the country, selling them to patriotic unionists. They created demand by advertising massively, including in foreign-language newspapers, distributing throwaways, knocking on doors, developing educational programs to explain the fundamentals of bond investment, and attracting great press coverage, perhaps the first modern propaganda campaign of this sort (Studenski and Krooss 1963). By early 1864 the entire issue had been sold, with Cooke's company responsible for well over half of it (Larson 1936). For the first time large numbers of Americans, many of them with modest means, invested in securities. Public finance, at least in part, had been mildly socialized. But at the same time, financial control was becoming more concentrated. Financing the war effort brought the federal government into the heart of Wall Street. By the end of the war, the federal government and its debt were a major concern and would continue to be so, with a total war debt over $2.5 billion. While the antebellum federal government (in contrast to the individual states) had little impact on the economy, either in the quantity of its transactions or institutionally in terms of money supply or debt, after the war its role was major and permanent.

In addition to the effect the war had on institutions of finance capital, it also forged a national banking system. The National Banking Act of 1863 had several effects on the development of the financial infrastructure that eventually underlay large-scale industrial corporations. These included the creation of a national currency and the development of a correspondent system of banking that helped channel capital into financial centers, especially New York, two innovations that were feasible only because of the wartime emergency. During peacetime, small-town banks, which made much of their profits by issuing notes, probably would have been able to block this sort of centralizing legislation (Myers 1970).

One of the changes now most taken for granted is the development of a national currency system. While the changes for the conduct of commerce were the most obvious effects of the creation of national currency, it contributed to the use of the corporate institutional structure by binding the system of commercial banking more closely to the structure of finance. Ending the antebellum system in which all paper currency took the form of bank notes that had to be transacted through an unwieldy system of currency brokers,[5] the National Banking Act and subsequent acts made national bank notes, that is, notes drawn on nationally chartered banks, a uniform national currency. Although issued privately, such notes circulated at par, without brokers, thus radically reducing the transaction costs of commercial exchange. But it was not their origins in national banks that made them universally legitimate; they were not legal tender. Rather, it was the fact that the National Banking Act required that they be secured with U.S. bonds.[6] Thus it was the linkage with the system of finance that legitimated the notes of nationally chartered banks.

The second major effect of the National Banking Act was to institutionalize the system of correspondent banking into the pyramidal structure that fed resources from America's hinterlands into the New York market of finance capital. After the war, the system by which local banks in small towns deposited funds in banks of large cities formalized and intensified. The Banking Act set up a three-tier system of national banks with New York, eighteen central reserve cities, and the rest. Country banks developed close corresponding relations to reserve city national banks, who in turn often had corresponding relations with New York banks. New York was not the only city where funds were deposited, but it was the largest because only its banks paid interest and notes drawn on banks there were more valuable. Although the act did not create this system, but gave legal form to a preexisting system (James 1978), there can be no doubt that it helped institutionalize the system and facilitate the centralization of wealth.

One of the most visible links between the system of commercial banking and corporate capital was the system of call loans, short-term loans that the lender could recall at any time. New York banks could use the funds deposited in them from regional centers to issue call loans to investors purchasing corporate and governmental securities, using the securities themselves as collateral (Myers 1970; James 1978; Berk 1990). The largest customers for call loans were stock brokers and investment banks, who used the loans to hold them over in the middle of transactions to buy and sell stock. The practice was institutionalized enough in 1857 to merit a post marking its place on the stock exchange floor (Chamberlin 1969). Call loans were a critical component of "bull" speculation in which an individual buys securities without the funds to pay for them in the expectation that the price will rise enough to repay the loan and make a tidy profit. However, when the stock market crashed, the bull speculators could not repay their call loans, the banks making them could not return the deposits to the small-town and rural banks, and the small-town and rural banks could not return the deposits made to them or redeem the paper they had issued (James 1978).[7] Increasingly over the course of the nineteenth century, this system was centered in New York, and increasingly it and finance capital overlapped. Conventionally, observers have emphasized the destabilizing effects of the call loan system. In 1857, when a panic on Wall Street prevented bull speculators from repaying their call loans just as rural banks were withdrawing deposits for the fall harvest, the system collapsed. Similarly, the inability of inventors to repay call loans in the panic of 1873 led to the bankruptcy of some of Wall Street's most prominent investment bankers, including Jay Cooke & Company (Larson 1936). Michie (1986) compares the American system of call loans with the more stable London system, where banks had ready access to outside sources to stabilize brewing panics. But the more important effects were longer-term historical developments. This sort of institutional structure, along with the many other practices that centralized wealth into New York, gradually built up the corporate system. Wealth flowing into New York and invested in securities generated profits that could be reinvested in the corporate system, leading to its further growth.

The relationship between the institutional structure and the growth of corporations was thus reflexive. Railroad corporations could be created because of the availability of capital through practices like call loans, while the growth of railroad corporations helped further build these institutional structures. These institutional structures, in turn, became the agents of their own reproduction. Through the development of this entire institutional structure, a new generation of financiers emerged during and after the war. According to Cochran (1955), "The handling of the contracting, selling, and refunding of these issues [national bonds] built up a few specialized houses that, with the exception of Jay Cooke & Co., were to dominate the security markets in the United States for the next sixty years" (357). These financial institutions, including Drexel-Morgan, J. & W. Seligman, and Kidder, Peabody & Company, dominated the merger movement at the end of the century by which industrial corporations were brought into the corporate system (Bruchey 1990).

J. P. Morgan typified this new generation. Before 1873, most American securities were handled by European banks such as Baring of London, Hottinguer of Paris, and Hope of Amsterdam. After 1873 American banks began to open branches in European cities, led by J. S. Morgan, who joined with the Drexels to form Morgan, Drexel & Company, which did business in London and Paris. It was this European link that gave Morgan both the edge over other bankers and the leverage to enter the railroad business. In the first few years after the war, many private banks avoided the relatively risky railroads in favor of the more secure government securities. Jay Cooke declined to help finance the Northern Pacific and Union Pacific railroads, while Joseph Seligman of J.& W. Seligman & Company wrote to his brother about railroad investments: "I consider this a speculation entirely out of our line. We can make enough money in a legitimate way without gambling hazard" (quoted in Greenberg 1980, 39). In 1879, as we have seen, when William Vanderbilt asked the younger Morgan to help sell some securities necessary to get the New York Central through a financial squeeze, Morgan sold the securities in England and obtained the right to select a director, initiating a pattern that would remake the American economic structure.

The changes in economic institutions were not unnoticed. It was clear to some that the new ways of conducting government business and the new institutions that financed both government and, increasingly, private business were grossly at odds with deeply held American republican traditions. Even during the war, the notoriety that Jay Cooke gained by marketing government bonds to a broad segment of the citizenry made him a target of public criticism. Although Larson (1936) estimates that he earned only one-sixteenth of one percent commission on selling the securities, the public outcry over perceived profiteering led to his being dismissed as a Treasury agent. Andrew Johnson, the postwar President, joined the criticism, charging that "an aristocracy based on nearly two and one half billion of national securities has risen in the northern states to assume that political control which was formerly given to the slave oligarchy" (quoted in Studenski and Krooss 1963, 161). But this ex post facto opposition was aimed at actions that were irreversible, at least in the context of the times. The criticisms were more plaintive lamentations of regret than calls to action, the ideological image more a sense of inevitability than a sense of injustice.

The war had several direct and indirect effects on the stock exchange. The stock exchange initially reeled from the beginning of the war. It had suffered devastating losses during the depression of 1857, which destroyed about half of the district's brokers, including such stalwarts as E. W. Clark & Company. The war eliminated all southern investing from the market, a not insignificant sum, while the general economy, before the stimulus of government purchases, suffered from the bankruptcy of six thousand firms of greater than $5,000 value (Sobel 1965). However, as the Union fortunes began to rise so did interest in the stock market. Investors soon found that there was considerable money to be made in wartime speculation, especially when the emergency encouraged innovative ways to finance purchases. For example, this was the first time that buying on a margin was used widely. Other exchanges like the Mining Board and Petroleum Board arose during the war, partly because the more conservative New York Stock Exchange restricted new companies and required tighter regulation of trading. One example was Gilpin's News Room, which specialized in gold and evolved into the Gold Exchange Bank.

In 1863 a rival exchange, the Open Board of Stock Brokers, arose, which sold securities at ongoing tables, one for each listed company, rather than the cumbersome company-by-company auction. Even though the older New York Stock and Exchange Board was renamed the New York Stock Exchange and adopted a new constitution that brought more order to business, including the scrutiny of securities and greater surveillance over members, by 1865 the challenger was conducting ten times the business of the older exchange. The two merged in 1869 and adopted the Open Board's method (Sobel 1965; Stedman and Easton 1969). By that time the basic contours of America's financial system were in place. Wall Street was no longer a street of shops and taverns, but one dominated by the stock exchange, investment banks, and brokers, highly institutionalized in a form that could later embrace America's growing industrial sector.

Foreign Capital

The rise of American corporations cannot be understood without taking foreign influence into account. American corporations would not have developed in the form they did if they had not arisen within the international economy. Corporations were not invented by American governments, but had long been used by European governments, including the trading companies American schoolchildren learn about such as the Hudson Bay Company, the East India Company, or the Jamestown Company. Early corporations were strategic for American governments because they not only could mobilize American wealth, but could tap into the already well-developed European investment capital market.

Any explanation of the rise of large American corporations must address the international dimension, which I will argue involves a process of power-based institutional diffusion more than a functional adaptation to the demands of technology and markets. At the core of this power-based process of institutional diffusion is *isomorphism*. As DiMaggio and Powell (1983) describe it, isomorphism is a constraining process that forces one unit in a population to resemble other units that face the same set of environmental conditions. In a developed field, diversity of organizations is a function of diversity of the environment, but in a developing field, isomorphism can reduce diversity and engender standardization of organizational forms. While isomorphism can be established by selective processes in which some organizational forms survive while others fail, it can also be created by the exercise of power. DiMaggio and Powell describe three processes by which organizations can become isomorphic. First, there is coercive isomorphism, by which one organization requires another to conform to its mode of interaction. For example, if those with capital are more inclined to purchase bonds of chartered companies than make commercial loans, parties seeking to accomplish tasks that need capital will be pressured to incorporate and issue bonds. Second, mimetic isomorphism is the process whereby organizations seeking to reduce uncertainty follow the lead of other similar organizations. Unlike coercive isomorphism, which would typically involve different organizations in a division of labor, mimetic isomorphism involves analogous organizational types. The influence that the Erie Canal had on the creation of canal development in other states is a form of mimetic isomorphism. Third, in normative isomorphism, leaders of organizations in a similar field share common values or understandings about how to solve their similar problems. By the end of the century, the large corporation was seen as the best way to avoid both the anarchy of unrestrained competition and the tyranny of state socialism, giving a normative basis to a standardized organizational form. The effect of foreign investors on the rise of large American corporations was primarily one of coercive isomorphism, although the term overstates the degree of compulsion.[8]

The American investment capital market developed in a form very similar to that of the European system, not only because the Americans copied the Europeans, especially the British, but also because the European system served as a template. If the Americans wanted to borrow European finance capital, they would have to offer bonds and other securities similar to those on the European markets. They would have to deal with investment bankers like the Rothschilds or the Barings and conform to the requirements that these conservative bankers proposed. The new, poor, and plebeian governments would have to provide interest rates and conduct their fiscal affairs in a manner that would win the confidence of the established, wealthy, and pedigreed Europeans. It was not that the Europeans dictated to the American governments how to run their financial affairs. Indeed, the Rothschilds, the Barings, and the European investing community did not need the meager American business enough to assert any such active direction. The Americans needed to join the European financial game and had to play according to the rules. States turned to Europe and England to sell their securities despite patriotic sentiments because it was there that they could find investors. Few Americans were willing or able to buy securities. There was no large class of persons willing to devote a part of their savings to risky investments (Callender 1902).

Europeans played a large role in American finance almost from the beginning and continued to dominate until the twentieth century (Adler 1970; Hidy 1949; Jenks 1927; Wilkins 1989 Callender 1902; Campbell 1938; Morgan and Thomas 1962). As early as 1808 an estimated three-quarters of the $10 million stock in the United States Bank was held by Europeans (Callender 1902). Eight years after it was founded, America's first major railroad, the Baltimore and Ohio, needed a million dollars of subscribed but unpaid capital for unfinished construction. It turned to the London market, initiating a new form of financing—borrowing with Maryland state bonds as collateral (Myers 1970). Many Britishers and Europeans were initially reluctant to invest in American railroads, which they deemed too risky. But they were willing to purchase state bonds that were used to finance railroads, and so that is the form by which many early railroads were financed, solidifying the relationship between government and corporate finance. From 1830 to 1843 American states increased their debt, much of it foreign, from $26 million to $231.6 million, about one quarter of which went directly to construct railroads. By 1843 Europeans owned about $150 million in state bonds, much of which had been issued to finance canals and railroads (Adler 1970). However, the financial embarrassment of many states and the strong records many American companies were showing induced more and more Europeans to invest in American railroads. Baring Brothers, the preeminent British house involved in American finance, was initially categorically opposed to investing in American railroads. But it changed its policy in 1852 for several reasons. Other banks like the Rothschilds

were becoming involved in railroads (mimetic isomorphism), fewer state securities were being issued, rail manufacturers were often willing to accept
bonds as payments, some British investors were requesting them, and the
bank's American correspondents, in whom it generally had great faith,
strongly urged it. Once Baring made up its mind, it "plunged into the railroad bond melee" (Hidy 1949, 413), purchasing $500,000 bonds of the
Eastern Railroad Company of Massachusetts and many others. Later that
year, when Thomas Baring was in the United States, he agreed to take a
share in a $3 million Pennsylvania Railroad issue of thirty-year 6 percent
first-mortgage bonds. By the mid-fifties, 26 percent of all American rail
bonds were owned by overseas investors, mostly English. The secretary of
the Treasury estimated that $222 million in American securities were held
abroad, of which half were state bonds, a quarter railroad, and the other
quarter bank insurance company and canal (Myers 1970). After the war
foreign investments in railroads increased even more. Greenberg (1980)
states that, by the lowest estimates, European holdings in American railroads grew from $50 million in 1866 to $243 million in 1869. Total foreign
investments in the United States grew from $1.4 billion in 1870 to $3.3
billion in 1890 (Carosso 1970). As late as 1890, railroad companies with
more than half their total capital owned abroad included the Illinois Central
(65 percent), Pennsylvania (52 percent), Louisville and Nashville (75 percent), and Reading (52 percent) (Williams 1929). But during the 1890s,
the depression gave Americans the opportunity to regain control of much of
the economy.

Americans were able to regain control relatively easily in the 1890s in
part because foreign investment was predominantly in the form of portfolio
investments (bonds or nonvoting preferred stock) rather than direct investment. Europeans preferred the reduced risk of bonds, which take priority
over all other forms of securities when allocating profits or liquidating assets, and left control to those closer to the site of the business. Dunning
(1970) estimated that 90 percent of all international capital before 1914
took the form of portfolio investment.[9] Portfolio investment was important
to the rise of large American corporations for two reasons. First, it helped
weaken the role of equity-owning securities in financing and operating large
firms, an important element in the redefinition of property rendered by the
corporation; that is, stocks became relatively less important than bonds.
When property became socialized, control became embedded in specific institutional spheres other than ownership per se. Foreign preference for
bonds over stocks was one major reason that railroads increasingly financed construction with bonds, marking a shift in the rights, entitlements,
and responsibilities of ownership. Stocks are formal titles of ownership,
originally parcels or shares of ownership, carrying the rights and some of
the obligations of ownership. Bonds were originally merely loans, obligations to pay interest and, at a specified date, the principal, much like ordi-

nary commercial loans but with the company's assets as collateral. But through the operation of finance capital and legal changes, each entity took on a very different meaning. Stock ownership lost many of the rights of ownership, including a much weakened right to manage. When corporations issued bonds, owners even lost some of their right to profit insofar as interest on bonds took priority over dividends on stock. And because interest on bonds was fixed and secured by the corporation's assets, bondholders, or the investment bankers that represented them, often gained the upper hand in directing the corporation.

This switch had substantial consequences for the distribution of profit and risk in American railroads. When people of modest means and local governments invested in railroads, it was typically as stockholders. Large investors, especially foreign investors, were more inclined toward bonds. Thus a shift from reliance on stocks to bonds also suggests a shift in the focus of control over corporations. The Pennsylvania Railroad, which controlled 13 percent of the nation's railroad capital, illustrates the shift. In its early years, its owners eschewed the obligations of fixed payments that bonds created. When the management developed an unprecedented $100 million bond issue, selling the first installment of nearly $25 million in England, stockholders mobilized to form an insurgent stockholders' committee. A lengthy report in 1874 criticized the centralization of power in the company's president and advocated returning more authority to the stockholders. It resolved that "the stockholders, under the charter of the Pennsylvania Railroad Company, were the owners of the corporate rights and property, and the original and only source of power and authority" (Schotter 1927, 164). It thus recommended that a committee of directors specifically represent stockholders' interests, and that issues of general policy be left to the directors. The rights of ownership that it felt were being usurped were decisions involving the assumption of obligations including bonds, leasing property of other companies, guaranteeing rentals to other railroads, the interest and principal on bonds, and the incurring of nonincidental liability. The report asserted that the powers of the directors should only be those that administer these general policies. The committee also recommended that the board include at least three members expert in railroad affairs, one of whom would be president. But the issue of real contention was bonds. It repeatedly condemned the amount of bonds that had been issued and strongly resolved that bonds be issued only temporarily and only for expansion and construction. It concluded by acknowledging the company's outstanding successes, including its contribution to building Pittsburgh and Philadelphia into great cities, and by praising its strong profitability, an average between 1853 and 1873 of 9.9 percent in dividends. In the 1875 annual meeting, the stockholders passed a resolution that the board of directors had already adopted several of the recommendations and that "it was their intention to adopt all of the recommendations that might be found of practical value to the company" (Schotter 1927, 172). But little actually changed.

On one level this can be interpreted as another chapter in the separation of ownership and control. But the complaint was more than loss of control to management as a matter of form or authority per se. The committee was formed to defend the stockholders more against bondholders than against management. It was a conflict between two groups external to the corporation that had conflicting proprietary claims on profits and authority, a conflict over the rights, entitlements, and responsibilities of ownership. But it was conflict with roots in the role of foreign capital in building American railroads more than any inherent efficiencies of managerial control or any invisible hand guiding capital markets to maximum earnings.

The role of foreign capital affected the relationship of finance to industry in yet another way. The railroads did not depend on foreigners only for capital. Until after the Civil War, most American rails were imported from Britain, often purchased with railroad securities. By 1853 an estimated half of the $70 million in American bonds held in Europe had been issued to pay for British rails whose manufacturers most often quickly sold them on the London market, usually through a merchant banking house (Adler 1970), thereby embedding the development of the American railroad system within the institutional structure of British corporate capital. The British rail-makers could have sold the rails for American securities only if they had access to the British securities market. The promise of American economic expansion could be manifested in railroads with real locomotives on real tracks only if the English institutional structure had developed fully enough to make it possible. American railroad builders did not experiment with different institutional structures and select the one that best suited the needs of the system, but pragmatically worked within the system that the past presented to them. They did not survey the terrain and map out the most efficient route to industrial development, but followed the path that had brought them to the present.

Although the institutions of finance capital in this country were molded after European models, the role of American government in corporations differed from those of Europe (Dobbin 1994). In France, the government actively engineered the entire system and induced private investment by guaranteeing a return on investment. The German and Belgian states each built their main railroad network. English railroads and canals were almost entirely financed privately without government assistance, made possible by the greater availability of capital (Goodrich 1960), institutionalized policy styles (Dobbin 1994), and the fact that development preceded railroads rather than followed them. The British could tap a developed economy rather than being a means of development because for them, rails and canals linked developed regions with one another. In America, especially, the railroads were built to link the frontier with fledgling cities. William H.

Seward stated in 1850 that "a great and extensive country like this has need of roads and canals earlier than where there is an accumulation of private capital within the state to construct them," while Henry Varnum Poor, who later published his annual *Manual of Railroads* to assemble pertinent financial data on companies, wrote, "No new people can afford to construct their own railroads" (both quoted in Goodrich 1960, 9).

The system of international finance had a long history in financing state building. Banking families like the Rothschilds had for centuries provided critical financial services for the states of Europe. At a time before the New York Stock Exchange had been created, when Americans bought and sold stock at the Tontine Coffee House, European governments could borrow funds to fight wars, build infrastructures, or turn over old debts by going to the Royal Exchange or the Change de Paris. And for international investment, it was governments that the investors preferred. The leading bankers like the Rothschilds and the Barings were especially conservative and only reluctantly handled international investments for risky private ventures.

Thus in the absence of European capital, American economic development would have unfolded much more slowly and in a very different form. Without European capital, builders of infrastructure would have had to rely on government mobilization of resources or they would have developed transportation and communication networks by linking locally financed projects together, a slower and more improbable alternative. However, foreign capital not only shaped the development of canals, turnpikes, railroads, and telegraph but profoundly shaped the institutional structure underlying all large-scale corporations.

CONCLUSION

The background of corporate institutions for the rise of large-scale socially capitalized industrial corporations is important for several reasons. The first is that the institutions were the fertile soil in which corporations were rooted. They constituted the social relationships through which capital resources flowed for large corporations. Second, institutions shape the taken-for-granted categories that reify frequently repeated social practices into "things" like money, markets, corporations, and institutions themselves. These practices, when they become reified as things, acquire ideological power by appearing as inevitable suprasocial developments. Finally, these institutions shape a historical—in contrast to a functional—explanation of the use of large, socially capitalized industrial corporations. The social structures that constitute the economy are shaped out of the raw materials available from the past, not the abstract needs of the future. The industrial corporations that arose at the end of the century could probably not have developed without the rise of institutions created to mediate between public finance and private wealth.

The Social Structure of Economic Reality

The elaborate system of practices that mediate social relations among actors in creating corporations differs fundamentally from that of the entrepreneurial world. Instead of cash, commercial notes, bank loans, profits, and deeds of ownership, we have a wide variety of stocks, bonds, purchase on margins, bull and bear markets, call loans, and dividends. Institutions create and enforce these media of interaction. Social relationships then can be seen in terms of the media bridging actors and the practices that validate or enforce these relationships. The more fully institutionalized such media are, the more "real" they seem. As the "new institutionalism" of organizations has argued, institutionalization thus becomes a historical force with a momentum of its own (DiMaggio and Powell 1991). When social arrangements are accepted as real, they become the default means by which people do things just because they are there, whether or not they are efficient. As DiMaggio and Powell argue, actors typically do not adopt institutionalized arrangements because they rationally and intentionally decide that the cost of innovation is less than the potential loss from accepting existing models; in fact organizations rarely make such calculated comparisons.

The social relations that build large corporations are different from those that build other enterprises, a distinction between "finance" capital and "commercial" capital. Finance capital is not just a different sort of entity from commercial capital, but a different set of relations and institutions, although it is sometimes convenient to talk about them as things. To understand the social nature of the relations and institutions of corporate capital, along with how they interact with other social relations and institutions, one must examine the stock market, investment banks, brokerage houses, and money system that spawned the system of corporate capitalism.

Thus it is that corporations have developed that can operate within social relations that grant them at least relative autonomy from product markets. They can be capitalized with relatively little cash as long as investment bankers agree to market their securities or contractors and suppliers accept securities for payment. Of course contractors and suppliers will accept securities only as long as they have a reasonable expectation that others will accept the securities as valuable. That is to say, the people making the decisions that enable companies to be formed are different from those who control commercial capital that entrepreneurs depend on. Socially capitalized corporations can continue to operate without profits as long as the investment community continues to buoy it by purchasing more securities.[10] And when that fails, investment bankers, bondholders, and stockholders can renegotiate with one another and the investment community through a state-regulated reorganization.

Thus large, socially capitalized corporations are more than the filing of papers with a secretary of state or the limiting of ownership liability and the prospect of outliving a founder. Corporate capitalism is an entire institutional system embodying a whole new set of social relations so firmly entrenched that we have reified corporations in our language by treating them as actors.

Comparative Logic and International Capital

The strategic role that New York played and the effect of foreign capital markets are important to the analysis of the rise of American industrial corporations not only for the historical preconditions of centralizing capital and eventually releasing it into industrial corporations but also for explaining the similarities between the American economic structure and that of other advanced economies. It has been argued that the convergence of corporate forms among the industrial nations validates the causal importance of technological factors. For example, the authors in Horn and Kocka (1979) seek to explain only the timing of legal and organizational forms. As Chandler and Daems state, "Thus, the historical story suggests that the modern business enterprise was the more 'natural' response to technological and marketing imperatives of modern mass urban and industrial societies. . . . The story also makes clear that the differences in timing of adoption of the administrative alternatives reflected differences in economic and legal environments" (Chandler and Daems 1979, 29). McCraw (1981) similarly reasons that the high level of fixed capital provided incentives for market cooperation found in American and European economies, although governments reacted quite differently. The reasoning is basic comparative logic: similar developments in different societies must reflect similar causes. Since different societies had different legal, political, and social environments, the common factor leading to a common corporate system is technology. The comparative case for a technological explanation would be quite strong except for one fatal logical flow: the "cases" were not independent. Such comparative causal logic is valid only if the causal mechanisms are endogenous to the societies. The rise of the modern corporation was not at all endogenous. On the contrary, its use in each major country strongly stimulated a rise in others. Business organizations interacting with one another tended to adapt to one another and organizationally converge toward similar structures by institutional isomorphism, not common exogenous causes. In terms of power, the behavior, including decisions concerning legal and economic forms, must be explained in terms of relationships with others, including foreign business. To be more concrete, American canals, turnpikes, and railroads adopted corporate forms, including the means they used to build and combine, because of their relations to others not only in this country, but also abroad. Not only did individual companies require foreign financing, but this system of financing was largely shaped to conform to the international financial system. Obviously foreign capital was not the only factor shaping the American corporate system, but it was strategic enough that the comparative logic of endogenous cause cannot provide an adequate analysis of similar outcomes in American and European systems. Rather, the corporate system arose in the context of international finance as much as national finance.

This chapter has focused on the development of corporate economic institutions in this country, emphasizing the continuity along preexisting paths. The stock market, investment banks, brokerage houses, and practices of capitalizing enterprise had their origins in government finance and foreign investment. But of course no institutions are entirely autonomous; they are situated within an institutional system. The previous chapters emphasized the role of government as initiator and financier of early corporations which then became privatized. The role of government and the operation of the institutional structure intersect in the law, which defines and enforces the entities that constitute the economy and the permissible relationships among them. It is to the law that we now turn.

CHAPTER SIX

Statutory Corporate Law, 1880–1913

I HAVE STRESSED throughout that the legal developments redefining the nature of corporate property and the corporate institutional structure were more than easy functional adaptations to any compelling logic of technological progress. This chapter will address the ways in which the law played an autonomous role in shaping the social relations institutionalized in the new corporate organization of property, and seeks to explain the legal underpinning of large corporations on their own terms.[1] It will elaborate three aspects of statutory law that helped redefine the rights, entitlements, and responsibilities enforced as property and show how variations among states helped determine the scope and nature of corporate organization at the end of the nineteenth and the beginning of the twentieth centuries. These three aspects of property and property rights are the legislated right of corporations to own stock in other corporations, the reduction of personal ownership liabilities, and the legal powers vested in the boards of directors, all of which varied from one state to another and affected the degree and form of businesses incorporating there. Variation among economically similar states in these important facets of corporate law suggests that corporate law was shaped by contingent political factors rather than by adaptation to economic forces. This chapter is about the effect of corporate laws in various states, not the reasons why they were passed: law is the independent variable. Although the laws were influenced by both structural and economic changes and by self-conscious actions of capitalists, their adoption cannot be reduced to structural or instrumental forces. That is, the laws cannot be explained as the process of a systemic adaptation of the law to exogenous economic change. If so, they would have been much more similar in various states than they were.

Theoretically the legal underpinning of the corporation is important for two issues, the institutionalization of the corporate form and the ways in which corporate property contributed to the process of formation of the capitalist class. Institutional theory emphasizes that the socially constructed sense of recurring social relations being "real" is a fundamental basis for the reproduction of those social relations with a minimum of ongoing exercise of power or self-conscious activity to sustain them (Meyer and Rowan 1977; Zucker 1977; DiMaggio and Powell 1991). When a set of relations or a way of organizing activity, such as a school, government, company, union, or voluntary association, becomes defined as a "thing," actors will tend to act according to the definition of that "thing." Students come to class, employers negotiate with unionized workers, or aggrieved citizens form lobbies to get the ear of legislators. The fewer alternative "things" that the institutional environment offers, the more constrained actors are in selecting how to organize activities. When the corporation becomes the only institutionalized way outside the state to organize large-scale economic activity, it will be adopted whether or not it is the most efficient of all potential arrangements. The state, through the activity of the law, becomes one of the fundamental determinants of what social relations and activities become defined as real (Coleman 1974; Jepperson and Meyer 1991).

The modern industrial corporation, to a greater extent than other forms of ownership, is a creature of the law. The law defines the rights, entitlements, and responsibilities of all forms of property, but it has little jurisdiction over the very existence of entrepreneurships and partnerships. Individuals and partners can form simple companies on their own, but a corporation does not exist unless the state says so. Legal treatises and sociologists have characterized the corporation as a "legal fiction" that has no existence without a charter from the state. [2]

As discussed in earlier chapters, property is a social relationship enforced by the state, creating a set of entitlements to goods and services and defining the different obligations and rights that people have to one another in relation to those goods and services. Property gives some people the right to use objects or to enter into contracts with others concerning the use of those objects or to decide how anything produced in the use of those objects will be disposed of. It also creates obligations and liabilities concerning the use of those objects if debts are incurred or people are injured by those objects. The exact nature of the rights, entitlements, obligations, and liabilities involved in property relations are defined and enforced by the state. It is the state that ultimately defines whether an economic system is capitalist, socialist, or communist, at least in the modern era. That is why revolutionaries who aim to create a new economic system generally target state power. As Polanyi (1957) has described and as the regimes of the former Soviet bloc have demonstrated, markets no less than state ownership are created and sustained by states. Thus any analysis of the rise of corporate capitalism must address the role of the law.

Corporate law contributed to creating the corporate form of property in two ways: by giving the corporation rights and entitlements not available to individuals or individually owned businesses and by solidifying institutional relations among corporations that are specific to the corporate system such as the stock market, investment banks, and interlocking directorships that structured the socialization of capital and of authority.

1. *Giving the corporation powers not available to individuals or individually owned businesses.* Because early corporations were created by governments to accomplish socially beneficial tasks like building canals, railroads, roads, and settlements, they were given special privileges, including legal monopolies, the right of eminent domain, and free land. Many of these privileges were discontinued when the right to incorporate became generalized, but some important ones continued: owners were not liable for the company's debts, companies were given the right to own stock in other compa-

nies, and managers could operate corporations without direct accountability to owners. Later writers would ahistorically interpret these privileges as inherent features of the corporate form, citing them as explanations for why the corporation was intrinsically a more efficient form of organization. By the turn of the century legal treatises were routinely explaining the rise of the corporation in terms of such "inherent features" as limited liability (Elliott 1900; Cook 1903; Burton 1911). Seager and Gulick, a few decades later, reflected the same perspective: "The reasons for this enormous development of corporate business are the advantages which corporations enjoy under present corporation laws and the absence of serious obstacles to the enjoyment of these advantages" (1929, 22).

2. *Solidifying institutional structures in which social relations among firms are specific to the corporate realm.* As we saw in Chapter 5, the large corporation was part of a new distinct institutional structure, including stock markets, brokerage houses, investment banks, businessmen's associations, and specialized mass media, all of which were separated from the realm of entrepreneurial capital. The social relations among the organizations in the corporate institution were not only enforced by law but also prevented by law from being used outside the corporate institution. Corporate securities developed as a self-contained market that was only loosely coupled to the ebb and flow of hard money or other currencies. Money could change hands at the margins of the securities market, as people entered and exited, but within the market, value could be created and exchanged on paper. People could make and lose millions on paper, with very little money changing hands. At least as important, firms could attain assets, including capital facilities and other firms, by exchanging stock, not money. At the same time, laws that vested power in boards of directors whose members could be recruited from outside the corporation made it possible to socialize authority across the corporate realm.

Chapter 3 argued that the antebellum experience of New Jersey, Pennsylvania, and Ohio created legacies for the permissiveness or rigor with which they regulated corporations at the end of the century. This chapter will describe how these three states varied legally and the effect this variation had on the development of large corporations. It is the consequences of differences in corporate law that are the issue here, consequences that not only affected the states individually, but altered the context within which other states made decisions about what corporations could be and do.

LEGAL AND ECONOMIC ORDERS

Weber (1978, vol. 2, chap. 1) makes the distinction between legal and economic orders. The former is the law as a system in itself, which is analyzed according to its internal relations. It is a purely normative order. In contrast, the economic order is how people actually behave. The two orders exist on different levels, and their subjects cannot come into contact with each other. Weber held that people obey the law less because of self-conscious decisions than because of either social norms governing specific behaviors or unreflective habit. There is considerable variation in the degree to which laws actually govern behavior. Some laws are "guaranteed law," which means that there are agents with coercive power whose job it is to enforce the laws. When he uses the term "law" without specification, he means norms which are directly guaranteed by legal coercion. Essentially, Weber is distancing sociological analysis from a purely jurisprudential analysis, which was the prevailing mode of analysis in his day. Most thinking on the law was based on textual analysis and logical construction, with little attention to the social consequence of the law.

On this side of the Atlantic, American "Legal Realists," led by Roscoe Pound, were beginning to distinguish between "law in books" and "law in action" (Scheiber 1975; Gordon 1983; Horwitz 1992). Like Weber, they argued that the effect of law on society is always refracted through social structure and culture. Textual analysis of legal treatises cannot tell us the actual effect of law, because the structure of the economy can strongly shape the effect of any law. However, this insight should not be pushed too far. By focusing on the ways that the economy determines how the law is manifested, one can easily slide to the conclusion that the effect of the law is determined by nothing but the economy. Horwitz (1992), describing how Legal Realism became a doctrine of inevitability, cites Cook's 1903 treatise on corporate law, which opened, "The laws of trade are stronger than the laws of men" (quoted on 85).

Weber (at least in this discussion) emphasizes that the social effect of law is mediated by the willingness of the state to enforce and the consonance of law with social norms, while the Legal Realists emphasized the fit between law and economic structure. The difference suggests that they were assuming different types of law. Weber assumed law defining the state's policing powers, that is, the power of the state to command or prohibit specific behaviors (consistent with his definition of power as the ability to maintain one's will over another, that is, to elicit or prevent specific behaviors, and his focus on authority as the basis of state power). Most people think of law—"Thou shalt not . . . kill, steal, exceed the speed limit . . ."—as manifested in its pure form in criminal law. The Legal Realists implicitly assumed a broader conception of law, including other types of law such as tort law or property law, whereby the state was adjudicating the ongoing relationships among actors involved in exchange or competition, areas in which the state has explicitly refrained from dictating the content of the interaction. For example, except for a few issues like restraint of trade, capitalist states have generally refrained from deciding whether contracts are reasonable as long as they conform to certain procedural standards such as honesty. It is up to the private parties, not the state, whether contracts are made for hog futures or hypercards. Both Weber and the Legal Realists were reacting to a scholastic mode of jurisprudential scholarship based solely on interpretive reading of legal texts, a mode of reading that drew unwarranted conclusions about social and economic consequences of the law. The analysis in this chapter draws on a reading of statutory and judicial texts, but bases conclusions about social and economic consequences on separate evidence. The issue is how the law can influence not only the specific behavior of actors or the state's powers to adjudicate relations between actors, but the very entities that can act or interact. The law is a constitutive element of what entities "exist," that is, the configurations of social relations among individual actors that become reified as social actors. The agenda here treats the law and the rights, entitlements, and obligations it defines in property primarily as an independent variable and the rise of the large-scale corporation as a dependent variable.

THE CORPORATION AS PROPERTY

Scholarship on the relationship between the law and the rise of the corporation has focused primarily on antitrust law, which was an important but limited part of the picture.[3] The three areas of corporate law analyzed here—intercorporate stock ownership, the powers of boards of directors, and the extent and limitations of owners' liability—all helped define the nature of corporate property. These laws even more than antitrust laws redefined the rights, entitlements, and obligations of ownership, and like antitrust laws, they selectively validated some forms of interfirm coordination (Fligstein 1990). They thus closed organizational options and weakened the competitive viability of individually owned firms while opening possibilities for corporations to become a more effective vessel for large-scale production by forging the new institutional structure of corporate capitalism.

Examining the corporation as a form of property involves a perspective fundamentally different from viewing it as an efficiency-seeking organization acting within the context of a market, especially when considering the role of law in the economy. As Campbell and his colleagues (1991) persuasively argue, previous analyses positing a weak American state fail to consider how the state's ability to define and enforce property rights determines social relations and the balance of power among economic actors in civil society. This underestimation of state power has been exacerbated by the tendency to focus on the American federal state, which had relatively little to do with the economy in general and property in particular, rather than the subnational state, which enforced property rights including the right to incorporate.

INTERCORPORATE STOCK OWNERSHIP

The law defines not only what unitary, singular organizations can exist and act with legal sanction, but also the relationships by which clusters of organizations can form larger entities. The corporation is defined in common law as a singular organization acting legally as an individual. But when corporations interact to form other sorts of organizations through mergers, trade associations, market or patent pools, joint ventures, employers' associations, or holding companies, the degree to which they form a new organization with the legal power to act in its own capacity is strictly constrained by law. In other words, the specific definitions of what rights, entitlements, and responsibilities were embodied in corporate property helped shape the social relations through which enterprise became concentrated into very large constellations of capital. As will be seen in the next chapter, the hostility of American courts to marketing pools severely constrained the ability of manufacturing companies to alleviate what they considered destructive competition. However, the law was changed in individual states to allow corporations to purchase the stock of other corporations, thereby permitting the creation of the giant corporations of today. What had been unitary, singular entities were combined proprietarily, sometimes combining their operations and other times not. It was the combination of capital that led to the giant corporations more than the combination of productive facilities, and it was changes in the law that made that possible. This variety of technical, managerial, and market relations within legally similar configurations of capital means that the explanation cannot rest entirely on technical, managerial, or market factors.

Although the law in many ways treated the corporation as an individual, with the same rights and privileges as individuals, common law restricted its right to own some types of property, especially other firms. Courts tended to rule that common law did not permit corporations to own stock in other firms, so they could do so only when permitted by statute (Buxbaum 1979; Freyer 1979; Haney 1917; Freedland 1955). Advocates favoring the legalization of intercorporate stock ownership successfully argued that insofar as corporations legally were individuals, they should have the same right to own both real and negotiable property as natural individuals. However, since this right was not available to an unincorporated business firm—a partnership could not own another partnership—the laws permitting intercorporate stock ownership created a power not available to entrepreneurships and partnerships.

Intercorporate stock ownership was not much of an issue until the second half of the nineteenth century, when industrialists were seeking legal means to control supralocal markets. Some railroad charters, such as the Pennsylvania Railroad's, which empowered the corporation to own stock in other railroads, offered a model that other corporations might follow when seeking a means of controlling competition. As the next chapter will elaborate, after the courts refused to enforce contracts that would have established accountability to collective control within industries, some industrialists attempted to use the powers of ownership to compel adherence to collective decisions about prices and production, resulting in the trust experiment. The prohibition against intercorporate ownership formed the common law foundation for outlawing trusts, even those that did not restrain trade (Boisot 1891).[4] As a contract among individuals, a trust was legally like a partnership, which did not have the right to own the stock of other firms. Only the individuals, as individuals, could own another firm. Statutes creating this power gave corporations the legal tool they needed to weld a binding association among firms so they could harness competition. The law of intercorporate stock ownership made it much easier to control another company than an outright merger, whereby the controller purchases the assets of the controllee. Most states strictly defined the circumstances under which a corporation could sell its assets, often requiring unanimous stockholder approval. Throughout the decades around the turn of the century, states eased these restrictions but still typically required a majority vote. To control a company through stock ownership, in contrast, required the purchase only of a controlling interest, which at a maximum meant a bare majority, and in actual practice a much smaller proportion. Moreover, if the controlling company paid for shares of the controlled company with shares of the parent company, as was typical, and if either company was chartered in a state that prohibited corporations from owning stock of other corporations, the transaction was illegal. However, if the purchasing company was buying shares from individuals, only the corporate law in the state of the parent company applied. The transaction, even if legal, would then render the controlled company a foreign corporation and often subject it to more restrictive laws (Hovenkamp 1991). For example, Pennsylvania foreign corporation law prohibited outsiders from owning coal mines, but could not restrict who owned the stock of domestic corporations. Without this legal change, the merger movement at the end of the century would have been virtually impossible or would have taken a very different form with unknown later consequences.

Ownership of other companies was one of the most controversial areas of corporate law, because it touched so directly on the issue of concentrated economic power (Seager and Gulick 1929; Bonbright and Means 1932; Sklar 1988). The debate posed two very different conceptions of economic organization. On the one hand, the economy was seen as an activity of individuals. Individuals owned factories, shops, and trading companies; individuals worked for other individuals; individuals aspired to get ahead by becoming owners. In this vision, the corporation was seen as a necessary but regrettable development by which individual resources were combined to do things that individuals by themselves could not accomplish. It logically followed that corporations were aggregated forms of property, a contract among individuals to pool their resources. As a contract among individuals, they should not be entities that themselves could hold property other than their physical assets. On the other hand, another vision viewed the corporation as an entity in itself. It was not only a legal fiction but a social reality, an entity that acted. Legally it was treated as an individual and given the power to do things that individuals could do. While much of this law was developed through judicial law (Horwitz 1992), even when the courts developed the legal conception of the corporation as an individual, it did not necessarily follow that corporations could fully engage in the most basic act that the law adamantly granted and enforced for natural individuals, that of owning any form of property. Although judicial law generally held that corporations could own physical property (although there were still strong limitations on their right to own real estate), there was a continuing debate over their right to own the stock of other corporations until the New Jersey legislature unilaterally invited corporations doing business anywhere to enjoy the authority to do so by the simple expedient of incorporating there.

The social structure of ownership permitted by intercorporate stock ownership sharply contrasted with that of individually owned businesses. Individually owned businesses were structurally atomistic, each firm being owned by one or a few individuals. The relationships among them were primarily through the market or through countermarket collective action like trade associations or pools. As individuals, the owners might try to control the market by regulating competition, but, as is well documented, such attempts rarely succeeded. In corporate capitalism, the social structure of ownership allowed firms to interact through networks of ownership as well as through the market. These proprietary relationships made it possible to control the market through two types of networks, holding companies and communities of interest.

When states began to allow corporations to own stock in other corporations, they gave birth to the holding company, a company that existed solely to own other companies. American Cotton Oil Company, American Sugar Refining Company, Standard Oil, and U.S. Steel, along with many other early corporate giants, were created in this fashion. The individual firms often continued to operate individually, maintaining their brand names and market shares, but operating as subsidiaries of the holding company. The degree of autonomy varied from those that merely set production levels and received reports from constituent companies, like American Cotton Oil, to those who homogenized production and accounting while maintaining tight routine control, like American Tobacco. But in all cases, the instability of industrial governance by markets was contained.

Communities of interest were a less common means by which the social structure of ownership permitted corporations to control the market more effectively than individually owned firms. In a community of interest, competitors own a noncontrolling interest in one another, giving each an incentive to maximize their mutual benefit rather than competing by undermining their rivals. This device was used most effectively by railroad companies, which by the turn of the century had coalesced into six major communities for the whole country (Roy and Bonacich 1988). In these ways the laws permitting intercorporate stock ownership helped solidify the institutional structure in which arose social relationships specific to the corporation.

While common law prohibited corporations from owning stock of other corporations, the states varied considerably in their statutory laws creating affirmative powers of stock ownership. At one extreme Virginia, in 1873 and 1887 statutes, expressly prohibited corporations from owning stock in other companies. In the middle of the spectrum, some states restricted either the type of corporation owning stock or the type of corporation in which stock could be owned. Ohio, in 1880, passed a law specifying that corporations refining or manufacturing coal, iron, petroleum, or manufacturing cotton or woolen fabrics could own certain kinds or classes of corporations. An 1874 Pennsylvania statute permitted companies to own stock in railroads, which was intended to allow companies to create little spur lines to link their factory, mine, or refinery to larger trunk lines.[5] Ohio's law permitting corporations to own stock in railroad companies was even more restrictive, specifying that the railroad connect the plant or adjacent land and requiring approval of two-thirds of the stockholders. Massachusetts in 1882 confined corporations to owning only 10 percent of a gas company in their hometown. Restrictions allowing corporations to own stock in other firms only if the other firms were in the same or related fields were relatively popular. Such provisions were passed by New York (1890) and Maine (1895). New Jersey is well known for setting the standard for the more permissive end of the scale, gaining notoriety for liberalizing its laws in 1888 and 1889, essentially legalizing the holding company form of organization. Despite their historical impact, these laws were virtually unnoticed when passed, with not a word in the financial press or national newspapers. But the consequences were quick and dramatic. By 1901, 66 percent of U.S. firms with $10 million in capital or more and 71 percent of those with $25 million or more were incorporated in New Jersey (*Manual of Statistics* 1901). Some praised the state for its modern, enlightened, progressive, and realistic vision (Keasbey 1899a). Others damned it as the Mother of the Trusts (Sackett 1914). Even though historians have argued that other states were compelled to conform with New Jersey's permissive corporate law (Grandy 1989b; Horwitz 1992), the response was neither automatic nor quick. New York passed laws allowing corporations to own stock in similar lines of business in 1890 and 1892. Connecticut emulated New Jersey's law in 1895, while Delaware explicitly challenged New Jersey's dominance as the home of large corporations in 1899. By 1903, when the corporate revolution was drawing to a close, only six states unequivocally permitted corporations to own stock in other corporations (Parker 1993).[6] It was not until the 1920s that as many as thirty states had passed similar laws allowing intercorporate stock ownership (Hurst 1970).

The differences among the states in the degree to which they allowed corporations to own stock in other corporations reflected fundamental issues about the nature of the corporation and the new institutional structure it was creating. Both proponents and opponents realized that these laws gave the corporations powers not available to individually owned businesses and heralded a new structure for organizing enterprise. Having abandoned the responsibility ethic that legitimated corporations on the basis of their public contribution to accountability (Hurst 1970), proponents celebrated the corporation as a necessary and progressive innovation providing an institutional framework for large-scale, technologically advanced, and efficient production. Edward Q. Keasbey declared before the Chicago Conference on Trusts, "The chief characteristic of this policy of New Jersey is that it is a policy of encouraging rather than discouraging the aggregation of capital. It regards the corporation as a means of bringing the savings of many into efficient use as capital for the development of resources and the promotion of industry" (Keasbey 1899b, 362). Lewis Haney praised the holding company form as the most effective means to maximize the productive use of capital, explaining that all that is necessary to finance a consolidation is to sell securities or exchange them for those of the company to be controlled, and, as a bare majority holding is generally all that is needed, the amount of capital required is reduced. He felt that the limits to the scope of combination were set only by the nature of the business. As a corporation, the holding company possessed a greater claim to legality than other forms of combination, while its ability to appeal openly to investors through the joint stock device, limited liability, and effectiveness in management enabled it to raise vast funds. Citing U.S. Steel as an accomplishment that would have been impossible under any other form, he concluded that the greatest advantage of the holding company lay not so much in the vastness of capital which can be amassed under it as in the economy gained in the use of capital (Haney 1917, 230–231). Opponents responded that intercorporate stock ownership concentrated economic power and enabled a small group of individuals to control the economy more completely than technology or efficiency considerations would warrant. For example, Edward S. Meade in his 1903 text on corporate finance stated what had become a very common opinion, that there had been no more far-reaching change in the organization of industry than that which converted an illegal combination in restraint of trade into a corporation authorized not only to manufacture and sell commodities but also to own the stocks and properties of other corporations engaged in the manufacture and sale of commodities. By reconstructing the trusts to conform to the law, by capitalizing these permanent pools, he wrote, the builders of the trusts made possible a widespread reorganization of competitive industry along more profitable lines and opened the way to create a huge mass of industrial securities, from whose profits the public had theretofore been excluded. Without this device of corporate organization, escape from competition would have been impossible (Meade 1903, 45). Another author, William Z. Ripley, described the New Jersey holding company statute in terms of "vast possibilities" involved in a "fundamental change" in American corporate law, which made it possible for corporations to serve the interests of bankers and promoters as well as efficiency (Ripley 1905, xix). Similarly, the legal scholar Theodore Burton in 1911 rebutted the claim that holding companies had benefited the country, arguing that it was not a natural way of attaining greater efficiency. He grounded his analysis within conventional corporation law, by which a business concern organized to engage in some branch of business must perform the functions for which it was created. Since the holding company produces nothing and performs no proper economic function, Burton could see no justification for its existence (Burton 1911, 119). By this time, both proponents and opponents not only agreed that the large corporation was a fact of life and the key to a new economic order, but also acknowledged that the law would be a critical factor in shaping the corporation.

THE POWERS OF THE BOARDS OF DIRECTORS

Like the issue of intercorporate stock ownership, the powers given to boards of directors also affected the extent to which the corporation was a distinctively new kind of organization in a distinctively new institutional structure. The existence of boards of directors is itself a distinctive feature of the corporation. There is nothing inherent in the corporation that would dictate that there be a board of directors. One could imagine firms in which owners selected their officers, in which officers were accountable directly to the owners. There is no necessary requirement that there be a mediating body between owners and management. Like the authority to purchase stock in other companies, the law regulating the powers of boards of directors created new organizational powers not available to individually owned firms (Keasbey 1899b; Horwitz 1992). Two discussed here are the autonomy that corporations potentially gained from owners and the ability to coordinate relations with other firms through overlapping directorships.

Autonomy from ownership is more commonly described as the separation of ownership and control. The boards of directors have the legal responsibility of representing the interests of stockholder owners. Control can be separated from ownership when either directors lose effective control over management or when they maintain control but become more oriented toward management than the stockholders. When authors like Berle and Means (1932) talk about the separation of ownership and control, they include not only the powers taken over by management but also those that directors took from owners. Berle and Means in particular focused more on how the law was vesting the power of ownership in the increasingly unaccountable boards of directors than on the operational dynamics that gave management practical control, making very little distinction between managers and directors. They saw the gulf in the separation of ownership and control less between managers and directors than between directors and owners. Although well known for promulgating managerialism, they were not entirely sanguine, charging that many boards of directors served the interests of managers and specifically large owners rather than all owners.

The small owners were the losers in their analysis.[7] Although the tendency was to slacken the hold of owners over directors, the trend was hardly uncontested. For example, the congressional Pujo Committee investigating the "Money Trust" recommended that minority stockholders be guaranteed representation on boards (U.S. House of Representatives 1913).[8]

In addition to the powers directly vested in boards of directors, the boards of directors indirectly created another kind of power not available to individually owned firms, power at the institutional level of interfirm relations. Individually owned firms related to other firms through the market and through the individual connections owners might have. Directors could not only govern the firm internally but mediate between the firm and the environment. Moreover, many directors could sit on more than one board, aggregating to form a system of interlocking directorates and making possible a degree of coordination and cohesion at the social level that individually owned firms could never construct[9] (Dixon 1914; Bunting and Barbour 1971; Mizruchi 1982; Norich 1980; Pennings 1980; Roy 1983a, b). Many directors were recruited from the outside to solidify relationships with key actors in the environment and to monitor or scan the environment on behalf of the firm (Useem 1984). Thus the socialization of ownership created by intercorporate stock ownership and common stockholders came to operate in tandem with the socialization of authority forged by shared directors, solidifying relations at the social as well as the individual level. Individually owned firms have never had this resource.

Interlocking directorates were another "currency" which corporations could exchange with one another. The power to recruit directors who sat on the boards of other companies or to gain the authority to name members to other boards was a means of intercorporate influence. Rather than affecting one another only through market transactions, corporations could affect one another through interlocked directorates. Moreover, interlocking directorates helped to control competition among the firms in a market, facilitate raising capital from commercial and investment banks, solidify and reduce transaction costs with suppliers and customers, and coordinate the activities among firms with common ownership. All of these activities were much more difficult among individually owned firms.

Although the existence of boards of directors was fully institutionalized by the late nineteenth century, states still varied in the powers given to the boards of directors. The people creating and controlling corporations wanted the boards of directors to be as strong as possible with the least accountability to the body of stockholders. Stockholders and legislators who believed in traditional property rights continued to advocate laws to protect shareholders' authority. Relative to other developed nations, the American states tended to increase the power of directors. They were less inclined to allow boards to delegate authority to management, which maintained powers in the board itself. Similarly for most of its powers, the board had to act as a unit, minimizing the powers of its chair or executive commit-tee. Finally, American states made it very difficult for shareholders to re-move directors, who increasingly were treated as equivalent to the corpora-tion entity, in contrast to treating the shareholders as the embodiment of the corporation (Horwitz 1992).

One consequential power about which states varied was the relative de-gree of discretion to distribute surplus earnings; at issue was the extent to which stockholders could demand dividends when directors preferred to re-invest for expansion. While discretion over surplus earnings was a positive power, some states gave directors more power by easing restrictions on di-rectors. Insofar as directors were held liable for debts, their autonomy was compromised, as when directors were held liable if stock was not paid in or if debt exceeded the amount of capital stock (Cook 1903). The powers given to directors were also limited or expanded by the power given to shareholders. The larger percentage of shareholders required to issue new stocks, the less discretion given to directors. When some states permitted corporations to issue no-par stock, directors became free to issue stock at will, since the mechanism by which stock had been capped had been author-ization for a given value at par (Buxbaum 1979). Shareholders were al-lowed to sue directors in some states but not in others, with important im-plications about the extent to which the corporation was an entity apart from the stockholders. All these issues defined powers that directors had relative to managers and shareholders, constituting the particular rights, en-titlements, and responsibilities enforced for the different actors involved in owning and operating socialized property. Some states more thoroughly supported the powers of directors; others were more prone to protect the property rights of stockholders. Stockholders' rights were actively protected in some states and ignored in others.

We will examine the powers given to directors by focusing on the power to assess newly acquired property. One of the chief ways that corporations grew was by issuing new stock for new assets. Sometimes they would pay construction companies or suppliers in stock, and sometimes they would take over the assets of competitors, suppliers, or sales companies by paying with stock. Different states established different criteria for assessing the value of the property or services received. The most common legislation re-quired that payment be for the actual value, which sounds fair enough, is straightforward, and provides legislative basis for penalizing fraud. How-ever, who is to say what the actual value is? When this was left unstated, the door was left open for stockholders to sue the directors for abridging their interests by paying too much, a device which became an effective strategy for any shareholder to obstruct directors' plans for expansion or acquisi-tion. Other states explicitly stated that the directors' assessment, unless clearly fraudulent, constituted a fair assessment and left virtually no provi-sion for the stockholders to contest the board's action. Thus what seems like a technical matter of who assesses value became an important issue of where power lay. In the period studied here, there was no consensus among the states on how the value of assets to be accepted in payment for stock was to be evaluated. The states with more permissive corporate laws vested the powers in the board of directors, stating that the value they decided was valid unless fraudulent. These laws placed the burden of proof upon those who might contest their assessment. This provision was passed by Colorado (1877), New Jersey (1896), Delaware (1899), and Virginia (1903). States that required only that property be evaluated according to market criteria of some sort included Connecticut (1880), Massachusetts (1882), Maine (1884), New York (1890), Pennsylvania (1894), Illinois (1905), and Texas (1907). Maryland had the most restrictive law. In 1908, when many states were closely examining their statutes to decide if they wanted to conform to the liberal standards of New Jersey and Delaware, Maryland required that stock be exchanged for property only at an assessment agreed upon by the majority of the stockholders.[10]

Between 1848 and 1882 three of the more restrictive states, New York, Pennsylvania, and Massachusetts, prohibited corporations from accepting notes or other stockholder obligations as payment for capital stock. This had the effect of barring consolidations in which the stock of a parent company could be exchanged for the stock of a company being taken over. However, over time, states explicitly permitted more and more types of payments for stock. For example, both restrictive states like Florida (1892) and Texas (1893) and liberal states like Delaware (1899) and New Jersey (1913) authorized capital stock to be exchanged for labor. States passed statutes permitting the exchange of capital stock for property generally, as far back as Colorado in 1877 and Connecticut in 1880 and continuing through Virginia in 1903 and Illinois in 1905. A few states placed restrictions on the kind of property that could be exchanged. Pennsylvania (1874) and New Jersey (1896) specified that a corporation could exchange stock only for property that it needed for its business; New York (1890) restricted exchanges to property that the corporation did in fact use in its business. Other states were more restrictive. Virginia (1887), before its more liberal 1903 law, allowed stock to be exchanged only for mines, mineral rights, or for leases, options, or rights of way or easement. Connecticut (1888) allowed corporations to issue stock for securing patents. These new options gave the directors more power to build and shape the company. Now the company could build new facilities, take over other companies, and in some states occasionally pay workers without borrowing or saving.

The powers that states created for corporations, including the power that permitted the directors to increasingly exercise the rights of ownership without accountability to stockholders, were not a natural result of the rise of the corporation. True, there is a structural tendency when hundreds and thousands of atomized individuals own stock to abdicate to full-time offi-

cers and highly invested officers. But the structural tendency toward centralization of power inherent in collective ownership was only part of the picture. Legislators, judges, and business practice gradually but actively
chipped away at the rights of ownership and fortified the powers given to
officers and directors (Berle and Means 1932). From the post–Civil War
period onward stockholders and directors have gone to battle over many
issues, and the directors have usually won.

LIMITED LIABILITY

One of the best-known features of corporate property is that owners enjoy
the right of limited liability. They have nothing at risk but the money they
have invested in purchasing their stock, so that if the corporation is sued by
creditors for debts or damages, the owners are immune. Indeed some observers identify this as the single greatest advantage of the corporate form,
the feature that explains the dominance of the corporation over individually
owned firms (Davis 1897; Smith 1912). Harvard's president, Charles W.
Eliot, effusively called limited liability "the corporation's most precious
characteristic," and "by far the most effective legal invention . . . made in
the nineteenth century" (quoted in Hurst 1970, 9). Owners of proprietorships or partnerships share all the rights and responsibilities of ownership.
They have full authority over the physical objects, including both the right
to determine how they will be used and the right to sell or bequeath them as
they choose, but they are also liable if the object damages others. Corporate
property carries a different responsibility. Even if a corporation negligently
or willfully damages others, its owners cannot be held responsible. Property
is thus transformed from a relationship in which individuals who hold title
to an enterprise exercise authority over all others involved in production
and distribution to a relationship in which individuals collectively invest
funds for which they are given nominal title, but individually lack both authority to manage and responsibility for debts. A new entity, the corporation itself, becomes the legal object into which the right to manage and the
liability for debt are vested. Thus limited liability is essential to the way that
property has become socialized. In the process, risk is transferred from
owners to creditors.

However, there is nothing inherent in collective ownership that makes
limited liability inevitable. The joint stock company was a legal form under
common law with all the powers of corporations except limited liability
(Seager and Gulick 1929; Bosland 1949). Limited liability was routinely
granted to corporations as far back as the eighteenth century. Davis (1917)
notes that only one company, the Hamilton Manufacturing Society, chartered in New York in 1797, was refused this privilege. Livermore (1939),
however, argues that in Massachusetts, limited liability was the exception
rather than the rule. In 1808 the legislature passed a law specifically estab-

lishing—not limiting—liability of manufacturing corporations. Investors could be levied to pay the debts of the company until the law was repealed in 1829. Connecticut during this period, even though it passed a law limiting liability, continued to stipulate in charters of specific companies that all investors were liable for debts. In general the status of limited liability as late as the 1820s was not at all clear. But over the course of the nineteenth century judges increasingly recognized limited liability, except when limited by charters (Hurst 1970). Many legislatures ratified limits on liability through statutes, but others continued to uphold investors' liability. Pennsylvania as late as the General Act of 1853 established individual liability in manufacturing and mining as well as banking, although the provisions were later restricted considerably. Hurst (1970) concludes, "Nonetheless, legislatures subjected corporate shareholders to enough liability through the span from about 1810–1860 that we must doubt the inducement of limited liability as the prime explanation for the growing popularity of the corporate form of business" (28). Moreover, especially for small corporations, lenders often required shareholders to cosign notes of indebtedness for the corporation. A New York law in 1890 required that corporations display the word "Limited" in all offices, advertisements, and correspondence so that potential creditors could be warned (*National Corporation Reporter*, Nov. 29, 1890, 1:226).

Much of the opposition to early corporations targeted the privileges such as monopoly protection, franchises, and limited liability that states granted in deference to corporations' public service. When the corporation privatized, some of those privileges were rescinded, especially grants of monopoly and franchise, while others were retained but redefined as rights or at least necessary features. For example, limited liability, despite the early controversy over its economic or moral wisdom, became seen as an inherent right when judges ruled that it was validated by common law.[11] But its validity depends on treating the corporation as an entity in itself. The liability of a stockholder at common law is determined and measured by the contract of subscription between the stockholder and corporation. When this contract with the corporation is fully performed, there is no further liability to the corporation or its creditors. In the second half of the nineteenth century, some state constitutions and legislatures imposed additional liability upon stockholders for the benefit of the creditors, which is called statutory liability (Elliott 1900).

Like other aspects of modern corporations, the most common explanation of the rise of limited liability follows a functionalist logic, reasoning that limited liability was a necessary component to a more or less naturally evolving organizational form: there could not be corporations without limited liability (despite the widespread availability of the full liability joint stock company); therefore limited liability had to arise. So its development is usually described but not explained. Hannah (1979) is representative: "In all countries it has been recognized that a necessary precondition for the widespread adoption of modern industrial organisation is the enactment of legislation facilitating what in English law is known as the joint-stock, limited liability company" (306). He goes on to explain that the joint stock, limited liability company was necessary for the expansion in size of operations and the divorce of ownership and control. Its main advantage has been that it facilitates raising capital for large-scale enterprise.

There is no doubt that limited liability solves a basic problem in socializing capital: how to induce individuals to invest capital without directly controlling how that capital is administered, or what economists call the agency problem. If a person is going to become involved in a risky endeavor—and all business enterprise involves some risk—a responsible person needs to maintain control over the endeavor or limit the risk. The more impersonal the relationship between the person who operates the business and the investors, that is, the less control people have over how their investment is used, the greater the investors will be motivated to have guarantees of reduced risk. If investors increase the level of risk by investing in an enterprise with unlimited liability, that is, if they place not only the investment but all their assets at risk, rational people are likely to want control over the investment. This explains a logic of risk, but not the historical process by which limited liability arose. Moreover, this logic takes only the investor's point of view. Limited liability basically shifts the risk of enterprise from the owners to the creditors, including construction companies, suppliers, lenders, and laborers. So it is not surprising that limited liability was not accepted without debate.

Thus the rise of limited liability has been neither automatic nor uncontested. Before the second half of the nineteenth century, some investors avoided corporations because they felt that full liability served as a check upon irresponsibility, that the more one had at stake the more carefully one would conduct business affairs. Others felt that abrogating liability was not only bad business but perhaps immoral. One should be responsible for one's actions. Only the immoral would not stand behind their investments and their actions. When corporations were quasi-governmental organizations to construct public works, liability could be dispensed with because the government presumably supervised corporate affairs and ensured proper business practices. But as corporations increasingly privatized, the legitimacy of limited liability remained contested, at least in part. It continued to be controversial at the end of the century, when William W. Cook, author of a widely cited legal treatise on corporate law, proposed in his book *The Corporate Problem* (1891) that stockholders of banks should be liable double their investment so that depositors could be compensated if a bank failed. He reasoned that the stockholders enjoyed the profits from using the deposits so they, not the depositor, should suffer from insolvency. He also suggested that the stockholders be liable for debts to laborers when a business failed, pointing out that Michigan and Ohio included such a provision in their constitutions and that New York had enacted such a law for railroads operating within its borders. California required the same liability for stockholders as for partnerships. But Cook noted that corporations were choosing to charter in states with more congenial laws. "There is nothing in the corporation form itself to justify the exaggerated application of limited liability. This pernicious movement has decreased the personal responsibility on which the integrity of democratic institutions depends, and has introduced into both investments and social services a dangerous element of insecurity" (Cook 1891, 288). Arguing that limited liability was not a feature of the earliest corporations, he maintained that "its prevalence in this century has been due to an overestimation of the importance of national internal development. . . . [T]he element of personal responsibility is gradually pushing its way back into the management of corporations so far that limited liability, instead of being an advantage, is often regarded by promoters and investors as a positive detriment" (288). Thomas Hogsett, speaking before the Ohio Bar Association in 1905, offered a contrasting criticism, that limited liability gave corporations an unfair advantage over individuals, and that if a corporation were to have unlimited powers, it should have unlimited responsibility. He acknowledged that limited liability had been a major incentive for the creation of corporations, but held that it had also been one of their great evils (Hogsett 1905). Herbert Knox Smith, later U.S. commissioner of corporations, felt it necessary to explicitly justify limited liability. Turning Hogsett's argument on its head, he reasoned that the application of this mass of capital must, for business efficiency, be centered in a few hands. "The many small investors, necessarily thus deprived of personal responsibility, control and supervision over the use of their individual contributions, must in equity also be relieved of personal responsibility for mismanagement" (Smith 1905, 388).

Hogsett and Smith agreed that the powers of ownership should match its responsibilities but differed over whether owners in fact enjoyed the powers of ownership. Both saw power moving to the corporate entity, but disagreed over the moral consequences. Both treated loss of authority and freedom from liability as two sides of the same coin. Limited liability was a logical precondition of establishing the corporation as a legal entity in itself, which was so important for socializing capital. Whereas earlier, legal doctrine had treated the corporation as a collectivity of owners, emphasizing its artificiality in the "legal fiction" doctrine, by the early twentieth century, the law was treating the corporation as a "natural entity" existing apart from the shareholders, who increasingly were endowed with neither the rights nor responsibilities of ownership (Horwitz 1992). Only the entitlement of profits remained, an entitlement compromised by bond capitalization and court decisions fortifying directors' authority to allocate net earnings as they saw fit.

In law, the owners *are* the firm. They initiate the activity creating a legal entity. They make decisions to take legal actions; they defend the firm if legal action is taken against it. And they enjoy the profits that the firm generates. But sociologically, the firm is an organization with a division of labor. Capitalist ideology may define the owners as the essence while Marxist ideology defines the workers—who create the value—as the essence, but sociologically, production is a collective activity. Sociological analysis thus should consider the roles of all participants: suppliers of raw material, equipment, or capital; workers, managers, and technicians; and distributors and customers. Their interrelationships may take the form of commercial transactions, sale of labor power, authority, or expertise. In this perspective, the legal definitions of the different participants' roles are something to be explained, not taken for granted. Why is a strike seen as the workers against the company rather than as an intraorganizational conflict? Why are workers considered a creditor when the firm goes into receivership? Why aren't the promising ideas of technicians considered an asset in bankruptcy proceedings, especially since "goodwill," a quality at least as elusive, is frequently considered?

The point is to shake the notion of limited liability loose of its doctrinal moorings, to view it as a historically developing legal principle that was only one of many sociologically possible definitions of organizational responsibility and accountability, not an inevitable development.

Variation among states in their laws covering liability did not affect the extent of socialization of capital as much as it did the nature of socialization. More stringent liability laws, at least within the context of the late nineteenth-century American polity and economy, discouraged socialization through the institution of large-scale corporate capital more than they discouraged the creation of small and medium-sized corporations. Even in states that required double liability like Ohio, small and medium-sized corporations were founded in large numbers (Evans 1948). When corporate stock was bought at small margins by investors with little personal knowledge of a firm or its managers, liability was riskier than investing fully paid in with companies that were known to be solidly financed and well managed.

Liability also affected the nature of socialized property, shifting some of the risk of enterprise from the owner to the creditor. The investor risked only his or her initial investment, but not additional costs incurred in the course of constructing or operating an enterprise or any costs levied against the firm for negligence. The American legal system through much of the nineteenth century protected creditors with the Trust Fund Doctrine, through which paid-in capital was treated as a fund to ensure that creditors were remunerated. It was by this doctrine that investors were held accountable for any subscriptions not yet paid in for capital stock (Horwitz 1992). Various states supplemented the common law with statutes prohibiting corporations from assuming debts greater than their capital stock. Debts were the most basic item of liability, especially if the corporation was reducing its capitalization, reorganizing, or going out of business. Would the people who owned the company and who had enjoyed its profits be responsible for paying its debts when it foundered? Or should creditors be left holding the bag, being forced to recover only a fraction of their legally contracted credit? Most courts held that common law limited liability so that if stockholders were to be liable beyond the value of their stock subscription, it must be established by statute (for example, *Carr v. Iglebart* 3 Oh. St. 458 1854; see also Marshall 1903, §3258, 153). Nearly all the states held stockholders liable up to the par value of the stock. If the stock was not paid in, the stockholder could be assessed up to the par value to pay debts. Some went further and held stockholders liable to an additional amount up to the value of their stock. Ohio's constitutional provision to this effect, creating double liability, was a major deterrent to large firms incorporating there. But the law generated controversy within the state. Even some who agreed that the principle fostered greater corporate honesty and discouraged overcapitalization argued that the state's exceptionally strict requirement penalized the state and encouraged firms to incorporate elsewhere (Bennett 1901). In addition to liability to debtors, some states held stockholders liable for unpaid wages. Nine states up to the end of the century, including New York (1848), Massachusetts (1860), and Pennsylvania (1874 and 1894), legislated that although stockholders were generally limited in their liability, they were individually liable for debts owed to workers (U.S. Industrial Commission 1902, 283–284).

With limited liability, the question arose of how to prevent innocent people from being taken advantage of by unscrupulous businessmen who might attempt to hide behind its shield. Most states held stockholders liable for debts expressly contingent upon failure of the corporation, its dissolution leaving debts unpaid, or return of an unsatisfied execution against it—including Maine (1871), Illinois (1872), Colorado (1877), Texas (1879), Massachusetts (1882), Connecticut (1888), New York (1896), and the two corporate "friendly" states, New Jersey (1896) and Delaware (1899).

One of the consequences of limited liability was that the corporation could to a much greater degree than otherwise act as an entity in itself, apart from its owners, both legally and practically. The concept that stockholders were not liable beyond the value of their stock subscription was closely connected to the concept that the corporation was an entity in itself. As the Trust Fund Doctrine was replaced by the Natural Entity conception of the corporation, stockholders without the traditional powers or liabilities of ownership were increasingly treated by the law as mere investors, legally distinct from the corporation itself (Horwitz 1992). As a legal individual the corporation had the right to enter into contracts, borrow funds, and conduct other economic transactions, just as natural individuals did. Practically, the individuals who controlled corporations could run them as they wished, knowing they were liable only for what they had personally in-

TABLE 6.1
Corporate Laws of Three States, 1900

State	Powers of Boards	Liability	Intercorporate Ownership
New Jersey	Liberal	Medium	Liberal
Ohio	Medium	Strict	Strict
Pennsylvania	Medium	Strict	Medium

Source: See Appendix 6.1.

vested in the firm. What was at risk were the collective assets of all the owners, the interests of the corporation itself. Limited liability contributed to the tendency to transform active owners into passive investors, a fact increasingly recognized by both firms and investors. At the level of the system, corporations could interact with one another, each one having limited accountability to stockholders.

CONSEQUENCES FOR INCORPORATION

The previous section described how the law governing liability, the powers of boards of directors, and the power of corporations to own stock in other corporations all created rights and entitlements not available to other business forms, that is, created distinctive corporate property rights, and also gave legal foundation to ways that corporations could interact with corporations differently than they interacted with noncorporations. The law thus helped established the corporate institutional structure. But how do we know that the differences in law had any effect on economic organization? Partly as a consequence of their different corporate laws, New Jersey, Ohio, and Pennsylvania, despite considerable economic similarities, exhibited very different rates and patterns of incorporation. Figure 6.1 displays the (logged) total capital of publicly traded corporations listed on the stock exchange for the three states. The shape of the trend over time is similar for all three states, starting from virtually nothing in 1890, rising slightly until the 1893 depression, falling thereafter until 1899 when it skyrocketed into the corporate revolution, and tapering off somewhat after 1904. But New Jersey's total corporate capital is about ten times that of Pennsylvania, which is about ten times that of Ohio. Table 6.1 summarizes the laws of these three states concerning powers of boards of directors, liability, and intercorporate stock ownership in 1900. As we shall see, businessmen were quite aware of the differences among the various states in corporate law and publicly cited them to explain their decisions about incorporation. The legacies of different antebellum experiences described in Chapter 3 were reinforced by subsequent political events to shape stark contrasts among state corporate laws.

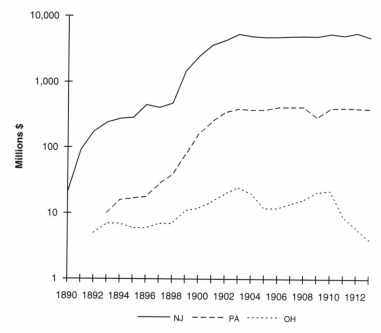

Figure 6.1. Total Capital (Logged) of Major Corporations Listed in Three States, 1890–1913. (Source: Data drawn from *Manual of Statistics*.)

New Jersey, the home of most of the giant corporations formed in the corporate revolution, was more liberal on all three types of law. Its tradition of congenial relations dating from the Society for Establishing Useful Manufactures through its virtual partnership with the Camden and Amboy Railroad was reinforced by postbellum political conditions that were inhospitable to the development of groups that might have counteracted the advocates of permissiveness. Especially important was the unusual vigor of interparty rivalry. Whereas the Democratic Party needed anticorporate sentiment to attract workers and farmers in most northern states, New Jersey Democrats were not shattered during the war. It was one of the few states where McClelland beat Lincoln in the 1864 election and where the Democratic Party continued to be strong after the war, in part because of its close relationship to the Camden and Amboy. Thus the corporation issue was much less politicized there than in other states (Parker 1993).

New Jersey's pioneering laws concerning stock ownership by corporations are, depending on one's point of view, widely celebrated or notorious.[12] Although now recognized as a major watershed in the law governing the American economy, the laws were barely noticed at the time, by either businessmen or journalists. The first law, passed in 1888, gave corporations the power to purchase stock in other corporations, but was "ambiguous almost to the point of unintelligibility" (Freedland 1955, 400). This law only permitted operating companies to hold subsidiaries and did not authorize holding companies, since a holding company exists only to own other companies. A second law of that year authorized intercorporate ownership only for hotel and water transportation companies. Both were passed without major debate or fanfare, mentioned routinely in New Jersey newspapers, and ignored entirely by the *New York Times*. At the behest of James Dill, of the major Wall Street firm Sullivan and Cromwell, representing the American Cotton Oil Trust, the legislature revised the law in 1889 to permit corporations to own stock of companies necessary for their business.[13] During the fall of 1889, the *Wall Street Journal* carried a series of stories about the Cotton Oil Trust and its change into a New Jersey corporation, but focused more on how it would be capitalized, with only one story noting that the company was denying rumors of legal impediments to incorporation. But corporate lawyers were taking note. The *National Corporation Reporter* noted that some firms were moving their legal domicile to New Jersey to escape rigorous laws in other states, but it remained skeptical about the wisdom of the move: "The advantages gained by these wandering corporations are counterbalanced by some hindrances which surround them as foreign corporations. They can not condemn lands without special legislative authority, and in some States the constitutions have hostile clauses against them" (June 13, 1891, 14:324). But until the century's end, the migration to New Jersey trickled as only a few very large corporations, like American Sugar Refining, American Tobacco, and United States Rubber, incorporated under the 1889 law. The law was further clarified in 1893, giving unqualified power to own stock in other companies,[14] and codified in 1896, unambiguously beckoning to New Jersey most of the large corporations founded during the corporate revolution. The law was important enough that the state sponsored a full treatise on it alone, Smith's *Nature, Organization, and Management of Corporations under "An Act Concerning Corporations (Revision of 1896)" of the State of New Jersey* (Smith 1912). By the time Woodrow Wilson tightened up New Jersey's permissive laws in 1913, other states, especially Delaware, were poised to take the mantle as the "home of the trusts" (Larson 1936).

In the laws allowing intercorporate stock ownership, New Jersey also liberalized its laws governing the powers of boards of directors. One of the more widely discussed provisions was a "good faith" doctrine giving boards the final authority to assess goods and services used to purchase stock, with judicial oversight only for fraud (Bostwick 1902; Stimson 1911; Chicago Conference on the Trusts 1900; U.S. Industrial Commission 1900b, 1:504). The practice was legitimated by judicial interpretation of the 1875 corporation act (Keasbey 1899b) and formalized in the 1896 statute. Buxbaum (1979) attributes this provision to the influence of James Dill, who wanted to counteract legal decisions made in favor of creditors and, to a lesser extent, defrauded stockholders. Testifying to the U.S. Industrial Commission, Francis L. Stetson, a lawyer for Federal Steel Company, the predecessor to U.S. Steel, cited this provision as one of the major advantages New Jersey had over other states (U.S. Industrial Commission 1900a). After Delaware emulated New Jersey's general corporation, Charles Bostwick, writing in the influential *Commercial and Financial Chronicle*, criticized Delaware's "true value" doctrine requiring that goods and services could only be purchased with stock at their true value. He argued that the threat of stockholder suits to block expansion or mergers posed an unnecessary risk and concluded that New Jersey's laws were still more congenial. So the Delaware legislature in 1901 altered its law to conform to New Jersey's (Larcom 1937). Others, however, looking from the perspective of potential investors rather than corporate directors, were less sanguine. U.S. Attorney General George W. Wickersham wrote in the *Harvard Law Review*: "Perhaps the great uncertainty, and the extremest interference with the finality of the valuation put by the stockholders and directors of a corporation upon property contributed to its capital, exist in New Jersey,—the last state where such conditions would be looked for; the favorite jurisdiction of the formation of large corporations or 'trusts' " (Wickersham 1909, 322). He felt that the law validating incompetent or irresponsible evaluations forced stockholders to take inordinate risk.[15]

While New Jersey was praised by corporate lawyers and directors for its liberal laws on stock ownership and powers granted to boards of directors, it was the moderation, not the liberality, of its laws on stockholder liability that made the state appealing for incorporators. The loose liability of states like Maine or West Virginia as well as the rigid liability law of states like Ohio were contrasted invidiously with New Jersey's middle ground. Charles N. King, secretary of the New Jersey Corporation Agency, testified to the Industrial Commission, "They are so liberal that they do not require anything down there; but I have always been given to understand that corporations organized in West Virginia have considerable difficulty in placing their stocks and bonds" (U.S. Industrial Commission 1900b, 1:1110). But by the turn of the century liability was less important to New Jersey's appeal than issues like intercorporate stock ownership and the power of boards of directors, because many states had liability laws acceptable to incorporators (Bostwick 1902). While New Jersey's liability laws were often cited as one of that state's advantages, it was not depicted as unique, unlike when intercorporate stock ownership was discussed, but in distinction to the few rigorous states like Ohio (*National Corporation Reporter*, Oct. 22, 1892, 5:147; Bostwick 1902; U.S. Industrial Commission 1900a).

Ohio's rigorous law on stock ownership, powers of boards, and liability, along with its occasionally vigorous prosecution of antitrust laws, gave it a reputation as being inhospitable to large corporations, motivating many large Ohio companies to incorporate elsewhere, especially New Jersey (*National Corporation Reporter* 1891, 3:245; Larcom 1937; Grossman 1920; Berle and Means 1932). Although its antitrust policy is often cited as the major factor driving out large corporations like Standard Oil, many large corporations who had no trust problems also left the state. For example Procter and Gamble, a Cincinnati partnership that incorporated in 1890, chose New Jersey because of its more liberal corporation laws (Schisgall 1981).

Ohio's laws governing intercorporate stock ownership restricted the privilege to very specific and limited circumstances. As already mentioned, an 1880 statute allowed corporations refining or manufacturing coal, iron, or petroleum and those manufacturing cotton or woolen fabric to own a railroad connecting their plant with a major line if two-thirds of the stockholders approved. The same law empowered these specific kinds of corporations to merge two at a time and only if two-thirds of the stockholders approved. Both provisions were considered restrictive at the time. By implication all other intercorporate stockholding was prohibited, placing Ohio among the more restrictive states. Nonetheless, these laws were not seen as major deterrents in and of themselves for the many large corporations that were operating companies rather than holding companies. Ohio's laws on intercorporate stock ownership by themselves may not have attracted large operating corporations, but apparently did not actively drive them away.

While the laws of intercorporate stockholding were strict, Ohio's laws on the powers of boards of directors were moderate, neither as restrictive as the laws in states like Massachusetts nor as liberal as those in states like New Jersey. It apparently was not a factor in either inducing large corporations to locate in Ohio or discouraging them from it.

It was Ohio's liability laws that distinguished Ohio from other states. Ohio was one of the few states to require double liability from stockholders. When the 1851 constitution was being debated, a Judge Ranney proposed that all stockholders be fully liable. Without this he feared that "they would usurp every branch of trade and business, intrude themselves into every nook and corner of the state, override all private enterprise, and become as troublesome as the lice of Egypt." He was especially alarmed to find that even taverns were incorporating, shocked that "we drank incorporated liquor without individual responsibility for its effects" (quoted in Bennett 1901, 157). Those like Judge Ranney who wanted full liability and those who wanted none compromised on a standard of double liability, policy enshrined in the state constitution and spelled out in an 1880 statute. Corporate lawyers and business leaders frequently cited Ohio's liability policy as a reason why corporations should avoid the state. Francis L. Stetson cited it before the U.S. Industrial Commission as one of the main reasons why Federal Steel had rejected Ohio as a site of incorporation. By the turn of the century, some Ohio lawyers were arguing that if all the states had enacted such a provision, corporations would have been more honest with less tendency to overcapitalization. But since no other state had any similar provision, the effect had been to penalize Ohio corporations and encourage firms to incorporate in other states. But the policy did have its defenders. Warner Bateman asked the 1895 Ohio Bar Association, "Why should they [the incorporators] enjoy exemptions that cannot be held by the individual transacting business in his own name? The franchise is granted for their convenience alone; the business is to be conducted in their interest and for their profit alone; the public derives no benefit or gain from it; and why should any portion of the risk of such business, or any liability for any of the losses which may result, be thrown upon the public, any more than in business by the owners in their own proper name?" (Bateman 1895, 166). Even the staid *National Corporation Reporter*, while affirming limited liability as an "essential feature" of the modern corporation, wondered how creditors were to be protected and cited Ohio's policy as one solution (Oct. 24, 1891, 3:126).

In between New Jersey's permissiveness and Ohio's rigor, Pennsylvania's moderate corporate policy was not very liberal on any of the three dimensions, but strict only on the liability dimension. The state's moderate corporate policy resulted in a moderate number of corporations being founded there. Pennsylvania permitted fewer forms of intercorporate stock ownership than New Jersey, but more than Ohio. As we have seen, the Pennsylvania Railroad was one of the nation's first holding companies, but it enjoyed that power through special charter, not general. A statute passed in 1874, when Pennsylvania led the union in petroleum production, granted petroleum companies the power to own subsidiaries in related lines of business. In 1887, when the state led in iron and steel production, it extended the privilege to that industry, and in 1895 to all manufacturing companies. Although some corporate lawyers like Frederic Stimson (1911) praised Pennsylvania as one of the more enlightened states on this important issue, it did not attract very many large corporations, in part because it still did not permit holding companies. The state specified that corporations could only conduct the businesses for which they were chartered, and corporations could not be chartered merely to own other corporations.

Relative to other states, Pennsylvania was moderately permissive about the powers of the boards of directors. Its 1874 statute allowed mining and other mineral companies to accept mineral rights or patents as payment for stock if necessary to the business, a fairly restrictive law, but it broadened the powers in 1894 to include other companies. However, that latter law was ambiguous about who had the authority to assess, specifying only that the value of goods and services used to purchase stock had to be the value taken generally, the basis of value not otherwise specified. It was not a provision that made the state attractive to corporations.

Liability is the area of law where Pennsylvania was most rigorous. While in many states the stockholders' liability was limited solely to the value of the stock, Pennsylvania held stockholders liable for debts due to mechanics and laborers for work performed for the corporation (although for iron and steel companies, the liability held for only six months). The *National Corporation Reporter* advised its corporate readers to avoid Pennsylvania, in part because of its "dangerous" liability provisions

(1891, 3:245). However, a decade later, some corporate attorneys were comparing Pennsylvania's "liberal" liability laws to those of New Jersey (Bostwick 1902).

Pennsylvania had three other unusual provisions that businessmen found onerous. One was that foreign (out-of-state) corporations were not permitted to own real estate, except what was directly needed for their business. This, of course, did not trouble domestic companies, but could deter large interstate corporations. Several large corporations evaded this law by creating Pennsylvania subsidiaries. The state attempted to retaliate, but the courts ruled that the state could not regulate who owned the stock of any corporation. The struck-down law was similar in spirit to Pennsylvania's restriction of any corporation to one line of business. Both laws were the legacy of the period in which corporations were seen as privileged organizations created by the state for public purposes. Both laws aimed to contain corporations within the specific functions for which they were created, emphasizing the distinction between corporations and ordinary business companies. Richmond Jones (1902) singled out these two "onerous" laws—unparalleled in any other state—for driving corporations to more liberal states like New Jersey. Advocating their repeal, he pleaded, "The popular prejudice against corporations should exist no more. It arose from the contemplation, not of associated capital, but of the special privileges and immunities with which corporations were invested by prerogative, and which could not be exercised by individuals" (348). But the law that irked businessmen the most was Pennsylvania's unusually steep corporation tax, which was cited frequently as an impediment to incorporating there (*National Corporation Reporter*, Dec. 5, 1891, 13:245; U.S. Industrial Commission 1900a; Larcom 1937). The fact that the state exempted corporations involved exclusively in manufacturing made the law more ambiguous, and as large corporations expanded by acquiring the stock of other companies, their status as manufacturing corporations eroded. The issue reached the courts in *Commonwealth v. Westinghouse Electric & Manufacturing* Co. The company's charter included a clause that one of its purposes was "to make purchases and sales of investments in the securities of other companies," but it had been exclusively a manufacturing company in practice. The courts ruled that this clause did not cancel its exemption, but that the part of the capital used for manufacturing should retain its exemption (*National Corporation Reporter* 1892, 5:221). The issue of corporate taxation became politicized sufficiently that the Pennsylvania legislature in 1909 created a commission to recommend a revision of its corporate statutes. The commission sent out 42,000 invitations to testify at hearings in Philadelphia, Williamsport, Scranton, and Erie. After hearing testimony from a variety of interest groups, commission members sided with farmers over manufacturers, cited the practice of other manufacturing states, and suggested that manufacturers' exemption from corporate taxes be discontinued while all corporations be taxed modestly.

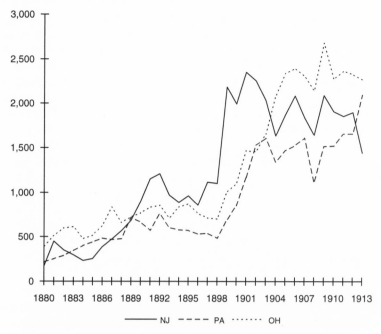

Figure 6.2. Total Number of Incorporations (logged) in Three American States, 1880–1913. (Source: Data drawn from Evans 1948, 126–143.)

The effect of these laws was stronger on large, socially capitalized corporations than small, closely held corporations, as seen in Figure 6.2.[16] Between 1880 and 1913, Ohio, the state with the most restrictive laws of the three states, annually incorporated an average of 1261 industrial firms, slightly more than New Jersey or Pennsylvania (Evans 1948).[17] Even after the turn of the century when New Jersey's permissive corporate laws were widely celebrated and condemned, more firms incorporated in Ohio than New Jersey. Thus Ohio's unusually restrictive legal climate did not deter small firms from incorporating there. Pennsylvania had nearly as many industrial corporations founded, an average of 549 a year, while New Jersey, which so dramatically overshadowed the other states in large publicly trade companies, trailed with only 420 companies a year (Evans 1948). The corporation was becoming institutionalized as the normal way of organizing industrial firms. But for most, the corporation was a legal detail with relatively little consequence for the way small companies did business. Most businesses, even when incorporated, were closely held by one or a few individuals, often members of the same family. The president would be the primary owner and the board of directors a mere formality, often only the major owners and a manager or two if the corporations were large enough.

The fact that these laws were more consequential for large corporations than small illustrates important qualitative differences that transcend size.

For small companies these provisions would have been rather meaningless. Few small corporations would have been concerned with the issue of whether they could own the stock of other companies. They were simple companies whose assets were confined to a physical plant, its inventory, and perhaps some moderate goodwill. The legal details of the powers of boards of directors were equally irrelevant. All the owners would typically serve on the boards of directors or be personally and socially close to them. There was no erosion of property rights for the owners of small companies. Only the issue of limited liability would have been germane to these owners. As is often stated, limited liability was one of the main incentives for individual companies to incorporate. Although in many respects a legal formality, incorporation did protect the owners' personal property and assets from the company's creditors if economic misfortune should strike.

CONCLUSION

This chapter has had two themes. First, the laws governing corporations, which were almost entirely state rather than national laws, gave corporations legal powers not available to partnerships. The corporation was a new type of property with a new set of rights and obligations vested in it. Thus the fundamental changes taking place as the nineteenth century gave way to the twentieth were not just a matter of increased scale and scope of production, deeper managerial hierarchies, intensified control over labor, or broadened national and international markets. These aspects have been well studied. But the legal underpinning of the corporation as a new form of property has been relatively neglected. Individually owned companies could not own other companies, a right confined to natural individuals. When corporations were given the right to own the stock of other companies, a whole new kind of organization, the holding company, was created. The powers given to the boards of directors changed the property rights of owners. The directors were legally charged with representing the collective interests of the stockholders, but increasingly they became more oriented to the interests of the corporate entity than of the stockholders, alienating corporate property from its nominal owners. The law of limited liability, in freeing stockholders of the responsibilities of ownership, helped erode their rights.

The fact that these legal changes disenfranchised nominal owners is, of course, well known, and is the empirical basis of Berle and Means's managerial model. Comparing the effect of the corporation on ownership to the effect of the factory on workers, they wrote that just as the artisan gave up independence in exchange for wages, the owner has become "merely a recipient of the wages of capital" (1932, 5). Berle and Means, more than most other managerialists, appreciated the importance of the historically specific nature of property and the role that law played in the corporate revolution, but, in failing to distinguish between small and large stockholders, overgeneralized the disenfranchisement of stockholders to include all of them: "In the corporate system, the 'owner' of industrial wealth is left with a mere symbol of ownership while the power, the responsibility and the substance which have been an integral part of ownership in the past are being transferred to a separate group in whose hands lies control" (1932, 68). Their arguments about managerial control have been vigorously debated (Allen 1981; Burch 1972; Daems and van der Wee 1974; Zeitlin 1980, 1989; Fligstein 1990). Zeitlin, in the most formidable critique of managerialism, called the separation of ownership and control a "pseudo-fact" based on faulty data and unfounded conclusions of sound data. Without examining this debate in detail, I can suggest that each of the characteristics of corporate property analyzed here affected large and small owners differently. The laws permitting corporations to own stock in other corporations made it possible to control corporations with a smaller proportion of total stock through the pyramiding of holding companies. An operating company can be controlled outright by owning 51 percent of the stock, which can be owned by a holding company, which itself can be controlled by a 51 percent interest. Thus with only one level of holding company, absolute control can be attained for a quarter value of the operating company. For example, a handful of individuals was able to use this and similar devices to control the American Tobacco Company, one of the largest companies in the world. Strengthening the powers of the boards of directors relative to stockholders means that control can be firmly secured by controlling a plurality of voting stock, enough to elect the directors. Berle and Means emphasize the influence that proxy mechanisms have given management in selecting directors, but the importance of proxy mechanisms is reduced in the face of organized major blocs of stockholders, especially if there is conflict between managers and large blocs. Large owners can more persuasively claim to be acting on behalf of all stockholders than can managers. The power of large owners relative to managers was further strengthened by the limits that boards had to delegate powers to managers (Horn and Kocka 1979). In the late nineteenth century American courts ruled that one of the differences between trustees and directors was that trustees exercised personal discretion, while directors were acting on behalf of stockholders (Heinsheimer 1888; Rogers 1915).[18] So while boards gained increasing power from owners, they were still somewhat accountable, especially to large holders. Limited liability similarly affected average stockholders more than large ones. It made one's stake proportional only to what one had invested, and unrelated to one's total assets, unlike entrepreneurial investments. While legally corporations were a reified entity apart from the natural individuals who owned it, sociologically, corporations were created by certain individuals who mobilized the resources of others to whom they could promise material gain without responsibility. But those who were creating the corporations continued to control them.

Nonetheless, examining the relative benefits and responsibilities among large and small stockholders misses the essential point about the corporation as a new form of property. The managerialists are correct that the corporation did undermine the importance of the relationship to ownership. Both legally and sociologically, whether one owned or did not own a particular enterprise became less consequential. But the managerialists myopically assume that power devolved to those who wielded formal authority within the corporation. This internalist perspective ignores the institutional level. Increasingly one's degree of control over production and access to the fruits of production were structured by one's relationship to the corporate institution, including investment banks, stock markets, and interlocking directorates.[19]

More than just a new kind of organization, the new institutional structure included new forms of interorganizational relations, new forms of "currency" that mediated exchanges among businesses, new kinds of organizations to facilitate growth and development, and a new set of understandings about the nature of capitalist enterprise. The laws permitting corporations to own the stock of other corporations meant that the relationship among companies became embedded in a network of property relations that transcended and at times controlled market relations. The powers given to the boards of directors facilitated and enhanced the importance of the structure of interlocking directorates. Limited liability helped stock ownership become a form of passive investment, lacking both the rights and the responsibilities of owners, in which the nominal ownership of productive property was embedded in a speculative securities market, an institutional structure very different from individually owned property.

While there were times that the law was shaped to intentionally conform to the perceived economic and technical needs, it did have a significant and substantial effect of its own. The changes created by corporate law were not necessarily conducive to greater efficiency, technological development, or managerial effectiveness. The explanations of the corporate revolution that focus on technological adaptation, managerial efficiency, or economic power miss part of the story, a part to which this analysis is intended to contribute.

APPENDIX 6.1: CRITERIA FOR CODING STATE LAWS

For Table 6.1, the laws of New Jersey, Ohio, and Pennsylvania with respect to powers of boards of directors, liability, and intercorporate ownership were coded as follows.

Powers of Boards

The only dimension coded was the power to assign value to property, labor, or other ways of paying for capital stock in a means other than money. States coded as liberal were those in which directors had full discretion to determine the value of those things paid with stock. The laws stated that, except in the case of fraud, the directors' assessment was authoritative. States coded as strict were those where the state continued to play a part in the process, for example, where the directors had to provide documentation validating their assessment. Otherwise, a state was coded as medium.

Liability

Common law held that stockholders were liable only for the funds invested in the corporation. Any further liability could only be established by statute (Elliott 1900, 591). Many of the state laws merely codified common law, but others increased liability. There were two specific differences in the coded states. One was double liability, as in Ohio. The other were liabilities for debts due to mechanics and laborers. States which specified additional shareholder liability for mechanics and laborers were coded as strict and all the other states in a medium category. No states were in a "liberal" category. Clearly, there is no point in giving shareholders freedom from liability for the amount of their stock subscriptions. The legal treatises of the time talk about the difficulties that corporations chartered in the "too liberal" states had in marketing their securities, but none fell in my sample.

Intercorporate Stock Ownership

There were the two completely unrestricted states, New Jersey and Delaware. The states which allowed intercorporate stock ownership under fairly liberal conditions (for example, corporations engaged in a similar business, or corporations useful and subsidiary) and the states which had no statutory provisions regarding stock ownership were coded as medium. Those states that prohibited intercorporate stock ownership or restricted it to very specific and limited circumstances were coded as strict.

CHAPTER SEVEN

Prelude to a Revolution

THE TROPE "CORPORATE REVOLUTION," used to describe the economic transformation at the turn of this century, is more than a casual metaphor. A revolution is a sudden change in which one group in power is replaced by the mobilization of another group (Tilly 1978). A *social* revolution entails a fundamental transformation in social institutions, not just a new set of incumbents in office (Skocpol 1979). With few exceptions (for example, Johnson 1968), academic theories of revolution reject functional theories and follow resolutely historical logics: the revolution and its consequences are the result of long-term institutional changes that become crystallized in the cauldron of intense conflict. Chapters 3–6 analyzed the long-term institutional change that set the stage for the corporate revolution at the end of the century. This chapter describes the events that immediately precipitated the revolution—how strategies adopted to govern industries in the 1880s created the conditions which made it possible for some businessmen to dominate their industries, thereby making it possible to coalesce with the corporate institutional structure in the 1890s—and the next chapter examines the revolution itself.

Asserting how profound the changes were in this period, of course, is very conventional. But I want to focus on an aspect of the transformation different from that emphasized by most of the literature. The conventional account is that the economy shifted from a market economy to an administered economy. What products were made, the relations between suppliers of raw materials and manufacturers, the relationship between producers and distributors, and the coordination of all the complex parts of the division of labor shifted from the invisible hand of the market to the "visible hand" of hierarchical bureaucracies (Chandler 1977, 1990). This description—although the terminology varies—is shared by most analysts, including Chandler's most ardent critics. The debate over transformation has focused as much on whether the participants were seeking market control or efficiency as on the characterization of industrial organization (see, for example, Duboff and Herman 1980; Perrow 1981). Chandler argued that far-sighted managers seeking efficient solutions to technologically induced problems of coordination should take the credit. Others have argued that the capitalists who destroyed markets to ensure monopoly profits should take the blame.

I will argue that the characterization of a shift from a market economy to an administered economy describes the rhetoric of economic theory more than the actual operation of the system. "The Market" was an effective ideological symbol and a convenient social construct to enable businessmen to make sense of their economic environment. But the social arrangements that governed American industry could only vaguely be described as a market. American businessmen have always been aware that they share common interests at least as much as they compete over conflicting interests. Moreover, they have rarely been what Granovetter (1985) describes as "undersocialized" utility maximizers, the atomistic, disconnected, homo economici. The social arrangements that characterize the relationships among the individuals and enterprises in those communities influence economic behavior at least as much as impersonal utilitarian decision making. Some relationships have been very tight, others very loose; some have been dominated by one or two individuals or firms, others have been more egalitarian; some have monitored the activities of participants closely, others have been more casual. Dynamics usually described as market dynamics are often present, and rarely entirely absent. Of course, people do pay attention to the prices that others are charging, they do sometimes seek to win customers away from others, they do raise and lower prices according to supply and demand. Enterprises unable to offer the kind of quality offered by others at a similar price do sometimes fail entirely. But those dynamics are only part of any governance structure. How much they fully characterize any industry is highly variable (Campbell, Hollingsworth, and Lindberg 1991).

The degree to which economies and industries within economies vary between competition and cooperation is due not only to institutional factors that undermine the operation of markets, but also to the systematic structuring of interests, that is, the contradiction between the interests that businessmen have in common and those in which they conflict. Concerning state powers, all capitalists have common political interests: political stability, a sound currency, and property rights that maximize their authority to manage and to appropriate profits. They are most likely to be aware of their common interests when class conflict is most intense (and it is possible that class conflict is most intense when they are especially aware of their common interests). The world economy has historically been organized into national economies in which the nation-state has raised tariff walls and subsidized the development of businessmen within their territorial boundaries, giving the businesses within each national boundary common economic interests vis-à-vis other national businesses. Similarly, businessmen in a particular industry share common interests relative to suppliers and customers; the competitive "game" in material and product markets is rarely zero-sum, so they often have more to gain by cooperating than competing. Chandler's thesis about how the "visible hand" of management has replaced Adam Smith's "invisible hand" of the market in coordinating the production and distribution of commodities emphasizes the gains to the system more than to any particular group, but he does acknowledge the costs of "unbridled" competition to businesses and agrees that the attempts of businessmen to form pools, cartels, and trusts was a rational response. Some economists, invidiously comparing our "managerial capitalism" with Japan's "collective capitalism" (Lazonick 1993), are now acknowledging that the enforced competition in the American economy has contributed to economic stagnation. While interests were systematically structured in this way, to the extent that the economy was governed by market dynamics, these interests do not explain the degree to which markets prevailed. It is overall governance of the economy that must be explained, not just the ways in which businessmen interact in the context of some assumed market.

The treatment of markets as a continuous variable rather than a dichotomy is, of course, hardly novel. There is a voluminous literature seeking to explain how concentrated or competitive industries are. The single dimension of market/concentration is important but by no means captures the widely varying sets of practices and relationships that underlie the operation of economic systems and theorizes only one alternative to markets—monopolies. The market/concentration dimension misses many alternatives to markets besides monopolies (Powell 1990; Campbell, Hollingsworth, and Lindberg 1991). Moreover, the conventional economic model assumes that the market/concentration dimension is also a natural/unnatural dimension, that markets are natural and anything else artificial. This chapter mirrors the emphasis in recent economic sociology that markets are no more "natural" than any other economic set of relations (White 1981; Baker 1990; Granovetter 1985). Insofar as market dynamics have governed economic relationships, they have been actively created and reproduced by explicit and intentional government regulation, especially through property and contract law. I will thus analyze how American industrialists, interacting with one another in the context of legal structures that permitted some relationships while prohibiting others, struggled to minimize the intrusion of market dynamics into their affairs.

During the 1870s and 1880s, market dynamics threatened several industries that had been organized in a number of regimes. As the contemporaries constantly complained and recent analyses have frequently validated, "ruinous competition" threatened to drive respectable businessmen into bankruptcy. Many devices were tried to contain the competition and reestablish industrial peace. But what most conventional accounts miss is that "industrial peace" in most cases did not mean returning to governance by market. The image in most conventional accounts is that a smoothly operating equilibrated Smithian market of small firms selling to small firms and consumers was disrupted by overproduction brought on by technological change. Technological change not only reduced the unit cost of production, but also increased the amount of fixed capital so that when demand fell below supply, firms could not cease production and wait for better times; they had to sell below cost to salvage whatever income was possible. I agree that technological change did have that effect in several important industries, but the problem with the conventional picture is the "before" account. Fully self-regulating markets were rare. Most industry was organized in local or regional communities that effectively prevented market dynamics from consistently undermining collective interests. During the 1870s and 1880s a number of factors coincided to undermine the local and regional manufacturing communities. The railroad made long-distance transportation cheaper and quicker; the national currency introduced during the Civil War made mercantile relations between states easier; the Civil War had enabled companies to expand far beyond the rest of industry; new technologies made it possible to produce large quantities with lower unit costs; new marketing strategies based on widespread advertising created brand loyalties for the first time; and new products were introduced that had no governance structure at all. But in most cases it was not that exogenous forces destabilized existing markets. The cartels, trusts, syndicates, and eventually corporations that businessmen tried were not intended to preserve markets; they were defenses against markets. The deviants who acted like Smith's atomistic maximizers were the threat. It was not unscrupulous rogues who threatened the orderly market, but the "undersocialized" utility maximizers who threatened the social administration of industrial affairs that precipitated the search for new modes of control. It is important to stress that these disruptive competitors were no more "natural" than other businessmen who sought to maximize their interests through cooperation. Andrew Carnegie, who consistently violated pooling agreements to drive his competitors out of business, was no more "natural" or "rational" than Albert Fink, who spent his career organizing and administering railroad pools to keep the average rate tariffs high for all companies in the industry.

My account of competition and merger in the late nineteenth century differs from that of efficiency theory in two respects. First, while I agree that technology was an important factor in many cases, I argue that both the causes and the effects of technology were refracted through the social relations within the industry and with other parts of the economy. For example, the American Tobacco Company, as discussed in the next chapter, not only was a response to dramatically enhanced economies of scale created by the Bonsack cigarette-making machine, but also depended on its monopsony with the company that made the machine along with its control and shutting down of competing machines. Second, like most economic sociologists, I treat the market not as an exogenous factor, but as itself a set of relationships constructed by participants and others, especially government. Instead of treating the market as a natural development that historically requires no explanation, the degree to which market dynamics characterize economic relations must be explained.

The conventional view of this period is also misleading insofar as it describes a stable economy disrupted by forces that stimulated innovations like cartels, syndicates, price fixing, and other cooperative activities. In the first place there was no stability in the economy. The American economy has always been dynamic. The first half of the century had seen handicraft industry replaced by factories, the development of turnpikes, canals, and later railroads that made regional trade possible, and the early industrial revolution that made cloth, shoes, soap, and other household items available to most households. If there was any single disruptive event during the century, it was the Civil War, which not only ruptured the national economy between North and South, but also created a national currency, fostered the centralization of production in large companies, spurred technologies to standardize production, ignited widespread population migrations, and decimated a shocking proportion of the labor force. Not only was there no equilibrium to disrupt, but the practices commonly cited as attempts to restore equilibrium were hardly novel. What was new was that price fixing, pooling, cartels, and eventually corporations were being organized on a national level, not just local and regional.[1]

While the events and practices were not new, the intensity and degree of threat to control were. As is well known, competition became more than inconvenient. It became ruinous. The old mechanisms of protecting industrial communities from the market failed. The manufacturers not only lost collective control of the industry governance; many of them lost individual control of their own enterprises. After trying many solutions, the only legal recourse seemed to be surrendering their companies to the collectivity, forming trusts and holding companies. Once that was done, many of them lost control of the collectivity, the corporation, to financiers.

The other factor neglected by most conventional accounts is the role of the state. In the usual image, the state responded to the effects of technological change and eroding markets, helping preserve markets (though inadvertently spurring tight combinations rather than loose ones), eventually validating while regulating the giant new corporations. The state was more than a bystander, legitimizer, or regulator, but was a constituent part of the corporate revolution. The state actively molded the economy by permitting some sorts of economic relationships and prohibiting others. State activity was just as important for market relations as collective activities, just as important for contracts among individuals as for corporations. As elaborated below, businessmen turned to the state for help in governing their relations with one another, but political events and the balance of power steered the American state down the historical path of judicially enforced markets and corporate property.

Although my emphasis is on structural factors, some of businessmen's actions at the end of the century—especially the nonrational pursuit of monopoly where it did not serve their interests—can be explained in no terms other than ideological. Only an ideology of monopoly can explain why some industrialists and financiers unnecessarily spent fortunes to underprice and buy out obviously unthreatening competitors. Monopolists and antimonopolists ironically shared the same model of the economy, but drew a different moral conclusion. Both assumed that total dominance of an industry was necessary for high profits and that monopoly was most effectively attained and preserved by nipping competition in the bud, even if one had to lose money to weaken upstarts and then pay exorbitant prices to buy them out. Neither realized that oligopoly could be both stable and prosperous. The *Wall Street Journal,* for example, editorialized in 1890 that it was "Bullish on Industrials," citing the high profits of the electrical, cordage, sugar, and distillery trusts and acknowledging that active legislation against those companies had "shaped them into permanently an attractive and legitimate form, while in no way reducing their efficiency" (4 [21]: 2).[2] While it would have been impolitic to publicly advocate monopoly, businessmen frequently decried competition as ruinous, with no guides to distinguish between healthy and ruinous competition. Gilbert H. Montague argued against the Sherman Antitrust Act: "Large business, and the temporal triumph over competition which it implies, is the crown of competition" (Montague 1910, 7). The same sentiment was expressed by government officials responsible for regulating monopoly. For example, Attorney General Wickersham defended the decision not to break the American Tobacco Company into small companies after its antitrust conviction, saying monopoly was preferable to "the general demoralization of business which would ensue were the business to be distributed between a large number of weak organizations with insufficient capital to maintain themselves in active competition" (quoted in Tennant 1950, 65). While businessmen often publicly justified their success in terms of efficiencies engendered by economies of scale, they often acted as if they didn't believe it.

Since the Progressive era, pools, cartels, and other strategies to collectively control prices have been discussed more for what they were not than for what they were. From the perspective of the idealized venerated market, they were immoral and unnatural. The language of economics, law, and morality have combined to paint a picture of acquisitive entrepreneurs defying the laws of nature and government to conspire against the defenseless consumer. The resolution creating a special committee of the New York legislature in 1897, for instance, gave as part of its justification the warning that "combinations of capital in the form of trusts or otherwise appear to exist and to be increasing in number and influence in this commonwealth, resulting in concentrating in the hands of a few, various important branches of industry, creating monopolies, shutting out competition, displacing labor and driving the citizen of moderate means out of business, with the effect that production and price are regulated not by the natural laws of supply and demand or the rules of normal and healthy competition, but by the arbitrary decision of combinations operating together to destroy competition and exact unreasonable charges from the people" (New York Legislature 1897, 3). Of course, pools had their supporters, especially among academic economists. John B. Clark, writing in the *Political Science Quarterly* in 1887, wrote, "Combinations have their roots in the nature of social industry and are normal in their origin, their development, and their practical working. They are neither to be deprecated by scientists nor suppressed by legislators. They are the result of an evolution, and are the happy outcome of a competition so abnormal that the continuance of it would have meant widespread ruin" (Clark 1887, 55). He thus reflected an equally pervasive sentiment that defined competition, not pools, as the evil. Ripley echoed the same belief almost two decades later: "The pool is probably the oldest, the most common and at the same time the most popular, mode of obviating the evils of competition" (Ripley 1905, xiii).

Chandler has helped us move beyond the moralistic treatment of pools and trusts to raise the question of why they arose and what consequences they had. As in his analysis in general, the two major factors he cites are markets and technology—markets in the form of falling prices and technology in the form of rapid expansion of output, which together squeezed businessmen into ruinous forms of competition and drove them to seek relief by controlling prices and output. But they had two serious problems: pools were not enforceable and, more important for Chandler, they did not allow any control of the internal operation of firms, only the price and output. Tight combinations were a solution to both; the holding company was legalized and provided a means of rationalizing production. So the process of controlling prices and output shifted from the invisible hand of the market to the visible hand of the firm (Chandler 1977, 318–319). However, Chandler's account is logically flawed. Rationalization was not a solution for the problems that Chandler identifies. Falling prices and overproduction did not dictate further rationalization within firms. In fact, rationalization was more likely to be a cause of increased output, which should have exacerbated the problem unless control of the market was achieved. The problem that pools were responding to was how to govern the industry, not how to organize the firm internally. My account also differs from his in that he does not problematize why enforcement of pools and cartels was illegal or whether it could have been different. He sees nonenforceability as a characteristic of the pool rather than of the state. But the most important difference between our interpretations of pools and cartels is that while he attributes them to a breakdown in an efficient market system, I argue that they were a defense against the intrusion of the market into socially embedded governance mechanisms in the industries where they were formed.

The importance of pools has been discounted by treating them merely as a transition from an economy of markets to one of hierarchies. Since they were neither the fish of markets nor the fowl of hierarchies, they are not accorded a respectable analytical status, but are only interpreted as evidence of market breakdown. The point usually made when pools, cartels, and other devices are discussed is that "ruinous competition" was destroying what is assumed to have been a stable market. For example, Ripley (1905) wrote that pools and trusts were important because they foreshadowed the future. Similarly for Chandler, they were a mere layover on the road to the holding company. But they were more than a transition and they were more than just a deviation from the market. They were a very common device to govern an industry to achieve stability, and they reflected the social relations among the businessmen producing a product as much as their individual motivations or moral outlook. Pools and trusts became a public issue only when the economy became nationalized, eroding the local and regional arrangements. In the 1870s and 1880s, businessmen in many industries attempted to create on a national scale a practice that lacked the social preconditions they had enjoyed on the local and regional level. Without the tight social organization they had there and without the legal support that might have substituted, competition did become ruinous for many industries.

While it is common to think of devices to control prices as a form of economic deviance, the sheer number of such devices, especially at the local and regional level, indicates that they may have been the norm rather than the exception. Local and regional markets were rarely comprised of atomistic producers facing an impersonal market of equally atomistic consumers. Rather, there existed a wide variety of governance regimes with varying degrees of market dynamics. But in many places and in many industries, the men who produced and often those who consumed products knew one another, socialized with one another, married into one another's families, worshiped together, and felt themselves part of a common industrial culture. Shoe men, textile men, cordage men, paper men, barrel men, and iron men (with few women in any group) were bounded and self-conscious social groups. Although they did compete with one another, they were also aware that their adversaries were just as often the common foes of undependable suppliers, untrustworthy and insubordinate workers, or fraudulent and irresponsible consumers. Even the discipline of the market could be mitigated. Many a bankruptcy was prevented or postponed by other manufacturers offering a loan, letting a factory building, and even steering customers to a troubled colleague (Scranton 1989). This is not to romanticize the harsh realities of doing business in a developing economy. Certainly bankruptcies, predatory raids, and the stealing of customers abounded, but they were no more typical than the tight social circles of producers. Altogether, the market was more an abstract moral principle than a description of the economy. The choice of what to produce and what price to charge was governed at least as much by the dynamics of social cooperation as by the impersonal laws of supply and demand. In other words, the visible hand, not of hierarchy but of shared governance, as much as the invisible hand of the market, orchestrated the economy.

THE POOL

The pool is one of the oldest, most common, and most popular modes of obviating the evils of competition (Ripley 1905). A pool is a way of socializing control over an industry's collective output. Producers agree to collectively set output levels and prices, sometimes turning over their product to a central distributing organization, at other times paying a fee to a coordinating agency that fines any firm that deviates from the collective agreement. However, if the contributions that firms make to the collective fund are less than the profit from violating the output and price agreements, pools are very difficult to sustain unless governments are willing to enforce the contracts that constitute them. Although this seemingly inherent weakness is often pointed out, industrial pools have appeared at every stage of economic growth since the Civil War. They were not even eliminated by gigantic mergers like that of U.S. Steel, which continued to participate in pooling arrangements with independent producers (Ripley 1905). As governments have become more hostile to them, they have become less frequent and more secretive, but they have not disappeared.

The analytical importance of pools in understanding the rise of the large industrial corporation is what they reveal about the interaction of law and social relations among businessmen. Any decisions they make regarding the market are refracted through the rights, entitlements, and responsibilities that the law enforces as well as the history of cooperation, trust, and loyalty to others in the industry. The agreements to surrender autonomy over prices and output that constitute pools are more than impersonal business decisions in the face of objective conditions. Although they are often treated as a form of deviance, they deviated more from an ideal that never existed than from the business practices of the mid- to late-nineteenth century. And while they are often treated as inherently unstable because of their lack of enforcement, they are inherently no more unstable than other contracts. Any contract is a restraint of trade because it restricts the buyer or seller from making the same deal with other sellers or buyers, even if a better price or product could be found. So the law was making distinctions about the types of relationships that could be enforced in contracts. In legal terms, partial restraint of trade was permitted but general restraint of trade was not. But it was only toward the end of the nineteenth century that pools and cartels were interpreted to be general restraints of trade. It was a change in the law as much as a change in economic behavior that accounted for the criminalization of pools and the subsequent search for other forms of industrial governance. The state was increasingly imposing its own definition of what was "natural" onto the economy, not a definition derived from businessmen's behavior in the absence of government interference, but a justification for interference based on an ideal of how they should act (Hovenkamp 1991).

Most accounts, including Chandler (1977), remark about how commonplace pools and cartels were in the latter nineteenth century. One of the earliest national pools was organized by the cordage industry about 1860. In the seventies and eighties, pools were as diverse as the Associated Pipe Works (cast iron pipes), Steel Rail Pool, Gunpowder Manufacturers' Association, Kentucky Distilleries' Association, Wall Paper Association, Sand Paper Association, Upholsterers' Felt Association, and Standard Envelope Company. The formal names indicate the public, unabashed nature of these organizations. The Michigan Salt Association was typical of these early pools that attempted to govern industry and illustrates the interaction of law and industrial governance. Michigan produced 40 percent of the national salt output and dominated markets west of Pennsylvania. In 1859 the state of Michigan exempted salt from all property tax and paid a bounty of 10¢ per bushel on all salt made in the state. The Saginaw Salt Manufacturing Company was incorporated in that year to dig a well and manufacture the product. Production in the Saginaw Valley increased rapidly and by 1862, there were sixty-six companies with a combined capital of $2 million. After the war ended in 1865 several companies failed and production fell somewhat, spurring them to formalize cooperation. In 1868 the Saginaw and Bay Salt Company (SBSC) was founded, a pool that handled four-fifths of the region's salt. It was basically a sales company, which standardized the product, inspected output, and ensured a dependable, quality commodity. It ran smoothly until 1871, when a personality conflict between some manufacturers and the management of SBSC destroyed the company. Competition increased, prices declined, and some companies failed. In 1876, J. E. Shaw, president of the Michigan Salt Association, called a meeting to coordinate the manufacturers' affairs, summarizing their experience: "Organized we have prospered. Unorganized we have not" (quoted in Jenks 1888, 83–84). The problem, he said, lay in marketing. The Saginaw Salt Company and the Michigan Salt Association were combined into a new Michigan Salt Association, a pool organized as a legitimately chartered corporation, with a capital stock of $200,000, divided into $25 shares. According to the by-laws, the shareholders were salt manufacturers with shares based on each company's output. A contract was made every year with each manufacturer to deliver all output to the association, or to lease all property to it. Any company that sold salt on its own account was required to pay the association 10¢ per barrel. On the state level, it worked well, but as manufacturers began to compete with producers from other states, governance became more difficult. When the Michigan pool raised prices too high, it invited new companies to form and manufacturers from other states to enter its markets. For example, in 1886, competition increased, with 600,000 barrels of Michigan salt sold by nonassociation members. The association lowered its price to meet the competition and by the end of the year most of the outsiders joined, at which time the price increased somewhat. Thus prices were not low, but according to Jenks (1888), not exorbitant. Moreover, they were generally declining, falling from $1.80 per barrel in 1866 to $.57½ in 1877.

Michigan was not the only state where salt manufacturers worked together. Thirty salt dealers and manufacturers in the salt-rich Muskingum and Hocking valleys formed the Central Ohio Salt Company to regulate prices and sustain quality. All salt made or owned by members of this voluntary association became the property of the company. The members were to continue to do business as before, except that sales and prices were to be controlled by the company. But as was typical of pools, enforcement was problematic. The company sued one of the manufacturers for violating the agreement by failing to deliver some of his salt. At issue was the kind of rights and responsibilities of production and distribution that the state would enforce. From the company's point of view, the manufacturer had violated a contract. So it turned to the state, which is generally responsible for enforcing contracts. The manufacturer defended himself by a common defense when contracts are violated, disputing the state's authority to enforce his responsibility to live up to the contract he had signed, claiming the agreement was illegal. The court ruled that agreements among manufacturers to employ common marketing arrangements were a general constraint on trade: "That all contracts in partial restraint of trade are not void as against public policy is too well settled to be gainsaid; while, on the other hand, it is fully established, as a general rule, that contracts in general restraint of trade are against public policy and, therefore, absolutely void" (*Central Ohio Salt Co. v. Stephen H. Guthrie* 1880 [35 O. St., 666], quoted in U.S. Industrial Commission 1900b, 205). Since public policy favors competition, the state refused to enforce the contract.

This case illustrates the pools' changing legal status. The fact that the pool would overtly form itself as a company and go to court to enforce the contract indicates that it had a reasonable expectation that the contract would be upheld. Moreover, the court drew the distinction between partial and general restraint of trade. Only the latter was considered illegal. But the distinction between partial and general restraint was vague.[3] The defendant had to establish that this case was one of general restraint. Thus what made this contract illegal was its multilateral social character. Even though a dyadic contract between a single manufacturer and distributor just as effectively prevented the manufacturer from selling the product to a higher bidder, thus restraining his trade, states vigorously enforced such contracts. But if all the manufacturers signed contracts with a single distributor, states generally refused to enforce them, defining them as a general restraint of trade. So multilateral relationships based on market cooperation were voided in the same jurisdictions that later permitted multilateral relationships based on ownership. The state was in the process of specifying the rights, entitlements, and responsibilities it would enforce.

Just as associations could sue members for noncompliance, members could take associations to court for failing to fulfill their side of the contract. In 1880 an unincorporated company, the Candle Manufacturers' Association, was formed to distribute 95 percent of the candles east of Utah. The members were required to pay 2.5 cents per pound on all candles sold in that territory. Each company then received compensation based on its former share of the trade, even if it produced nothing. The Ohio Candle Company joined in 1883, withdrew the next year, and then sued for the $2,000 that the association owed it in back profits. The association defended itself on the grounds that by withdrawing, the company had violated the agreement to participate over the life of the contract. The court ruled that the contract was contrary to public policy and therefore not enforceable (*Emery et al. v. The Ohio Candle Co.* 1890 [47 O. St., 320], discussed in Davies 1916). What made this case notable was that neither plaintiff nor defendant had questioned the legality of pooling output and fixing prices. The Ohio court autonomously and proactively judged the content of the contract illegal, taking the question of the fairness of the contract outside of the two parties making the contract and ruling that parties outside the contract had an interest. In effect, the court was saying that the state would not permit the industry to govern itself through contracts with an otherwise legal company. Manufacturers could not collectively integrate forward by using contracts. The state would compel them to compete, because, it said, markets were natural.

The state similarly asserted its prerogative to define whether contracts were legitimate in a case involving a pool among the white lead manufacturers (*McBirney & Johnston White Lead Co. v. Consolidated White Lead Co.* 8 Ohio Decisions reprint, 762 [1883]). The manufacturers of white lead west of Buffalo formed a corporation, with stock apportioned to the manufacturers on the basis of previous output. They agreed, but did not establish by contract, that each member could produce white lead proportionate to this same portion and no more. They still sold their own products, but at prices fixed by the corporation. Members failing to sell as much as they were entitled turned over their surplus for the average price they received from others. Members disposing of more than their allotted proportion would receive from the corporation the amount turned in by unsuccessful dealers. The suit was an ordinary dispute between the plaintiff and defendant over the price for lead turned in. But the court found that the agreement was entered into for the purpose of controlling and restricting manufacture and controlling prices so that they should not fall below a certain figure. It thereby held that the contract, being an essential part of an unlawful scheme, could not be enforced. (Davies 1916, 48–49). Thus courts increasingly declared that the state had an interest in actively creating markets. They would dictate what was "natural," with "natural" defined in terms of preconceived notions of what businessmen should do, not in terms of how they acted when free from government interference. Government "interference" was thus actively shaping markets, not just permitting them.

Other formal pools and cartels were a reaction to a breakdown in more informal means of controlling prices and achieving stability. For example, before 1873, wallpaper manufacturers had made simple agreements to maintain scheduled prices without any need for enforcement or penalty provisions. The panic of 1873 depressed prices and precipitated a breakdown in the manufacturers' agreement, allowing market forces to temporarily govern the industry. In 1880 they formed the American Wall Paper Manufacturers' Association, a "modified profits" pool. A schedule of prices was agreed upon and each manufacturer deposited a sum with the association to ensure good faith. They calculated how much profit each manufacturer should make on the basis of his capital investment. If the profits of any manufacturer fell below this amount, the other establishments were assessed on the basis of what they might have earned above the estimated amount, and the money was turned over to the manufacturers who earned less. But the pool did not last long. A number of manufacturers sold below the schedule prices, and when the imposition of fines failed to stop the practice, the association was dissolved in 1888 (Carlson 1931, 70–71; U.S. Industrial Commission 1902, 13:282–283).

Prices were not, of course, the only object of cooperation. In competitive markets, one would expect firms to closely guard and protect any technological advantages over competitors. Patents in fact are one of the few monopolies that the law routinely protects, giving producers an exclusive right to use or license new technical knowledge. However, the degree of exclusivity or sharing of technological information is quite variable. Patents have been used to create and sustain monopolies, not only by using new techniques, but also by purchasing potentially competitive technologies. For example, the American Tobacco Company not only controlled the patent for the highly productive Bonsack cigarette-making machine, but also bought the patent for competing machines (Jacobstein 1907; Jones 1929). But in other industries, especially on the local and regional level, technology was more shared, occasionally altruistically (Scranton 1989) and at other times as a means of control. Pooling patents under common control could be used to help govern industries by providing a weapon to discipline businesses that deviated from agreed-upon prices or a means by which a dominant firm could police the rest of the industry. The "Great Sewing Machine Combination" was the first national patent pool (Hounshell 1984). Elias Howe received a fee for every sewing machine produced with his patented grooved, eye-pointed needle used in conjunction with a lock-stitch forming shuttle. Similarly, as early as 1869, manufacturers formed a patent pool in paper bags. Union Bag Machine Company was created to fix prices and allocate territory, enforced by controlling all manufacturing patents, which were then leased back to constituent companies. Each company paid 4¢ royalty to the Machine Company on every one thousand bags manufactured, money that was used to buy and contest patents (Carlson 1931). Patents were thus a mechanism by which governments unwittingly enforced centralized industrial governance regimes.

Although the Union Bag Machine Company did not evolve into a major corporation, other new industries that were eventually dominated by large corporations could trace their roots back to early patent pools. Charles Goodyear, long before anyone could imagine the blimp that bears his name, had the original rubber patent. In 1843 he transferred the patent to Leverett Candee of New Haven, Connecticut. In 1848 the six companies licensed to make rubber shoes under the patent formed a voluntary association, the Goodyear Associates and Licensees, and agreed to pay 3.5 cents per pair of

shoes into a common fund which could be used to prosecute patent infring-
ers, in addition to a half-cent royalty. They also agreed on minimum prices
and maximum discounts and decided to meet annually to set prices. This
patent pool was not a device to keep new companies out of the industry, but
only to govern prices and production. Through the 1850s the industry was
governed by eight large companies. At one point a committee representing
all companies recommended forming a company to buy all the companies,
purchase the Goodyear patents, and eliminate duplicate products. They estimated that they would double their profits to about 80 percent a year. The
organizers reported, "We should then have in reality what we now have but
in name, one interest and no competition" (quoted in Babcock 1966, 23).
However, they did not carry through the idea, but only continued to issue
an annual list of prices. When the patents expired in 1865, the manufacturers created a pool that governed by assessing severe cash fines for deviating
from the set prices, a structure by which the Associated Rubber Shoe Companies successfully maintained prices for more than two decades, illustrat-
ing that not all pools quickly failed. In 1892 these companies completed the
merger they had contemplated four decades earlier and combined into the
U.S. Rubber Company (Babcock 1966). If there was any equilibrium in this
industry, in the sense that disequilibrium provoked actions to reestablish
the status quo, it would be cooperation rather than free markets.

Because the social management of manufacturing industries was not de-
viant, the participants did not act furtively or deviously. Setting prices was
overt and public. Trade journals, ordinary newspapers, association minutes, and other public activities openly and unabashedly discussed price setting. In the 1870s, the Articles of Association of the Gunpowder Trade
Association of the United States forthrightly announced, "This Association
shall meet quarterly . . . for the purpose of establishing prices if need be, of
hearing and deciding appeals, and determining all questions relative to the
trade that may be submitted to it" (Stevens 1913, 2–3). Another leading
industry journal, the highly circulated *Iron Age,* in 1880 noted, "The manufacturers of Augers and Bits held a meeting in this city [New York] to-day,
at which the price of Augers and Bits was advanced to discount 40 per cent.,
instead of 40 and 10 per cent, as formerly, and Hollow Augers were advanced to discount 15 per cent., formerly discount 20 per cent. . . . At a
meeting of the American Ax Manufacturers' Association, held at the Astor
House, New York, February 40, 1880, the price of Axes was fixed as follows: 4½ to 5½ lbs. and under, $11 per dozen, net; 4½ to 6 lbs. and over,
$11.50 per dozen, net; Beveled, 50 cents advance per doz., respectively"
(Feb. 5, 1880, 25:6). Prices of specific companies were listed. Even as late as
1888, when national pools were condemned by legislation, court decisions,
and newspaper editorials, old practices continued. The *Proceedings* of the
Kentucky Distillers' annual meeting in Louisville noted that the members
had "Determine[d] the quantity of whisky to be made in 1889. On this
point 11,000,000 is recommended as the maximum" and then listed the

number of gallons each member of the pool was authorized to produce during the year. Whether or not the pooling was effective, it was overt and normal, not the act of capitalist miscreants.

By the end of the 1880s, especially as national pools and trusts were publicized, the moral and legal climate changed dramatically. The rights, entitlements, and responsibilities the government had enforced among the members of an industry changed. Since that period, it has frequently been pointed out that pools and cartels failed to stabilize prices and tended to quickly dissolve because they were not legally enforceable (Keasbey 1899a, b; U.S. Industrial Commission 1900a, b; Ripley 1905; Stevens 1913; Seager and Gulick 1929; Hurst 1970; Chandler 1977; Hannah 1979). These accounts contrast the legal response to these agreements with more "natural" market mechanisms. However, there is nothing more unnatural about these transactions than those conforming with the socially constructed image of what a market should be. If governments did not enforce contracts between buyers and sellers, markets would collapse by the same sort of opportunism that wrecked the pools. Contracts for promises to deliver goods or pay for goods delivered would be at least as tantalizing to break without external enforcement mechanisms as contracts to follow a collectively mandated level of production or price. It is difficult to imagine that markets could operate without some external coercive force to prevent buyers and sellers from opportunistically breaking promises normally embodied in contracts. Markets can exist only when governments actively decide that markets constitute an industrial governance structure preferable to other means (Polanyi 1957). To label contracts between producers and retailers as "natural" but label equally voluntary contracts among producers or between producers and a single wholesaler as "unnatural" must be recognized as an ideological statement of preference, not a statement of fact. I do not deny that contracts between producers and retailers are socially or legally equivalent to contracts among producers. American law has made this distinction a fundamental tenet of antitrust law. But the justification of this distinction on the basis of natural or unnatural markets is the issue. To treat the market as "natural" relieves the analyst from having to explain it; one must only explain deviations from the market. The businessmen of the time seem to have felt that they were acting in accordance with the laws of nature and that the state would enforce those laws. When businessmen could no longer trust "gentlemen's agreements" on prices and output, they created various forms of contracts for enforcement, contracts between producers, or contracts with selling agencies, contracts they expected to be enforced by the power of law. It is significant that many of the celebrated cases that outlawed pools, cartels, and price fixing, that eventually left holding companies and consolidation as the only enforceable mechanisms of industrywide governance, were initiated by parties in the agreements. Some were instigated by state officials, but many involved litigation among the participants, who were confident enough in the legality of what they were doing to present the matter to the courts. Moreover, many of these cases were the precedents for later decisions—they were creating new law. That is not to say that anti-competitive contracts had confidently enjoyed the unequivocal force of law before that, but there was enough ambiguity that it was not unreasonable to expect that breaches of contracts would be condemned by the law.

It was not just the courts, of course, that were actively attempting to enforce market mechanisms upon American industry. Legislatures at both the state and the federal level were passing antitrust laws to prevent manufacturers from governing themselves by nonmarket mechanisms. However, the political system interacted with the economic system in two ways that undermined these attempts and had the effect of accelerating the corporate revolution. In the first place, states were powerless to influence enterprise beyond their own borders, and many states were vulnerable to competition from other states' more permissive corporate law. In several states, the issue became defined as a choice between economic development within their states or the principles which would have demanded that corporations sustain greater public accountability. By the end of the century, states were rarely using the powers they had through corporate law and through the regulation of foreign corporations operating within their border. Second, courts, especially federal courts, were interpreting federal law to apply only to the regulation of interstate commerce, that is, market relations, not to issues of property or production (McCurdy 1978b, 1979).

Although many jurists felt that the common law was a satisfactory weapon to fight the increasing number of large-scale pools and trusts, legislators still passed laws, sometimes to give the common law a stronger punch and sometimes to demonstrate their dedication to a competitive economy. Some states—Illinois (1891), Ohio (1898), Massachusetts (1903), Florida (1907), Colorado (1911), and Texas (1911) were among the more rigorous—explicitly decreed that violation of antitrust laws could be grounds for revocation of a corporate charter, although the ultra vires principle that corporations could only act in ways that they were explicitly empowered to act could probably have provided ample legal justification to revoke the charters of unlawful companies without legislative justification.

At the same time the national government, through the courts and through legislation, was intentionally attempting to undermine the social relationships among manufacturers. Whether such a policy was constructive or destructive for business or for consumers is less important here than the consequence that the policy had on the development of the American business structure. Businessmen and their lawyers set about to find the legal means to organize themselves or to change laws by legislative and judicial action. They eventually found that the corporation offered a set of property relations that the government itself had created to supersede the limitations of individual ownership. Manufacturers had increasingly used the corporate form to organize their businesses, but without drastically changing their property relations. The corporate form as it existed before the late

1880s did not provide the means for stabilizing governance within industries. The manufacturing corporation was already widespread in the 1880s and in public discourse often equated with "trusts." But since manufacturing firms were rarely part of the institutional structure of the large publicly traded corporations based on financial capital, the legal form of the corporation was used for several kinds of property regimes, including entrepreneurships, industrial trusts, and occasionally experiments like profit sharing. It was only when other means of organizing their industries were prohibited that they began to use corporate structures in a way that ironically reflected the original conception of corporations as supracompetitive, socially owned, financially capitalized, large-scale enterprises. To get a fuller picture of the economic landscape on the eve of the corporate revolution we need to explore the nature and the scope of all industrial corporations—not just large ones—at that time.

THE ORGANIZATION OF ENTREPRENEURIAL INDUSTRY

Most industrial corporations before 1890 (as they are today) were still essentially entrepreneurships, owned by individuals or families who adopted the legal form for the conveniences it offered such as limited liability, the ease of passing the firm on to heirs, and in some states, tax advantages. But the organization of ownership remained individual or familial rather than social. Small and medium-sized firms generally did not incorporate for the purpose of mobilizing capital, although minority holdings might be sold to friends, associates, and occasionally strangers. Capital was raised primarily through commercial loans, family wealth, or internal accumulation. Altogether in terms of their operation, organization of ownership, and means of raising capital, these corporations were little different from unincorporated proprietorships and partnerships.

An unexceptional manufacturing industry before the corporate revolution, the brewing industry had many of the qualities that efficiency theory suggests would make it a likely industry for large corporations. Prior to the entrance of British capital in the late 1880s, the large American brewing companies were closely held corporations with stock owned by one or two companies and control vested in two or three executives. "Management was strictly a family affair, and problems actually could be settled at the family dinner table" (Cochran 1948, 80). Table 7.1 shows some of its major features.

The industry defined by the census as malt liquor, which was overwhelmingly beer, in 1880 was large, highly productive, and capital intense. The aggregate capital was nearly $100 million, about nine times that of an average industry, or nearly three standard deviations above the mean.[4] Between 1880 and 1900, the industry mushroomed by a factor of more than four, its aggregate capital growing to more than fourteen times the mean of all in-

TABLE 7.1
Economic Characteristics of the Malt Liquor Industry, 1880, 1900

Year		Establishments	Capital (000)	Average Capital / Estab. (000)	Productivity	Capital Intensity
1880	Malt Liquor Industry	2,191	$91,208	$41.6	1.69	7.48
	Standard deviations from the mean of all industries	0.61	2.95	−0.03	1.43	1.91
1900	Malt Liquor Industry	1,507	$413,767	$274.56	4.70	16.05
	Standard deviations from the mean of all industries	0.36	4.87	0.35	2.97	2.16

Source: U.S. Bureau of the Census 1914, 650.

dustries. Its market was clearly large enough to support large corporations. Productivity, operationalized as the total value of product/total number of workers, was well above the mean, as was capital intensity. Both statistics in 1900 were further above the mean than in 1880. By efficiency theory, the industry's productivity and capital intensity should have provided fertile conditions for large corporations. However, a critical structural factor that Chandler generally downplays mitigated these tendencies: the number of establishments in the industry. The social density of ownership[5] was too great for brewers to organize themselves into a cohesive social unit. In 1880 there were over 2,500 separate establishments with an average size just under the mean of all industries, too many owners to effectively govern their industry. By 1900 it was an even stronger candidate for large corporations. Not only had the number of establishments declined by about 40 percent and the average size increased—both absolutely and relative to the mean—but the industry had also concentrated with the rise of nationally sold brands whose companies were building large processing plants and building national distribution networks. Yet even after substantial concentration, malt liquor remained outside the corporate institutional structure and organized in family firms. This can best be explained, not in terms of objective economic characteristics, but in terms of the social ties among its leading owners.

One of the nation's largest brewers in the last quarter of the century was the Phillip Best Brewing Company, led by "Captain" Frederick Pabst, with ownership controlled by the Pabst, Best, and Schandein families, all of whom were active in its management. Emil Schandein, the vice-president, had married Phillip Best's daughter Lisette, bringing Best into the brewing business. When Schandein died in 1888, his widow Lisette took his position as vice-president, which she occupied until 1894, probably the only female major officer of a large brewery. When Best resigned because of ill health in 1890, Pabst appointed Best's son Gustav as secretary. Even when the company expanded by acquiring other firms, it remained out of the orbit of large-scale corporate capital institutions. In 1892 Pabst acquired the property of the Falk, Jung, and Borchert brewery, which had suffered two major fires and was unable to continue on its own. The acquisition enabled Pabst to increase sales by 180,000 barrels in 1893. Although the deal let Ernest Borchert become vice-president and Frank R. Falk treasurer, eroding the family nature of the firm, it remained solidly under the control of "Captain" Pabst.

Contrary to efficiency theory's contention that large corporations were more efficient in processing industries, it was Pabst's autonomy from large-scale corporate institutions that gave him a competitive advantage.[6] The company's singular control structure gave it greater maneuverability and flexibility. "As a result, incorporation and growth produced no bureaucratic red tape to handicap Pabst in competition with smaller partnerships" (Cochran 1948, 83). Another advantage of close control was that there was no demand for steady dividends, freeing profits to be effectively reinvested for growth. The company expanded its net worth from $600,000 in 1873 to $12 million in 1893 without selling any securities or contracting long-term debts. The value of the stock was increased to $2 million in 1884, $4 million in 1889, and $10 million in 1892, in each case by distributing new thousand-dollar shares to the existing stockholders. Growth was financed through stable social/financial ties. In contrast to corporations that borrow to expand and use cash for operation, Pabst tended to avoid tying up cash in working capital and borrowed for most of its operating funds, a policy viable primarily due to close relationships with the Second Ward Saving Bank (SWSB) and the Wisconsin Marine and Fire Insurance Company. From 1866 to 1894, the president of the Second Ward Saving Bank was a brewing competitor, Valentine Blatz. As in many industries, manufacturers often assisted one another. Pabst's relationship with his fellow brewer became a positive social tie rather than an impediment. Pabst himself was a bank director from 1869 to his death in 1904. By the 1890s loans were running as high as $1 million during the spring season, when brewers were busiest. The strength of the social ties worked in both directions. When the bank was in trouble, the brewery scaled back its loans and offered its own company notes to help the bank meet eastern obligations (Cochran 1948). Pabst has continued to prosper a century later.

The Anheuser-Busch Brewing Company is now a big-name corporation, but when organized in 1857 E. Anheuser & Company was a typical St. Louis manufacturing enterprise. When it incorporated in 1875 as E. Anheuser Company's Brewing Association , it continued, like most pre–corporate revolution corporations, to operate more like a partnership and remained outside of the corporate infrastructure.[7] One of five St. Louis brewers to incorporate in that year, it was chartered for a twenty-five-year term with 480 shares of $500 par for a total capital of $240,000, making it a solid medium-sized firm. Eberhard Anheuser held 140 shares, Adolphus Busch had 238, Lilly Anheuser Busch 100, and for a taste of profit sharing, the brewmaster Erwin Spraul was given 2 shares. President Anheuser, Vice-President Adolphus Busch, and Spraul were the only directors. Like many partnerships, shares of stock could not be transferred without approval of the board of directors. The new corporation purchased the entire property and assets of the old company and assumed all debts and obligations. In 1879 it changed its name to Anheuser-Busch Brewing Company when Busch took over active management on Anheuser's retirement. In 1895, it renewed its corporate charter for another thirty years. Incorporation had little effect on how it operated or who controlled the firm. The legal form was less consequential than the institutional setting, which in this period remained constant.

In the late 1880s and early 1890s, English capital attempted to penetrate the American brewing industry, exporting to this country the property regime of English brewers, but the close social ties among brewers and the entrepreneurial institutional structure were able to defend against the assault. In contrast to America, brewing was one of England's most highly concentrated and incorporated industries (Keller 1979). Many English investors were favorably inclined toward American brewers, but they shared a general distrust of American industrial securities. In 1891, the *National Corporation Reporter* reprinted an article from the London *Financial Times* defending investment in American brewing companies, a defense against apparent charges of corruption by English-owned breweries in America: "There are to be found all the elements of prosperity and rapid progression, and Americans are most anxious to attract English capital, as they find cash, especially in the west, very scarce and difficult to obtain. Surely men of our own race are better worth trusting than the Spanish races of South America, and I say most emphatically that the ordinary businessman in America is as well worthy of trust as the same class in this country" (1:387). The article went on to explain that the recent problems in American brewing companies had come mostly from overcapitalization by English promoters. Thus English investors, who had invested so heavily in American railroads on the eve of the corporate revolution, were still being persuaded that American industries were sounder investments than those of South America.

But, just as social factors can facilitate cohesion and consolidation, social conflict can undermine fertile economic conditions. At the same time that the English were defending American breweries, several leading Chicago and Milwaukee breweries announced the formation of a brewing combination with close ties to the St. Louis Brewers Association. It was to be known as the Milwaukee and St. Louis Brewers Company Ltd., capitalized at $7.5 million and led by Valentine Blatz. However, the combination ended in litigation when brewers started charging Blatz and others with reneging on promises concerning the amount they would receive for their properties

(*National Corporation Reporter*, Feb. 21, 1891, 1:466, 2:267; May 30, 1891, 267). Several of these companies were bought by English investors anyway, but did not consolidate. Despite an estimated $60 million in English capital (*Iron Age* 1890, 45:641), in contrast to English industry, which had the same technology as American breweries, the American beer industry remained relatively local and medium scale until well into the twentieth century. The contrast highlights the way in which a single industry, holding technology and markets constant, differed because of the social relationships within it.

The contrast between large socially capitalized corporate manufacturing and persisting entrepreneurial business can be seen in another industry that incorporated on a large scale in some places but not others—textiles. Although textiles was the type of standardized article of mass consumption appropriate for the large-scale continuous-process technologies that Chandler sees as the foundation of large-scale corporations, and although the textiles were among the earliest manufacturing corporations, they remained at the periphery of the corporate revolution, especially outside of New England. Scranton (1989) describes how the textile manufacturers of Philadelphia used techniques of flexible production and autonomy from financial control to develop an alternative way of doing business from the corporation-dominated textile manufacturers of New England. The organization of firms in the two regions, producing the same basic product, differed for social reasons. For example, in 1885, John Gay's Sons was founded by John H. Gay and his sons, James and Thomas, and operated the Park Carpet Mills, a mid-sized establishment with 86 power looms. They added 22 more looms in 1887, 22 more in 1889, and built a new mill in 1892, expanding capacity to 160 looms with more than three hundred workers. Then they incorporated, with $300,000 capital, after the period of expansion, a move Scranton characterizes as "defensive" (114), and which seemed to have little effect on their operation. Their production had already been partially integrated as they dyed their own yarns before weaving.

The Philadelphia textile men interpreted the differences between themselves and the New England manufacturers in terms of corporate organization. The *American Wool and Cotton Reporter* wrote in 1907 about Philadelphia: "There are no corporations, as mill corporations are classed up in New England, and there are but few large companies. The [incorporated] companies are practically as closely held as the individual enterprises, and no shares are offered the public. . . . There is a refreshing lack of red tape in the conduct of the business, the proprietors often being found in overalls, running or directing the operations of looms or spindles, and personal knowledge and application to one department are believed by a majority of the manufacturers to be the sole cause of their success. . . . Pay of operatives is higher than ever before, and higher than in many other textile centers. . . . 57 hours is now a standard week's work" (quoted in Scranton 1989, 242).

They also emphasized easy entrance into the industry and the predominance of skilled labor (mostly immigrant, especially English and Irish). Thus even after the corporate revolution a major industry was citing efficiency considerations to justify its choice of an alternative to large corporations, emphasizing that for small firms, incorporation was but a mere formality. Like the brewing industry, a single technology that differed in this country and England because of different social organization, the textile industry exemplifies how a similar technology can be organized in different regions with very different organizational forms.

The open-ended nature of corporate property can be seen in profit sharing, an experiment in which ownership is socialized not exclusively in the capitalist class, but throughout both classes. In the 1880s the notion of profit sharing gained wide currency, primarily as a means of convincing members of the working class that they shared interests with owners. It was especially popular after 1886 and even gained the muted approval of the *National Corporation Reporter,* which reported that one of the large paper companies in Maine was successfully adopting profit sharing. "As the paper mill in question is sagaciously managed on broad views, and is able to earn large dividends, it is safe enough to say that the profit sharing is of that modified kind which is as just to the brains as it is to the muscle of the establishment" (July 1, 1893, 17:465). It was adopted by firms as prominent as Procter and Gamble (Procter and Gamble 1954). None of the plans, however, survived the depression of the 1890s. Then in 1902 U.S. Steel began a widely imitated plan to sell stock to its workers. By 1927, two-and-a-half million wage earners worked in firms with such plans. Although not true profit sharing, these plans were widely hailed in similar terms, calling workers the "real partners of owners" (Rodgers 1978). Without detailed case studies of their operation, it is impossible to establish whether the experiments failed because they were inherently inefficient or because of hostility from suppliers, customers, and lenders. It is clear that neither the legal system of property rights nor the institutional structure of support provided a hospitable environment, in contrast to that of large socially capitalized corporations.

THE 1890s: MANUFACTURERS LOSE CONTROL OF INDUSTRY

When the Sherman Antitrust Act was passed in 1890, it was clear that American industry had changed dramatically. The limp legislation was as much an admission that the changes were irreversible as it was a futile gesture to restore a competitive world that had never existed. The bill merely put businessmen on notice that the federal government was joining state governments in prohibiting manufacturers from governing themselves on their own terms. In the name of preserving markets, industries were being forced to choose between the anarchy idealized as the free market and the new corporate order. The former would have entailed heavy reliance on government activism to preserve the market in an era when laissez-faire ideologies reigned; the latter would have required abandoning any pretense of a market and reorganizing within the institutions theretofore confined to railroad and related corporations. At the same time, the institutions of corporate capitalism, which had long spurned industrial corporations, faced with the prospect of a saturated railroad industry, saw an opportunity for new conquests. Manufacturers, tempted by the prospect of Morgan's millions, made their Faustian bargain. Industrial capital merged with investment capital and sparked the corporate revolution.

Trailblazers are especially important to a historical and institutional approach, in which the causes of early adopters can be quite distinct from that of late adopters. The metaphor of trailblazer is appropriate because the structure built by the early incorporators was a major cause of later incorporation. They not only served as an example, but established networks of interaction that later incorporators tied into. Firms did not incorporate in isolation but became socially and economically linked to a growing institutional structure. One of the main differences in the cause of early and late adopters is that for the late adopters, the existence of the early adopters is a major cause, so the factors that explain the rise of the late adopters differ from those of the early adopters (Tolbert and Zucker 1983). Most of the early large corporations followed a similar scenario: industrialists who were unusually cohesive on the basis of geographical proximity, few firms, or friendship or solidarity from fighting common enemies attempted to govern themselves among themselves through such devices as pools and cartels. These devices usually failed when governments declined to enforce them or prohibited them outright. Often an industry leader emerged who used a combination of the carrot of lucrative buyouts and the stick of predatory competition to induce most of an industry or sector of an industry to join a tighter combination such as a trust or holding company. This leader often acquired the resources for the carrot and stick through networks with the theretofore nonmanufacturing corporate segment. The stories discussed here emphasize the dynamics of power and social relations rather than the technology and adaptation that characterize efficiency theory accounts. The American Cotton Oil Company was not a large powerful industry at the center of the industrial system, but a southern industry processing a byproduct of a major commodity, the cotton seeds that Eli Whitney's famous gin extracted from the bolls. But its Wall Street lawyers instigated a change in New Jersey corporate law that altered the course of economic history. However, it is difficult to effectively rebut efficiency if one cannot control for technology and market factors. The sugar industry demonstrates how different subindustries of the same product yielded different materials, but were organized very differently until the eastern sugar monopoly took control of the western branch. The sugar industry more than cotton oil was the archetype of the first generation of corporate giants, a regionally based industry whose small number of leading industrialists failed to govern themselves by pools or trust, then incorporating as a holding company only to lose control to financiers within two decades. Its huge financial success and its ability to withstand legal challenge created both motive and opportunity for the hundreds of large industrial corporations that followed.

Cottonseed Oil

At the end of the 1880s, the institutional structures of American corporate capitalism and American manufacturing were still quite separate. Wall Street was still the center of railroad and government finance but not of manufacturing. The only industrial stocks listed were closely related to the railroad. The *Wall Street Journal* had no listings of "Industrials" but did have stories on some of the trust certificates that were being traded on the "curb." In 1889, the American Cotton Oil Company was founded as a New Jersey holding company, a pioneering corporation that set the example for the hundreds that were to follow in the next decade or so. American Cotton Oil blazed two important trails, the New Jersey law permitting intercorporate stock ownership and the willingness of investors to purchase the securities of industrials as well as of railroad companies.

The epochal New Jersey holding company law was not developed for any of the great and celebrated companies that come to mind when we think of the corporate revolution, but for the American Cotton Oil Company, a firm that did not produce any fundamental industrial product but crushed cottonseed into oil, cottonseed cake, and a host of minor by-products. It did not dominate any great industrial centers, but owned many plants scattered throughout the South. The cotton oil industry was economically ordinary, hardly a prime candidate to blaze the trail of corporate development, as shown in Table 7.2. In 1880 it had less than $4 million total capital reported to the census, compared with more than $10 million for the average-sized industry. The typical cotton oil plant was slightly larger than the industry as a whole, but its productivity of $783 value added per worker was less than the average. Its capital intensity of $4.38 in capital for every dollar in wages was just above the mean. But it had one consequential feature: it had only 45 establishments, compared with the average 669 for all manufacturing industries.[8] This made it feasible to manage competition. While most industries attempted to limit competition through self-governance, the more separate establishments there were, the more difficult this would be. Nonetheless, in terms of the factors emphasized in efficiency theory, the industry was altogether an unlikely candidate for institutional pathmaker.[9]

Like many other industries in the 1880s cotton oil attempted to govern itself through a trust and was declared illegal in a case that set a precedent for other antitrust legal actions (Larcom 1937). The suit that the state of Louisiana filed against the trust had many of the common features of anti-

TABLE 7.2
Economic Characteristics of the Cotton Oil Industry, 1880, 1900

Year		Establishments	Capital (000)	Average Capital / Estab. (000)	Productivity	Capital Intensity
1880	Cotton Oil Industry	45	$3,862	$85.8	0.78	4.83
	Standard deviations from the mean of all industries	−0.25	−0.23	0.63	−0.29	0.71
1900	Cotton Oil Industry	369	$34,451	$96.4	1.23	10.96
	Standard deviations from the mean of all industries	−0.13	0.06	−0.12	−0.11	1.12

Source: U.S. Bureau of the Census 1914, 663.

trust litigation, charging that the trust was motivated by monopoly, that it restrained the trade of others, that it reduced the price of raw materials, hurting a major industry in the state, and that it hurt consumers by charging high prices. The New Orleans *Times Democrat* articulated popular sentiment: "Louisiana wants no Standard Oil Company to override the law" (April 15, 1887). But the charge that was most serious, and the grounds on which the state sought to ban it, was that it had no legal standing. Because a trust was neither a partnership nor a corporation, the state petitioned that it be declared a fraudulent association with no right to issue certificates of ownership. In other words, it did not conform to any existing institutional structure of property. It "sprang into life as an association under an agreement and by-laws kept to this day a profound secret" (*Times Democrat,* April 15, 1887).

The state's case raised two objections to this lack of legal definition. The first was that there was nothing for the state to communicate with, no one on whom taxes could be levied or to whom charges could be filed. So the suit was filed against both the American Cotton Oil Trust and an individual, Jules Aldige, one of its vice-presidents and its agent in New Orleans. Aldige defended himself in the suit by basically conceding this charge, claiming that he lacked any authority to control any alleged actions restraining trade or to produce any subpoenaed papers. In the course of preparing for the trial, the state attorney general asked for authority to send lawyers to get interrogatories from several officers of the trust in New York. Many of the questions in his agenda concerned questions of basic organization, such as the nature of the formal structure, the powers of the officers, and their relationship to the certificate holders, the men who had owned the constituent companies (*Times Democrat,* May 27, 1887). The trust's institutional ambiguity clearly troubled the government.

The other objection to the trust's lack of institutional definition was the secrecy with which the trust conducted its affairs. The fact that the by-laws had never been made public, that there was no way to know how the trust conducted its affairs, violated the traditional theme of accountability. The state's lawyers viewed the trust as a sort of incorporation, not a partnership, and reasoned that therefore it should be accountable to the public as much as other corporations, even though the demands of accountability were rather feeble at that time. When the trust announced that it was going to reorganize as a holding company, the *Times Democrat* interpreted the change as a reaction to negative public opinion and the falling prices of its certificates, although it is not clear which was thought more decisive: "The continued assaults on the trusts of late have undoubtedly had some effect on them. The depression in the Sugar Trust and Oil Trust certificates compelled the engineers of those concerns to recognize the public opposition to and prejudice against them. When these affect the pockets of the stockholders, it is not to be wondered at that they realize the evils of trusts and go to work to reorganize on a new basis" (Oct. 21, 1887). While the editorial acknowledged that the new company would maintain some monopolistic features of the trust, it welcomed what it saw as a big improvement. In other words, cotton oil's ambiguous property definition as a trust seemed to be more serious than its monopolistic practices. In the long run, these journalists may have been correct. A monopoly could have been eroded with the emergence of new competitors. But the solution to the problems of its ambiguous property status changed the entire economic and social system.

To fight its legal battles, the Cotton Oil Trust hired William Nelson Cromwell of the eminent New York firm Sullivan and Cromwell. His initial tactic was to cut the feet out from under the suit by removing the defendants from Louisiana's jurisdiction, selling outright all the property in that state to the Rhode Island Company, a corporation chartered in the so-named state. The *New York Times* reported that "Wall-street, or so much of Wall-street as has been admitted to an advance view of this sharp practice, is chuckling over what is termed the smartness of the tactics" (Feb. 10, 1889). The tactic failed. Louisiana courts had issued an earlier injunction that prohibited any transactions with the trust. So Cromwell proposed a more radical means of removing the trust from the jurisdiction, dissolving it and reorganizing as a corporation. But the problem was where such a corporation would be legal. An outright merger was not practical because the trust did not entirely control all the constituent corporations. A single stockholder could keep any company from merging. Common law did not permit either partnerships or corporations to own stock in corporations, which is why the trust form had been invented. At Cromwell's initiative, New Jersey had amended its corporation laws to permit corporations to own stock in other corporations. So in 1889 the officers of the Cotton Oil Trust decided to reorganize as a legal corporation under the laws of New Jersey. But they did not merely form a simple corporation. They appointed a committee of men with strong connections to corporate capital to reorganize along the lines of railroad corporations. E. P. Olcott, president of the Central Trust Company, chaired a committee that included E. D. Adams of the investment bank of Winslow, Lanier and Company and W. L. Bull, president of the New York Stock Exchange (*New York Times,* Nov. 2, 1889). The new industrial corporation would be a full-fledged participant in the institutions of corporate capitalism. The reorganization committee designed a plan that would squeeze some of the "water" out of the company's capital structure. Holders of trust certificates could exchange them for common stock valued at 50 percent of their certificates and preferred stock valued at 25 percent. The new corporation would reduce total capitalization from $42 million to $32 million (*Commercial and Financial Chronicle,* Oct. 26, 1889, Nov. 9, 1889).

Not only did the legal assault on the trusts induce them to reorganize as holding companies, as emphasized in conventional accounts, other actors wielded other kinds of power to foster incorporation. The trust's institutional ambiguity created more than legal problems. The ill-defined nature of the property insulated the trust from accountability to both government and investors. At the same meeting in which the American Cotton Oil Trust appointed a reorganization committee, it was disclosed that previous announcements had overestimated profits by a million dollars and that the president and another officer had used company funds improperly, losing about a half-million dollars. Although they apparently were acting in the company's interest rather than their own, they spent their entire personal funds to compensate the company, admitting misjudgment, not corruption, thus assuming liability as though it were a partnership. The *New York Times* took this occasion, in the light of recent losses in the price of certificates of several trusts, to ask "Who Owns the Properties?": "The proceedings at the recent annual meeting of the Cotton Oil Trust have enlightened a good many people as to the real nature of a Trust and the danger to which the buyer of a Trust's certificates is exposed. One inquiry that is suggested by the recent movement of certificates deserves the attention of all who are interested in what have euphemistically been called 'the industrial stocks' " (Nov. 4, 1889). Even the *Times* viewed the socialization of industrial capital suspiciously, at least until the property was administered within an established institution.

The trust organization assumed that the owners of the constituent plants would continue to operate them while still being partial owners. In other words, ownership and authority would be socialized within the group, but the powers of ownership and the authority of management would not be divorced. But when the price of certificates rose to three, four, or five times the value of the plants, many owners took advantage of the opportunity and sold their certificates, which then circulated speculatively in the stock market. The *Wall Street Journal* carried regular headings on "American Cotton Oil" and "Sugar Refineries" about the two trusts, but still had no general heading for industrials. However, the *Times* worried about whether these "mysterious associations" could operate effectively if ownership were separated from control. "What will be the attitude of a Trust manufacturer toward the property he seems to own, but does not own? What will be the attitude of so-called Trustees toward the mills which they no longer own, and the industry in which they no longer have a large pecuniary interest? What are the rights of the new owners of certificates and how are they to exercise those rights in these blind pools?" (Nov. 4, 1889). Even General Samuel Thomas, one of the trust's organizers, advocated reorganization, proclaiming that he had never believed in trusts, which he felt "were not fitted for straightforward business conduct. They were evil in abundant ways. The public rightly suspected every such organization. They were un-American—they ought to go. It would be suicidal policy to attempt to continue the Cotton Oil Company in its trust guise" (*New York Times*, Nov. 2, 1889). So it is not surprising that the staid *Commercial and Financial Chronicle* congratulated the trust for its "business-like action" to reorganize as a corporation (Oct. 26, 1889, 539). Within a year, Sullivan and Cromwell could certify in the American Cotton Oil Company's annual report and announce to the legal and investing public that "the legality of this organization has been passed upon on behalf of the bankers by Messrs. Bristow, Peet and Opdyke and Olin, Rives and Montgomery, who state, under date of September 5, 1890, their opinion 'that the American Cotton Oil Company is a legally organized corporation of the state of New Jersey.' " They had paved a road to legality that many others would follow.

Sugar

Although the American Cotton Oil Company can show us how a socially cohesive industry, with the help of Wall Street lawyers and financiers, helped create a new form of property, its story does not help us analytically isolate the role of technology or markets. In the sugar industry, a technologically homogeneous industry was divided into two regional subindustries with very different organizational forms. Their differences were due less to the functional imperatives of technology than to the historical setting of their origins, the social networks among their owners, and their different relationship to the state. Their eventual integration into a single company was due to the financial power of one branch to subsume the other. While the American Cotton Oil Company created a legal form for others to emulate, the American Sugar Refining Company was the object of two momentous court decisions, including the one that is generally credited with legitimizing the very large, monopolistic corporation and thwarting the federal government's modest attempts to constrain economic concentration.

Although we commonly think of sugar only as an ordinary food commodity, it was once one of the largest and most powerful industries in the country. While a bit of an overstatement, and more positive than contemporary public opinion, this statement reflects commonly held sentiments at the turn of the century: "The exploitation of no other product has influenced the political history of the western world, and in the United States it holds the unique position of having ushered in an era of corporation development and control unprecedented in the history of the world" (Surface 1910). In the first decade of this century, the American Sugar Refining Company was the nation's sixth-largest industrial corporation, exceeded only by Standard Oil, American Tobacco, and three of Morgan's giants (Eichner 1969). Editorials lambasted it and cartoons depicted its monstrous arms crushing the consumer. Although not directly at the industry's behest, America's foray into colonization acquired primarily raw sugar producers. But it has been sugar's historical importance as one of the first trusts and first holding companies as well as the object of precedent-setting court decisions validating the corporate organization of property that has made it the focus of considerable scholarship and debate over the causes and effects of its concentration and incorporation.[10]

Nearly all accounts of the industry have focused on the Sugar Trust and its successor, the American Sugar Refining Company (ASRC). While they were indisputably the dominant force in the industry, this is not the complete picture, but primarily the sugar industry east of the Mississippi River. The West Coast industry was organized in a very different fashion and had a very different history. The contrast provides a useful case study to examine the effect of situational social and historical factors, holding technological factors constant. It challenges Eichner's technologically based explanation of the industry's concentration and incorporation. Producing precisely the same product, the East Coast and West Coast branches of the industry sharply contrasted with each other in several respects. The East Coast branch spawned a monopoly that eventually controlled virtually the entire country's production including the West Coast, while the West Coast branch was organized in a sequence of oligopolies. The East Coast branch confined itself entirely to refining with occasional, typically unsuccessful, forays into the control of the raw product, while the West Coast branch had, from its beginning, been vertically integrated, first with Hawaiian cane sugar and later with domestic beet sugar. The East Coast branch formed one of the first publicly traded corporations with strong ties to finance capital, one of the first large industrials listed on the New York Stock Exchange, while the West Coast branch remained privately held with close ties to agricultural interests, until the dominant East Coast company assertively gained partial control. Finally, government played a central role in the life of both sectors, but in a very different way. From the 1880s to the 1920s, the eastern Sugar Trust and its corporate successor contended with state and federal governments over antitrust law, which very much influenced what they did and how they were organized. They also frequently had to contend with the government's policing function, facing charges of bribing public officials, cheating customs agencies, and other

TABLE 7.3
Economic Characteristics of the Cane Sugar Industry, 1880, 1900

Year		Establishments	Capital (000)	Average Capital / Estab. (000)	Productivity	Capital Intensity
1880	Cane Sugar Industry	49	$27,433	$559.9	1.84	9.54
	Standard deviations from the mean of all industries	−0.25	0.63	7.64	1.71	2.84
1900	Cane Sugar Industry	657	$184,033	$280.1	1.30	26.60
	Standard deviations from the mean of all industries	−0.01	1.96	0.36	−0.05	4.31

Source: U.S. Bureau of the Census 1914, 697.

forms of corruption, although these problems were less consequential for their basic operation and organization. They were concerned about tariffs on raw and refined sugar, but more as another cost of production, not as a matter of life or death as with the West Coast branch, which depended on the tariff for its livelihood. The federal tariff and bounties, not antitrust laws or corruption charges, were the most immediate object of the western branch's relation to government.

Looking back at the economic characteristics of the sugar industry in 1880, efficiency theory and power theory would agree that it fit the profile of an industry likely to become dominated by large corporations.[11] As shown in Table 7.3, the sugar industry was large, productive, capital intense, and had few firms.[12] Observers inclined toward efficiency theory would point out that the average establishment was capitalized at more than a half-million dollars, suggesting substantial economies of scale, and that its capital intensity was nearly three standard deviations above. In 1880, cane sugar was produced in very large plants, with the average establishment costing more than a half-million dollars when manufacturing as a whole operated in establishments less than a tenth of that. The average worker produced $1,841 of value, double all manufacturing. The capital intensity for the industry was $9.54 capital for every dollar in wages, about three times the average industry. Those working from a power perspective would emphasize that the small number of establishments might enhance social interaction among the manufacturers. However, the change between 1880 and 1900 would challenge any perspective that explains the industry's organization in terms of its economic characteristics. In those two decades the industry grew tremendously, expanding the capital invested by nearly seven times. It was still a very large industry in the aggregate, and the average firm was still greater than most industries, but its productivity had fallen below the mean for all industries. Thus for the industry as a whole, the large scale did not translate into economies of scale, at least as measured by productivity. My account follows a historical more than a functional logic. The East Coast branch was characterized by a small cohesive group of owners with a history of tight governance and strong leadership, whose network connections gave them access to the corporate institutional system and its largess of finance capital. The West Coast branch was also led by a small cohesive group, whose members were tied more closely with western capital and the Mormon church than with eastern capital. It was the eastern branch where the large publicly traded corporation was founded. Once the industry concentrated and organized in corporations, the institutionalized economic power reproduced the structure. Contrary to the assumptions of efficiency theory, the power of the market was not sufficient to erode the power of the organization. This hypothesis is borne out by examining the cane and beet sugar branches.

Chandler cites sugar refining as one of the new industries in which the economies of scale and high productivity inherent in continuous-processing technology fostered economic concentration and, after horizontal mergers failed to sustain monopoly power, vertical integration, which underlay long-term oligopoly. Technology and markets are again seen as the driving forces of change. However, he uses them in an ad hoc manner, citing them when they fit, and discounting them when they do not.

In the first place, the technological changes creating continuous process occurred several decades before the East Coast branch consolidated. In the early 1830s Robert L. and Alexander Stuart developed a method of refining sugar based on steam energy, enabling them to dominate the industry. By the 1850s they were producing 40 million pounds per year and employing about three hundred workers (Eichner 1969). Following another technological advance simplifying production in 1851, many new refineries were established. By 1869 there were forty-nine independent refineries in Boston, New York, and Philadelphia, where East Coast refiners continued to congregate thereafter. Unlike the Bonsack machine for cigarettes or the open hearth for steel, there were no major technological advances after this time, but the shape of the industry changed dramatically and varied greatly between east and west. The trust, monopoly, and late oligopoly developed with relatively constant technology. Chandler identifies the coming of steam refining in the 1850s as the most consequential technological breakthrough, but discounts the forty-year delay until consolidation by invoking market forces, arguing that increasing demand ensured continuing profits until the 1870s (1977, 257). While it is true that the demand for sugar did not grow during the depression-filled years of the 1870s, demand did continue to expand thereafter. In the 1880s, the years leading up to the formation of the trust, per capita consumption grew from forty-three pounds in 1880 to fifty-five pounds in 1890, continuing to grow over the next two decades. The New York wholesale market price fell considerably from 14 cents in

1870 to 6 cents the year the trust was formed (American Sugar Refining Company 1911), but this was more than two decades after the technological achievements over a period of widespread deflation. While I do not dispute that sugar producers faced declining margins between raw and refined sugar, I do question whether their behavior was determined by any productivity-enhancing technology.

The story of the Sugar Trust is well known, especially from Eichner's (1969) excellent account. He calls the 1870s the Golden Age of Competition, when entrance was relatively easy, with a new plant requiring about $500,000 to $700,000 in investment, a substantial but not prohibitive amount. In New York alone, about three or four new firms per year entered the market. But the failure rate was also fairly high with a net loss of firms over the decade, including the once dominant Stuarts, a casualty of the 1873 depression. Because the supply exceeded the demand, profit margins for the industry as a whole remained relatively low. Eichner (1969) and Zerbe (1970) have debated whether the competition was ruinous or healthy, with a corollary debate about whether antimarket devices were appropriate or pernicious, but both are measuring the industry by the abstract concept of Adam Smith's free market. Eichner's evidence for ruinous competition is the refiners' antimarket behavior, including not only pools and trusts but fraudulent customs procedures, political mobilization to change tariffs, attempts to adulterate their product, and accusations of predatory practices that manufacturers lodged against one another. Zerbe (1970) responds that fraud and cheating are also found during strong economies and that the rate and scope of failures were merely the market's natural discipline eliminating the unfit. However, both assume that antimarket collusion was extraordinary enough to require an explanation in terms of atypical events. Neither considers whether refiners' behavior was the very ordinary means of governing the industry. In one sense Eichner and Zerbe may both be correct. The refiners felt that the competition was ruinous and must be managed, but they may have felt that all open competition was ruinous. The market may have been seen as ruinous precisely because it was so free. Whether or not the competition was "objectively" ruinous or merely free is less important than the fact that it was seen as ruinous and that the sugar men acted collectively to contain it.

During the seventies, the East Coast refiners were not cohesively organized, but split into two groups. The refiners in Boston, New York, and Philadelphia were frequently in conflict with the smaller inland refiners whose attempts to fix prices failed when the former group refused to participate. But by 1880, the coastal refiners themselves came together to form a pool, agreeing to pay 1 cent per pound of sugar into a common fund, which would be split at the end of each week in proportion to each manufacturers' previous output. An executive committee, including Henry and William Havemeyer, two cousins who controlled refineries producing more than three-quarters of the nation's sugar, was elected to administer this pool. But the legally unenforceable agreement was soon broken and fell apart.[13] A year later, a verbal agreement to try again also failed. In 1882, the Havemeyer and Elder refinery, the nation's largest, burned down, temporarily reducing aggregate supply and allowing profit levels to rally, but when the rebuilt, state-of-the-art replacement entered the market, profits again fell. In 1886 the refiners agreed to a ten-day suspension of production, but few honored it. The following year, William Havemeyer asked John J. Searles, Jr., a banker and corporate lawyer associated with the earlier negotiations, to begin discussions to reproduce in sugar what John D. Rockefeller had accomplished in petroleum. The smaller refiners agreed quickly, and the Sugar Trust was founded. George Moller, the manager of the North River Sugar Refining Company, later testified to a congressional committee, "We were all practical men, all sugar refiners . . . as far as we were concerned, we did not consider any discussion necessary. We all knew that the only way to make sugar refining pay was to stop overproduction" (quoted in Eichner 1969, 71). Thus the trust was seen not as an organization that would supersede the individual companies, but as a device by which each company would trade some of its economic sovereignty for greater profits. The other Havemeyers, however, resisted, reasoning that their new factory was the most efficient concern going and could come out on top of any competitive struggle. However, on the condition that all the other major refiners would join, they agreed (even though some major refiners in Boston and Philadelphia did not participate, at least at first). By April 1887, all but one of the East Coast refiners joined the trust. John R. Dos Passos, a leading corporate lawyer, drew up the papers.

Moller's explanation that they were all "practical men, all sugar refiners," expresses not only a description of their economic orientation, but also a consciousness of commonality and cohesion. An industry with only forty-nine establishments in the entire nation in 1880 would not have had a difficult time establishing close ties, especially since nearly all major refiners were in Boston, New York, and Philadelphia, with most of the trust members in New York. The Havemeyers, one of New York's wealthy families, were the social and political center. Henry O. Havemeyer, who eventually became president of both the trust and the ASRC, was the leading voice. His cousin and business partner, William F. Havemeyer, was a three-time mayor of New York. At the time the trust was created, the family owned three of the four largest refineries in the country, accounting for 55 percent of the national refining capacity (Zerbe 1969). Not only were six of the eleven original trustees associated with the Havemeyer interests, but the owners were linked together in other ways. George Moller, already mentioned, was from a family that had joined the Havemeyers in partnership before the Civil War (Mullins 1964). When he decided to step out of the trust, he sold his North River Sugar Refining Company to John Searles, an act which, as we shall see, had an important impact on the trust and on trusts in general when New York sued the company for joining. Even the refiners who refused to join the trust did so more for personal reasons than for business ones, again reflecting the tight cohesion in the industry. Theodore Havemeyer had formed a partnership with the Philadelphia refiner Charles Harrison, but subsequently withdrew, creating sufficient animosity that Harrison not only kept his Harrison, Frazier & Company out of the trust, but convinced his friend Joseph B. Thomas of Boston to refuse until Henry Havemeyer asked a common friend, Lowell Palmer, to intervene (Mullins 1964).

The other important social factor besides the cohesion of the sugar manufacturers was the immediate institutional ties with institutions of corporate capital. John Searles, who had negotiated the formation of the trust, had long-term ties with Wall Street as both banker and lawyer. John R. Dos Passos, a Wall Street promoter and lawyer, with the help of John E. Parsons, a founder and active member of the New York City Bar Association, drew up the legal documents. Kidder, Peabody, one of the first investment banks to promote industrial offerings on the major stock exchanges, administered the trust's formation (Navin and Sears 1955). Even before the trust, Henry Havemeyer had run his business from a Wall Street office which became the trust's headquarters as well. Thus while earlier trusts like Standard Oil had been almost solely a matter of governing relations within the industry, the Sugar Trust, from the first, served a dual purpose—industrial governance of the various sugar refiners and linking the industry to the emergent corporate institutional structure. The combined value of the firms was set at $3.5 million and represented in preferred stock. The common stock of $19.5 million was considered the value of the combination—what its members would profit from their organization together over and above what they would earn individually. It was clear that they saw solidarity, not technology, as the key to prosperity. These two kinds of trust shares were exchanged for the stock of the constituent companies, several of which had incorporated only to joint the trust. A board dominated by Henry O. Havemeyer took over the administration of the new organization that controlled firms refining 85 percent of the sugar east of the Rockies. But the organization was still very loose. The trust had no office and no records, never met as a group, kept no minutes, took no votes, and eventually did little more than control the quantity of output. Daily reports were sent to Havemeyer's Wall Street office, which allocated weekly quotas. Except for the plants that were closed, daily operations, along with the right to all profits, remained with the constituent companies (Eichner 1969; Mullins 1964), with no managers designing more efficient means of production. But the meaning of ownership in the new property regime had changed. The refiners still operated their refineries, hiring workers, securing raw supplies, and selling their product for the best price they could negotiate. But two of the prerogatives of ownership had been surrendered. The quantity of production and the price of sale was dictated by the trust.

If the industry's consolidation was a functional adaption to technological advancement and growing markets, the new organizational structure should have rationalized production and distribution. If, as Chandler contends, the great advantage of the trust over the looser forms of collective action was that it could exercise authority inside the individual companies to increase efficiency for the whole, why didn't it? The visible hand did little to foster greater efficiency other than to limit production, sustain prices, and close down a few plants that the invisible hand of the market would have soon swept aside. Chandler again turns to the ad hoc, concluding that the Sugar Trust did not "feel the same pressure to integrate forward" (1977, 320) while offering no evidence that it did not feel the pressure to integrate other than the fact that it did not integrate. The visible hand was used more to continue controlling the market, offering a hefty discount to wholesalers who promised to sell the trust's products exclusively (New York Legislature 1897). Each proprietor of the constituent companies produced sugar in the plant he formerly owned outright, now held in trusteeship, but the profits were shared by all owners. Efficient operation of each plant meant profits for all owners, including those whose obsolete and inefficient plants had been shut down. The profits were socialized, long before production was consolidated or rationalized. The trust achieved no economies of scale, only the socialization of ownership.

Ownership, however, took on a new dimension, one with contradictory effects. In addition to ownership of the physical assets, it was now ownership of negotiable securities that could in itself, with only an indirect connection to production, be a source of wealth. The trust certificates they had exchanged for the stock of their individual corporations could be sold. The distinction between enterprise for production of a commodity and enterprise for profit from securities was novel enough to be newsworthy even to the *National Corporation Reporter*. It cited a New York State legislative investigation of the Sugar Trust that included a discussion of speculation in trust certificates, which were being traded on the "unlisted" section of the New York Stock Exchange. "It may well be questioned whether the Trust was not organized more for the purpose of enormous speculations than for the advantages to be obtained by a combination of refineries in the legitimate refining of sugar. That the chief object of the Trust was for the purpose of speculation is quite plainly shown by the inflated values placed upon the property of the constituent corporations upon which certificates were issued. Had the aim been solely a more economical and profitable refining of sugar this result would have been obtained without an increase of the capitalization of the properties of the constituent corporations" (May 23, 1891, 2:229). Whether or not speculation motivated the trust, the result was that it became integrated into the corporate infrastructure. It discovered a new source of profits from a very different property relationship.

The trust organization lasted only a short time, not because of any considerations of efficiency but because it was declared illegal. Like Ohio's battle against Standard Oil, the state of New York filed suit against one of the constituent companies, seeking to nullify its charter on the grounds that it had stepped beyond its legally granted powers by joining a trust (*New*

York v. North River Sugar Refining Co. 1890 [121 N.Y. 582]). And as in oil, the Sugar Trust defended itself by reorganizing as a holding company in New Jersey after an aborted attempt to incorporate in Connecticut.[14] The first annual report of the ASRC was quite explicit about the effects of legal action on forming the holding company: "To the Holders of Certificates of the Sugar Refineries Company: The decision of the Court of Appeals in the case of the North River Sugar Refining Co. necessitates a dissolution of the existing arrangement and the formation of a new organization" (American Sugar Refining Company *Annual Report*, 1890). Henry Havemeyer affirmed the same motive verbally; when asked why the trust had incorporated he replied, "Well, from being illegal as we were, we are now legal as we are; change enough, isn't it?" (quoted in Mullins 1964, 73). In retrospect we can see that change from trust to holding company was pivotal and far reaching, changing the relationship among the constituent companies from a coalition in which each had strategically exchanged sovereignty for profitability and stability into one in which the full powers of property were vested. A coordinating agency that set production levels was replaced by one with the authority to fully manage. At the time, this was seen as another strategic maneuver. But it was a step from which there was no going back.

Although *New York v. North River* was a decision of a state supreme court, not the U.S. Supreme Court, it was widely cited by courts and the public. It was one of the definitive decisions concerning the relationship between individuals and the corporation and it emphatically put the business world on notice concerning what kinds of social relations the state would enforce among owners, thereby redefining the nature of productive property. The state claimed that by joining the trust, the North River Refining Company was ultra vires, acting beyond the powers granted in its charter, since the company did not have the authority to delegate the responsibility of managing the property to an external agent, the trust. The defense argued that the trust was formed by the individual owners, not the constituent corporations; the owners had exchanged their stock certificates for trust certificates. The individual companies, many of which had incorporated only for the purpose of creating stock to be exchanged, were still operating legally since, as corporate bodies, they had no control over who owned their stock. Ownership was vested in the individuals; the stock was their property to sell for any price in any medium of exchange they saw fit. Articulating a principle of profound sociological importance, the court rejected this argument, ruling that there is no distinction between the collectivity of the stockholders and the corporation. This is the flip side of limited liability. Limited liability protects the ownership from some of the responsibilities of ownership. But the corporation also alienates some of the rights of ownership. Presumably, if the owners had kept their companies as partnerships and had fully merged into a new company in which they were all partners— apart from the issue of monopoly, a distinction the court seemed to accept—the actions would have been legal. The court ruled that the trust was illegal per se. Even if the North River Company had not participated in a monopoly, it would have been illegal. By forming the trust the owners suggested that they were not yet willing to combine their property. They wanted the cake of ownership over their firms, even if temporarily alienated to a trust, and to eat the profits from a centrally governed industry. The state would not enforce this kind of contract among owners. The property rights of individual ownership or corporate ownership would be enforced, but not the hybrid form of the trust. Only when owners incorporated would the state enforce a new social relationship among them, socializing capital and institutionalizing different rights and privileges (Beach 1891; Jones 1895; U.S. Industrial Commission 1900a, b; Davies 1916; Eichner 1969).

The court ruled that the corporation—the North River Sugar Refining Company—had acted illegally not only when it participated in a partnership, but also when it colluded to restrain trade. Thus the court was defining not only the legal form it would permit and enforce as property, but also the content of the contract among corporations. Since the time of Jackson, American courts had generally avoided dictating the permissible content of contracts apart from fraud, allowing individuals to decide on the content of contracts. But antitrust law was the major exception. It proscribed a particular motivation: individuals could not do anything *intended* to restrain trade. The New York court in *North River* articulated a principle more characteristic of the first half of the nineteenth century than the turn of the century, writing that a corporation was created solely for the public benefit and if the incorporators acted contrary to the public, they no longer deserved a charter. By placing itself in subservience to another organization that was intended to injure the public by creating a monopoly, the corporation violated ultra vires, the court reasoned in revoking the charter. The court was saying that corporate property was a different kind of property with different rights and privileges. When partnerships violate laws, the individuals may be penalized, but they cannot be deprived of property rights per se—only some of the profits of that behavior. In contrast, a corporation which violated the common law concerning restraint of trade could be denied the right of existence. In the words of the decision, "It is quite clear that the effect of the defendant's action was to divest itself of the essential and vital elements of its franchise by placing them in trust; to accept from the State the right of corporate life, only to disregard the conditions upon which it was given; to receive its powers and privileges merely to put them in pawn; and to give away to an irresponsible board its entire independence and self-control. It has helped to create an anomalous trust which is, in substance and effect, a partnership of twenty separate corporations. It is a violation of law for corporations to enter into a partnership" (quoted in Jones 1895, 419–420).

When the New York court prohibited the sugar manufacturers from governing themselves through the trust, one option would have been to return to the earlier competitive situation. But other businessmen, most notably the cotton oil manufacturers, were abandoning their home states and taking advantage of the new law in New Jersey to form holding companies. At the time, the difference between the trust and the holding company must not have seemed that great. Instead of trust certificates for one's company, one received corporate stock. The larger refiners would continue to govern the industry through their elected board of directors. The company headquarters would set output and pricing levels, but, except for the few plants closed, most refineries would continue to operate their factories. In short, companies were not relinquishing ownership, but socializing it on terms that they collectively still controlled.

However, legal uncertainty remained, though not of the form of property per se, since there was no serious legal challenge to New Jersey's authority to permit holding companies. In the face of public outcry about monopolies, the Cleveland administration initiated a suit against the E. C. Knight Company, one of the constituent companies under the new Sherman Antitrust Act (*United States v. E. C. Knight Co.* 156 U.S. 1). Again the legal action was taken not against the combination, but against a constituent company. The U.S. Supreme Court ruled that the Antitrust Act prohibited certain actions in restraint of trade, that is, as part of commerce, but that merely being a monopoly was an issue of manufacturing, not commerce. McCurdy (1979) has persuasively identified serious flaws in the conventional interpretation of this decision as a conservative assertion of *laissez-faire* principles. He explains that, in contrast, the decision was an affirmation of the legal authority of individual states to police corporations, to decide whether property rights included the right to produce the total national supply of a particular commodity. The Commerce Clause of the Constitution explicitly gave the federal government jurisdiction over relations in the national market. But states had jurisdiction over production, over property. McCurdy (1978a) argues that the Court expected the states to exercise that authority, but they failed to live up to those expectations. State-level politics and lack of will, not constitutional constriction, accounted for the feeble defense against the concentration of economic power. But virtually all authors discussing the two sugar cases, one outlawing the trust, the other validating the holding company, agree that they opened the door for the merger movement. Thus there was no natural economic logic blazing a path to the large corporation. The government was quite specific about what rights property entailed, including the differences between the rights of individuals in contrast to corporate property.

Thus while the history of the East Coast branch of the sugar industry did conform to the efficiency model in some respects—it was a capital-intensive industry in a growing but competitive market—there are both anomalies in the history of the industry and the presence of other important factors that conform to a power model. The long delay between technological changes and consolidation, the fact that attempts to restrain competition were normal, and the lack of change in productive relations after consolidation all

challenge an efficiency argument. The close social ties of sugar manufacturers before the trust, the immediate affiliation with institutions of corporate
capital, and the fact that the formation of the trust and holding company
did more to change the nature of property than the nature of production all
lend support to a power argument. However, since the assertions of both
perspectives are implicitly comparative—oriented toward explaining variation in the likelihood of economic transformation—this single case study
can only suggest rather than confirm. A comparison with the western
branch of the American sugar industry thus provides an illuminating contrast which holds technology constant.

The course of development of West Coast sugar was very different, resulting in oligopoly rather than monopoly. Three ownership interests pre-
dominated, with a shifting series of coalitions and competition. Hawaiian
cane sugar growers led by Claus Spreckels were the first West Coast refiners, followed by beet sugar interests including Spreckels and later the
Church of Jesus Christ of Latter-Day Saints (Mormons). When the West
Coast industry developed enough to compete with the East, and when
Spreckels made a foray to the East, the American Sugar Refining Company
became a major factor in the West.

Claus Spreckels began his sugar career on the East Coast, but as a young
man traveled to Germany to learn the technology there, then set out for the
West where he began a refinery in San Francisco. In 1876 the United States
signed a reciprocity treaty with the Kingdom of Hawaii that permitted
sugar to be imported duty free. Spreckels sailed to Hawaii on the ship carrying the news of the treaty, but before general word could spread, he bought
half the anticipated crop. At the time, Hawaii supplied only about 1 percent
of America's sugar, but by the time of annexation in 1898, it would supply
10 percent, most of which would be controlled by Spreckels. While gaining
control of Hawaiian land and water, partly through payments and loans to
the king, he expanded his refining apparatus in San Francisco. In 1878 he
formed the Hawaiian Commercial Company, with an authorized capitalization of $10 million—far larger than any East Coast refinery—with Spreck-
els holding a controlling interest. The operation at Spreckelsville was the
most modern and efficient possible, with electric lighting as early as 1881,
only a few years after Edison perfected it. And unlike the eastern refiners,
Spreckels's operation was vertically integrated. But he was not able to maintain control of his company. The stock went public, selling in 1882 for
about $60, and within two years, with the company deeply in debt, it
plunged to 25 cents, rebounding to $10 by 1885. The *San Francisco Chron-
icle*'s allegation that Spreckels was manipulating the stock infuriated his
son so much that he shot and killed the editor in an argument. He was
acquitted, partly on the defense that the charges were false and the shooting
justified. But his stalwart defense of his father's honor did not stand in the
way of his gaining control through legal action against the elder Spreckels,
who then turned to other sugar projects. In 1888 he constructed a refinery

at Watsonville, California, to refine sugar imported from Hawaii, mostly on his own steamship line. Competitors soon appeared, but over time he gained control of all but the American Sugar Refinery (not to be confused with the East Coast's American Sugar Refining Company), of which he owned a third and with which he cooperated closely. For a while it was able to dictate the price to other Hawaiian growers, but when the relationship with the independent company broke down, he sold his share and lowered the price of his own sugar. Other Hawaiian planters gained control of the American Sugar Refinery, recapitalizing and expanding its facilities. In the midst of this conflict, John Searles, who had engineered the East Coast's Sugar Trust, went west to invite Spreckels to join. He refused. The Sugar Trust then bought a controlling interest in the American Sugar Refinery, provoking the state of California (with Spreckels's encouragement) to file suit against the company for being a member of the trust, and forcing the company to vacate its charter (Surface 1910; Adler 1966; Eichner 1969; Zerbe 1969). All these adventures had little to do with efficiency and much to do with economic power.

Spreckels did not remain on the West Coast. In 1890, after the trust had raised the margin between raw and refined sugar from .768 cents to 1.207 cents over two years, he built the Spreckels Sugar Refinery in Philadelphia, producing three thousand barrels a day, and began another one in Baltimore. By the next year the margin had dropped below the pretrust level. Like the pattern in many of the early consolidations, when faced with competition, the ASRC bought out the competition, taking control of the two companies. The following year a national modus vivendi was reached when the Western Sugar Refining Company combined with the Spreckels Sugar Company and the ASRC-controlled California Sugar Refining Company into a new Western Sugar Refining Company, with ownership evenly divided between the two and management by the Spreckels family. This company dominated West Coast refining until 1902. This coalition with the Spreckels marked the ASRC's high point, giving it control over 98 percent of the country's refined sugar. Thus a market mechanism (enforced by government, not "naturally" occurring) did contain ASRC from unlimited price increases by inviting new entrants. The policy of absorbing competitors could not be a viable long-term strategy and the ASRC eventually accepted an oligopolistic governance structure for the industry (Eichner 1969). But market forces only explain why monopoly was unstable, not the industry's overall property relations.

The comparison of cane sugar and beet sugar organization shows the limitation of efficiency theory and the importance of social and political factors. Although the raw product differs between beet and cane sugar, the two products become identical quite early in the production process. The initial milling is done near the site of harvesting, because both beets and cane are bulkier and more expensive to transport than partially refined raw sugar. The initial product is dark brown, graded for price and import duty by degree on the basis of color.[15] So even raw sugar is indistinguishable between cane and beet sources, which means there is no technological reason why one branch should be more vertically integrated than the other. Only historical and social differences provide an explanation. The beet sugar industry matured in this country after the beginning of the trust. Its development was led by individuals who had refined sugar in the East and moved west after their companies were incorporated into the trust. By the time rapprochement was reached between the two branches, beet sugar was thoroughly integrated from planting to refining.

Efficiency theory treats the degree of vertical and horizontal integration as a function of the operation of the market. In both Chandler's and Williamson's perspective, companies will bring within a single organizational umbrella their sources of raw material or competing firms when economic efficiency so dictates. Chandler argues that technologies based on the continuous processing of materials from raw material to manufactured product are more productive when the various steps of manufacture are integrated in the same firm. Williamson argues that when sources of raw material are uncertain or untrustworthy, it is rational for firms to create a vertically integrated hierarchy. But the sugar industry reversed the causal direction. The level of vertical integration in the two branches shaped the competitive dynamics. Since the technology was basically the same in the eastern and western branches, they were differentially vertically integrated for very contingent historical and social reasons. But this difference, in the context of a fluid political environment on which they were very dependent, created intense conflict between the two branches. The conflict in turn coalesced the western sugar companies, overshadowing whatever competitive tendencies there might have been.

The eastern refiners never thoroughly integrated although, at times, the American Sugar Refining Company acted to stabilize or control the sources of its raw materials. Raw sugar from cane for the East Coast came from three sources: the southern United States, especially Louisiana; Cuba/Puerto Rico; and Hawaii. As a virtual monopsony, the ASRC seemed to follow a policy of pragmatism, buying where it was cheap, acting politically to reduce the tariff on raw sugar, and occasionally investing or intervening on one front or another. But eastern sugar refining remained nonintegrated less because of efficiency considerations than because of the struggle for power with supplying regions in the American South and Cuba (Sitterson 1953; Hitchman 1970).

The first permanent beet sugar factory in the United States was built in 1870 in Alvarado, California, by two Germans, Bonesteel and Otto, but played only a minor role in the industry's development. In addition to Claus Spreckels, the two most influential individuals were Henry T. Oxnard and Thomas R. Cutler. Like Claus Spreckels, Oxnard began his career refining sugar on the East Coast and traveled to Germany to learn about beet sugar. He had been with the Oxnard Brothers Refinery in Brooklyn when the trust was formed and after his year abroad, along with his brothers and the Cutting family, he created the Oxnard Beet Sugar Company to refine sugar from beets in Grand Island, Nebraska (Blakey 1912). Cutler began refining beets into sugar in Utah in 1891. From virtually nothing, by 1902 nearly two million tons of beet sugar (Surface 1910) were being refined into over thirty thousand tons of refined sugar in forty-six factories (*Willet and Gray's Weekly Statistical Sugar Trade Journal,* May 21, 1903). For Colorado, which had about a third of the total sugar beet acreage, the crop was the leading agricultural source of wealth in the state.

In 1899 beet sugar manufacturers consolidated, created a trade journal, founded a trade association, and went on the warpath against the eastern "trust." Their consolidation, the American Beet Sugar Company, capitalized at $20 million, was created at the height of the corporate revolution. Although financed by eastern bankers including Kuhn Loeb & Company and Spencer, Trask & Company of New York, the stock was owned almost entirely by the beet manufacturers. The company was primarily a California operation, with the largest beet sugar factory in the world at Spreckels, California, but included refiners from other states.

The war with the eastern cane refiners, especially the ASRC, was fought over the tariff and control of beet refining companies. The cane refiners wanted the elimination of the tariff on raw sugar with increased protection on refined sugar. The beet growers/refiners continued to advocate a high duty on both raw and refined sugars. The newly acquired colonies of Puerto Rico, Hawaii, and the Philippines, along with the protectorate over Cuba, posed a grave threat to protected sugar. The pages of the *Beet Sugar Gazette* pitted Henry Oxnard, president of the American Beet Sugar Company and the American Beet Sugar Association, as a gallant David against the Goliath Henry Havemeyer, president of the American Sugar Refining Company: "Seldom was a young industry beset by so many dangers as the beet sugar industry, and seldom was a business in [its] infancy called upon to meet adversaries of such gigantic dimensions as the Sugar Trust, the relentless enemy of the American [beet] sugar industry" (Oct. 1899, 5). It called on the industry to rally around the association, joining together with the cane growers to protect the company from cheap colonial sugar. In December, the refiners founded a second association, the American Beet Sugar Manufacturers' Association. These two associations, along with numerous state associations and associations representing other commodities threatened by the colonies, including the Grange, formed the League of Domestic Producers, which the sugar growers dominated. "Our purpose is to put into the pockets of the farmers, capitalists, and laborers of these United States the $100,000,000 now exported annually to pay for imported sugar, and thus also vastly benefit the general welfare of the whole people without injury to any" (quoted in *Beet Sugar Gazette,* Oct. 1899, 6). After a bill for reciprocity with Puerto Rico was defeated, the journal turned its attention to the kinds of technical matters usually found in trade journals, until Congress considered a reciprocity treaty with Russia two years later. The level of rhetoric escalated again. "Nothing is of greater importance to the beet sugar industry at this juncture than a strong organization. . . . The beet sugar men must present a solid front. Their enemies are many and shrewd and unscrupulous. A solid phalanx alone can protect them" (*Beet Sugar Gazette*, Feb. 1901, 1). The ASRC responded by issuing $15 million of additional capital stock to operate in Puerto Rico and Cuba. The company had decided to vertically integrate for reasons far removed from efficiency. At the same time it lowered the price of refined sugar sold in the West to drive the beet sugar companies out of business. The rhetorical response escalated further: "Seize the Opportunity! If the enemy can be successfully beaten off this time there will be a magnificent opportunity to carry the industry into new districts, and on the strength of the agitation growing out of this fight, to conquer new fields and extend the industry in a measure that would not be possible in the ordinary course of development" (*Beet Sugar Gazette*, Aug. 1901, 131). A later article asked, "Shall American Farmers compete with Naked Cuban Laborers?" (Sept. 1901, 221). At this point, western grocers joined the battle, when the Denver Retail Grocers' Association adopted a resolution to buy no sugar from the ASRC, but only beet sugar. The rhetoric and lobbying paid off. The tariff remained. The issue of the *Gazette* celebrating a victory against a proposed reduction in the tariff on Cuban sugar also noted that the ASRC had bought a controlling interest in several beet factories, including the American Beet Sugar Company. But the belligerent tone had subsided. The trade journal even conceded that it was possible that the company might be sincerely interested in developing the nation's sugar industry, although it recommended continued vigilance (May 1902).

Although the beet sugar industry was led by a few large companies like the American Beet Sugar Company, it remained competitive. In 1905 there were about fifty-four factories listed by the primary sugar trade journal, owned by as many as thirty companies (Zerbe 1969). The distribution of output among factories was remarkably even, suggesting that there were no strong economies of scale. The largest single factory was the Spreckels Sugar Company plant in Spreckels, California, with a daily capacity of three thousand tons. Thirteen of the fifty-four plants had a capacity of greater than half a ton, and only eight produced less than a quarter ton. Consolidation did not change the size or organization of production, but was more a reorganization of ownership, bringing together the producers of a region, after the turn of the century often under the aegis of the ASRC.

The ASRC's temporary foray into beet sugar was driven not by the forces of technology but by the exercise of economic power. In 1890 Henry Havemeyer, in part because he was persuaded by Wallace Willett of the leading sugar trade journal, had decided to enter into beet sugar. Within two years ASRC bought out half of Thomas Cutler's Utah Sugar Refining Company, and over the following three years other companies were formed, especially in Idaho, controlled by ASRC (Eichner 1969). The president of these companies was the president of the Church of Latter-Day Saints, and Cutler was a bishop in that church.[16] In 1901, the ASRC formed a special committee chaired by Havemeyer to acquire a controlling interest in the beet sugar industry (U.S. House 1911). Their takeover of the Michigan Sugar Refining Company, a 1907 consolidation of six small refineries in that state, illustrates how they operated. The Michigan company's president, Charles B. Warren, testified to a congressional committee that he had been holding a major block of stock for unknown individuals at the request of Havemeyer, later learning they were owned by Havemeyer himself (U.S. House 1911). By 1907 the ASRC had invested close to $30 million in beet sugar, well over half the total investment in sugar (Eichner 1969). The two halves of the sugar industry reached agreement to divide the country, with the ASRC predominantly in the East and the beet sugar growers in the West. The westerners with eastern interests like the Spreckels deferred to ASRC in the East and took a back-row seat in the West, while ASRC gradually reduced its influence in the western companies and stood by while the beet companies increased their national market share.

Thus the contrast between the East Coast and West Coast sugar refiners demonstrates the limitations of an efficiency-based theory to explain the organization of the industry. The East Coast branch had been socially cohesive from its early days and formed pools, a trust, and later a corporation as a means of controlling competition and socializing its profits. The West Coast branch, however, initially importers of Hawaiian raw sugar, turned to domestically grown beet sugar to take advantage of government decisions to pay a bounty and increase tariffs. Its war with the eastern refiners was structured equally by different interests relative to government policies and mutual hostility, resolved only by the victory of one over the other. The eastern branch was much more geographically cohesive and the relationship between controlling competition and cohesion was reflexive, with each attempt to pool or create a trust being both a factor and a result of cohesion. The western producers were spread across several large states at a time when communication and transportation were primitive, and were integrated by the Mormon church as much as by an explicitly business organization. The main incentive they had to become more cohesive was their conflict against eastern refiners. An illustrative contrast is provided by the trade journals of the two branches. The *Beet Sugar Gazette* regularly exhorted readers to solidarity and clearly saw its job as creating cohesion. The eastern *Willett and Gray Sugar Statistical Weekly,* the only trade journal for much of the period, even as early as the eighties, well before the trust, merely printed prices and the output of each firm, a way to set prices as well as report them, information useful for no purpose other than setting prices, and effective for setting prices only if there is already tight cohesion within the trade. In the end the dynamic was as much social as economic: alliances, coalitions, conflict, and domination describe the events better than technology, productivity, efficiency, or market incentives.

After the *E. C. Knight* case validated the legal status of the large industrial corporation, Ardemus Stewart, the associate editor of the *American Law Register,* wrote, "It is enough to say that if this decision stands, and it is true that the national government is powerless to protect the people against such combinations as this . . . then this government is a failure, and the sooner the social and political revolution which many far-sighted men can see already darkening the horizon overtakes us, the better" (quoted in Paul 1978, 287). Unlike the obscurity of the initial New Jersey holding company laws, *E. C. Knight* was widely recognized at the time as epochal. But Stewart was wrong on two counts. First, the effects of the government were not so much from its passivity as from its affirmative definition and enforcement of laws defining what sort of entities could exist and what their powers were.

Second, the revolution incited by *E. C. Knight* was less a matter of armed citizens in the street than of owners and managers in board rooms. The *E. C. Knight* case was one of the decisive points of the process that this chapter has described by which there arose an organizational option that would soon be institutionalized. The large corporations that followed were not pioneers like American Cotton Oil or American Sugar Refining. Industrialists seeking to govern their industries, financiers hunting for alternatives to the saturated railroads, and states searching for a judicial and statutory resolution to the question of how to conceive of collective actors within a jurisprudence that recognized only individuals created a new form of property that socialized capital across the capitalist class. Like the camel sticking his nose into the tent, the national and regional pools helped coalesce networks of industrialists and contributed the social ties that made "tight" combination a more viable option than destructive competition when courts thwarted their attempts. American Cotton Oil made a strategic maneuver to take advantage of the little-noticed change in New Jersey's corporation laws. The men of the Sugar Trust similarly made a tactical change to replace their trust with a holding company. But doing so moved them from the institutional structure of manufacturing into that of corporate capitalism. The New Jersey holding company law can be compared to the calling of the French Estates General, a decision taken to solve a specific problem with little intuition about its long-term consequences. The American Cotton Oil Company was the storming of the Bastille, the initial foray into the old order, while *E. C. Knight* was the execution of the monarch, the point from which there was no turning back, sweeping in a new regime and opening the floodgate for the changes to follow. But there is still the question of why the corporate revolution affected some sectors so much more thoroughly and immediately than others, which the next chapter will address.

CHAPTER EIGHT

American Industry Incorporates

ALTHOUGH CHANDLER substantially advanced social science beyond the debate over whether the first generation of corporate leaders were robber barons or captains of industry by opening the agenda to the question of why some industries spawned large corporations rather than others, Chapter 2 showed that his predictions were not borne out by empirical tests. Large corporations were found in industries with large firms and high capital intensity, but were no more likely to be in highly productive industries than low productive industries and no more likely in quickly growing industries than stagnant ones. That chapter demonstrated the need for an alternate explanation, to which the body of this book has been addressed. Subsequent chapters have described the gradual changes over the nineteenth century that set the stage for the corporate revolution—the development of the public service corporation for canals, turnpikes, and banks, its privatization into railroad corporations, the emergence of a corporate institutional structure, and the changes in law that defined the nature of socialized property in the corporation by establishing new powers that corporations uniquely enjoyed. As of 1890, there were very few large, socially capitalized industrial corporations. Manufacturing was still primarily entrepreneurial, even when adopting the legal form of the corporation, while the corporate institutional structure was overwhelmingly oriented toward railroads and related industries. The question that this chapter addresses is why large socially capitalized industrial corporations, which virtually did not exist in 1890, came to dominate the economy by 1905. It will show why and how, within the context of the legal structure that created entities with corporate rights, entitlements, and responsibilities, the institutional structure of securities markets, investment banks, and mobilization of capital, and the existing institutional structure of manufacturing property and markets, the corporate revolution unfolded as it did. It will offer a very different rendition based on a historical logic and an institutional perspective, in contrast to the conventional account based on functional logic and a managerial perspective. The experience of several key industries will illustrate how the dynamics of power as much as those of managerial rationality forged the corporate system. Much of my case will rest on contrasts within different sectors of industries, some where technologically similar sectors adopted very different property regimes and others where divergent technologies were combined under one property regime.

Efficiency theory explains the shape of economic organization in terms of technological development and market dynamics. Chandler states, "Markets and technology, therefore, determined whether the manufacturer or the market did the coordinating [within an industry]. They had a far greater influence in determining size and concentration in American industry than did the quality of entrepreneurship, the availability of capital, or public policy" (1977, 373). Firms are assumed to be organizational forms rationally adapting to the imperatives of new technology and the opportunities of enlarged markets. My alternative power theory account not only treats action in terms of rational decisions, but also explains action in terms of the actor's relationship to other actors.

The previous chapters, describing how the institutional structure of socialized capital arose, have brought us to the brink of the corporate revolution itself. By the early 1890s, the legal apparatus for corporate property had been achieved by the privatization of corporate property, the corporation's definition as a legal individual, and the New Jersey holding company law, which the American Cotton Oil Company had employed. The institutions of finance capital provided the vehicle for regulating the relationship among putative owners. The railroads had pioneered the organizational forms and had centralized the quantities of capital needed for corporations large enough to dominate their national markets. The pools and trusts ended serious attempts for alternative forms to govern nationalizing markets, especially after the federal government's suit against the American Sugar Refining Company legitimized even monopolistic corporations. While this book has stressed that the explanation of the large socially capitalized corporation must include long-term institutional factors, this chapter focuses on the corporate revolution itself, highlighting a few strategic examples that reveal patterns faced by the manufacturing sector as a whole. The tobacco industry illustrates how two very different technologies and markets could be molded into a single organization. The American Tobacco Company used its power to gain control of all branches of the tobacco industry except cigars, in which it controlled the largest company, but did not dominate the market. Cigars were a subindustry where small-scale, labor-intensive production set limits on the organization of large corporations. The paper industry illustrates the divergent experiences that different branches had with large corporations. The International Paper Company nearly monopolized the production of newspaper until newspaper publishers financed a rival. Wallpaper, however, had one of the era's well-known failures. Through these intra-industry comparisons we can see how factors other than technology and markets shaped the process of socializing capital into corporations.

To understand the explosive transformation by which large, socially capitalized corporations that were originally distinctly outside manufacturing came to dominate it, we must identify who the actors were, and how property rights and institutions affected their relationship to one another as they collectively worked to create and distribute the things that people bought and consumed. The immediate factors that shaped the transformation to large, socially capitalized manufacturing corporations were: (1) the ability of businessmen producing a product to act collectively; (2) the elimination of forms of collective governance other than corporations; (3) the networks that gave some industrialists access to corporate capital which they could use to secure dominance within their industry; (4) the ideology that dictated that competition was basically destructive and that monopoly was necessary for sustained profits; (5) the collapse of the American railroad industry precipitated by the 1893 depression, freeing massive amounts of capital for industrial corporations; and (6) the process of organizational institutionalization that made the creation of large corporations a "rational" and "timely" activity. The case studies that follow illustrate the operation of these factors.

TOBACCO

Although the American Tobacco Company was created about the same time as the American Sugar Refining Company, it adopted corporate forms rather than blaze any institutional trails. In the sugar industry, the different subindustries were technologically similar; in the tobacco industry, the different subindustries contrasted in both technology and property regime until they were subordinated within a single corporation, the American Tobacco Company. If we can think of technology and market structure as independent variables hypothesized by efficiency theory to explain variation in economic organization, my strategy for the sugar industry was to show that similarity in the independent variables was associated with differences in the dependent variable; for the tobacco industry, I will show that differences in the independent variables were overwhelmed by the exercise of economic power.

The story of the tobacco manufacturing industry during this period is primarily the story of the American Tobacco Company.[1] Before the 1880s, manufacturers tended to specialize in one type of tobacco product such as smoking, plug, snuff, or cigars. Originally the work of manufacturing was cutting, curing, and packaging the tobacco leaf in labor-intensive factories, but during the 1880s some of the branches started to adopt machines to do more of the work. The most dramatic change was in the production of paper-wrapped cigarettes, a new product dominated by a handful of companies selling to a national market. In 1890 five of these companies merged into the American Tobacco Company (ATC), which was led by James B. Duke, a North Carolina cigarette maker. Over the course of the following decade, ATC moved assertively into other branches of the industry through aggressive competition and acquisition of surrendering companies. It succeeded in virtually monopolizing all branches except cigars, in which it nevertheless became the largest producer, controlling about a seventh of the national market. In 1911 the U.S. Supreme Court upheld an antitrust decision against it and ordered its dissolution into three full-line companies, the American Tobacco Company, R. J. Reynolds, and Liggett & Myers, which are, of course, still major tobacco companies. During the first decade of this century, the American Tobacco Company was one of the largest corporations in the country, and one of the most consistently profitable.

My account will emphasize the role of corporate capital in governing the industry. Those who focus on the role of technology assume that competitive practices and corporate capitalists were incidental, that technology determined the shape of the industry, so that the industry would have developed the same structure regardless of how corporate capitalists operated. However, technology *interacts* with property. Without the large socially capitalized corporation, the industry might well have remained in medium-sized companies. It was its capital structure that enabled the ATC to compete as successfully as it did, to develop its productive capacity ahead of demand, and perhaps most important, to develop the demand that made the new technology profitable. The interaction of property and technology can be seen in the different role the American Tobacco Company played in the different branches of the tobacco industry. ATC began as a producer of cigarettes, which it developed from a marginal branch of the industry into the core of the economy. The enterprise was not created to meet an inherent "need" to supply America with cheap cigarettes, but continued James Duke's campaign of stimulating demand. Only after the corporation was established did it move into the other branches of the tobacco industry. It brought no technological advantages to the other branches, but offered financial backers the prospects of monopolistic profits in plug tobacco, smoking tobacco, and snuff.

Whereas Chandler focused on cigarettes, where a single invention unequivocally revolutionized production, I will contrast cigarettes with the plug tobacco branch of the industry, which had no technological or market factors making it suitable for incorporation but shows the visible hand of financial power fully ungloved. Finally I will examine the cigar industry, the exceptional branch of the tobacco industry, both because of its large aggregate size and because it was the only branch where the ATC failed to dominate. Analysts since that period have observed that the cigar industry remained in relatively small factories with few large corporations because it lacked inherent economies of scale. The American Tobacco Company created a large cigar subsidiary, the American Cigar Company, that, despite entirely inappropriate technological or market conditions, continued to exist. It never dominated the market and never was as profitable as other branches, but was the nation's largest producer of cigars, a position it enjoyed primarily because of financial power, not economies of scale or technological need.

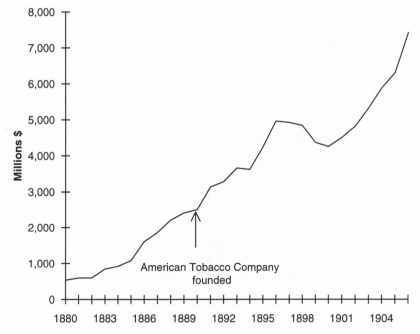

Figure 8.1. Annual Output of Cigarettes and Little Cigars, 1880–1906. (Source: Data drawn from U.S. Bureau of Corporations 1909, Part I, 53.)

Cigarettes

When we think of the tobacco industry today, we think primarily of cigarettes. Plug (chewing) tobacco is associated primarily with baseball players and cigars with men displaying hyper-masculinity. But it is anachronistic to equate the tobacco industry with cigarettes before this century, when most Americans who smoked tobacco enjoyed cigars, pipes, or rolled their own paper-wrapped cigarettes. Before 1880, few people bought prewrapped cigarettes. After the invention of cigarette-making machines, the industry took off, as seen in Figure 8.1. But it still was a minor branch, as seen in Figure 8.2. In 1904, the fifteen million dollars in cigarettes produced was far overshadowed by the nearly two hundred million dollars in cigars or the more than one hundred million dollars in chewing and smoking tobacco (U.S. Bureau of Corporations 1909, 28).

The cigarette industry is an example where the effects of a new productivity-enhancing machine on the consolidation of an industry seem most straightforward. Largely as a result of the Bonsack machine for automatically making cigarettes, the cost of cigarettes fell from 96.4 cents per thousand in 1876 to 8.1 cents per thousand in 1895 (Jones 1929). There are virtually no accounts of the industry that do not acknowledge the important

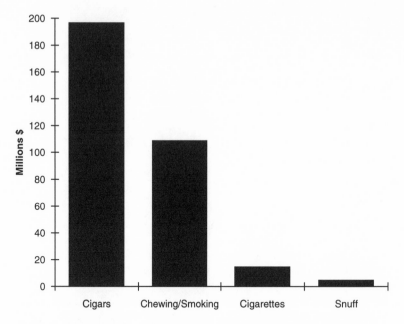

Figure 8.2. Value of Products of Branches of the Tobacco Industry, 1904. (Source: Data drawn from U.S. Bureau of Corporations 1909, Part I, 52.)

role of this new technology. But just how the Bonsack affected the industry's organization has been a matter of debate since the turn of the century. Some have emphasized solely the effects on economies of scale of production (Burns 1983). Chandler (1977, 1980, 1990) frequently cites this industry in support of his general argument about the integration of production and distribution. He argues that James Duke's special talent was to take advantage of the new machinery to create large-scale production units while instituting new distribution organizations that could effectively reach the consumer. His "success resulted from his realization that the marketing of the output of the Bonsack machine required a global selling and distributing organization. Duke became the most powerful entrepreneur in the cigarette industry because he was the first to build an integrated enterprise" (Chandler 1977, 382). In contrast, other accounts have acknowledged the role of the new machinery in increasing productivity, but have emphasized the dynamics of competition in explaining the American Tobacco Company's supremacy. Jacobstein (1907), writing at a time when the ATC was facing antitrust litigation, rejected the efficiency arguments (without, of course, using that terminology), arguing that the ATC dominated the industry because of its unfair methods of competition. Echoing the analysis (1909) of the U.S. Bureau of Corporations, Jones's (1929) classic book on trust problems in the United States acknowledged the existence of some economies of scale in both production and management, but emphasized the company's practice of buying up the competition.

What was the relationship between the formation of the gigantic American Tobacco Company, the technology of cigarette production, and the size of the cigarette market? Chandler writes that the fundamental causal force was technological, arguing that the massive output by continuous-process machinery "caused and indeed almost forced" (1977, 390) the creation of a worldwide integrated organization. His functionalist logic presents an image of an established industry that rationally adapted to the new technology by changing its organizational structure. However, Chandler reverses cause and effect: he depicts a preexisting industry adopting an integrated structure and a marketing strategy. Historically, ATC's marketing strategy constructed the market that sustained the industry. There was no inherent cigarette industry niche waiting for the technology to produce the product, no preexisting demand for cigarettes waiting for a marketing structure to meet. The technological ability to make cigarettes in great abundance did not "almost force" anything. The marketing structure made the industry when the innovative advertising strategies created the demand for cigarettes.

Duke originally located his headquarters in 1881 in Durham, North Carolina, where the university bears his name, and in 1884 installed the phenomenal Bonsack cigarette machine, which could produce as many as 120,000 cigarettes a day compared with a worker's 3,000. Three operatives and the machine could do the work of forty to fifty hand rollers. Because cigarettes at that time were virtually unknown, creating demand became the key to success, a key Duke found. He built an extensive organization, creating sales offices in major cities with salaried managers, and advertised heavily. W. Duke, Sons & Company increased production from $200,000 in 1883 to $4,500,000 in 1889 (U.S. Bureau of Corporations 1909).

Most accounts agree that advertising was the key to ATC's success (Jones 1929; Chandler 1977, 1990; McCraw 1981). ATC was one of the first companies to heavily promote brand names, use all media for advertising, and employ such devices as distributing matches featuring advertisements, as when it placed an order for 30 million books of Diamond Match's new paperback matches with the company logo (Manchester 1935). Figure 8.3 demonstrates the close relationship between advertising and the net receipts American Tobacco Company received for its cigarettes. Advertising costs per thousand cigarettes varied from $.01 to $.60 or about .5 percent to 17 percent of total costs (U.S. Bureau of Corporations 1915). When advertising costs were low, net receipts fell. When advertising rebounded, so did net receipts. Thus I do not dispute the details of Chandler's account; I question his invocation of Duke's marketing accomplishments to support an efficiency argument. Creating demand for a product fundamentally contrasts

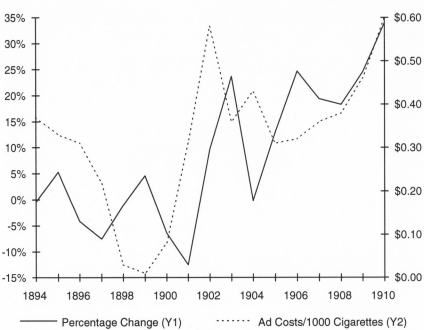

Figure 8.3. American Tobacco Company Advertising Costs and Percentage Change in Net Receipts, 1894–1910. (Source: Data drawn from U.S. Bureau of Corporations 1915, 87–89.)

with developing technology to more efficiently meet an existing need. There may be economies of scale in marketing and advertising, but they do not necessarily correlate with economies of scale in production. A closer look at how ATC grew to dominate the entire industry reveals that the dynamics of power overshadowed those of efficiency.

Duke was not the only manufacturer to build cigarette production and distribution systems. The cigarette industry was already concentrated before it consolidated. The five companies that formed the combination were centered in three cities and produced 90 percent of the national market (U.S. Bureau of Corporations 1909). Several attempts to consolidate the tobacco industry failed, until Duke persuaded the four other major cigarette makers to join his company in the American Tobacco Company in 1890. It was difficult to see any compelling economic logic in this action other than the benefits of windfall corporate capital and monopoly profits. All accounts, including Chandler's (1977, 292), agree that the combination was intended to control the competition in the industry. The industry had been profitable, with spirited but not ruinous competition. Incorporating in New Jersey like the other large holding companies, the ATC issued $15 million in common and $10 million in preferred stock, subscribed entirely by the men controlling the five constituent companies. The windfall corporate capital came from the inflated assessment of the properties that were merged into the combination. Since, of the $25 million in capital subscribed by the founders, over $21 million was carried on their books as "goodwill," by their own accounting the tangible assets represented only about $4 million. The Bureau of Corporations estimated that the original cash purchase value of goodwill for the combination was about $9 million, based on the ATC's own tally. So the $12 million overvaluation represented what the founders anticipated they would gain by the combination, their expectation of monopoly profits (U.S. Bureau of Corporations 1911). Such were the dividends of the ideology of monopoly. With 95 percent of the national market, and their contract for exclusive use of the phenomenal Bonsack cigarette machine, they initially had little trouble in achieving that.

If American Tobacco Company's dominance was based solely on technological superiority and greater efficiency, it should have been able to easily outcompete other companies. But their market share declined. Although ATC monopolized the Bonsack machine and had bought the patent for the competing Allison machine solely to prevent its use by competitors, smaller companies were using the Elliot machine, which had been released from ATC control by the courts. ATC was able to regain some of the market share, mainly through using financial power to purchase independents more than through winning customers with good products and low prices. It used the standard monopolistic competitive practices, selling in targeted areas below cost, making exclusive contracts with jobbers, and gaining control of raw products. For example, in 1901, the company was selling "American Beauty" cigarettes for $1.50 per thousand, which just covered taxes, but only in areas where Wells-Whitehead Company was marketing "North Carolina Bright." Sometimes new brands were introduced that were very similar to those ATC was trying to gain market share from, as when it introduced "Central Union" to compete with "Union Leader." This latter practice was often administered by subsidiaries it secretly controlled. When consumers boycotted ATC because it was considered a monopoly and hostile to unions, they were wooed with "Nontrust" and "Union labor" advertising of products the combination secretly controlled. These methods were combined with legitimate techniques that required considerable capital up front, such as extensive advertising and offering coupons for premiums. When successful at defeating competitors, ATC bought the companies, including major competitors like National Tobacco Works of Louisville, T. H. Hall Cigarette Company of New York, and the Consolidated Cigarette Company of New York (Jacobstein 1907). It bought others for as little as the $24,000 it paid in cash for the A. H. Motley Company of Reidsville, North Carolina, or the $60,000 it paid for the American Eagle Tobacco Company of Detroit. The point is not moral—to condemn predatory tactics—but analytical: ATC's profitability and growth were not due to its efficiency.

It is difficult to imagine that the $25 million American Tobacco Company with its virtual monopoly could take these small companies seriously as competitors. The only plausible explanation is that ATC's leaders believed the ideology of monopoly, that high profits required monopoly control and that any small pesky independent represented a potential threat. So it paid the cost of price cutting and buying the independents even if it only intended to eliminate their plants, because it feared that the small companies might grow into substantial competitors. It may have also been concerned that these little companies would be taken over by larger independents. Since other capitalists shared the ideology of monopoly, they knew that ATC would be willing to pay premium prices to eliminate competition, and they moved quickly to form companies primarily to sell them to ATC. In 1892, the National Cigarette and Tobacco Company was founded to obtain control of two fairly successful machines, the Elliott and the Baron, and was able to successfully compete with the ATC. It produced "Admiral" cigarettes at 5 cents for a package of twenty, in direct competition with ATC's "Sweet Caporal" at 5 cents for a package of ten (Jacobstein 1907). Although the combination continued to acquire competitors throughout the next two decades, its market share of cigarettes fell to about 83 percent in 1906.

I have noted clear flaws in the efficiency argument: that economies of scale engendered by advertising do not imply efficiency, the unwillingness of the ATC to depend on higher productivity or economies of scale to outcompete the independents, and the fact that despite greater resources for advertising and a monopoly over the Bonsack technology, ATC failed to sustain its market share. But other features of the industry fit efficiency theory. There were definite economies of scale which drove down the unit price of cigarettes and made it difficult for more than a few firms to maintain profitability. Neither my argument nor the efficiency account is validated prima facie. The causal direction between market domination and corporate structure still remains somewhat debatable, as does the question of whether the marketing structure and emphasis on advertising was a crucial causal factor in the industry's growth or merely a mediating structure between technology and market share. However, comparison between the cigarette branch and the plug and cigar branches does make a stronger case that the prime mover was financial power set within the corporate institution. In plug tobacco, the American Tobacco Company started with virtually no market share and came to dominate the industry almost entirely by purchasing existing companies. If efficiency theory can make a plausible but flawed case for explaining the structure of the cigarette subindustry, it fails altogether to explain why the other branches of tobacco industry came to be dominated by large corporations.

Plug Tobacco

The plug (or chewing) tobacco industry was much larger than the cigarette branch. As shown in Figure 8.2, in 1904 chewing and smoking tobacco produced nearly $110 million, of which half the volume was chewing, compared with only a little over $15 million in output of cigarettes. Plug output was thus three to four times as large as cigarettes. By 1906, ATC controlled 82 percent of the plug market, but the history of its domination was very different from its experience with cigarettes. Whereas the American Tobacco Company was created as a combination of cigarette manufacturers, making plausible the argument that it resulted from economies of scale, especially in distribution, the company began with virtually no plug business and built its plug business by acquisition. Domination by the combination offered no technological advantage. There was no functional equivalent to the Bonsack machine cigarettes, and ATC made no major technological changes when acquiring plug factories. The plug manufacturers were not engaged in ruinous competition that might have motivated them to seek a stabilizing force through merger. But the acquisition of the plug companies did have one major effect on ATC. It brought into the central leadership a group of financiers that thereafter shared power with the tobacco manufacturers, solidifying the link between manufacturing and finance capital. Financial power, not technology or markets, was at work here.

In the 1880s the plug industry looked much like the cigarette industry. The industry was dominated by a few large companies that tried unsuccessfully to combine. In 1884 they organized the Trade-Mark Protective Association of Plug-Tobacco Manufacturers, but it did not have much effect on the organization of the industry. Around 1890 they organized the Manufacturers and Buyers' Association of the United States, including P. Lorillard, Liggett & Myers, Drummond Tobacco, J. G. Butler Tobacco Company, Catlin Tobacco, P. J. Sorg Company, Wilson & McCallay Tobacco Company, Harry Weissinger, John Finzer & Brothers, and the National Tobacco Works. Its purpose was to prevent price cutting by jobbers, and did little to control the overall market for plug. It was rumored that P. Lorillard and P. J. Sorg were attempting a combination around 1890, but were prevented by the opposition of Liggett & Myers and Drummond companies.

Almost immediately after initial incorporation, the American Tobacco Company began to use some of the capital mobilized in its consolidation to acquire subsidiaries in noncigarette branches of the industry. In 1891 it bought the National Tobacco Works of Louisville, an important producer of plug tobacco, for $600,000 in cash, $400,000 preferred, and $800,000 common stock, giving it the brands "Piper Heidsieck," "Newsboy," and "Battle Ax." These brands became the beachhead from which to launch the "Plug Wars," when ATC began to sell plug tobacco at greatly reduced prices in 1894.

The Battle Ax brand, aptly named for the belligerent policy for which it was being used, sold for 13 cents a pound, below the cost of production, a price made possible only by ATC's generous capitalization. An expensive advertising campaign accompanied the price campaign. In areas where P. Lorillard and Liggett & Myers were strong, salesmen circulated, passing out free samples of Battle Ax to every man they saw to reinforce the barrage of billboard and wall space advertisements. Jobbers who exclusively sold Battle Ax were offered lower prices. In 1895 several plug manufacturers met in St. Louis and, while rejecting a proposed combination, decided to defensively enter the cigarette market. By 1897, Drummond and Liggett & Myers accounted for 15 percent of the cigarette output. ATC continued to gain a larger share of the plug market and by 1897 controlled more than a fifth of the national output. In the process, however, it had lost more than $3 million dollars (U.S. Bureau of Corporations 1909; Jones 1929).

In 1898 it looked like the war was over. Several competitors had decided to give in, but when the tax on tobacco was hiked to pay for the Spanish-American War, financiers pulled out, fearing a loss of profits. ATC bought out two leading competitors anyway, the Brown Brothers and Drummond Tobacco companies of St. Louis. With the additional artillery, ATC escalated the war, lowering the price on "Horse Shoe," the Drummond brand. Within a month the major plug companies caved in, except for Liggett & Myers. The Bureau of Corporations (1909) concluded that ATC had prevailed, not because of superior technology or organization or even size, but because it had access to financial resources that the others lacked. But although ATC had become a major producer of plug, it still did not control the market. Its strategy to achieve monopoly made it vulnerable. Four financiers, including the New York transit magnate Thomas F. Ryan, along with three tobacco manufacturers, gained control of the Liggett & Myers Tobacco Company, reasoning that if they held it out of the combination, ATC would be forced to buy them out at a premium. Adding the National Cigarette and Tobacco Company, the only formidable rival to ATC in the cigarette business, in October 1898, they created the Union Tobacco Company.

Union soon acquired a controlling interest in Blackwell's Durham Tobacco, one of the largest smoking tobacco firms outside of ATC, then combined with the North American Commercial Company and increased its stock to $24 million. In early 1899 it gained an option on a controlling interest in Liggett & Myers from the Ryan group, the nation's largest independent plug manufacturer, at which point the two giants came to an agreement. ATC increased its stock by $35 million, of which it used $12.5 million to purchase the stock of the Union Company, which was dissolved in July. The remainder of the new stock was used to declare a 100 percent dividend on existing stock. At the next annual meeting, the number of directors was increased from twelve to fifteen to include three of the financiers who controlled Union. Before that time, most of the directors had been practical tobacco men. Duke testified before the U.S. Industrial Commission that he bought the company to bring its owners into ATC for their financial resources. Later acquisitions would not have been possible without financial assistance. Several of the minority holders of Blackwell's Durham Tobacco Company were unhappy about the acquisition and petitioned for appointment of a hostile receiver. ATC as majority stockholder petitioned for a friendly receiver, which was granted. ATC then created a New Jersey corporation with the same name and reduced the stock from $4 million to $1 million, all of which was controlled by ATC. Blackwell was later used by ATC as a holding company to secretly control other tobacco companies.

The men who controlled ATC then created a new company, the Continental Tobacco Company, to handle the plug business. It bought ATC's plug business, for which ATC received a profit of $12,000,000—the benefits of combination, not efficiency. The new plug combination was capitalized at $62,290,700, which was soon increased to $97,690,700 with the acquisition of Liggett & Myers. All the common stock ($48,846,100) was bonus, that is, water. In 1901 the American Tobacco Company in cigarettes and the Continental Tobacco Company in plug and smoking were combined under the umbrella of a holding company, the Consolidated Tobacco Company.

Thus the plug tobacco branch of the industry came under the control of the same large corporation that dominated the cigarette business. But the reasons had little to do with efficiency, economies of scale, or integrated production and marketing. They had a lot to do with economic power, especially financial power. Plug production had been produced in large factories and had already achieved economies of scale when organized in partnerships and closely held corporations. It did not need to be integrated into the institutions of corporate capitalism to serve national markets. The cigarette branch and the plug branch by the end of the first decade of this century were thoroughly controlled by American Tobacco Company, both concentrated production in large factories and both sold through extensive distribution facilities adopting name-brand marketing with heavy advertising. They were both organized along the lines of modern business enterprise. But their histories had little in common in terms of any technological need for large-scale production or for integrated production and marketing in large corporations. What they had in common was integration into the corporate structure, using financial resources to consolidate into a single corporation the various businesses that had previously competed with one another. The constituent companies had faced the choice of either going it alone against intense competition or enjoying both the larges of corporate capital, by selling their properties for far above their cash value, and the prospects of continuing profits in the form of dividends on any stock they held on to. The widespread ideology of monopoly undermined resistance to selling out and attracted resources from other corporate capitalists who wanted to share in the promise of monopoly profits. So both cigarette and plug tobacco in turn became part of the giant corporation.

The history of these companies also illustrates how the manipulation of corporate securities can create control and profit for strategically placed individuals with the use of other people's money. While the socialization of capital can potentially contribute to a broader distribution of wealth beyond those conventionally considered capitalists by allowing anyone with a few hundred dollars to share in corporate profits, the actual operation of corporate capitalism has concentrated control in fewer hands and created colossal individual fortunes. The rights, entitlements, and responsibilities of ownership are divided among the different types of securities defining new relationships among owners and creditors. In 1901 the inner group of leaders moved to further cement its control of ATC and Continental Tobacco Company by acquiring nearly the entire common stock of both. Consolidated's original capital of $30 million had been paid in cash and had increased to $40 million by 1902. Soon thereafter it offered to exchange 4 percent bonds for stock of Continental Tobacco and $200 in bonds for $100 of American Tobacco stock. The offer was accepted by nearly all stockholders, resulting in the issuing of $157,378,200 in Consolidated bonds split more or less equally for the stock of the two companies. At the time the issue appeared very advantageous for the stockholders. Continental stock had never paid a dividend and had been selling on the market for $20–$30 per $100 share. American stock had been paying about 6 percent, but the two-for-one exchange guaranteed an 8 percent return on original investments. However, the men who controlled Consolidated and who engineered the deal knew that the revenue tax on tobacco was about to drop, giving the company windfall profits. When the taxes had been levied during the Spanish-American War, the increased costs had been passed on in higher prices; but when they were repealed, prices were reduced only in part. For Consolidated's $30 million original investment, it enjoyed profits of $23 million during its first year. After paying $6 million in dividends, it had $17 million in surplus. More than half the shares were controlled by Duke, Brady, Payne, Ryan, Widener, and Whitney. As the Bureau of Corporations observed, "Most of these men, it will be observed, were the financiers who had entered the Combination in 1898 and 1899. They and a few associates had supplied the greater part of the new capital now made available for the expansion policy; but they did so only because it was evident that, through the organization of the Consolidated, they might enormously increase their power and their share in the prospective profits of the business" (1911, 9).

In 1904, the Supreme Court decision against the Northern Securities Company alarmed many corporate capitalists who feared that the holding company would be declared illegal, just as the trust had been. So the combination organized a new corporation, also named the American Tobacco

Company, which took over the properties of the Consolidated Tobacco Company, the Continental Tobacco Company, and the old American Tobacco Company, dissolving all three. The new ATC operated both as a holding company and as an operating company. The new organization further concentrated control in the hands of the inside group and simplified the organization. New ATC stock was exchanged for stock of the constituent companies. Only $242,000 of old ATC and Continental common stock had been in the hands of the public. It along with closely held common was exchanged for new common ($40 million). All old ATC and Consolidated and most of Continental preferred stock had been in the hands of the public. It was exchanged for new ATC bonds, which of course lacked any voting power. The immense Consolidated 4 percent bonds were exchanged, half for new ATC preferred stock paying 6 percent dividends and half for new 4 percent bonds. Thus the new ATC issued $40,242,400 common, $78,689,100 preferred, and $136,360,000 bonds. The preferred stocks had no voting power in the new company, which meant that power was even further concentrated in those who controlled the common stocks. The actual effect of the reorganization upon the capital obligations standing against the business and assets was not great, but the control of the company by the small group of insiders became nearly absolute. Thus those with title to the vast majority of ATC capital had no authority over its management. Five men holding title to less than a sixth of its capital exercised full control, a distribution of power possible only in the corporate system of property.

Cigars

The cigar branch is widely cited as the most unprofitable branch of the tobacco industry. Because cigars were generally made by hand, except for the cheapest types, they continued to be manufactured in small plants with no dominating companies and no economies of scale. Chandler states the conventional wisdom: "Since these processes did not lend themselves to high-volume throughput, administrative coordination did not reduce costs and so raise barriers to entry. Neither massive advertising nor effective organization could bring the dominance of a single firm in the cigar business" (1977, 390). However, American Tobacco did succeed in creating a corporation that became the nation's largest maker of cigars. It did not monopolize the market, but did account for about a seventh of all cigars sold. It did not make high profits, especially compared with the other branches of the tobacco industry. The cigar industry is a prime example of a business that lacked all the fertile conditions for large-scale corporations but still gave birth to a corporation that did not greatly prosper, but did survive. It survived only because of the financial transfusions ATC gave it until it was able to stand on its own. The social relations institutionalized in the corporate infrastructure were used to create and sustain an enterprise that would have otherwise failed. In the end its integration into the corporate system was more consequential than its unfit objective conditions.

At first, the American Tobacco Company had dabbled only in cheroots and other small cigars, but in 1901 it decided to move into the cigar business. Just as it had created the Continental Tobacco Company to administer its plug business, it created the American Cigar Company, a $10 million corporation, of which 70 percent was owned by American Tobacco and Continental Tobacco. With James B. Duke as its president, it bought American Tobacco's cigar business for a little under $4 million, which more or less offset the price American had paid for its cigar company stock. Like the plug branch, it expanded by buying the leading companies, not by building new factories. One of the company's first purchases, Powell, Smith & Company, was then producing about 100 million five-cent cigars a year at three plants, including a Kingston, New York, factory employing 1,600 workers. The new subsidiary received a little over $2 million for less than a million dollars of tangible assets. American Cigar then proceeded to buy other companies, spending in the first year $12 million for about $7 million of tangible assets. By 1908 its book assets exceeded $40 million, but the Bureau of Corporations estimated the true value to be less than half of that. At that time American Tobacco controlled five cigar combinations: the American Cigar Company; the American Stogie Company, making a cheap cigar sold primarily in Pennsylvania and surrounding states; the Havana-American Company, which made cigars in the United States from Cuban tobacco; the Havana Tobacco Company, operating in Cuba; and the Puerto Rican–American Tobacco Company

When it decided to move into the cigar business, American Tobacco and its subsidiaries controlled only a little over 2 percent of the market but assumed that the techniques that had served them in cigarettes, plug, and the other branches would work in cigars. As American Cigar acquired new companies, it launched extensive advertising and promotional campaigns, by 1903 spending as much to advertise cigars as to manufacture them. The results were disastrous: three straight years of major losses, including a 1902 loss equal to a quarter of its tangible assets. However, it continued to purchase other companies and issue new stock, transactions that represented social relationships possible only within the institutional structure of corporate capitalism. For example, in 1902, when its operations lost more than $3.6 million, its books showed a surplus of nearly $1.5 million, because $1.5 million of the recently acquired Cabanas y Carbajal stock was exchanged for $6.6 million in stocks and bonds of the American Cigar subsidiary Havana Tobacco. In 1905 American Cigar issued $10 million in preferred stock with which it paid an $8 million loan from American Tobacco (U.S. Bureau of Corporations 1911). After the splurge of advertising and the heavy losses, it continued to buy companies, but reduced the advertising and enjoyed modest profits. From 1904 to 1908 the American Cigar Company made profits of about $10 million. Overall American Tobacco profits from its cigar subsidiaries were about a third of those from other branches, and slightly less than those of major independents (U.S. Bureau of Corporations 1915).

The point here is not that these transactions are corrupt or unethical or that only socially capitalized corporations employ accounting sleights of hand. The point is that these particular forms of manipulation were possible only within the corporate system. Partnerships can be owned by the same individuals and assets can be transferred at nonmarket values, but it is assets of the companies, not pieces of companies themselves, that are being transferred. Moreover, the techniques that corporations use are presumably temporary fixes; eventually enterprises that don't turn a "real" profit will fail. The piper must be paid. However, the link between short-term manipulation and long-term market discipline is much shorter for privately held companies than it is for sprawling publicly held corporations. In the meantime, those who control corporations can gain enormous short-term profits from new capital infusions from outside investors. The relationship between investors and beneficiaries is thus very different.

It is widely acknowledged that the cigar industry offered no economies of scale. But American Cigar did operate in large factories. Between 1901 and 1906, it decreased the number of operating factories from forty to twenty-nine, while steadily purchasing new companies. In the latter year its two largest factories were more than four times the size of those of any independents. American Cigar's largest plant, at Jersey City, produced nearly 200 million cigars a year. The average American Cigar Company plant produced 18 million cigars, compared with 300,000 for the industry as a whole. Part of this difference was due to the acquisition of the larger independents, but part was due to increased concentration among its plants. Yet it gained few economies from this scale. Its operating costs were similar to those of the leading independents, and its rate of profits lagged behind theirs. In the first decade of the century, the profits of major independents were slightly higher than the combination and tended to increase, and in 1909 and 1910 were about twice those of the American Cigar Company. Part of the difference was that American Cigar spent relatively more on selling. The combination in the years 1907–1910 spent an average $1.13 per thousand cigars on sales while the leading independents averaged only $.96. The combination averaged $1.19 per thousand for advertising compared with the independents' $1.03 (U.S. Bureau of Corporations 1915). These are the areas in which the combination was supposed to enjoy economies of scale. While it did not have any special economies of scale in production, it should have enjoyed greater economies in distribution. Thus it was the corporate structure that created its scale of operation, not any economies of scale that accounted for the corporate structure.

If the dynamics of efficiency had determined the structure and operation of the tobacco industry, its history would have looked very different. Efficiency theory holds that organizations arise or adapt to more effectively meet existing needs. But the cigarette industry created its demand by advertising and promotion. If the product had never existed, nobody would have missed it. It is implausible to hold that the process of creating demand through advertising meets any need but that of profit. If the efficiency account is correct, supply and distribution should have followed demand, not created it. The producers would have joined together after a huge market justified a level of scale that technology would economize. More important, if the merged corporation enjoyed truly substantial economies of scale in production and distribution, it would not have been necessary to resort to predatory competition. The discipline of the free market should have eliminated smaller, less efficient competitors. American Tobacco would not have needed to sell below cost in areas where other brands thrived or buy competitors at inflated prices to shut their factories. When efficiency accounts concede that ATC was engaging in such practices, they are, in effect, saying that the creation and growth of ATC was overdetermined—that it would have happened even if ATC had not engaged in such practices. Some of this behavior may be explained by the tobacco leaders' belief that monopolization was necessary, but this also undermines the assumption of efficiency theory that managers rationally maximize their utilities. Moreover, even if efficiency explained the formation of ATC to manufacture cigarettes, there is no necessary reason why the corporation would aggressively take over the other branches. Plug tobacco companies were acquired for no economies of scale in production or distribution. Without technological marvels like the Bonsack cigarette-making machine, the advantages achieved by merger into the cigarette company could only have come in purchasing raw materials, but different products used different types of tobacco. The only advantage would have been monopsony power, the power of a single buyer to dictate price. If efficiency theory operated, the plug manufacturers should have independently and endogenously merged to create single production or distribution facilities. They didn't do that. They were taken over by ATC, which made a policy decision to acquire them one by one. Only when a few manufacturers joined with financiers to force ATC's hand did they merge on their own. It is ATC's size and resources that explain the plug manufacturers' organization into a large corporation. Finally, if efficiency dynamics operated, cigar making would have remained entirely outside the corporate order. It was ATC's financial power and aggressive acquisition that made it possible for it to enter and become the largest manufacturer in an industry wholly unsuited for large corporations. Technology and economies of scale may have limited ATC's ability to monopolize the cigar business, but had no effect on its ability to form a large, enduring corporation.

In both the sugar and the tobacco industries, different parts of the industry were transformed into the property relations of socialized capital by integrating them into corporations that dominated their entire industries. In sugar, the different parts of the industry were technologically similar, but were organized in very different property regimes until the dominant eastern cane sugar branch temporarily gained control of western beet sugar companies. The tobacco industries were technologically highly diverse but homogenized into the American Tobacco Company by the exercise of market and financial power. In contrast, in the paper industry, different parts of an industry were organized into large corporations, each of which dominated only their part of the industry, but with different degrees of success. This industry allows us to examine another facet of efficiency theory, that of survival. Chandler, for example, concedes that large corporations were established for a variety of motivations, but maintains that they persisted only where the technological and market conditions made them appropriate: "[V]ery few American mergers remained large or profitable unless they . . . moved beyond a strategy of horizontal combination to one of vertical integration. Even then they rarely became and remained powerful business enterprises unless they were in industries employing mass production technologies for mass national and global markets" (1977, 316). The paper industry permits us to examine why corporations in different subindustries fared very differently, and especially to ask whether markets and technology or networks and power more accurately predict the winners and losers.

PAPER

Chandler (1990) discusses paper along with other producers of industrial materials such as stone, clay and glass, and metals, arguing that large integrated firms first appeared in the subindustries where economies of scale were largest and whose products went to the greatest number of companies. Although the most important technological innovations, those permitting paper to be made with wood pulp rather than rags, were widely adopted as early as the 1870s, he asserts without evidence that gradual improvements throughout the 1880s and 1890s created economies of scale. Nonetheless, he admits that the largest consolidation, the International Paper Company, moved sluggishly to rationalize production and build its sales arm (Chandler 1990).

A comparative analysis of the different parts of the industry challenges Chandler's interpretation. Since in all branches, a tradition of close cohesion and strong industrial governance fostered the creation of major socially capitalized corporations, the point of contention among explanatory theories is why some succeeded while others failed. Chandler explains the difference between the successful and concentrated newspaper or heavy kraft paper subindustries and the relative stagnation of the American Writing Paper Company or Bemis Paper Bag Company in terms of vertical integration. While the successful companies integrated backward, the unsuccessful ones integrated only forward into distribution, and therefore "found they had few advantages over small, non-integrated companies" (Chandler 1977, 354). Similarly, he attributes the dismal failure of National Wall

Paper to "the costliness of a strategy of horizontal combination and the ineffectiveness of the holding company in carrying out that strategy" (334), drawing the conclusion that successful mergers "operated in industries where technology and markets permitted such integration [with marketing and purchasing organizations] to increase the speed or lower the cost of materials through the processes of production and distribution" (336). While he is no doubt correct that the cooperation between suppliers and distributors enhances the success of new corporations and that outright ownership effectively secures their cooperation or, if necessary, their subordination, I would challenge the assumption that the relationship among suppliers, manufacturers, and distributors is determined by the objective needs of production and distribution. Close relationships did not necessarily develop "in industries where technology and markets permitted such integration," but in industries where networks and power created cooperation or compliance. Even if technological and market factors may have made integration easier in some subindustries than others, it was the social relationships that determined whether integration was actually achieved. The paper industry also illustrates a very different point—that corporations could be effectively integrated into the social institutions of corporate capitalism, thoroughly changing the social definition of ownership, with little active involvement of investment bankers.

Most of the branches of the paper industry were technically similar and papermakers could with only modest investment shift from one kind to another, but the established social relations with customers ensured a stable division of labor among newsprint, writing paper, envelopes, straw (wrapping) paper, and so forth. All were long established in this country. Unlike petroleum, electrical machinery, or chemicals, which were born in the second half of the century, paper was as old as any commodity known to humanity. Each of the branches had a traditional and established social basis that greatly facilitated its governance. By the turn of the century most of the branches had been organized into large socially capitalized corporations, although some had reverted to proprietary control.

The paper industry, lacking colorful figures and great scandals, is not as widely discussed as other, more innovative or notorious industries. There were no J. P. Morgans, John D. Rockefellers, or Thomas Edisons. The best-known consolidation, the International Paper Company, was a routine merger in the midst of the great merger movement, neither a pioneer nor a mammoth. There was little that fired the imagination of the chroniclers of this period; but, for that very reason, there is much that should interest the sociologist. Statistically the industry was very typical of manufacturing corporations. Table 8.1 shows some of its major features. In both 1880 and 1900, it was within a single standard deviation to the mean on nearly all pertinent characteristics, including number of establishments (virtually at the mean), productivity (slightly lower), capital intensity (slightly higher), and growth over the previous decade (substantially lower, but still less than

Table 8.1
Economic Characteristics of the Paper Industry (except wallpaper), 1880, 1900

Year		Establishments	Capital (000)	Average Capital / Estab. (000)	Productivity	Capital Intensity
1880	Paper and Wood Pulp Industry	742	$48,140	$64.88	0.88	5.37
	Standard deviations from the mean of all industries	0.03	1.38	0.32	−0.12	0.95
1900	Paper and Wood Pulp Industry	763	$167,508	$219.54	11.44	8.07
	Standard deviations from the mean of all industries	0.04	1.75	0.2	−0.36	0.53

Source: U.S. Bureau of the Census 1914, 666.

a standard deviation on a skewed variable). Only for the aggregate capital was it more than one standard deviation above the mean, which was due to the fact that the industry boundaries included all types of paper rather than categorizing each type separately.[2] In many ways, paper is our industrial "everyman."

The largest and best-organized branch was newsprint, which spawned the best known of the paper corporations, the International Paper Company. The International Paper Company exemplifies the effects of long-established tight cohesion, leading, in the face of only moderate hardship, to a consolidation that effectively governed the industry with relatively little enhancement of productivity. A glimpse of the paper industry in the years before the consolidation can be seen in the correspondence of Herbert A. and Charles T. Wilder, proprietors of the Wilder Paper Company of Boston (Baker Library, Harvard University, MMS 491). One brother handled production at their plant, the other sales from their Boston office. This medium-sized firm sold paper to such sizable newspapers as the New York *Tribune* and the Chicago *Herald*. The letters reveal that both brothers paid very close attention to all phases of the operation, monitoring such aspects as quality control, especially when receiving complaints from customers. For example, Herbert wrote Charles that "Lessor [an employee] is here today and says 5 lbs Acetic Acid [vinegar] to 1000th Engine, is better to use with Aniline to brighten up color, than Sulphuric Acid." They were very attentive to competition, especially price competition, but also collegial toward the competition. "I did not find what price Montague had offered them [the Washington *Star*] but incline, more and more, to think that it is less than my quotation, viz 3¼ less 2 off cash. . . . Think I may have to revise the price to the Star" (Feb. 9, 1893). The competition between the two companies for the business of the *Star* was mentioned in several letters; they finally concluded that the only way to get the business was to go far below Montague, which they were unwilling to do, finally being resigned to losing: "Should rather be beaten by them than any one else, I know of" (Feb. 27, 1893). Thus the competition was spirited, but hardly reckless.

The papermakers were more inclined to view the 1890s as reckless in retrospect than when they were living through it. The decade began on a high note. The *Paper Trade Journal* reported, "It will be conceded by most members of the trade that so far as the aggregate volume of business is concerned the year which closed this week has been far in advance of its predecessors for several years past. . . . Manufacturers of News have had their product well under control of orders during the greater part of the year, and in fact some mills have been pretty steadily crowded" (Jan. 3, 1891, 20:1). There had been only two bankruptcies, both companies founded by lawyers who didn't know the paper business. When competition heated up the *Journal* remarked on it, noting, for example, that the makers of paper bags were at war, or that the envelope combination had failed to control the market, although it continued to do business as a company (Jan. 3, 1891, 20:1), but such sentiments of alarm were rare. Another indication that the competition was not ruinous was the number of companies doing business. In the dozen years prior to the formation of the International Paper Company, the total number of paper companies operating was nearly constant. In 1886, an even 1,000 plants operated, and in 1897, it was 1,067.[3] There had been a slight rise in the early nineties and a slight drop during the depression, but for every company that folded, whether by bankruptcy, the death of the owners, or altering the factory to make a new product, someone was confident enough in the industry's profitability to begin a new plant. At the same time, demand for paper was growing. Except in the depression years, the industry did not feel that it was experiencing unusually hard times. For example, in 1896 only five companies in all branches of paper went bankrupt, all of which were valued at less than a million dollars (*Paper Trade Journal*, 26:34).

Despite these objective conditions and a long history of collegiality, the paper manufacturers publicly justified the creation of International Paper (IPC) in much the same terms as other consolidators. Overproduction had driven gentlemanly competition into reckless rivalry. As Hugh Chisholm, the IPC president, testified to the Industrial Commission, low returns on invested capital and the real prospect of bankruptcy were engendered by "unbusinesslike methods" (U.S. Industrial Commission 1902). True, prices were falling, as they were generally in that period. From 1880 to 1897, prices had fallen from 9 cents a pound to 1.6 cents a pound. But there is no evidence that the "reckless" competition was qualitatively any different from "natural" competition. The pages of the *Paper Trade Journal* were filled with more news about sociability than about trade wars or bankruptcy.

Unlike earlier consolidations such as American Tobacco or American Sugar Refining, no single company or personality dominated. Hugh Chisholm was the industry's leading figure, but he led through the voluntary American Pulp and Paper Association rather than through domination by competition. Of the twenty-one companies that constituted the consolidation, no single company was worth as much as $5 million, out of a total of a little over $38 million total (*Paper Trade Journal,* Oct. 15, 1898). Three companies, including Glen Falls, Chisholm's company, had only a short time before been combined at just under $8 million. Including these three, there were twelve companies greater than a million dollars. Thus International Paper was a more egalitarian consolidation than many, formed to take advantage of a new institutional system rather than to solidify a victory of a dominating force. IPC was taking advantage of an institutional structure rather than constructing one.

The consolidation was a complete merger, not a holding company. The industry's prominent producers, led by Hugh Chisholm, formed a committee to negotiate with the other manufacturers. After appraising each property on the basis of machinery, access to water and timber, and goodwill, an offer was made to buy the company outright, payable in stock of the new company. Eighteen companies, almost all in the Northeast, merged into the new company. The company's officers took great pride in the fact that no promoters were involved and that no funds other than routine lawyer's fees were paid. Paper men engineered the consolidation, paper men controlled it, and paper men profited from it. The nature of the profits was debated between the companies and critics. Although the company claimed that its $55 million authorized capital included no water, it admitted at the time of formation that at least $20 million represented goodwill. For the paper men who sold out to the firm, their profits would come from selling the company's securities along with any dividends the company might pay before the stock was sold. The company admitted that several of the mills had been grossly undercapitalized, especially older plants that had not updated their books to reflect new investment. Many proprietors at that time did no capital accounting, calculating their profit rate only relative to revenues and current expenses. Each manufacturer now received IPC securities in payment for his property; he no longer received the profits from his individual plant, but did gain the dividends from the entire IPC, which, because of its control of the market and its negotiating power with customers, was able to increase the profit rate for the aggregate. When he sold the securities, he received the considerable profits from that, almost certainly more than the cash value of his plant. Thus the largest source of profit would be from the securities market, not the direct profit of making and selling paper. Of course, at the same time, he lost the other privileges of ownership, especially the authority to make strategic decisions. Only if he stayed on to manage the plant that he formerly owned would he retain any authority at all.

While Chandler points to the paper industry as an example of the way in which the number of customers influences the propensity to consolidate, a comparison between newsprint paper and writing paper challenges such a generalization. Newsprint was sold to newspapers, and writing paper to individuals. In contrast to newspaper, writing paper did not fit the model of the low-quality, mass-produced product. It was the most craftsman-like branch of the industry, requiring greater quality control and greater skill for cutting and fine engraving. But writing paper had the social conditions for consolidation. It was geographically concentrated, with 60 percent of production in the state of Massachusetts, notably in the Holyoke region, and had a long history of industrywide governance (*Paper Trade Journal* 1893). Writing paper manufacturers had cooperated closely since the depression of the 1870s, setting prices and controlling production levels, but the introduction of "engine-sized" mass-produced writing paper during the 1893 depression ended the unanimity of interest (Lamoreaux 1985). But even then this section of the industry was able to respond to the depression by maintaining prices and reducing output, unlike the newspaper manufacturers, who maintained production while reducing prices (Scranton 1989). According to efficiency theory, writing paper's actions should have reduced its need to consolidate. Nonetheless, in 1899, thirty-three manufacturers formed the American Writing Paper Company, capitalized at $25 million and controlling three-quarters of the national market (U.S. House of Representatives 1909). They originally used a Providence, Rhode Island, bank to finance the consolidation, but found the arrangement unsatisfactory and turned to Lee, Higginson & Company, an investment banker more experienced in consolidations. These matters were best administered within the organizational structure already in place. Thus a part of the industry even less economically suited than newspaper spawned a major corporation based on social cohesion, taking advantage of a maturing institutional structure of corporate capital.

One of the smaller branches of the paper industry was box board or pulp board. It had no new productive technologies, no expanding market, no special economies of scale—none of the factors that under efficiency considerations would warrant consolidation. But it did have trouble governing its industry, and the corporate form offered what was becoming considered to be an effective form of governance. Pulp board makers' dissatisfaction with their inability to govern the industry had provoked attempts to integrate as early as 1895, when the leading companies created the National Pulp Board Company, which controlled 90 percent of the national output and was "the organization which has regulated the market for pulp board" (Oct. 15, 1898, 27:735). It was more of an association than a company, and its role was to regulate rather than to make profits. The *Paper Trade Journal* reported the consolidation attempts as a mundane matter, telling a story, not of efficiency or technology, but of control. In 1898 a dozen makers of box board—all members of the National Pulp Board Company—met in New

York to discuss forming a company along the lines of the International Paper Company, "to control the pulp board interests of the country" (Oct. 15, 1898, 27:735). The monopoly ideology suggested a means to satisfactorily govern the industry. In contrast to descriptions of the newspaper industry, the *Journal* reported that "[t]he pulp board market is in a very unsatisfactory state, and some of the manufacturers have come to the conclusion that the only way to properly regulate the manufacture and sales of pulp board in this country is to form a big company and buy the plants outright" (Oct. 15, 1898, 27:735). As discourse within the industry, the *Paper Trade Journal* would have no need for euphemisms to rationalize the company's purposes. But its deliberations had faltered over the price to be paid for the properties. "Indeed it is said that the discussion on this point became so warm at one stage of the proceedings that it looked as though some of the manufacturers might come to blows" (Oct. 15, 1898, 27:735). This describes a conflict among people well known to one another. Conflict among strangers is more like to engender exit rather than voice. But it is not surprising that the industry would be difficult to govern. There were many companies, none of which dominated. The two largest, the Uncas Paper Company of Norwich, Connecticut, and McEwan Brothers Company of Whippany, New Jersey, accounted for only as much as 15 percent of the productive capacity. Thus this subindustry had a different story with the same ending, a small industry with no dominant leaders but a long history ending contentiously in yet one more socially capitalized corporation.

Strawboard was the industry's largest branch among those producing a product not destined to be written on. Unlike most of the other branches, which were centered in the Northeast, most strawboard manufacturers were located in the Midwest, especially in Indiana, Ohio, and Illinois, which accounted for three-quarters of the market. The strawboard manufacturers had long been one of the more active groups in the American Pulp and Paper Association. Their geographic proximity and history of associational activity were fertile soil for combination. In 1889, before most of the other industrial corporations, and a year before the Sherman Antitrust Act, the larger midwestern producers formed the American Strawboard Company (Lockwood Trade Journal Company 1940; Smith 1971). Although its $6 million capitalization pales relative to the consolidations a decade later, when formed it was gigantic compared with other manufacturing firms. From the point of view of efficiency theory, it was an anomalous industrial pioneer. Its product was a simple one with no recent technological advances, no inherent demand for great capital, and no economies of scale.

The wallpaper industry is one of the well-known examples of corporate failure during this period. In many ways it conforms to the efficiency theory model of failure: a product that had no particular economy of scale combined to control the market, pursued monopoly profits, inviting new competition, which it tried to buy out at any price, driving itself out of business. But this is not the entire picture. The reasons for its failure were as much social as economic. For thirty years, the manufacturers of wallpaper combined from time to time to maintain uniform prices and terms of credit. At first they made a simple agreement on a schedule of prices and terms that despite lack of enforcement mechanisms, was generally honored. Hard times after 1873 eroded the system, and it was finally abandoned, giving way to an open market, depreciation of prices, and unprofitable business. After new attempts to govern the industry failed, most of the nation's producers created a pool in 1880, the American Wall Paper Manufacturers' Association. Each company paid a security deposit to bind it to the agreed-upon prices. A commissioner was appointed to enforce agreements by appropriating the security violators had paid in. However, the profits to be made by breaking agreements exceeded the fines for violation, and the system broke down when manufacturers sold for less than the agreed-upon price and failed to report sales.

During this period, there was no growth of outside competition despite high profits to the industry. "During the next 5 years there was an open market; prices were greatly reduced, and several manufacturers retired from business" (U.S. Industrial Commission 1902). But the open market was not celebrated in the spirit of Adam Smith. Apparently these manufacturers found unacceptable any competition in which any manufacturers failed. In what they characterized to the Industrial Commission as terrible times, only four out of twenty-five or twenty-six left the industry. The most progressive companies prospered, but it was the dealers who were hit the hardest. Prices were generally falling, and dealers found themselves with overpriced inventories and fixed contracts for overpriced wholesale goods. They wanted relief as much as the manufacturers. The National Wall Paper Company was created in 1892, capitalized with $30 million in common stock and $8 million in bonds, and controlled 60–65 percent of output (New York Legislature 1897). The stock was taken entirely by the manufacturers with no promoters. Manufacturers agreed to refrain from reentering the industry on their own except in the state of Washington, and placed their stock in a trust fund for ten years. Another clue that hardship had not fostered the merger was that most of the manufacturers said they would be satisfied if the profits equaled what they had earned before the merger (U.S. Industrial Commission 1902, testimony of Henry Burn). They were more interested in realizing increased economies in distribution than in production, attempting to eliminate the middle men and jobbers. They established branches in all the major cities, lowered prices so the consumer could enjoy the profits that had gone to the jobbers, and offered the product at a standard rate. They also closed some of the smaller and less efficient plants.

However, without government enforcement of the contracts, the pledge to refrain from competition was not honored. The displaced managers joined forces with the jobbers to attract capital and successfully compete on the basis of antitrust sentiment. The challenge in the midst of the depression undermined National Wall Paper's profitability. In response the company reversed its policy of eliminating jobbers, bought up some of the competition, and tried to rebound, but more competition arose. Convinced that only monopoly control could succeed, National Wall Paper, along with the new companies, created the Continental Wall Paper Company to market all the product of all the companies. After a year of profit, new challengers, guaranteed of selling their product, arose, further depressing the industry. National Wall Paper's share of the business fell from 75 percent to 60 percent. No dividends were ever paid on the stock. Henry Burns, the company's president, testified to the Industrial Commission that the enmity produced by cutting out the jobbers was a major factor. Customers had built cordial relations with jobbers whom they trusted to sell them a good product at a reasonable price. Without this link with the customer, manufacturers could not sell their product. The timing of the depression also prevented them from establishing a good reputation. Another factor was labor costs. Prior to National Wall Paper, most companies had operated about nine months a year. At the end of 1894, during which most factories had operated a relatively short time because of the depression, the workers demanded an eleven-month year. The following year they demanded and won a twelve-month year with increased wages. Burns felt that the combination benefited labor by allowing it to focus its demands on one company, and making it more difficult to replace unruly workers.

In the different branches of paper examined here, all were organized into large, socially capitalized corporations that attempted to monopolize their markets, regardless of the different technologies and different types of markets. They succeeded where they were able to form uncontentious oligopolies with solid working relationships with suppliers along with cordial relations with investors that could help weather the storms of hard times. Certainly there was a threshold of technological conditions and minimal profits necessary for survival, but for most, success or failure easily surpassed that. Social and political factors then were more important for determining survival or persistence.

THE BIGGEST MERGER OF ALL: FINANCE AND INDUSTRY CONSOLIDATE

The social organization of enterprise under any economic system is constrained by the social organization of property. The social relations among the individuals participating in the various aspects of conceiving a plan, bringing together materials, transforming and assembling goods, and distributing products are fundamentally property relations. These social relationships include not only the relations among the different participants in the division of labor—under capitalism, owners and workers—but also social relationships among individuals in the same part of the division of labor, such as workers and workers or owners and owners. The relationships among owners in the market and the relationships that constitute the relations among different owners of the same enterprise are property relations. What types of relationships will be legitimated and enforced by the state thus constitute the nature of the economic system and structure how it operates. As has been stressed throughout this work, the corporate revolution was a transformation of property relations and a new social organization of capital. The American Sugar Refining Company, the American Tobacco Company, and the International Paper Company were more than just the merger of the sugar men, tobacco men, and paper men who had owned the constituent companies. They were a new type of property and defined a new social relationship among those sugar men, electrical machinery men, and steel men. The transformation could not have happened without a new legal framework allowing collective ownership and the socialization of property. It could also not have happened without the availability of large amounts of capital. The availability of capital means the existence of not only an aggregate amount of capital in the economy but, at least as important, the institutional structures to mobilize that capital and make it available in an accessible form. The new enterprises did more than amalgamate the capital of the constituent companies into a larger company. To label them mergers only describes the most superficial facet of the process. The specific institutional form that the new property took was corporate capital—capital organized and administered through the specific institutions of investment banks, stock markets, and brokerage houses—which investors then invested in socially capitalized large corporations.

The corporate revolution did more than aggregate productive units together into larger and more integrated units. As capital was socialized, the forms of capital were changed in at least three ways. First when corporations combined productive units, they also changed ownership into a more liquid form that was much more fungible and more easily transferred from one person to another.[4] Second, the process created new capital that achieved its value less out of physical assets than by socially legitimated agreement. Finally, it mobilized new capital from outside the party of owners and promoters, from other individuals and organizations.

If a new corporation was created as a merger of existing companies, as most of them were during the corporate revolution, the owners of the constituent companies sold their property to the new corporation for securities of the new company or, less frequently, for cash. Pieces of capital that had been separate were combined into a single organization, but ownership of that organization was divided into easily sold parcels. The most common pattern was to assess the value of the property and pay for it in preferred stock or a combination of preferred and common stock of the new company. This had the effect of dividing two of the prerogatives of property. Preferred stock gave the possessor a prior claim on profits; common stock gave the possessor the right of control, at least in theory. At the same time, the deeds that had represented physical property that could only be transferred to others by the clumsy and difficult processes of sale for cash or inheritance were replaced by the more liquid form of corporate securities. The representations of ownership became easily fungible, split into very small pieces which could be easily sold on an active and readily accessible market.

Incorporation not only combined and reorganized existing capital, but also generated new capital that represented value created by the institutional framework of corporate capital, value that depended not only on physical assets but also on socially legitimated agreement to its value. For example, when the American Sugar Refining Company was created to replace the Sugar Trust, it issued $25 million in preferred stock, which was distributed to the sugar men who owned the constituent company. It also issued $25 million in common stock, which represented nothing but the promise of future earnings. Securities that represented no physical assets were known as watered stock, a metaphor for the earlier practice of gorging thirsty, scrawny cattle with water before weighing them for sale. "Watered stock" had no "beef." As standard histories describe, the practice of watering stock was a major issue of the day, an object of intense criticism on behalf of the small investor most likely to suffer when watered securities returned to their "true" value, but interpreted by pro-corporate economists and lawyers as anticipated profits from the combination, either the monopoly rent or the fruits of economic scale (Cook 1903). Since the time of the corporate revolution, some economists have argued that the debate is misplaced, since the value of any commodity, including corporate securities, has only the value set by the market. In this line of reasoning, par value is always a fiction, as attested to by the growth of "no par" securities, which operate on the market no differently from securities with an official par value. They conclude from this argument that it is pointless to distinguish between securities that represent "real" value and those that represent fictional value or "water" (Bosland 1949; Buxbaum 1979; Grossman 1920). In terms of the dynamics of the securities market, this is reasonable. But in terms of the social relations of property, it is essential to distinguish between the value that physical assets would have if administered through the social relations of an entrepreneurial economy (which is not necessarily any more "true") and the value that they would have when administered through a corporate economy. Both modes express value in terms of dollars, but they are socially quite distinct. It was the existence of the second mode of value that provided the incentive for many of the industrialists to sacrifice the ownership of their property. They could obtain not only the value of the physical plant but also the speculative profits, the value that was created within the institutional structure of corporate capital. A man with a million-dollar factory could sell the factory not only for the million dollars in preferred stock, which gave him the right to continued and presumably increased profits, but a million dollars in common stock, which could be sold on the market, although the market price might deviate. But many owners of stock expected to make more profits from selling than from dividends. As long as the community of investors was willing to buy securities, the profits from dividends could be at least temporarily ignored.

In addition to capital that represented the value of the assets and capital that represented socially legitimated value, there was often new capital infused into the corporation from outside the company from the investment community, wealth mobilized previously and available for new assignment. Most often this took the form of bonds rather than preferred or common stock. This was the new capital that often provided the funds for new equipment, new factories, or new distribution facilities. Common stock and preferred stock could have conceivably been invented de novo. People could have in principle agreed to merge and to issue new securities that others could have agreed to "purchase." But entirely new capital required a history, the prior accumulation and concentration in a few hands of wealth for reinvestment. This was one of the reasons the railroad was so critical to corporate history. It was through the railroads that most of this capital was mobilized. When the railroads ceased to be as dependable as previously believed, investors were willing to invest in industrial securities (Navin and Sears 1955).

No one disputes that investment bankers played an important role in the rise of the large corporation in general or the merger movement in particular. This was the age of finance capitalism, when financiers like J. P. Morgan, Jay Gould, August Belmont, and Jacob Schiff administered huge fortunes and oversaw the creation of multimillion-dollar corporations, when a committee of the U.S. House concluded that there was in America a "money trust" (U.S. House of Representatives 1913). But there are two debates concerning the role of finance capital in the American economy. The first is the causal direction of the relationship between the size of firms and the movement of finance capital into the industrial sector. The second is whether the power of financiers relative to that of other economic actors was transitional, a temporary stage of finance capital between family capitalism and managerial capitalism, or a fundamental feature of corporate capitalism that persisted after the passing of the prominent financiers gave way to the anonymous managers who administer most of today's corporations. It is clear from the history of the first generation of large corporations that the concentration and mobilization of investment capital and the novel willingness of financiers to invest in manufacturing had an independent causal effect on the size, shape, and operation of large corporations. Further, this effect was fundamental enough that the modern corporation operates in an environment where the criteria for success accepted by managers and owners alike are defined in terms of the dynamics of investment capital at least as much as technical rationality.

The efficiency theory of the corporation holds that the important role of finance capital in the years around the turn of the century can be accounted for by the increased demand for capital stimulated by new technology and new marketing strategies. Chandler notes: "When their requirement [for capital] had outrun local sources, industrialists had turned to wealthy individuals who had made fortunes in railroads or traction companies, in industry, or (to a lesser extent) in land, commerce, and banking" (1990, 80). Or as James states: "The development of large-scale industry with its increased demands for external financing required the raising of unprecedented amounts of capital. One result was the rapid growth of the open market for funds in the late nineteenth century, especially the New York stock and bond markets, which were no longer limited to railroad issues" (James 1978, 8; see also Navin and Sears 1955; Carosso 1970). In this perspective, the dynamic element in economic production is technology. Organization and the flow of resources, including capital, adapt to changing technologies. When new technologies create economies of scale that stimulate larger firms, the capital markets respond by making more capital available.

Others have disputed this argument, asserting that the availability of capital actively encouraged the growth of corporations and affected the form they took (Nelson 1959; Markham 1955; Smiley 1981; Scott 1986). For example, Ransom writes: "[I]t was the success of the large firms such as railroad companies which provided the economic stimulus for the acceleration of incorporation during the post-bellum period. Spurred on by the ease with which railroads sold their shares of stock to the public, entrepreneurs engaged in all sorts of ventures that required the large acquisition of capital" (Ransom 1981, 56). In this perspective, the flow of capital is the dynamic element in economic production. The concentration of capital into a few hands created a leverage for economic power that enabled bankers and financiers to gain control over a major segment of the economy by extending the corporate form into the industrial sector.

Neither of these perspectives can be wholly sustained because they both oversimplify the process and miss the deeper underlying issue: it is not so much whether the causal direction was from size to demand for capital or from concentration of capital to concentration of the economy, but the way that investment and organization reflexively interacted with each other. The consolidation movement in industry could not have happened without the prior development of large firms and some of the technologies that facilitated large firms. As the case studies and the statistical analysis demonstrate, consolidation was much more common in industries that already had large firms. By the same token, if firms had been able to grow only through internal financing or commercial loans, they could not have developed as quickly or as commonly, and they certainly would not have taken the same organizational form. The "demand" for capital discussed by efficiency theory is not a need for a neutral resource like raw materials, but involves a set of social relationships that define the nature of property.

Thus any effects that "objective" factors like markets or technology might have had on the organization of business was refracted through the institutional structure. The institutionalization process is seen especially clearly in the timing of the corporate revolution. Figure 1.1 displayed the virtual explosion in the amount of capital (book value) of large corporations listed on the stock exchange, creeping from near zero in 1890 through the nineties and then detonating after 1898. Figure 8.4 breaks down this pattern by major industries. This seemingly chaotic jumble of lines is presented to demonstrate one very important point: industry after industry simultaneously adopted the corporate form, indicating a process of institutionalization, not a process of adaptation to factors like market expansion or efficiency-enhancing technologies. While many industries had one or two trail-blazing corporations before 1898, all of them that enjoyed a major takeoff did so between 1898 and 1903.[5] Figure 8.4 extracts a few industries that have been discussed earlier.

In the chemical industry, the only companies other than those associated with the American Cottonseed Oil Company to list their securities on the major stock exchanges (as ascertained from the *Manual of Statistics*) were National Linseed Oil, capitalized at $18 million, and Procter and Gamble, the Cincinnati soap manufacturing partnership that kept effective control. Then four companies joined the corporate institution in 1899, followed by ten in each of the next two years, by which time the industry controlled nearly $350 million in corporate capital. After the E. I. Du Pont de Nemours Powder Company was founded the following year, the level of aggregate capital in the industry remained stable for at least the next decade. So even though the decades around the turn of the century were technologically the "second industrial revolution" that firmly established chemicals as a fundamental essential of modern productive life, the institutionalization of the corporation within the industry was concentrated in just a handful of years.

The food industry, in which the American Sugar Refining Company loomed so large, displayed a similar pattern. Before 1898, besides ASRC, only the National Starch Manufacturing Company, a Kentucky corporation capitalized at under $15 million, was listed on any major exchanges. After two companies (the Glucose Sugar Refining Company and the Hawaiian-Commercial & Sugar Company) came on board in 1898 and four more the following year, an average of nine companies did so in each of the next years, followed by three years (1904–1906) in which no new food companies did so. For the next decade or so, the aggregate amount of corporate capital held steady at just over a half-billion dollars. While food was not central to the second industrial revolution, as chemicals were, Chandler treats it as an archetype of the type of processing industry preparing a standardized product for a mass market that is especially suitable for vertical integration and modern business enterprise. But like chemicals, the institutional change in the system of property structuring the industry was concentrated in just a historical blink of an eye.

Since American Tobacco Company so thoroughly controlled the tobacco industry, there were no unrelated companies in the corporate system. The financiers who were trying to challenge James Duke put P. Lorillard Com-

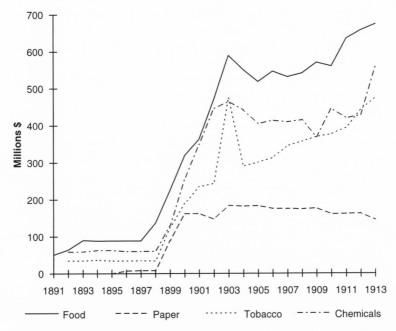

Figure 8.4. Aggregate Capital of Firms in Four Industries Listed on Major Stock Exchanges, 1891–1913. (Source: Data drawn from *Manual of Statistics*.)

pany on the public market, when ATC took it over. A medium-sized company, the Union Tobacco Company appeared in 1898, but only for a year. Some ATC subsidiaries such as the 1901 American Cigar Company were listed on the exchanges. Nonetheless, the aggregate amount of capital, as seen in Figure 8.4, fits the pattern of other industries, indicating that the corporate revolution stimulated not only the creation of hundreds of new corporations, but a vast expansion of some of the companies that had pioneered the new form of property. The aggregate capital in the industry increased from just under $35 million in 1898 to nearly $125 million the following year and over $235 million dollars two years later. When ATC reorganized in 1902, the industry's capital shot up temporarily to nearly a half-billion dollars but then leveled off and started a gradual climb over the next decade. In other words, the process of institutionalization that was spawning new corporations in so many industries was also affecting the property relations in the corporate trail-blazers. The leaders of ATC were taking advantage of a system that ATC had helped to create, a system that could construct wealth from the operation of the institution.

The paper industry lives up to its characterization as our industrial "everyman." Before 1898, only one company, the American Strawboard Company, capitalized at a modest $6 million, was listed on major exchanges. In 1899, the major International Paper Company, the National

Paper Company (founded in 1892), and the U.S. Envelope Company all listed securities. By 1900, the aggregated capital for the industry surpassed $160 million, which although unimpressive compared with food or tobacco, dwarfed the figures the industry had commanded before 1898. As in the other industries, the level remained stable for the next decade or so.

We could repeat this exercise for all the industries in which major corporations were founded. All would show the years 1898 to 1904 as the watershed. Another way to illustrate how focused the period of institutionalization was is to note that between 1905 and 1913 only six new companies entered the corporate system.[6] Three of them were connected with the burgeoning automobile industry: B. F. Goodrich Company in rubber; Studebaker Corporation, which was making the shift from wagons; and General Motors Company, organized in 1911 with $75 million. Another, the Central Leather Company, was a successor to the U.S. Leather Company; one, Liggett & Myers Tobacco Company, was a result of a government antitrust suit against American Tobacco; and the final, Baldwin Locomotive, was the move of an old and established company into the corporate system. These companies were incorporated within the context of business as usual. The corporate system was institutionalized. Whether reorganizing a failed company, preparing to ride the wave of the industrial future, administering the breakup of an illegal monopoly, or outgrowing an old institutional skin, companies would thenceforth do so as socially capitalized corporations.

As discussed in Chapter 4, the operation of the system of finance capital tended to centralize and concentrate capital into a small group of New York–based institutions. The railroads were key to this process. At first the ownership of American railroads was quite widespread. Many local and state governments along with merchants and industrialists in cities seeking railroad lines invested in railroads as an inducement to locate. Many railroad companies skillfully played local communities against one another to gain financing and other incentives such as tax breaks and free land. But many American railroads overcapitalized, issuing common stock, preferred stock, and bonds, creating a heavy load of obligations. Throughout the eighties and nineties, major American railroads were allocating as much as half of their gross revenues to fixed payments, most of which went to New York or foreign bondholders.

The New Order Stabilizes

By 1905 the corporate revolution had subsided. In the previous year only 6 new corporations that would become listed on the stock exchange were founded, 2 of which were reorganizations of existing companies. In the six years previous to that an average of 54 corporations were founded annually, peaking at 130 in 1899. From 1904 to 1912, an average of just under 9 new corporations of this sort were founded each year (computations from

Manual of Statistics, passim). Even after the institutions of corporate capital had become the accepted, taken-for-granted means of creating and capitalizing major industrial enterprise, there would still be privately held companies, including some industrial giants like Ford Motor Company and later Hughes Aircraft, but these would be the exception rather than the rule. When a group of entrepreneurs wanted to establish a large-scale industrial enterprise, henceforth the standard procedure would be to mobilize the resources of the corporate institutions by recruiting investment bankers, brokerage houses, and the investment press in order to attract sufficient capital.

Chandler treats the period immediately after the corporate revolution as a period of shakedown. "Unless the newly formed consolidation used the resources under its control more efficiently than had the constituent companies before they joined the merger, the consolidation had little staying power" (1977, 338). Merely having a coherent strategy and organization were not sufficient for success; a company had to use mass production and serve mass markets to reduce unit costs. He states a basic contention of his study: "Modern business enterprise became a viable institution only after the visible hand of management proved to be more efficient than the invisible hand of market forces in coordinating the flow of materials through the economy. Few mergers achieved long-term profitability until their organizers carried out a strategy to make such integration possible and only after they created a managerial hierarchy capable of taking the place of the market in coordinating, monitoring, and planning for the activities of a large number of operating units" (1977, 339). By World War I the constraints of technology and markets on growth were manifest, and by 1920 the shakedown was complete, when successful firms had become established and unsuccessful firms had failed. In a chapter entitled "Integration Completed" Chandler writes, "Modern business enterprises dominated major American industries and most of these same firms continued to dominate their industries for decades" (1977, 345). The functional logic here is clear: a new social form, initially created for a variety of reasons which may or may not have been rational, proves more efficient at performing a vital social function—producing and distributing material goods and services. The evidence is the greater survival of the new social form—the large-scale, vertically integrated, modern business enterprise—over the old social form, the entrepreneurial, unitary business. Because it has proved its greater effectiveness, the new form ceases to be experimental and becomes the standard model for creating new business organizations.

Although Chandler and I agree that the causes of the first generation of large-scale corporations differ from the causes of subsequent generations, we differ over how and why the new social form became the standard. In contrast to his functionalist model, the account offered here is an institutionalist perspective that emphasizes the dynamics of power. The resources necessary to construct a major enterprise became embedded within the institutions of corporate capital, and only under exceptional circumstances could large-scale production develop outside these circles.[7] An institutionalist perspective challenges the rationalist assumption underneath the functionalist account.[8] The large corporation became the taken-for-granted mode of organizing large-scale enterprise, not because it was rational, but because it became required whether it was rational or not, fitting DiMaggio and Powell's (1983) definition of institutional isomorphism, a constraining process that forces one unit in a population to resemble other units that face the same set of environmental conditions. Moreover, the process conformed less to competitive isomorphism, which operates most where there is free competition and works through a selective process (as Chandler describes the selection of more efficient vertically integrated firms), than to institutional isomorphism, by which political power and legitimacy define which organizational forms are appropriate for a given organizational field. In particular, the centralization of capital into the institutions of corporate capitalism illustrates DiMaggio and Powell's proposition that "[t]he greater the extent to which an organizational field is dependent upon a single (or several similar) source of support for vital resources, the higher the level of isomorphism" (1983, 155). As Fligstein (1990) has argued, with the development of corporate capitalism, the relevant organizational field for American business shifted from the industry to the institutions of corporate capitalism, especially in terms of legal form and organizational structure. As firms less and less used other firms making the same product as the decisive reference group in deciding how to finance growth and expansion, structure a division of labor, or integrate with suppliers and distributors, they increasingly turned to the corporate field as a whole.

CONCLUSION

These case studies illustrate how the events recounted in the earlier chapters came to fruition in a fundamental transformation of the way that America produces and distributes many basic commodities. The corporate form of property was developed when the boundary between public and private spheres was fuzzy at best. The rights, entitlements, and responsibilities that the state enforced for those who controlled corporations could have only arisen for enterprises infused with a public purpose. The corporate form privatized or, as most accounts would have it, "matured" when the giant railroad companies developed as singular organizations that could rival the state itself in terms of resources and consequences. But even until the end of the century, the railroad was considered more accountable to the public than other forms of business, a principle embodied in the law through the numerous state and federal regulatory agencies instituted at the height of laissez-faire ideologies. When the industrial corporation became part of the corporate institutional structure and fully socialized large-scale capital, the privatization was complete. The law was used more to protect corporations from direct state regulation than to ensure any accountability, as manifested most clearly in the definition of the corporation as a legal individual protected by the same rights as natural individuals. In contrast to the accounts of efficiency theory, this chapter and the preceding one describe how the actions taken to create the large socially capitalized corporation were not taken by managers acting to rationalize production or distribution or even to serve their specific needs, but were taken by owners, using the rights, entitlements, and responsibilities delegated by state law, reallocating the material resources mobilized by the railroad corporations, and acting within the institutional structures that had arisen to build canal and railroad companies. Each of the aspects of corporate law discussed in Chapter 6 played important roles in the case studies. The New Jersey law permitting intercorporate stock ownership was used first by the American Cotton Oil Company, whose lawyers helped refine the law for general use. This law could not be used as a general basis for creating large corporations until the Supreme Court validated the Sugar Trust in the *E. C. Knight* case. The new liberal powers of the boards of directors were used by the leaders of the American Tobacco Company to recapitalize the company, making the most of the companies as nonvoting bonds, while a few individuals ended up controlling a majority of the voting stock with relatively little total capital. Liberal liability laws are generally held responsible for the routine indifference of stockholders to corporate management, allowing men like Henry O. Havemeyer to continue controlling the American Sugar Refining Company long after he had sold his initial controlling interest.

The narratives told here illustrate Marx's observation that people make their own history, but not under the circumstances of their own choosing. The earlier chapters described the circumstances within which the owners, financiers, and investors were acting to make the late nineteenth century a liminal period for the American economy. Rather than orderly change within an existing institutional structure in which many tactical adaptations accumulated into substantial change, change took the form of restructuring the American industrial order. American businessmen, sensing acutely that the old industrial order was evaporating, turned to the corporate system just as the men who controlled the corporate structure, sensing that it had saturated the transportation and communication spheres, were seeking new fields to conquer. The greatest irony, one that efficiency theory misses in its celebration of American economic growth, is that the merger of entrepreneurial industry and corporate property arose from weaknesses on both sides. The prevailing interpretation that ruinous competition had terminally infected the entrepreneurial system of manufacturing was confirmed by the worst depression America had known, which shattered the American dream of fulfillment through owning one's own business. The legacies that businessmen had labored to pass on to their sons and sons-in-law were liquidated into lucrative but abstract securities. The system based on railroad corporations, which as much as anything caused a depression in which at one point a quarter of all railroad miles were in receivership, both weakened the industrial order and offered to be its redeemer.

From the perspective of survival, the new system worked. Although some individual firms failed while others prospered, it is more important that virtually all large-scale enterprise was constructed within the framework of corporate capitalism. Contrary to Chandler, survival cannot be taken as evidence of the efficiency of the system as a whole, but only the efficiency of particular firms within a given institutional order (if at all). The corporate system created around the turn of the century is the new context within which economic activity transpires, the stage upon which the twentieth-century economy has played.

CHAPTER NINE

Conclusion: A Political Sociology of the Large Corporation

THREE INTERRELATED concepts—power, history, and the state—have shaped my account of the institutions that have structured corporate property. Property, I have argued, is the major relationship connecting the intersection of state and economy. The concept of power highlights the question of *who* is determining the behavior of social actors. But power relationships that create new structures become embedded within social institutions that take on a life of their own, a process set within history, so that to understand the reasons why a system like corporate capitalism arose requires that we understand its roots as well as its immediate precipitants. Within this framework, I explain how efficiency theory itself can be reconceptualized within a framework of power.

POWER

Power is the most fundamental concept distinguishing my perspective from that of the efficiency model. When power is defined as it is here, as the degree to which the behavior of one actor is explained in terms of another actor's behavior, it is a methodological perspective—an agenda. To explain why an actor behaves a certain way within a certain context, one must ask who else's behavior must be included in the explanation, with the assumption that the answer matters. Efficiency theory theorizes about "who" only in terms of the technical process of production and distribution—owners, suppliers, consumers, and most centrally, managers. Who acts is of little consequence because change is explained as the rational adaptation to asocial exogenous forces like technology and markets. Technology is treated as a dynamic with its own logic; markets are seen as the result of so many individual actions that no single actor matters. Throughout this work, however, we have seen that the decisions that led to the organizational, legal, and economic changes underlying the development of the large industrial corporation have been shaped by the social relations within which actors were embedded, in contrast to efficiency theory's focus on the relative effectiveness with which owners and managers were able to arrange the internal structure of firms to maximize output relative to input. For example, the early canals were built at the behest of the New York, Philadelphia, Baltimore, and Cincinnati merchants, who then turned to railroads as a form of investment. The Wall Street institutions that capitalized canals, railroads, and belatedly manufacturing were developed to administer and profit from the allocation and circulation of government securities. The conflict over the role of states in underwriting and operating quasi-public corporations for infrastructural development may have been framed in terms of the natural role of government and the inherent superiority of private enterprise, but the outcome was determined by the contending group that prevailed politically, not the inevitable forces of destiny. The winners were not always at the top of the social pyramid. The antistate strand of the anticorporate movement led by Jacksonian democrats ultimately prevailed over the strong-state strand of anticorporatism, resulting in general incorporation laws and the demise of government ownership. Although not as democratic as its ideology proclaimed, the movement's popular support was a major factor in its prevailing over the strong-state opponents of corporate privilege. Even though I have argued that the creation of competitive national markets was less pervasive and more transitory than described in conventional accounts, the markets that did develop were fashioned by governments that increasingly enforced market relationships to the exclusion of other economic relationships, thereby undermining traditional relationships, and that permitted—and at times assisted—dominant businessmen to become giants.

Similarly, the actions that constituted the corporate revolution at the end of the century must be explained by reference to the social relationships within which the actors were exercising power. New industrial giants like the American Sugar Refining Company and the American Tobacco Company may have adopted new technologies and benefited from economies of scale, but the advantages of size were at least as much a matter of the power they wielded as any efficiencies they may have enjoyed. The organizers of the Sugar Trust and the tobacco combination were able to offer deals too lucrative to refuse easily because they were able to draw on the resources of corporate capital while controlling the monopoly profits gleaned from consolidations. The decisions of most of the incorporators of corporations like American Tobacco or American Sugar Refining are thus explained in terms of their relationship to the dominant movers. The decision of the various sugar refiners and tobacco manufacturers who later joined the combinations, that is, the western beet sugar manufacturers and the plug, smoking tobacco, and cigar companies, must also be explained in terms of their relationship to others. They could attempt to compete with a giant corporation that controlled the resources to undermine the market or they could become part of those combinations, a choice that had little to do with efficiency. If they lacked the power to beat them, their decision to join must be explained in terms of the corporations' power.

Others have emphasized the operation of power in the rise of large industrial corporations, but have treated power as a motivation for actions rather than as a dynamic of the underlying social relations. The essential issue in the conventional debate about whether the first generation of corporate leaders were robber barons or industrial statesmen centered on the issue of motivation, a debate framed in Populist and Progressive critiques of the large corporation. Because that debate was so explicitly ideological, the issue became whether those individuals were good people or bad people, which was reduced to the issue of whether they were motivated by power and greed or order and efficiency. Reflecting the assumption of American individualism that historical events are crystallized in the actors that shape them and the instrumentalist assumption that outcomes are explained by the motivations of participants, generations of opinion makers, politicians, and historians have judged the large industrial corporation by judging the motivations of corporate leaders. Dudley G. Wooten, a Texas legislator, expressed this perspective to the Chicago Conference on Trusts in 1900:

> Side by side with the natural man created by God, there has arisen an artificial person, conceived by the mischievous ingenuity of mercantile greed, created by the capricious legislation of human assemblies, protected by the fictions of fallible tribunals, vested with practical immortality, endowed with every attribute, power and function that may belong to the natural person, and exempt from every limitation, influence and restraint that render human nature honest, charitable, generous and conscientious (Chicago Conference on Trusts 1900, 48).[1]

The attack on evil motives has persisted since the time of Ida Tarbell's indictment of John D. Rockefeller up to the present day. Duboff and Herman (1980), for example, challenge Chandler by arguing that "the struggle for market control may have been at least as important as any quest for efficiency" (91). The perspective on power taken here, however, is less concerned with the motives for action than with the social relationships within which action is embedded. Whether businessmen were motivated by greed, control of the market, or efficiency, they had to contend with circumstances beyond their control: early nineteenth-century states decided that they had to compete with other states by building physical infrastructures; corporations were politically more feasible than taxation and direct ownership; the canals and turnpikes suffered from bad timing and fiscal collapse; the antimonopoly movement for extending corporate privileges was stronger than the movement against those privileges; governments refused to enforce manufacturers' attempts to govern themselves collectively; states redefined the nature of property by legally equating corporate and natural individuals; government-facilitated competition was collectively defined as ruinous; and the late nineteenth-century collapse of railroad capital created a dilemma for struggling businessmen, who would risk failure if they insisted on remaining capitalists or enjoy windfall profits if they sold out to new corporations. I am interested less in the particular motivation than in the complex and illusive relationship between motivation and behavior. Whatever one's goals are, the explanation of behavior must include the relationships that define what actions will achieve those goals. The way that men pursued wealth, achieved social order, or contributed to social welfare in 1800 was very different than in 1900. Whether James B. Duke and Henry O. Havemeyer were motivated by greed, order, or charity is less important in explaining the rise of the large industrial corporation than the fact that the economic resources they could draw on, the economic relationships that states enforced, and the institutional forms they could adopt to achieve wealth, order, or charity resulted in the large industrial corporation as we know it. Power operated less through motivation than through interaction and the control of resources. Thus the issue of who makes history is more a sociological than a moral or psychological issue.

The "currency" of power, by which the behavior of an actor is to be explained by his or her relationship with other actors, is the capability of one actor wielding power to mobilize resources and then make the allocation of those resources contingent on the behavior of another actor. Resources here are defined very broadly to include such nonmaterial resources as the ability to define the nature of the interaction, any persuasive powers an actor might wield, and the support of other actors to reinforce or legitimate authority. I have emphasized two especially critical resources in explaining the rise of the large industrial corporation, the control of capital and the power of the state, especially as inscribed in property and corporation law. The capital for early large corporations to build canals, turnpikes, and bridges came from governments, wealthy merchants, foreign investors, and towns anxious to be linked to broader markets. Explaining the rise of these corporations requires considering the behavior of those organizations that controlled resources. But increasingly the purposes and structure of the large corporation were shaped by those who controlled the distribution of large amounts of capital, especially the large investors in American and European cities. At the end of the nineteenth century, the decision of investors like J. P. Morgan to broaden corporate financing from the railroads and government securities to industrial combinations was an emphatic turning point, sparking the explosion of mergers we call the corporate revolution. Similarly, property and corporation law became a resource that could be used by those who, for whatever reason, wanted to harness large-scale industrial enterprise. The creation of the business corporation, its privatization from public accountability, its status as a legal individual, and its endowment with such powers as limited liability and the right to own the stock of other corporations all help explain why large socially capitalized corporations became the form by which industrial enterprise was conducted. These developments are part of an explanation based on power.

Although capital and the state were the two most important resources for those shaping large-scale historical change in the nineteenth century, the factors emphasized by efficiency theory, technology and organizational hierarchy, can also be seen as resources that could be used in relationships of power, thereby reconceptualizing efficiency within power theory. While I dispute that technology and efficiencies of organizational hierarchy ade-

quately explain the rise of the large, socially capitalized industrial corporation, it would be foolhardy to claim that technology and organizational
hierarchy are irrelevant to the way the modern economy operates. Developments such as Bessemer steelmaking, the Bonsack cigarette-making machine, the continuous process, multiple-state distilling of petroleum, and the
many cumulative innovations that made mass production possible, along
with the advances in transportation and communication from the railroad
to the telephone that facilitated the creation of national markets, all affected
the context within which people made decisions and struggled over the
shape of the economy. Similarly, the creation of large-scale organizations
with multiple levels of authority, the adoption of the line and staff system,
the functional form of organization, the vertical integration of production,
and rise of middle management as a new stratum in the occupational structure are vital consequences of the rise of the large industrial corporation.
Any complete account of the economy in the second half of the nineteenth
century must discuss and analyze these developments.

As I have contended throughout, however, technology is not a "factor"
that autonomously or exogenously affects society. People use technology as
a resource that can give some a material advantage over others. Whether or
not a broad range of other people might benefit from lower prices, new and
useful products, or even longer life is less relevant to the effect of technology
on organizational structures than whether technology helps certain actors
accumulate resources needed by other actors. By using the Bonsack cigarette-making machine, James Duke may have gained an edge over his competitors that helped him mobilize enough resources to induce other cigarette
manufacturers to join his plan for the American Tobacco Company. The
technology did not determine the outcome; it could have been used in other
ways. There was no technological reason why the various tobacco factories
had to be owned by the same entity. Moreover, within other institutional
and legal contexts, Duke would have been more likely to use the resources
gained from lowering his production costs in ways other than buying out
his competition. When seen as a resource rather than a factor, technology
can be analyzed within social relations rather than as exogenous to them. In
this way it becomes theoretically decoupled from efficiency. Edwards
(1979) and Noble (1977) have described how new technologies were
adopted to wrest control of the work process away from skilled workers.
McGuire (1990) gives an account of the electric utility industry that explains the adoption of such features as centralized generation stations rather
than household generators in terms of the conflict between Thomas Edison
and financiers. As Sabel and Zeitlin (1985) argue, "which technological
possibilities are in fact realized depend[s] crucially on the distribution of
power and wealth in society: those who control the disposition of resources
and the returns from investments choose from among the available applica-
tions of technology the one most favorable to their interests as they define
them" (161).

Moreover, while technology is not independent of organization, many technologies can operate within a variety of social forms. Sabel and Zeitlin (1985) show how the United States adopted mass production systems for industries that France organized in flexible production systems. Weiss (1988) has similarly described how the Italian political environment has effectively promoted the proliferation of a dense network of high-technology firms linked by a variety of nonhierarchical relationships. The fact that some technologies were used primarily in large-scale organizations does not ipso facto indicate that they created compelling economies of scale. Scale and economies of scale are not synonymous. The quantitative results presented in Chapter 2 indicated that industries with large corporations had larger establishments, but were not necessarily more productive. Scale can create at least as many diseconomies as economies. John Searles, the architect of the Sugar Trust, testified before the New York legislature that the American Sugar Refining Company had to charge more for sugar than smaller companies because producing multiple grades of sugar was more expensive than producing single grades (New York Legislature 1897). Many of the new industrial giants of the late nineteenth century secured their advantages more through marketing than through technology. Hounshell (1984) and Chandler (1977) agree, for example, that Singer Sewing Machine, one of America's first multinational corporations, had no special technological advantage but effectively created a marketing structure that ensured its growth. Likewise the cigarette industry was created as much by marketing as by technology. The technology made large-scale production feasible, but extensive advertising and promotion were necessary to create a market where there had been none. Finally, large size can be as much the result of economic power as its source. The other branches of the tobacco industry became part of the corporate system by the actions of the American Tobacco Company, not by their technologies. With few technological changes, they were transformed from a competitive market to a virtual monopoly and then to the stable oligopoly that has governed the industry since then. Thus to explain the rise of large corporations one must address the issue of how the industrialists used technologies and the resources they offered, but within the framework of power, not by denying or neglecting power.

This line of reasoning can be extended to consider efficiency itself as a resource in at least two senses. First, efficiency can increase the material resources used in exercising power. Technology is only one means of increasing the relative output from a given set of inputs. The science of management is based on the premise that some organizational structures are more productive than others (Lazonick 1993). Most of what managers do is arrange social relations among those who make and distribute products in order to maximize the ratio of output to input. Authors from Weber on have discussed the way that worker consciousness can enhance how much can be produced from given material inputs. Regardless of the source, greater efficiency can give actors greater resources for exercising power. Thus ceteris paribus, more efficient organizational forms are more likely to survive and spread than inefficient forms. However, not only are the "ceteris" rarely "paribus," but more important, the effect of efficiency is mediated by the way in which the beneficiaries of efficiency use the resources that efficiency bestows.

Besides increasing material resources usable for exercising power, efficiency can constitute an ideological resource. As Fligstein (1990) has explained, there are competing definitions of efficiency. He has described how the meaning of efficiency has changed with different kinds of CEOs. When CEOs came from production departments, efficiency was defined by costs of production and increasing output.[2] When men with a sales background gained ascendancy, efficiency was defined by gross revenue and related indices. More recently, when a background in finance has become the primary route to the executive suite, efficiency has become defined in terms of how well the company's securities are doing on the stock market. Fligstein has argued that part of the stagnation of American business is due to the fact that corporate decision makers have paid closer attention to short-term fluctuations in stock prices than long-term planning and investment in more productive technologies. Thus efficiency itself has a political content. Those in power are able to define the criteria by which performance will be judged. Efficiency is an effective ideological resource because of the belief in efficiency cultivated by efficiency theorists. The belief in efficiency has been an important part of the institutionalization process underlying the rise of the large corporation. From this vantage point, efficiency is only one factor in mobilizing resources that can be used in different ways, not the primary causal force in determining organizational change.

SOCIAL INSTITUTIONS

Out of this general relational perspective on power, we can derive several propositions about the institutionalization of the large socially capitalized industrial corporation. The overarching principle is that the ability to exercise power inheres less in the characteristics of the power wielder than in the relationship between actors. This social dimension means an explanation is to be found in the interaction of real actors, what happens between them, and organizations and institutions that embody interpersonal interaction, more than in the impersonal operation of immanent underlying forces like efficiency or technology. Five dimensions of the social were especially important for the rise of the large industrial corporation: (1) Institutions are constructed by extensive and complex interaction of many parties with a variety of motivations and resources, not just those with positions of formal managerial authority. (2) Within this complex, multifaceted social world of differentially motivated actors the terms by which interaction takes place are very uneven, and this unevenness is intimately connected to the way people are tied into the social structure. (3) Accordingly, different actors have different abilities to benefit from technological and organizational innovations. (4) The institutional structure at any point in time is the context within which actions are set and shapes the consequences of any behavior, which in turn reflexively perpetuate that institution and create change. (5). The large corporation did not dissolve the dynamics of property; it socialized property, socialized not within the institutional structure of publicly accountable government, but within the institutional structure of corporate capitalism; thus it did not render class irrelevant so much as it changed the particular social relationships within which intraclass and interclass relations were framed. These five propositions help us assess the social significance of socializing capital in the large corporation.

1. *Institutions are constructed by extensive and complex interaction of many parties with a variety of motivations and resources, not just those with positions of formal managerial authority.* Investors, bankers, workers, lawyers, and political figures played critical roles in the rise of the large corporation, acting out of logics of action very different from the logic of efficiency. Efficiency theory focuses almost entirely on the actions and decisions of managers, who are treated as synonymous with the corporation. For example, Chandler (1990) defines "modern industrial enterprise" as "a collection of operating units, each with its own specific facilities and personnel, whose combined resources and activities are coordinated, monitored, and allocated by a hierarchy of middle and top managers. It is the existence of this hierarchy that makes the activities and operations of the whole enterprise more than the sum of its operating units" (15). This is basically a technocratic definition, in the sense that running the organization is equated with governing the technology.[3] The organization is merely a collection of operating units. "Facilities and personnel" are logically equivalent, reducing labor to another asocial factor of production along with capital and raw materials. All other actors, such as government, investors, and consumers, are treated as exogenous. What managers do is maximize the productivity of these various factors; their interests are seen as ultimately compatible with those of workers, investors, consumers, and the public.

Chandler describes the rational manager as "a new subspecies of economic man, the salaried manager. With their coming, the world received a new type of capitalism—one in which the decisions about current operations, employment, output, and the allocation of resources for future operations were made by salaried managers who were not owners of the enterprise. Once modern transportation and communication systems were in place, the new institution and the new type of economic man provided a central dynamic for continuing economic growth and transformation" (1990, 2). In efficiency theory, on the one hand, managers are seen as attempting to maximize productivity, and efficiency and success are validated by survival. Productive and efficient firms survived while inept and wasteful firms failed. The perspective thus assumes a smooth congruence between the internal operation of the firm and the environmental dynamics. A relational perspective, on the other hand, assumes that outcomes are determined by the interaction of many actors with many motivations, in contrast to efficiency theory's singular, asocial technological determinism. Managers, owners, workers, consumers, politicians, judges, and others have interacted together, some motivated by financial gain, some by personal stability, some by quality considerations, some by a sense of justice, and some by a desire for control. The politicians who committed state and local governments to create and finance canals in the name of public prosperity, the entrepreneurs who organized the construction companies in the name of family enterprise, the judges who molded the corporation as a private legal individual in the name of ancient tradition, the financiers who reinvested their railroad profits into industrial mergers in the name of economic order, the workers who reinforced the process of combination in the name of solidarity all played a role. Whether they were truly motivated by the principles they were acting in the name of is less important than the dynamics and outcome of this multifaceted interaction.

2. *Within this complex, multifaceted social world of differentially motivated actors the terms by which interaction takes place are very uneven, and this unevenness is intimately connected to the way people are tied into the social structure.* Insofar as power operates, people vary in the extent to which their behavior must be explained in relation to other actors. Some people can define the terms of interaction, including the definition of the situation, the nature and quantity of resources to be exchanged, and the eventual outcomes, more than others. Governments were able to dictate the terms on which early canal and railroad companies were chartered, but when the canal companies were rendered unprofitable by poor planning, political logrolling, an unforeseen depression, and competition from railroads, the governments could only react to minimize their losses and cede active control to private interests. As more and more productive activity produced articles for markets rather than consumption, legislators and judges used market criteria as the standard by which to judge personal disputes. As capital became concentrated through the institutions of Wall Street, journalists and politicians used stock prices as a measure of prosperity. When canals and railroads were being built, towns were set against one another to see which could offer the most lucrative package to locate there. When national courts weakened the ability of states to regulate out-of-state corporations while refusing to hold these same corporations accountable to federal law, states were pitted against one another to see which could offer the most permissive legal environment.

Altogether the large corporation itself—or, more strictly speaking, the individuals who could use the corporate form to pursue their own interests—was increasingly able to dictate the terms of interaction with other

individual and collective actors, including governments, workers, customers, and even investors. But it was able to do so primarily because it was
historically constructed with the legal and financial resources to do so. Its
right to act as an individual apart from the individual owners, the shield of
limited liability its owners enjoyed, the particular rights, entitlements, and
responsibilities it embodied, along with the theretofore unimaginable concentration of economic and human resources, made it a formidable social
contender indeed. So the corporation itself was the ultimate social relationship through which some people were able to dictate the terms of interaction with others.

   3. *Accordingly, different actors have different abilities to benefit from
technological and organizational innovations.* Efficiency theory assumes
that technological and organizational innovations are generally beneficial,
benefiting society as a whole and, by implication, everyone in society. For
example, Chandler describes the use of large firms: "[M]anufacturing enterprises became multifunctional, multiregional, and multiproduct because the
addition of new units permitted them to maintain a long-term rate of return
on investment by reducing overall costs of production and distribution, by
providing products that satisfied existing demands, and by transferring facilities and skills to more profitable markets when returns were reduced by
competition, changing technology, or altered market demand" (1990, 15).
The implied beneficiaries are the investor, for whom lower costs imply
greater profits, the consumer, who gets lower prices and the products desired, and the society as a whole, which benefits from quick adaptation to
changed conditions. In contrast, a power perspective would be more inclined to examine the relative benefits and costs to different actors. Certainly some technological developments benefit a broad range of people.
Many people benefited in some way from the railroad. But the distribution
of costs and benefits was uneven. A few individuals became very wealthy
and powerful. All shippers potentially benefited from faster and cheaper
transportation, but John D. Rockefeller and Henry O. Havemeyer were
each able to gain control of their industries at least in part because they
secured special transportation rates on products for which transportation
was a substantial part of total costs. For many of the early trusts, the relationship to the railroad was a determining factor in both the rise of the trust
and the individuals who gained control. Those who profited the most from
railroads were able to shape and profit from the corporate revolution. Not
all Americans agreed that they benefited from the railroads. Certainly Na-
tive Americans, whose way of life was destroyed by the flood of easterners
who invaded their land, did not benefit. And many of the farmers who
joined the populist movement to fight the railroads felt that any benefits
they enjoyed were overshadowed by the costs they endured. We could examine other innovations in a similar light. All the innovations that are commonly cited to explain new economies of scale underlying the growth of
large corporations brought both costs and benefits. It was the distribution

of costs and benefits and the way that people and organizations differentially interpreted and reacted to the innovations that explain transformations like the large corporation. Whether the innovation was the railroad, the Bonsack cigarette-making machine, Bessemer steel, the vulcanization of rubber, the electric dynamo, or the telephone, the extent to which people benefited or suffered was structured by their place in society and, increasingly, their relation to the corporate institution.

4. *The institutional structure at any point in time is the context within which actions are set and shapes the consequences of any behavior, which in turn reflexively perpetuate that institution and create change.* Legislators building turnpikes, bridges, and later canals and railroads could not rely on state resources and so turned to the institutions that had supplied financial resources for other state projects like war, that is, the institutions of government finance. Construction was thus funded with stocks and bonds rather than with new taxes. Stock markets, private banking, and brokerage houses developed from casual and auxiliary sidelines into major economic actors. The infrastructure builders used the legal form that had been used for education, religion, and municipalities, creating legally constituted bodies with delegated legal powers such as absolving owners of liability, but securing public accountability by limiting the purposes for which the organization could be used and requiring elected boards of directors to act as quasi-republics. The corporation developed as an institution in its own right and took on a life of its own far removed from the intentions or the original public uses for which it was first adopted. It was only after the corporation became fully institutionalized as a private, autonomous, self-reproducing organizational form embedded within a larger institutional structure of laws, banks, stock markets, and managerial professions that it became plausible to explain its adoption in particular cases by efficiency considerations.

A relational power perspective of the rise of the large socially capitalized industrial corporation gives us not only a richer and more realistic view of the social interaction underlying economic transformation, but also a more dynamic and sophisticated perspective on institutions. Efficiency theorists are part of the "new institutional economics," which differs from neoclassical economics by explicitly including institutions in their models and explanations. The new institutional economists differ from sociological institutionalists in several important respects.[4] In the first place, the new institutional economists define institutions more in terms of what they are not—markets—than in terms of what they are. They treat institutions as any site of transactions in which nonmarket dynamics are present. Firms are institutions because the transactions within them operate according to authority relations rather than according to the laws of supply and demand. Thus institutions are a residual; they are explained by the incompleteness of market forces. Hierarchies and institutions are something to be explained; markets are not. A political sociological perspective would define institutions more broadly as any set of organizations that has been socially constructed to perform a social task in a taken-for-granted set of behaviors and interactions. Thus the market itself is an institution that must be explained just as thoroughly as hierarchies. Institutions are not residual, but are the basic foundation of society. Any sociological explanation of macrolevel phenomena should include institutional factors. Courts, legislative bodies, banks, organized capital markets like stock exchanges, families, and the press are just a few of the institutions that help shape both markets and hierarchies. The emergent corporations were both shaped by them and in turn profoundly affected them.

Second, the new institutional economics still sees market forces and efficiency as the most basic and central causal force in social and economic change. Williamson states, "whether a set of transactions ought to be executed across markets or within a firm depends on the relative efficiency of each mode" (Williamson 1975, 8), a hypothesis that this book has directly challenged. The new institutional economists hold that institutions are invented and changed to compensate for market failures. They argue that economic actors act rationally with little nonmarket interference and without any social environment to mediate their interaction, and thus they discount such nonmarket phenomena as trade associations, interlocking directorates, and family-based credit associations (McGuire, Granovetter, and Schwartz forthcoming). In other words, institutions are still fundamentally economic, formed by exchange transactions and embodying exchange transactions. Sociology is more inclined to see institutions as fundamentally social, caused by a broad variety of social processes, including power and affiliation, and embodying behaviors and relationships in taken-for-granted categories and patterns of interaction.

5. *The large corporation did not dissolve the dynamics of property; it socialized property, socialized not within the institutional structure of publicly accountable government, but within the institutional structure of corporate capitalism; thus it did not render class irrelevant so much as it changed the particular social relationships within which intraclass and interclass relations were framed.* Increasingly the decisions that shape economic life (and much of political and social life) are made within the context of the corporate system. To understand what products are produced, the fate of occupational and professional groups, the job and career opportunities of gender and ethnic groups, the choice of new technologies and work processes, and the distribution of wealth, one must take into account the organizational and institutional structures of socialized property. In twentieth-century America, the road to individual wealth and national prosperity has passed through Wall Street. But socialization brought a certain organizational irony. It did spread nominal ownership among a much broader range of the population. More people had a proprietary stake in America than ever before. Factory workers and consumers could get a piece of profits.[5] However, as Berle and Means (1932) pointed out, the separation

of ownership and control came at the expense of equity owners, especially small ones. As ownership was dispersed by socialization, control was concentrated. It was concentrated not only because the dilution of influence among numerous owners made it possible to control firms with smaller and smaller proportions of total equity, but also because control operated increasingly through the institutions of socialized capital. Investment bankers, the stock market, brokerage houses, and the financial press mediated the relationship of owners to enterprise. The ability to mobilize increased capital, adopt new product lines, initiate new marketing campaigns, and even select top management and directors has become accountable to the institutions of socialized capital.

If class is defined as people's historically constructed relationship to the means of production, those relationships are embodied in the rights, entitlements, and responsibilities enforced by the state, that is, property. Most fundamentally, the corporation has transformed the dynamics of social class by defining people's relationship to production less in terms of the formal title they hold than in terms of the social relationship they have to networks of social capital and the institutions that administer them. My legal analysis has described how—as capital has become socialized and administered through the institutions of corporate capitalism—the rights, entitlements, and responsibilities have changed and been redistributed, but have not disappeared. The corporation itself has acquired many of the legal rights, entitlements, and responsibilities formerly held by individual owners, but that merely creates a new set of relationships that individuals have to one another. Although the law treats the corporation as a legal entity in itself, separate from the natural individuals that own it, sociologically, the corporation describes and structures relationships among individuals. Reifying the corporation may mystify the relationship among individuals and the way individual interests are structured, but cannot deny these realities. Socializing capital has socialized the capitalist class, solidifying it rather than dispersing it. It has coalesced its common interests and dissolved its conflicting and competing interests. Rather than hundreds of iron and steel manufacturers competing with one another, the formation of U.S. Steel gave all previous owners whose companies were purchased with corporation stock a common interest in the success of the merger. Those who managed the companies they had previously owned became accountable to corporate managers who were accountable to the board of directors, which was accountable only to the largest owners. So people's relationship to the corporation structured the relations of class. The way that the corporation developed and the form and content of the corporation's accountability to owners, bondholders, managers, workers, creditors, and the state itself was ultimately enforced by the state. People still have very different relationships to the corporation with very different interests. Whether one is a stockholder, bondholder, manager, worker, customer, or supplier means that one has very different interests in what the corporation does. And insofar as the corporation is one of the two most powerful institutions in modern society, those contending interests become very consequential.

Thus the concrete process by which the corporation was created was a class-forming process. The creation of corporations was accomplished by collective activity and in turn further solidified the corporate class. The individuals who organized and operated canal companies and railroad companies cooperated with the investment bankers, stock brokers, financiers, and investors to mobilize the funds, secure the charters, neutralize opposition, and build the organizations for the first generation of large corporations. These people became tied into a network and constructed central institutions that formed the scaffolding for a national class. In the latter part of the nineteenth century, the large corporation moved into industry by bringing industrialists into the core of the corporate class and extending the reach of the core into industry. John D. Rockefeller epitomized the movement of an industrialist into the core of the corporate class, a move solidified by his close alliance with the National City Bank and the numerous corporate boards the Rockefeller family and partners sat on. J. P. Morgan led the financial community into the industrial realm, underwriting and controlling the formation of General Electric, International Harvester, U.S. Steel, and other corporate giants. The power that I have focused on throughout is class power, power that is derived from people's property relationships and administered through institutions that embody class relationships.

Socialized capital in this respect is like other forms of socialized activity in that all forms of socialized activity require an institutional framework spanning the scope of the activity. Socialization by government requires a state apparatus that can administer all the activities it brings with the social network it is trying to organize. For example, socialized agriculture requires a system of farming collectives, storage facilities, distribution systems, and consumer outlets to make it possible. The Veterans Administration, one of the world's largest organizations of socialized medicine, has built giant hospitals that articulate closely with that very anti-individualistic institution, the modern military. Similarly the many forms of private socialization are set within specific institutional structures. Insurance companies, one of the preeminent socialized institutions in capitalist economies, require mechanisms for recruiting members, investing the aggregated premiums, deciding the validity of claims, and allocating resources to pay claims.

The large American corporation arose during a period sometimes called the organizational revolution, when many areas of social life were becoming socialized (Boulding 1953; Stinchcombe 1965; Galambos 1970; Meyer and Scott 1983; Hannan and Freeman 1987). The emergent system of professions was for the first time socializing the control that occupational groups had over their work and embarking on campaigns of collective social mobility (Abbott 1988). Workers were organizing to socialize the sale of labor power, defensively pitting a united labor force against a united capitalist class. Philanthropists were creating foundations to combine the resources of the wealthy into more rational and sustained programs. And governments were forming a new type of organization, different from executive, judicial, and legislative bodies that had previously governed: "independent" regulatory agencies that were socializing the monitoring of food production, transportation, commerce, and the production of social statistics. Individualism was increasingly a hollow, albeit still formidable, ideology beckoning more toward a past that had never really existed than affirming the present. Thus socialized activities are more than networks; they are organized in institutions.

History

My orientation to sociology is fundamentally historical. This means first of all that explanations of events must treat their context in historical terms: How did the context itself get created? How does the explanation of similar events change under different historical situations? How does the long-term trajectory of structural change affect particular events? It is the consideration of power—the ways in which the actions of some are explained in terms of their relationship to others—that provides the dynamic dimension to a historical perspective. Who is able to determine the outcomes? What resources and capacities can they mobilize that determine the outcome? And how did they acquire those resources and capacities? As the configuration of power changes so moves history.

Throughout this analysis, references have been made to the immediate context within which people were making decisions, and attention has been paid to explaining who was able to influence how those circumstances were constructed. It is not enough to posit that new technologies "required" more capital, depicting firms unproblematically adopting the corporate form, analogous to buying a new coat if one needs to warm oneself. The need for a coat does not explain why some people own coats and others do not. Setting aside the knotty issue of whether the "need" was an objective situation determined only by technology, a full explanation would still have to address the issue of why the needed capital had been mobilized and why incorporation was necessary to gain access to it. When states "needed" to build canals and railroads, why did they turn to investment bankers and bond markets? The immediate context was that investment bankers and bond markets were already the institutionalized means by which governments raised funds for specific projects like fighting wars. To understand when and why railroad companies privatized, one must take into account the immediate context of the depression of the 1830s, the ascendance of the antistatist branch of the anticorporate movement through the rise of Jacksonian democracy, and the interpretation of corruption and failed canal ventures in antistatist terms. Such events set the context for the development of the institutions of corporate capitalism that were there in the late nineteenth century when industrialists "needed" them. As with the discussion of power, my approach to history also yields general propositions underlying the account in earlier chapters: (1) Institutions change the context within which people act so that causes of the first appearance of a phenomenon differ sharply from later appearances. (2). Because institutions tend to make taken-for-granted relationships seem natural and consensual, a longer-term trajectory of explanation is necessary to reveal underlying power relationships.

1. *Institutions change the context within which people act so that causes of the first appearance of a phenomenon differ sharply from later appearances.* This is a central insight of the institutionalization perspective in organizations (Meyer and Scott 1983; DiMaggio and Powell 1983; Tolbert and Zucker 1983; Zucker 1983; Powell and DiMaggio 1991). The very fact that new organizational forms appear becomes part of the context within which later organizations are created. When new organizational forms are institutionalized, they are adopted with much weaker external causation. The new organizational form takes on a self-reproducing power (Meyer and Rowan 1977). The historical forces that shaped the Baltimore and Ohio Railroad, the first major railroad company, including the competition among seaboard cities for access to the hinterland, the coalition of merchants and city officials that mobilized the capital, the willingness of the city and state governments to contribute capital, the semipublic rights, entitlements, and responsibilities defined in the charter, and the developmental strategy that created infrastructure ahead of demand, were very different from the forces that shaped later railroad companies. Later railroads could be established and expanded within the structure of finance, law, technology, and organization institutionalized by the earlier railroads.

Similarly, the explanation for the development of American Cotton Oil, American Sugar Refining, and American Tobacco must take into account that these early corporations dominated growing industries with a history of dominant players solidifying cooperation among a small number of large owners, that they were able to overcome Wall Street suspicion of industrial securities by validating the common belief that monopolies, while not entirely ethical, were certainly profitable, and that the relationship among owners, managers, and creditors was determined by conflict and competition as well as by cooperation and mutual interests. For later large industrial firms like International Paper or U.S. Steel, the mold was already set. The large corporation by the end of the 1890s was institutionalized sufficiently that large-scale enterprise taking other forms was the exception rather than the rule. At that point it became plausible to explain the adoption of the corporate form in terms of the advantageous features that the corporation offered, such as limited liability, perpetual existence beyond the life of the founders, ease of transferring property, or ease of raising capital. But such a choice can only be made among well-institutionalized forms. Until the corporation was institutionalized, it is inaccurate to explain its adoption as though incorporators were rationally making this sort of choice. The fact that as of 1890 there were so few large industrial corporations despite the form's common usage in railroads indicates that it was not institutionalized in manufacturing. Thus explaining how it originated and became institutionalized is different from explaining its adoption once institutionalized.

This is one reason why institutions—the sets of organizations that fulfill a task and provide taken-for-granted routines and categories for fulfilling that task—are so important to my explanation. Institutions are fundamentally historical: they do not just exist, but are constantly being created, reproduced, and transformed. The actions of actors can typically be explained only by reference to their relationships with others. This is of course clearest in the creation of institutions. The business corporate institution was created by the interaction of governments and financiers to promote economic development by erecting an infrastructure of roads, canals, bridges, and banks. The early semiprivate corporations were set within the institutions of government finance primarily to link them to sources of capital in American and foreign financial centers. Such activities could have been developed by fully public agencies or, if they had developed later, by fully private agencies. But they took the particular form they did because the stock markets, investment banks, and brokerage houses, with their existing practices, were the only practical means of raising the capital, thereby further building those institutions.

When the corporate institution embraced manufacturing enterprise at the end of the century, the dynamics of power were perhaps at their most transparent. Most of the industrialists who dominated their industries gained a competitive edge from a relationship with the corporate institution. The relationship was sometimes financial, like that of James B. Duke, the New York–based tobacco man who first dominated the cigarette industry and then used access to ready capital to take over the other branches of tobacco manufacture. Or the relationship could take other forms, especially discriminating relationships with the railroad, as with John D. Rockefeller's and Henry Havemeyer's rebates, or Augustus Swift's refrigerator cars. But once institutionalized, the dynamics of power are less visible. The interests that are vested become embedded in the institutional structure and taken-for-granted routines and categories (Roy 1981). These interests that became vested are not as much those of particular individuals as they are the interests structured by particular categories of social relationships (Friedland and Alford 1991). When people's economic interests have increasingly become structured by their relationship to large corporations, categories like "owner," "manager," "creditor," or "consumer" have served the interests of their incumbents in new ways. For most of the twentieth century corporate capitalism has been the only game in town for major economic activity—the only source of large-scale capital, the only legitimate organizational structure for major enterprise. Wealth has been created primarily by owning or speculating in corporate securities; economic power is achieved by being or controlling corporate board members or officers. And as has been demonstrated in the last decades of the twentieth century, American business is very self-reproducing and slow to adapt to changed conditions.

2. *Because institutions tend to make taken-for-granted relationships seem natural and consensual, a longer-term trajectory of explanation is necessary to reveal underlying power relationships.* Even if the precipitating causes of organizational change centered on rational adaptation rather than conflict and power, the time frame of efficiency theory is inadequate.[6] The conditions that firms were adapting to and the choices that were available to the adapters themselves must be explained. Thus when I argue that the rise of the large-scale socially capitalized industrial corporation must be explained as much by state action as by private action, I am referring not only to the specific changes in the meaning of property at the end of the nineteenth century, but also to the political origins of the corporate institution and the political roots of the "free" market earlier in the century. Even if the participants saw themselves as rationally adapting to technological change that created economies of scale in industries like tobacco or petroleum, even if they saw the legal changes like the holding company laws as tactical maneuvers to legalize economic reality, in retrospect we must explain how the context they were acting within was historically constructed.

STATE

I have emphasized the role of the state. Since the 1970s, political sociology has placed increased emphasis on what the state does as well as who it serves (Alford and Friedland 1985; Mann 1984; Evans, Rueschemeyer, and Skocpol 1985; Lehman 1988; Campbell, Hollingsworth, and Lindberg 1991). We have moved from an emphasis on the kinds of decisions that the state makes, as debated by the pluralists and power elite theorists in the 1960s (Mills 1956; Dahl 1961, 1967; Domhoff 1967), to an agenda that emphasizes state functions like legitimation and accumulation (Offe 1972; Offe and Ronge 1975; O'Connor 1973), to a focus on the organizational capacity of the executive branch (Evans, Rueschemeyer, and Skocpol 1985; Skowronek 1982; Skocpol 1980).

However, political sociology may be entering a new stage in its view of the state, especially in terms of its relationship to the economy. At the heart of this new perspective is an agenda that asks how the relationship between state and economy is historically constructed, focusing on the legal definition of that relationship (Campbell, Hollingsworth, and Lindberg 1991; Creighton 1990; Fligstein 1990; Sklar 1988). The boundary between state and economy is a set of distinctions and definitions about the rights, entitlements, and responsibilities that people have relative to production and distribution, that is, to property. Private property means that the state will enforce the rights of individuals (including corporate individuals) to acquire, control, and dispose of productive facilities and the goods thereby produced without accountability to anyone except those directly involved in the act of acquiring, controlling, and disposing, that is, those supplying capital. An owner has the right to use his or her property with wide discretion, limited by the relatively weak restrictions of zoning laws and prohibitions on harm to others. He or she is entitled to the fruits of using the property, and has responsibility only to those from whom the property is acquired, those who enter into agreements about using the property, and the state itself. Public property means that the state itself has rights to acquire, control, and dispose of productive facilities and the goods thereby produced. At a time when the boundary between public and private is being actively reconstructed in former communist states, it is not surprising that social scientists are discovering the historical roots of a boundary once considered natural and inevitable (Campbell, Hollingsworth, and Lindberg 1991; Block 1990; Maier 1987). Two propositions logically follow: (1) There is no such thing as a noninterventionist state; property underlies all social and economic relationships and is defined and enforced by the state. (2) In addition to the content of law, the scale and scope of the state apparatus influences the scale and scope of such organizational offshoots as large corporations.

1. *There is no such thing as a noninterventionist state; property underlies all social and economic relationships and is defined and enforced by the state.* Thus even when the state is not actively regulating or administering economic activities through the executive branch, it is creating the conditions within which economic activities take place. This defines a very different relationship between state and economy. Initiative for particular economic activities may arise outside the state. The state may not dictate the use of any particular resource or the content of any particular contract but indirectly defines the kind of social relationships within which economic activity can take place. An economy in which individual owners are liable for all debts of companies they hold title to, in which owners have the right to veto liquidation of assets, and in which one company cannot exercise ownership rights of another is very different from one in which the owners bear little responsibility for the actions of a company, in which assets can be sold if some of the owners agree, and in which companies can own other companies.

The conception of property found in recent economic and political sociology (Horwitz 1992; Campbell, Hollingsworth, and Lindberg 1991; Calhoun 1990), which emphasizes the positive rights, entitlements, and responsibilities that the state enforces, contrasts with a more conventional political philosophy conception of property that pits property rights against the state (Ryan 1987). Property rights are seen as a form of freedom—a shield against government intrusion into private life. In this conception, the stronger the property rights, the weaker the government. A more sociological perspective would go beyond the individualistic assumption that the only theorized interaction is between the individual and the state to consider how the state affects the way that different people interact with one another.

Thus my perspective, along with other recent sociological work on the relationship between state and economy, places much greater emphasis on the law (Fligstein 1990; Creighton 1990; Campbell, Hollingsworth, and Lindberg 1991; Berk 1990). I have emphasized statutory law, especially at the state level, rather than the more common focus on national judge-made law. While legal scholars for at least the last century have recognized the difference between the law in the books and the law in reality (Horwitz 1992), the law in the books does set limits on the law in reality. Moreover, I have emphasized broad trends rather than nuanced interpretation. What historical detail there is has come from the broader historical context rather than from the subtleties of legal interpretation. For example, of all the legal changes that underlay the modern corporation, the right to own stock in other companies is important less because of its formal legal significance than because of the way that it was used. It is an excellent example of the state's ability to define rights, entitlements, and responsibilities in relationship to production and distribution without determining the way that they would be used. The right to own stock in other corporations is a widely cited legal change, often given too much credit for creating the large corporation, that I have attempted to put into a broader legal historical context. But it does focus our attention on the strength of the judicial state in America, even if the executive state was weaker than its European counterparts.

Property law, especially at the state level, has been more important than antitrust law in determining the shape of the large industrial corporation. To be sure, antitrust law has altered the course of economic development at certain critical turning points, especially in terms of the public debate on the corporation (for example, see Sklar 1988; Fligstein 1990; Campbell, Hollingsworth, and Lindberg 1991). I have treated antitrust law as but one form of property law; it specifies the kinds of rights, entitlements, and responsibilities among those engaged in production and distribution. It was widely used to prevent certain kinds of relationships among producers and distributors, such as contracts to restrict production and manage prices or the trust form itself. The spotlight has been focused on antitrust law because, as Sklar (1988) as argued, it was at the center of public discourse on the relationship between the state and the economy. At a time when the legal profession was working valiantly to institutionalize the objectivity and neutrality of the legal profession by promoting a science of law (Gordon 1983; Horwitz 1992), antitrust law was unabashedly moralistic, an instrument to eradicate the evils of large-scale industrial enterprise. But two factors mitigated the degree to which antitrust law could effectively contain corporate power. The first was that antitrust was primarily federal law rather than state law, and the national government refused to exert the jurisdiction beyond commerce and into production. The *E. C. Knight* case crystallized the federal government's diffidence, interpreting the Sherman Antitrust Act to prohibit only specific acts of restraining trade, not the existence of monopoly power, that is, restraining commerce, but not regulating productive relationships. The Court held that only the states had the power to regulate production (McCurdy 1979). At the same time the Court was weakening the ability of the states to regulate foreign corporations operating within their borders by fortifying the principle of comity, by which states were required to permit corporations of other states to do business within their borders (Thacher 1902; Smith 1905; Hurst 1970; Scheiber 1975).

The other fundamental weakness of antitrust laws was that they were inherently blind to distinctions between corporations and other forms of ownership, a stance of neutrality which sanctions forms of power by denying their existence. In the decades around the turn of the twentieth century, the federal government became increasingly blind to differences between entrepreneurial and corporate property. The first national laws to contain the power of economic giants were aimed quite specifically at particular organizational forms. The Interstate Commerce Commission was created to regulate railroads, and the Sherman Antitrust Act aimed to regulate trusts like the Standard Oil Trust and the American Sugar Refining Trust. For all its obvious weaknesses, the Interstate Commerce Commission did slow the growing power of railroads and according to some may have hastened their erosion (Martin 1971). Since the trusts immediately circumvented the Antitrust Act by changing into holding companies, the act probably did more to motivate the creation of large corporations than to regulate them. The federal response was to form a Bureau of Corporations with weak regulatory powers but strong investigative powers. It conducted several consequential studies on the petroleum industry, the tobacco industries, and others, several of which provided evidence to dissolve the combinations. But when the bureau was replaced with the Federal Trade Commission, intended to update the antitrust laws and provide a more reasonable instrument of regulation (Roy 1982), the specific reality of large corporations was no longer institutionalized in government organization. The federal government would regulate "trade" in a way that treated corner grocery stores and automobile manufacturers as functionally equivalent. While the Bureau of Corporations had conducted an investigation of the "Big Five" meat-packing companies, the FTC would conduct a study on the meat-packing industry as a whole. Antitrust law would remain a specialized branch of law primarily reacting to complaints of competitors about specific anticompetitive practices and occasionally sanctioning a large corporation like AT&T or IBM. But the corporate system per se was beyond its jurisdiction.

2. *In addition to the content of law, the scale and scope of the state apparatus influences the scale and scope of such organizational offshoots as large corporations.* The state, as the most formidable organization in mod-

ern Western civilization, in terms of its sheer size, its legitimated claim to embody the nation, and its coercively enforced claim to sovereignty, has enormous capacity to build other large and powerful organizations. When states forged early business corporations to perform tasks beyond the ability of existing organizational forms including the state itself, they endowed them with the resources and authority they needed to accomplish those tasks. States delegated some of their sovereign powers and redefined the rights, entitlements, and responsibilities of enterprise and contributed public funds in order to get these things done. Corporations did not arise and then become large. Size and economic power were central to their creation. Only when the large business corporation had been institutionalized could political conflict extend some of its legal features to smaller businesses. Like Dr. Frankenstein, the state created a creature which it lost control over and which grew formidable enough to challenge the power of its creator.

Political sociology since mid-century has hotly debated the extent to which national power is concentrated in the hands of the few or widely dispersed among competing interests. The history of the corporation has revealed how historically contingent the nature of power is. Insofar as a few individuals do wield extraordinary power, their power is neither omnipotent nor inevitable. Although history does create structures that reproduce themselves, social structure is inherently plastic. Corporations did not have to develop the way they did and will not necessarily persist in their current form. But the sense of inevitability, the aura of invincibility, the image of hard and fast structure contributes to their ability to hold their power.

CONTINGENCY

So the rise of the corporation was neither inevitable nor natural. It was the work of specific individuals and groups acting within the context of constraints and facilitators, setting goals, mobilizing resources, and influencing others to act in concert, shape meanings, and mobilize resources. The existence and form of the modern industrial corporation abounds in contingency. If New York had not built the Erie Canal, it is doubtful that the other states would have been compelled to create canal corporations. If the canals had not been completed just as railroads were becoming practical, and just when the transatlantic economy plunged into depression, the canal companies might have been profitable enough to reinforce government enterprise rather than to discourage it. If these events had not happened at the height of Jacksonian antistatism, they could have been interpreted, as in France, as proof of the need for more government involvement in the economy. If railroads had been built when governments had greater administrative capacity and greater resources, they might have built the railroads themselves, as many European governments did, or at least might have been able to sponsor private enterprise in an institutional setting other than the

Wall Street apparatus for government finance. If the Civil War had not accelerated the centralization of national power, states might have been able to keep a rein on corporations in their own borders and to regulate foreign corporations more thoroughly within their borders, making it more difficult for corporations to play one state off against another. If state and federal governments were truly controlled by business or if these governments had not been so thoroughly committed to enforcing market relationships to the exclusion of others, industrialists might have been able to govern themselves effectively without resorting to coalescing ownership in trusts and later holding companies. If New Jersey had not passed its holding company laws when it did, the trusts might have dissolved back into competing independent entities. If the railroads had not performed so poorly and had not become so overcapitalized, the depression of the 1890s might have been weathered without wholesale flight of capital into industrial mergers. We might have still had large companies, but organized like Carnegie Steel, Andrew Carnegie's limited partnership that expanded internally by driving down costs and adopting the latest technologies, rather than U.S. Steel, J. P. Morgan's billion-dollar corporation that grew by acquisition and stagnated technologically.

Simply listing the contingencies, however, does not adequately capture the role that contingency plays in a fully historical analysis. Dichotomously juxtaposing contingency and determination posits a false antinomy that makes sense only in an ahistorical, short-term perspective. Whether events are contingent or predetermined is a question that makes sense only when a time frame is fixed. If one goes back far enough, all events are contingent. If one shortens the time frame sufficiently, all events are determined (except events that are so accidental or capricious as to defy social scientific explanation). Instead of debating whether or not events were contingent or determined, it makes more sense to establish the factors upon which events were contingent and the point at which they became determined—or to be more precise, how the occurrence of some events narrowed the degree of contingency and made events more probable.

By 1890, the large-scale socially capitalized industrial corporation was probably destined to dominate American manufacturing. Only a few events, which were themselves already largely determined, might have undermined its rise. The Supreme Court might have legalized pools and trusts, allowing manufacturers to govern their industries without mergers. There might have been more unsuccessful large corporations like National Wall Paper or the Distilling Company of America, and fewer like the highly profitable American Tobacco or American Sugar Refining. The depression of 1893 might not have happened and thereby might not have taken the luster off railroad investments. A populist regime might have fostered agrarian cooperative capitalism at home and moved the nation toward economic autarky, cutting off European capital. It probably would have taken several of these events to undermine corporate ascendancy.

If we go back to 1860, we see that the rise of the large industrial corporation was much more contingent than it would be later. The South might have won the Civil War, creating two nations, each economically dependent on Europe and investing most of its resources in chronic war to rule the rest of the continent. It is unlikely that either would have had enough political stability to sustain long-term economic development. Even with the northern victory, it is possible that the Union would have nationalized railroads (especially if the war had continued longer), short-circuiting the development of the institutional framework of corporate capitalism including the stock market, investment banks, and brokerage houses. The legal framework that treated the corporation as a legal individual could have departed from the way it developed. If the national banking system had not served to centralize capital resources into New York and other large cities, a greater proportion of economic resources would have remained under the control of local commercial banking. While an informed and creative observer in 1860 might have reasonably imagined that the corporate form would eventually dominate manufacturing, I doubt that many individuals would have been willing to stake much money or personal credibility on it.

Going back another forty years, very few in 1820 could have imagined an economy dominated by large private corporations. In retrospect we can see how contingent and how little determined the corporation was in that agrarian, mercantilist, decentralized, and economically primitive society. The only factor necessary for a corporate economy established at that time was that the nation had a predominantly capitalist economy. The rights, entitlements, and responsibilities of private property were highly institutionalized, although it was far from the only economic arrangement. State enterprise was both common and legitimate. The corporation itself was as much public as private in an economy not significantly more developed than that in parts of South America. It is easy to imagine a variety of different economic forms that might have lain in the future, including workers' cooperatives, state enterprise, or economic activity embedded within other institutions such as religious or fraternal bodies. The *Dartmouth College* case of 1819 had just established that corporations had private rights, including protection from changing the content of a charter. If the Court had decided on the basis of the equally plausible principle that the state had a continuing interest in holding the corporation accountable to the public, corporate history would have been very different indeed. There might have never arisen an entity with the rights, entitlements, and responsibilities that we recognize as the modern private corporation, much less one that would have come to dominate the economy and society.

History moves like a boat sailing upstream. Each fork closes off possible destination points, decreasing contingency and increasing determinacy. Often when we look at where we are and where we are going, forgetting the forks passed by, we notice only the solid banks we move along and imagine that we came to this point on a continuous single stream. In contrast to societies that visually depict time as someone looking backward, able to see where one has been but not where one is going, we emphasize the alternatives ahead of us, but not those we have rejected. Our culture depicts a person looking forward, facing the future, with his or her back to the past. Yet, there are two ways the river metaphor fails. The first is that in history, the tributaries are not set in advance, but constructed as we go. Social power is a matter not only of steering the boat up one tributary rather than another, but also of determining what the alternative courses are. Second, we never reach the final destination. We can attempt to make stops in ports to refuel, reflect, and plan for the route ahead, but the boat does not stay anywhere very long. History waits for no one.

As social scientists, however, our object is not just to reflect on the nature of contingency and determination, but to specify and systematize what it is that classes of events are contingent upon, that is, to theorize and verify causes and effects. My thesis has been that the rise of the large-scale, socially capitalized industrial corporation in America is more accurately explained by the dynamics of power as theorized within political sociology than the dynamics of efficiency as theorized by economics and the historians and sociologists who accept that logic. For social science, the arbitration between these two competing perspectives is in empirical research. My goal has been to provide an alternative empirical account of the rise of the large industrial corporation. Chapter 2 demonstrated that large corporations were more likely to be found in industries with already large and capital-intense establishments than in industries that were highly productive, profitable, and rapidly growing. Socially capitalized incorporation was highly uneven among industries that had substantial scale, but not economies of scale. The other chapters, discussing the factors other than efficiency that the rise of the large corporation was contingent upon, have emphasized the dynamics of power, the rise of corporate institutions, and the role of the state, especially law.

THE TIMELINESS OF CORPORATE HISTORY

While my analysis has been historical, and indeed I have attempted to examine the events discussed as much as possible from within the framework of time and place, an analysis of the rise of the large-scale, socially capitalized industrial corporation is quite timely because its dominance is currently challenged on a variety of fronts. We are on the verge of a new mix of property regimes in which the large corporation will be just one of many interacting and interdependent forms. Corporate giants like General Motors, General Electric, and even such previously progressive firms as IBM are now losing money and are increasingly viewed as economic dinosaurs rather than vital, dynamic leaders on the cutting edge of the economy. As recently as the mid-1980s, even their critics focused on their success, worrying that their power was approaching omnipotence. Now even their supporters acknowledge that their ability to remain economically viable has been jeopardized.

What is emerging is a complex of new entities and new relationships among entities, both in the West and in the former Soviet economies. The long-term trend toward vertical and horizontal integration has been reversed as large companies have divested divisions that made components and unrelated products. Flexibility rather than integration has become the organizing principle, flexibility both in production (Piore and Sabel 1984; Scranton 1989; Weiss 1988; Noble 1984) and in the new forms of integration among firms that are replacing both markets and hierarchies (Weiss 1988; Powell 1990; Campbell, Hollingsworth, and Lindberg 1991). Many of these new relationships are being forged in the context of the changing rights, entitlements, and responsibilities of production. For example, Weiss's (1988) state-centered perspective on small business in Italy describes how a wide range of market-based, contract, and proprietary networks by which small firms collectively produce a broad range of product has been fostered by government policies in both property and commercial law. Campbell and his colleagues (1991) have argued that multilateral forms of economic cooperation have penetrated a large variety of industries from electronics to high-quality shoes. What this adds up to is a partial deinstitutionalization of the corporate form. This is not to say that the corporate form is about to disappear, but that the taken-for-granted nature of the large-scale, vertically integrated, socially capitalized corporation is being called into question. What once appeared inevitable and omnipotent is now being seen as contingent and vulnerable.

The analysis here also has implications for the reconstruction of politics and economics in the former Communist bloc. Capitalism is not a state of nature that will inevitably manifest itself once the "artificial" barriers of state regulation are removed. Capitalism was historically constructed in the West by affirmative activities. Markets were intentionally created by the active elimination of alternative modes of exchange and cooperation and by forging a legal and financial system in which the market became the only viable structure for economic activity. The states liberalizing their economies would thus be ill advised to accept the suggestions of ideologically laissez-faire consultants who promise economic vitality by merely removing state restrictions. The result is more likely to be economic anarchy than vigorous growth. Liberalizing states will have to actively create the institutional structures within which market economies operate and redefine the particular rights, entitlements, and responsibilities that underlie economic activity. Moreover, capitalism is not a system with a Platonic essence that uniformly manifests itself in various political and social contexts. The specific logic by which it operates and the specific relationships that give it substance are shaped by specific historical events. Insofar as there is similarity among different national economies, it results from structural isomorphism

engendered by interaction. In other words, capitalism is a historically specific world system. If the emerging capitalist economies in Eastern Europe
resemble those of the West, it is more from interaction than from the effer-
vescence of a compelling economic logic. Just as the emerging corporate
structure in the United States was shaped by its relationship to European
capital, the new capitalist institutions taking form today are shaped by their
relationship with Western capital. Not only does Western capital serve as a
model to emulate, but until the markets in Eastern Europe are more fully
developed, it will supply most of the capital as well as the demand for economic growth. If Eastern European states put their faith in the inevitable
sprouting of endogenous capitalism, the former Second World will drift
more toward the Third World than the First World, underdeveloping and
becoming dependent.

The changes in the former Soviet bloc have also affected the dimensions
of discourse about the large corporation in the United States. The occurrence of such profound, epochal transformations that few could have imagined within our lifetime spotlights how contingent history can be. We are
not only watching allegedly omnipotent structures disappear, we are watching the faltering, rudderless shaping of new societies, polities, and economies. It is clear that systems cannot be made from blueprints, but that those
who are making the future must use the resources that the past has left. One
can choose to walk down a new path, but each step is taken only from
where the last one left off.

Although there has been a continuity since Progressive times in seeing the
large corporation as the horn of plenty that created an unprecedented standard of living as well as the tyrant that gave enormous power to a lucky
few, in the last several decades those legacies have been adapted to cold war
imagery. Anticommunists have depicted the corporation as the foundation
of a vital economy that has provided the material resources for economically, militarily, and morally combating the assault of communism, as the
proof that freedom is not only right but more efficient. The left has accepted
the imagery in all respects but morally, emphasizing the power exercised
and the wealth centralized, juxtaposing the reality of corporate America
with an image of a socialist future (although there is little consensus about
what that image is). The American corporation has been portrayed as both
the strength and the evil of the American economy. Both sides have overem-
phasized the difference between state and economy in capitalism, treating
the economy as truly "free" and independent of government influence. The
dichotomous imagery that treats the American corporation as the foundation of capitalism has thus been sustained by the ideological battle waged in
the cold war, with both sides conveniently adopting the same implicit model
of capitalism. The end of the cold war, which has so thoroughly forced a
reconsideration of socialism, might also force a reconsideration of capitalism. I have argued throughout that there is no such thing as a "free" economy operating independent of the state. All economic systems involve spe-

cific rights, entitlements, and responsibilities enforced by some institutional mechanism embodied in political institutions. As we see former Soviet states attempt to make "free" economies, we see how difficult and how very contingent the process is. As Americans struggle to recover the level of prosperity many once considered their birthright, we should learn from both our own history and the epochal history-in-the-making in the land of our former enemies how open the future can be. We need not accept fulminations that any particular set of economic arrangements are natural, inevitable, or "American." By looking at the path that has brought us to this point, we can see the multitude of paths that lead to the future.

There is one caveat about knowing where we will go. The path to the present was not determined by the dynamics of efficiency, but the dynamics of power. Simply knowing what will bring the most material bounty for the most will do little to actually foster positive change. Many people with diverse and conflicting goals and aspirations will participate in shaping the future. Some will succeed more than others. Those who understand and appreciate the reality of power will be better equipped to prevail than those who naively trust in the inevitability of efficiency.

NOTES

CHAPTER 1

1. These figures do not mean that half the economy was in large corporations; the value of securities was often grossly inflated relative to the value of capital assets.

2. Strictly speaking, Chandler does not claim to explain the rise of the large corporation per se, but instead speaks of modern business enterprise (1977) or modern industrial enterprise (1990). Nonetheless, it is appropriate to contrast my perspective with his for two compelling reasons. First, we are trying to explain the appearance of the same empirical referents: U.S. Steel, General Electric, American Tobacco, and similar entities, around the turn of the century. When I discuss specific cases in Chapter 7, I will examine several of the same firms that he does. More important, any poll of business historians or economic sociologists, if asked to name the most influential analysis of the rise of the large corporation in America, would almost certainly single out Chandler's. One leading economic historian has written, "Virtually every work now written on the history of modern, large-scale enterprise must begin by placing itself within the Chandlerian analytical framework. Over the course of more than three decades . . . Chandler tenaciously pursued the large corporation. He sought to answer these questions: When, where, and why did it arise? How did it persist? Where did it spread? How was it organized? What functions did it perform?" (Porter 1992, 128). Nonetheless, it will be necessary at times to distinguish between his arguments that seem to apply to large corporations and those that seem to be specific to managerial hierarchies.

3. Computed from U.S. Census (1914); see Chapter 2 for details.

4. Socialization does not necessarily mean government ownership, but is the opposite of individualization. It only requires that some institution act to synthesize input from individuals and distribute output to individuals. Private health insurance is a form of socialized medicine. All persons pay premiums whether or not they are ill and draw benefits regardless of how much they have paid in.

5. To note that ownership was legally separated from control does not necessarily endorse a managerial perspective. Managerialism assumes that the legal separation from ownership and control (administration of daily affairs) means that managers became autonomous from capital and free to be even "soulful." While most owners lost authority over administration and strategic planning, managers, especially those without a major ownership share, remained beholden to capital and the class that controlled it. The fact that smallholders were generally disenfranchised does not mean that large holders or bondholders were enfeebled. Zeitlin (1974) has labeled the separation of ownership and control a "psuedofact" which he disputes by showing how few late twentieth-century corporations were truly management controlled.

6. The contested implication of this statement is the managerialist contention that only owners and workers are classes, and that insofar as authority passes to managers, class dynamics are extinguished as managers are seen to exercise authority as they see fit, as likely to be "soulful" as to maximize profits (Berle and Means 1932; Drucker 1946; Chandler 1977). My point here is that the relationship of man-

agers and owners to workers is not fundamentally changed by the rise of the corporation. The degree to which that relationship is exploitative is beyond the scope of this work.

7. One might argue that behavioral power can be reduced to structural power, since making a command is a way of setting alternatives. The subordinate has a choice of obeying or not and will face different consequences depending on his or her choice. However, the dynamics of exercising by command and by merely setting consequences are different enough to warrant this basic distinction.

8. The law specifies the circumstances under which new stock can be issued, setting a limit on "authorized" capital. Issuing stock beyond that authorized requires the approval of some percentage of the voting stock (the percentage varies from state to state). If stock has no par value, there is no way to calculate authorized stock, which means that directors can issue as much stock as they wish without accountability to stockholders.

9. Like my basic model of historical change applied to the rise of the corporation, the logic of selecting these three states is "historical." This study began as a quantitative study of the decisive period from 1890 to 1914. New Jersey, Pennsylvania, and Ohio were the states for which detailed industry-level data were available for the number and aggregate capital of corporations formed. As the study evolved into a more narrative account, these three states were retained because they embodied the full spectrum of legal attitudes toward corporations among industrialized states.

10. Even now there continue to be large firms outside of this structure, firms that are privately owned and do not publicly offer stock, such as Hughes Aircraft and Bechtel. However, I would argue that these large privately held companies could not exist without the larger economic system made up of the corporate segment. Moreover, to the extent that these firms wander beyond the orbit of the central institutions, they are handicapped. Glasberg (1989), for example, has documented how Howard Hughes lost control of TWA by disregarding powerful banking interests. I am not implying that institutions like banks control manufacturing corporations, but that dominant corporations and the institutions constitute a distinctive structure within which there is cooperation and interdependence.

CHAPTER 2

1. Chapters 7 and 8 employ the industry as a unit of analysis to examine case studies of incorporation, but there I treat the industry as a socially constructed entity in which industrialists themselves created variable degrees of boundedness and internal cohesion.

2. It might be argued that the relevant time frame should be 1898–1904, to span the entire period of intense corporate formation. While 1898–1904 does form a cohesive era, I decided to adopt a methodologically conservative strategy, setting the temporal sequence above the substantive considerations of the "natural" era. In fact, the time frame of the dependent variable makes little difference in results because there is a nearly perfect correlation between the total capital of large corporations in 1898–1904 and 1900–1904.

3. This threshold was selected because a few industries happened to have one very small company listed, presumably for arbitrary reasons. The results were slightly stronger with this threshold than using a dummy variable indicating whether there was any corporate capital at all.

4. Industries with extreme outliers on the independent variables were omitted from the analysis: iron and steel, distilled liquor, illuminating and heating oil, and fruit and vegetable canning. Their exclusion does not substantively change the results.

5. This is used as an independent variable rather than making the dependent variable into a ratio variable of corporate capital/establishments because doing so would distort the results. The model as I have specified it, using only one additional independent variable is:

$$y = a_1 + b_1 x_1 + b_2 x_2 + e \qquad (1)$$

where x_1 is number of establishments and x_2 represents another independent variable. If equation (1) is the "true" model, and y/x_1 were made the dependent variable, I should then in fact be estimating this equation:

$$\frac{y}{x_1} = \frac{a}{x_1} + b_1 + b_2 \cdot \frac{x_1}{x_2} + \frac{e}{x_1} \qquad (2)$$

So I control by making it an independent variable.

6. It is true that a desire to achieve some of the qualities in the independent variables may have constituted something close to reciprocal causation. For example, if incorporators desired greater productivity, one might argue that productivity was a cause as well as a consequence of incorporation. However, in testing such a model, one would have to separately measure productivity and the desire for productivity. In the absence of data on desire, we test only the effects of actual productivity. Nonetheless, it would be interesting to examine whether incorporation had any independent effects on qualities like productivity.

7. There was a bicycle "craze" in the 1890s, one of the very first mass consumer fads self-consciously promoted by business with heavy advertising, shows, competitions, and auxiliary paraphernalia.

8. One variant of structural theory in sociology does emphasize the importance of size per se. Blau (1970) has argued that size has a fundamental influence on the operation of organizations. For example, the more members, the greater the extent of differentiation and the more levels of hierarchy required. The reasoning is similar to that of efficiency theory, but the specific variables differ. The theory has not been explicitly tied to the corporate revolution, and this finding is too slender a reed to make such a connection very strong. Many other concomitants of size have been suggested that still await systematic analysis.

9. The data for 1904 are drawn from the *Manual of Statistics,* and I originally examined the same publication to discover corporations' fate in 1912. However, the coverage had been reduced so that many smaller firms were no longer included. In the meantime, *Moody's Manual of Railroad and Corporation Securities* had expanded its coverage, and therefore I used it to supplement the data. It is possible that some small firms may have been missed by *Moody's,* but the fact that it systematically gathered its information from stock market agencies and financial press, plus the fact that it was substantially larger than the *Manual of Statistics* ever was suggests that the number of omissions would not compromise the conclusions.

10. Since the issue is the success or failure of large corporations, I am examining only those industries with large corporations in 1904, not all those with large corporations in 1912. There are two ways to interpret the independent variable, capital in 1904: (1) Chandler's logic suggests that capital in 1904 embodies the effect of ex-

ogenous conditions at that time; industries would tend to have a similar level in 1904 and 1912 because the independent variables were relatively stable. Thus industries would be as highly capital-intensive in 1912 as in 1904. This variable would therefore have no substantive meaning in and of itself, but only as a proxy for other effects. (2) In contrast, I argue that it is important to distinguish between how firms' relative size in 1904 would give them the resources and influence to reproduce their position in 1912 on the one hand, and the conditions that explained their level of capital in 1904, on the other. The tendency for firms in 1904 to survive through 1912 could be due to the persistence of the conditions that facilitated their existence in 1904 or to the power to reproduce themselves whether or not the causes of their existence in 1904 persisted. The exogenous causes and the power to reproduce are not, of course, exclusive.

11. Tobit is a statistical procedure for analyzing "left censored" dependent variables, that is, variables that are cut off at the low end of a threshold. It assumes that subjects falling below that threshold do have some real value on the dependent variable, but that it is not measured. The technique was developed by econometricians to examine such issues as the factors determining consumer expenditure on major items during a specified time period, for example, the amount spent on a new automobile during the previous year (Tobin 1958). However, since most people do not buy a new automobile during any one year, most respondents report zero. One might assume that they still had some propensity to buy an automobile, but it fell short of the threshold needed to actually make a purchase. Thus it is assumed that the same factors determine whether any purchase is made and how much is spent (Tobin 1958; Maddala 1977).

12. My reasoning is theoretical and empirical: we might expect some factors to affect both the propensity to have any corporations and the amount of capital incorporated. This would be especially true of factors that generate very large firms, for example, the proportion of fixed capital. However, other factors, especially those related to power, such as falling profit, would tend to determine whether or not an industry contained corporations, but by themselves would not determine the amount of capital.

The most compelling theoretical reason for rejecting Tobit is the argument that corporate capital was a qualitatively different form of capital, not just a different amount. It is quite possible that characteristics such as capital intensity may not determine whether or not major corporations are formed in an industry, but if they are, would determine the level of capitalization. Whether or not corporate capital is a different form of capital should be a matter of empirical investigation, not an a priori assumption.

The empirical justification for separate analyses is that results *do* differ when the dependent variable is a dichotomous variable indicating whether the industry had any corporations and when it is a continuous variable indicating the amount (including only cases with any capital).

CHAPTER 3

1. Littlefield's account, however, does not demonstrate that anyone assumed that major public works projects could be completed except with major government support. Most of his account concerns efforts to mobilize support from the bordering states and federal government, all of whom passed the buck to other jurisdictions.

2. Delaware, which a century or so later would become a corporate haven, had only three business corporations; only Georgia and Kentucky had fewer.

3. The responsibility principle contrasted with a utility principle that framed debate in the second half of the nineteenth century, by which corporations were legitimated on the grounds that they maximized productive capacity, that is, that they were more efficient than other forms.

4. That is to say that "state" and "society" were increasingly treated as distinct categories. At the same time, the market was being treated as an autonomous system within itself, apart from society (Polanyi 1957). Sociologists have recently renewed Polanyi's challenge to the alleged self-contained market logic (Granovetter 1985; Block 1990).

5. Different authors have different variations on the name. Keasbey (1899b) and Smith (1912) refer to the "Society for the Establishment of Useful Manufactures," Cadman (1949) to the "Society for establishing useful Manufactures," Hindle and Lubar (1986) to the "Society for Encouraging Useful Manufactures," and Davis (1961) to simply the "Society for Useful Manufacturers."

6. Whereas railroads had supplied 90 percent of state revenue as recently as 1865, by 1870 they had fallen to 40 percent. Over the next two decades the state attempted to reassert its authority over the railroads. In the 1880s it allowed railroad corporations to broaden their charter only in return for surrendering their tax-exempt status (Grandy 1989a).

7. The institutionalization process involved here is not simple diffusion among discrete entities independent from one another. Law is institutionalized in such a way that states directly influence one another through the practice by which decisions in one state can be used as a precedent by others. Although statutory law is less uniform than case law, legal differences among states create pressure for uniformity.

8. Sobel (1965) and Adler (1970) report nine states defaulting.

CHAPTER 4

1. Berk (1990) explicitly challenges Chandler on this point, reversing the causal arrow and arguing that "[m]ore than technology alone, capital-market organization, investor entitlements, and national policy encouraged railroad growth and corporate investment over other strategies of national economic growth" (137).

2. There is a kink here in the functionalist logic. When it fails to readily fit the facts, Chandler's explanation moves outside it: the interfirm coordination was "needed" but failed. "To control and allocate the flow of traffic across the transportation network of a major region was a complex administrative task requiring more men and managers than [pool manager Albert] Fink and his counterparts in other associations ever had at their disposal. The pooling and allocating of income, while a more modest effort, was still administratively difficult. . . . Most important of all, however, was the relentless pressure of high constant costs. The need to meet these costs intensified the pressure to use excess capacity by subverting the cartel arrangements" (Chandler 1977, 142–143). Why were the resources not forthcoming? Throughout most of *The Visible Hand*, the very need for innovation explained its development. But when a clear need fails to stimulate appropriate innovation, the outcome is explained by an ad hoc turn to logic of collective action. He also invokes the failure of the government to facilitate coordination, implying that political processes can undermine functional processes, but not explain them.

3. Although in comparative terms the American state played a smaller role than European states like France (Dobbin 1994), the railroads would have developed at a much slower rate in a very different form without government involvement.

4. Although railroads were always more tightly regulated than other industries, in the twentieth century it has been their function as common carriers that was regulated, not their corporate status.

5. One might define a crisis as a socially constructed arena of decision in which proponents of previously rejected alternative courses of action are able to successfully convince those with decision-making power or those whose approval is needed that the new course is plausible or necessary. The "impossible" or "unviable" becomes "viable." The unthinkable becomes thinkable. The "normal" circumstances that have prevented the innovation are suspended. Thus wars, depressions, and other calamities have been fundamental switching points of history.

6. The railroad executives were not entirely unequivocal, as Seavoy (1982) points out. Many of them were reluctant to surrender the legal privileges they enjoyed, such as certain monopoly rights and the right of eminent domain, a very lucrative feature when a substantial part of their profits typically came from land sales and speculation. Many continued to favor defining the railroad as a public utility.

7. Salsbury (1967) questions the use of the term "mercantilism" to describe the postrevolutionary policies, arguing that states were motivated more by pragmatic considerations than by ideological commitment to government activism. But his analysis also shows that states took for granted their responsibility to foster development by proactive institution building.

8. This chapter also draws heavily on the experience of Ohio, Pennsylvania, and New Jersey, but to illustrate general points, not to apply a comparative causal logic to explain differences, as in other chapters.

9. The private sector probably did not lack the resources in any absolute sense. The amount of capital needed for the small railroads being built then was frequently mobilized from state finances.

10. Ohio passed a general corporation law in 1848, but nearly all the lines operating at the beginning of the Civil War were built before it was passed (Scheiber 1969).

11. See Creighton (1990) for a thorough analysis of antebellum charters across the United States.

12. Nonetheless, several towns that had been given the right to hold referenda passed an additional $3 million in local investment after the constitution went into effect.

13. Chandler (1977) emphasizes the innovations and downplays the borrowing, noting that few of the leaders were military men. The preeminent model of organization was based on engineering knowledge, however, and many of the early leaders had engineering backgrounds. West Point dominated engineering training and the Army Corps of Engineers was the leading agency of engineering practice. Ward (1981) has argued that the first generation of military leaders saw themselves and their organizations more in statelike terms than in economic terms, using such imagery as war, conquest, territorial control, and authority, but that this imagery gave way to economic images in the next generation.

14. I also avoid the terms "finance capitalism" and "finance class" to distinguish my perspective from two uses of "finance capitalism." One is the theory of finance

capitalism (Hilferding 1981; Lenin 1971; Rochester 1934; Perlo 1957), which reduces the dynamics of production to the institutions that administer the flow of liquid capital. As Soref and Zeitlin (1987) and others have pointed out, corporate capital is the merger of finance capital and industrial capital. The other use is that of managerialists who write off finance capitalism as a transitional stage between family capitalism and managerial capitalism. My terminology highlights the permanent features of the corporation.

15. In 1892, the year before the depression, the Santa Fe, the Erie, the Union Pacific, and the Northern Pacific owed for operating expenses and fixed debt 95 percent of their revenues, which meant that a loss of 5 percent in revenues would trigger insolvency (Campbell 1938).

16. Bankers had occasionally taken an active role in railroad companies as early as the 1860s (Greenberg 1980), but their systematic, pervasive role became activist only in the seventies and eighties.

17. See Chapter 7 for a discussion of the legal issues in accepting securities for currencies other than cash.

18. While Fogel (1964) sparked an important and lively debate over the counterfactual contention that other means could have spurred equivalent growth, there is still a general consensus that railroads contributed to American economic development (Lightner 1983). Bruchey (1990), for example, estimates that by 1890 the railroad's lower costs of transportation accounted for as much as 10 percent of the gross national product.

19. The Baldwin Company had a special relationship with the Pennsylvania Railroad, supplying it with locomotives from the very first. Matthias Baldwin was a close personal friend of J. Edgar Thomson, with whom he vacationed and invested.

20. Not all concentrating industries fit this pattern, of course. Tobacco, for example, had relatively low transportation costs (Jacobstein 1907).

21. Mercer (1982) is one of the few to systematically examine the question of public versus private benefit, but he only looked at federal investment in transcontinentals, and defined efficiency in terms of return on capital. He found that some railroads brought a higher rate of return on capital than those not receiving federal subsidies and concluded that overall, public efficiency was served.

CHAPTER 5

1. For example, Block (1990) criticizes both neoclassical and neo-Marxist perspectives for assuming that politics and economics operate according to not only different but contradictory logics, an assumption underlying their explanation of economic stagnation in the last few decades. He insightfully explains that the reification of these distinct logics has been itself a contributing factor in economic malaise. Insofar as his argument is persuasive, it will help erode the walls between economy and polity and become part of the historical process by which institutions are built and rebuilt.

2. Other theories are, of course, also concerned with reproduction, especially functionalism in both its Parsonian and its Marxist variations. The difference is that a historicist argument focuses on how a new social form creates the conditions for its own reproduction, while functionalists explain reproduction in terms of how external factors at the level of the system ensure reproduction.

3. Katznelson (1981) has used the analogy of trenches to describe a similar structuring of social formation that set the context for later developments, but "path" has become the more familiar image.

4. There has been considerable debate over the economic effects of the Civil War, but it has concerned the rate of growth more than the institutional structure of the economy. See, for example, the debate concerning Williamson's thesis that the war retarded the rate of growth (Williamson 1974; Livingston 1987).

5. There is a certain irony in our view of the prewar system, which seems so unwieldy because of the lack of national currency. Commerce today, including consumer purchasing with checks, credit cards, and charge accounts, probably is transacted with less currency than at any other time in our history. But institutionalization is so much more standardized and routinized with enforcement agencies that facilitate transactions across political boundaries that it appears seamless.

6. There is some disagreement about whether state bank notes would have thrived otherwise. Myers (1970) feels that the 10 percent tax on state bank notes effectively squelched their issue. James (1978) counters that state banks could find ways around the tax. He argues that if state banks had secured their currency with bonds, they would have been just as reliable and would not have needed to be brokered and discounted.

7. This system in which banks made investment loans on commercial deposits was one of the main reasons commercial banking and investment banking were separated in the New Deal (Hollingsworth 1991).

8. DiMaggio and Powell do not restrict the term to outright coercion.

9. Buckley and Roberts (1982) challenge that figure as perhaps twice its actual value, but agree that prior to 1914, portfolio was the predominant form of foreign investment.

10. It is therefore ironic that so many contemporary American corporations are so short sighted as to neglect long-term planning in order to maximize quarterly profit rates. Corporation financing ought to make it possible more easily to sacrifice short-term profits for long-term development.

CHAPTER 6

1. There are two ways that "autonomy" has been used to describe the relationship among institutions. The strong version of the concept would maintain that the law develops on its own with little input from society. Few social scientists today would accept this view. A broad range of social and political forces, including business in general and corporations in particular, helped shape the law. The weaker version is that the law can be an independent variable in explaining economic change, a perspective that suspends the question of why the law changes. The point of this version is that any explanation of economic change based only on economic analysis is incomplete and inaccurate. As a provisional perspective to begin analysis, I would hold that economy and politics are intimately tied up with each other, but that neither can be reduced to the other. Nonetheless, such a formulation tells us virtually nothing except the kinds of questions to ask.

2. The "legal fiction" doctrine in law had a very specific meaning that had fallen from legal favor by the turn of the century, replaced by an "entity theory" by which the corporation, rather than being a "fiction," was legally defined as a real entity in and of itself, endowed with individual rights (Parker 1911; *National Corporation*

Reporter 1892, 5:124; Horwitz 1992, chap. 3). While legally it became less of a "fiction" and more of a "real" entity, sociologically it remained no less a creature of law. Ironically the corporation became more of a social fiction through the law's treatment of it as real and mystification of its legally constructed nature.

3. There are three plausible reasons scholarship has focused on antitrust law. (1) It was the most visible and controversial law concerning corporations when they were rising. Sklar (1988) argues that the debate over antitrust crystallized the conflict over the corporation itself and analyzes the debate in those terms. (2) The basic constitutional issues concerning the corporation revolved around antitrust law. Legal scholarship has exalted the place of constitutional law, overshadowing other types of law (Gordon 1983). (3) Since the corporate revolution was a national phenomenon, there has been a tendency to focus on national-level factors. Although most corporate law is at the state level, state law is more complex and less prestigious to study.

4. Surprisingly, the legal status of intercorporate stock ownership was still ambiguous enough that the Illinois Supreme Court set a precedent as late as 1889 in a widely cited case (*People v. Chicago Gas Trust Co.*, 130 Ill. 287, 22 N. E. Prep. 798), which established that corporations did not attain the power to own other companies by virtue of including such a clause in their articles of incorporation. The court ruled that only the legislature could grant corporations this power, and it had not done so (*National Corporation Reporter*, Sept. 27, 1890; see also Jones 1895; Larcom 1937).

5. The Pennsylvania Railroad, under special legislation, had owned the stock of other companies for decades, but there had been no general legislation permitting railroads to own stock.

6. The U.S. Industrial Commission's analysis of how states defined the power to own the stock of other corporations included the following categories (with the number of states and territories in that category as of 1899): corporations are expressly prohibited from owning the stock of other corporations (2); corporations have the same power to acquire property as private individuals (1); any corporation may own the stock of any other corporation (3); certain kinds of classes of corporations may own the stock of any corporation (4); any corporation may own the stock of certain kinds or classes of corporations (2); a corporation may own the stock of another corporation engaged in a similar business or in a business in some way useful or subsidiary to the first corporation (11); no statutory provision with regard to such power (29) (U.S. Industrial Commission 1900b, 288–289).

7. Berle and Means are quite severe in their conclusion that the stockholder is being economically disenfranchised by the aggregation of power: "The only example of a similar subjection of the economic interests of the individual to those of a group which appears to the writers as being at all comparable, is that contained in the communist system. It is an odd paradox that a corporate board of directors and a communist committee of commissars should so nearly meet in a common contention" (Berle and Means 1932, 278).

8. The committee was alarmed that "[n]one of the witnesses called was able to name an instance in the history of the country in which the stockholders had succeeded in overthrowing an existing management in any large corporation, nor does it appear that stockholders have ever even succeeded in so far as to secure the investigation of an existing management of a corporation to ascertain whether it has been

well or honestly managed" (U.S. House of Representatives 1913, 146). It is interesting that committee members were equating management with the board of directors. Moreover, they must not have searched very thoroughly, since the Pennsylvania Railroad owners had launched a well-known investigation in the 1870s, as mentioned in Chapter 4.

9. While there has been a debate about whether interlocks form a system of power in late twentieth-century America, there is little doubt that they did in the nineteenth century. Mizruchi (1982), for example, frames his analysis of this issue in terms of whether interlocks have been transformed from a system of domination to a more benign system.

10. The U.S. Industrial Commission's analysis of state corporate laws defined the following variations for the method of valuation where the stock is not paid for in money (with the number of states and territories in that category as of 1899): generally the basis of value not being otherwise defined (3); at the actual value (1); at the true money value (2); at the fair cash value (4); at the reasonable value (1); at the appraised value (1); at the valuation mutually agreed upon between the subscriber and the incorporators (3); at the market price (1); at the value bona fide determined by the directors (3). One state (Montana) permitted the value to be arbitrary with no requirement that the assets of the property match the value of the stock with which it was bought (U.S. Industrial Commission 1900b, 281–282).

11. Smith (1905) explains that many of the corporate powers were in derogation of the common law, citing how limited liability contradicts the common law requirement that everyone doing business is liable for his or her debts. Thus corporate law has developed on its own quite apart from common law. Horwitz also advises to distinguish between statutory and common law on limited liability, stating that, while most states recognized a common law basis of limited liability, many continued to qualify the limitations in their statutes up until the end of the century (1992, 94).

12. Prior to New Jersey's statutes legalizing the holding company, its courts were little different from other states' in their interpretation of common law. In 1879, the state courts explicitly ruled that a corporation could not, in its own name, subscribe for stock or be a corporator under the general railroad law, nor could it simulate compliance by authorizing agents to act for it (*Central Railroad of New Jersey v. Pennsylvania Railroad,* cited in the *National Corporation Reporter* 1895, 9:357–359).

13. William N. Cromwell was the president of the Cotton Oil Trust (*Wall Street Journal,* Oct. 18, 1889, 88:1).

14. Freedland (1955) argues that the holding companies like American Sugar Refining or American Tobacco incorporated in New Jersey before this time were technically illegal.

15. Larcom (1937) agrees that New Jersey was perceived as too lenient and was a factor in the relative rise of Delaware as the favored state of incorporation. However, most large corporations continued to choose New Jersey until Wilson tightened the New Jersey law in 1913 (*Manual of Statistics,* passim).

16. Note that Figure 6.1 included the amount of capital, while Figure 6.2 tallies the number of corporations.

17. Evans lists the number of corporations broken down by size and by industry, but not by both, so it is impossible to state exactly how many small industrial corporations there were. For all Ohio corporations, 82 percent were small. The figure for

Pennsylvania was 79 percent. But in New Jersey, only 47 percent of new corporations were small.

18. The relationship of boards to stockholders was discussed in terms of whether directors were trustees—acting at their own discretion in interpreting the interests of the trust beneficiaries—or agents, acting not only on behalf of, but also at the behest of principals. The law specified a relationship with aspects of both (Rogers 1915).

19. Berle and Means acknowledge that the large corporation was a new institution: "The corporation has, in fact, become both a method of property tenure and a means of organizing economic life. Grown to tremendous proportions, there may be said to have evolved a 'corporate system'—as there was once a feudal system— which has attracted to itself a combination of attributes and powers, and has attained a degree of prominence entitling it to be dealt with as a major social institution" (Berle and Means 1932, 1). But, by their formulation, this new institution seems to be the sum of all the individual corporations, each operating according its internal dynamics, with the law being the only institutional-level factor.

Chapter 7

1. To be more precise, what was new was the national attention focused on such practices. Many of the industries and practices commonly cited as national in fact remained regional.

2. Ironically, two of the four that they were so bullish about later failed and are now remembered as object lessons on inappropriate monopolization.

3. The distinction between partial restraint of trade, which was legal, and general restraint of trade, which was not, resulted in very different standards in different jurisdictions. While Ohio courts concluded that the intrastate Consolidated White Lead Company was a general restraint on trade, New York courts ruled that the Diamond Match Company, which dominated all match production except two non-manufacturing states of Nevada and Montana, was only a partial restraint because it was not fully national (*Diamond Match v. Roeber,* 1887 [106 N.Y. 487]; see also U.S. Industrial Commission, 1900b; Dwight 1888).

4. Table 7.1 shows the statistics for the industry along with a measure of each statistic standardized on the mean and standard deviation of all industries. For some of these statistics, the standard deviation exceeded the mean, so that even though an industry may be several orders of magnitude larger than the mean, it may be only one or two standard deviations larger than the mean because few very large industries skewed the distribution. I could have eliminated those very large industries, but since I am dealing with a population rather than a sample, such a procedure would have introduced a bias in the direction of the point I am making. In emphasizing that the beer industry was larger than average, it is better to present data that show it was only a few standard deviations above the mean than to eliminate the outliers and "inflate" the difference between it and the mean.

5. Social density here is used in the sense that population ecologists use the term, to mean the total number of firms. It is somewhat counterintuitive if one thinks of density as the degree of interaction each firm has with other firms. In the latter sense, a small number of cohesive firms would be very dense, but as the term is used here, a large number of firms is more dense than a small number.

6. Chandler (1977, 1980) cites Pabst as an example of a company that grew in the 1880s through technological development (the development of the pneumatic

malting process and refrigerated tank cars), vertical integration (barrel making and branch distribution offices), and name-brand advertising. However, he gives no systematic comparative evidence that link cause and effect. More important, the use of advertising and distribution networks is consistent with both a power and an efficiency explanation.

7. One recent historian anachronistically draws on present-day business thinking to suggest the factors which "may have influenced" Anheuser to incorporate in 1875: "self-perpetuation, better financial protection in case of bankruptcy, to use stock as collateral for loans, increase capital by sale of stock, and tax exemptions" (Plavchan 1976).

8. Because the census amended the categories from one census to the next, the industry categories are altered to create a single scheme that could be used for all censuses from 1880 to 1914. The averages for all manufacturing may differ slightly from that computed directly on published figures.

9. In 1890 these characteristics had not changed dramatically. There were more plants, 199, and the average establishment had increased to $107,639, still hardly large. Productivity ($842 value added/worker) was still below the mean, although capital had nearly doubled to $8.57 capital/$1.00 wages. Despite more than a half decade of trust management, value added increased by a factor of only 2.32, compared with 3.25 for all manufacturing. Thus the trust did not have a major effect on the industrial performance.

10. Eichner (1969) and Zerbe (1969, 1970) have focused entirely on the sugar industry, Eichner offering a Chandlerian interpretation and Zerbe a critique. Most standard histories of trusts and antitrust include an account of the Sugar Trust's organizational and legal history. See also Blakely 1912; Vandercook 1939; Sitterson 1953; Adler 1966.

11. Beet sugar census statistics are not comparable until 1900. The two subindustries were enumerated separately in 1880, but the beet sugar industry was minuscule, with only four small establishments. Conventional histories date the industry as beginning with the sugar bounty of 1890, when the federal government began to pay beet growers a cash subsidy for each pound they grew. In that year, beet sugar was not enumerated separately. In 1900, it was smaller than cane sugar in the aggregate, but comparable in its characteristics. Cane sugar was somewhat more capital intensive, but beet sugar was produced in larger plants. Its level of productivity was virtually identical with cane sugar, both slightly below the mean for all industries.

12. The great increase in the number of firms is apparently attributable to a change in the definition of the industry, which starting in 1890 included mills that produced raw sugar from cane.

13. This might be seen merely as a "free rider" problem, an inherent problem in any collective action when the existence of a collective good depends on individual contributions (Olson 1971). However, the analysis of the free rider problem assumes that there are no enforcement mechanisms. The issue here is why there is no enforcement mechanism. The existence or nonexistence of enforcement mechanisms is something to be explained.

14. According to the journal *Iron Age,* "The Sugar Trust seems to have become hopelessly involved in litigation. It was lately understood the purpose of its managers was to obtain a charter as an incorporation under the laws of Connecticut, but it was believed that no attempt would be made at any conversion scheme pending the action of the Court of Appeals upon the case now before it—the case decided

against the trust originally by Judge Barrett, whose decision has since been confirmed by the General Term, by which the trust has been held to be a criminal enterprise. There was some surprise therefore, when it was announced in Wall Street on Thursday, that Judge Ingraham had issued a formal injunction to restrain the trust from making a conversion, it being alleged that the proceedings looking to that end were now actively under way. It was also ordered that no more moneys be paid out in dividends pending the decision by the Court of Appeals. The effect of this action was seen in the immediate fall of Trust stock to 51⅝, the lowest price it ever touched, indicating a shrinkage of $37,500,000 from the recent market value of $62,500,000" (Jan. 16, 1890, 45:94–95).

15. The American Sugar Refining Company had its own loading docks and customs inspection, arousing the criticism even of the conservative *Commercial and Financial Chronicle*. The government eventually found that the company had for decades been cheating by artificially dyeing its imported raw sugar, thereby incurring lower tariffs. The company was fined and several executives received jail sentences.

16. In 1907 the Utah Sugar Refining Company was consolidated into the Utah-Idaho Sugar Company, of which ASRC owned 51 percent.

CHAPTER 8

1. The accounts of other industries summarized the economic characteristics of the industry as enumerated by the Census of Manufactures. In tobacco, however, the census combined cigarettes and cigars, two radically different industries in terms of both economic characteristics and social organization, rendering the results meaningless.

2. Although the difference was slight, it is significant that in average size of firm, capital intensity, and productivity, the paper industry grew more slowly than the rest of the economy. That is seen in the fact that the deviation of the paper industry from the mean of all industries is lower in 1900 than in 1880 on these measures. It can also be seen in the separate computation of growth rates. For example, productivity for all industries increased by a ratio of 1.7 while paper industry productivity increased by only 1.3. These are not the figures that efficiency theory would expect to create large corporations in all an industry's branches.

3. The discrepancy between these figures and those of the census are due primarily to a different unit of analysis. The census counted "establishments," which meant separate business units at one location. A plant denoted a building. Since an establishment could have several plants, the number of plants making newspaper exceeded the number of establishments for the paper industry as a whole.

4. It is possible—in fact probable—that, ceteris paribus, fungible ownership is more efficient than impartible ownership. To the extent that it is, this would be a consequence of the large-scale corporation, not a cause of it.

5. The industry categories are very broad, a total of twenty-two industries as categorized by Evans (1948).

6. There was additionally one Canadian company, the Dominion Steel Corporation, Ltd.

7. For example, Schwartz and Romo (forthcoming) describe how the automobile industry became concentrated in southern Michigan with relatively little capital from eastern financiers, who were convinced that the eastern producers of luxury

cars were more lucrative investments than companies like Ford or Chevrolet that were more oriented toward a middle-class mass market. However, General Motors during its largest growth period in the 1920s was widely traded on the stock market. Only Ford departed from the corporate mold, growing by pouring most of its net revenues back into expansion and using short-term loans for operating expenses. The quantity of commercial capital available in an economy like southern Michigan's could not have supported many more major companies. Ford was unique because its presence precluded other similar companies.

8. To question the "rationalist assumption" does not mean to assert that economic actors are irrational, but only to question whether the assumption of their rationality can serve as the foundation of viable explanations. Questioning the rationalist assumption means that rationality becomes an empirical issue, not a presumption.

CHAPTER 9

1. But the emphasis on evil motives could also be used to protect corporations from government. J.B.R. Smith stated a widely held view at the time: "The remedy [of corporate excesses] is the only remedy ever found for evil. Remove the evil by placing good in its place, by evolving a higher standard of ethics in the individual. . . . Vice is purely personal and can only be changed by changing the nature and purposes of individual evil doers" (Smith 1912, 41).

2. If this is correct, it implies that even if Chandler has accurately identified the criteria by which large companies made strategic decisions, that is, factors such as the rate of throughput, the reduction of costs, and the integration of the productive process, this would have been only a temporary stage in the rise of the large firm, applicable only to the period when men from manufacturing backgrounds were in charge.

3. The term "technocratic," in contrast with "technical," is used here to indicate that it is a form of rule, as in democratic or autocratic.

4. For sociological critiques, see McGuire, Granovetter and Schwartz forthcoming; Granovetter 1985; Campbell, Hollingsworth, and Lindberg 1991; Zukin and DiMaggio 1990; Powell and DiMaggio 1991.

5. This does not mean that the interests of workers and consumers who hold shares are the same as that of large shareholders. A worker would need to own a very large block of stock to compensate for a wage reduction, as would a consumer to compensate for a price increase.

6. Even though Chandler (1977) begins his account in the eighteenth century, the period before the second half of the nineteenth century is treated as the "before" in a before/after story. The causal dynamics, that is, the transformations of technology and markets, occurred in the second half of the century. The events and structures of the first half are not part of the explanation, but just the setting for the dynamic events of the second half.

REFERENCES

Abbott, Andrew. 1988. *The System of Professions: An Essay on the Division of Expert Labor*. Chicago: University of Chicago Press.

————. Abbott, Andrew. 1990. "Conceptions of Time and Events in Social Science Methods: Causal and Narrative Approaches." *Historical Methods* 23:140–150.

Adams, Donald R. 1978. "The Beginning of Investment Banking in the United States." *Pennsylvania History* 45:99–116.

Adler, Dorothy R. 1970. *British Investment in American Railways, 1834–1898*. Edited by Muriel E. Hidy. Charlottesville, Va.: University Press of Virginia.

Adler, Jacob. 1966. *Claus Spreckels: The Sugar King in Hawaii*. Honolulu, Hawaii: University of Hawaii Press.

Alford, Robert, and Roger Friedland. 1985. *The Powers of Theory: Capitalism, the State, and Democracy*. New York: Cambridge University Press.

Allen, Frederick Lewis. 1965. *The Great Pierpont Morgan*. New York: Harper & Row.

Allen, Michael Patrick. 1981. "Managerial Power and Tenure in the Large Corporation." *Social Forces* 60:482–494.

Aminzade, Ronald. 1992. "Historical Sociology and Time." *Social Methods and Research*. 20:456–480.

American Sugar Refining Company. 1911. *A Statement in Regard to the American Sugar Refining Company*. New York: American Sugar Refining Company.

Ardent, Gabriel. 1975. "Financial Policy and Economic Infrastructure of Modern States and Nations." In *The Formation of National States in Western Europe*, edited by Charles Tilly, 164–242. Princeton: Princeton University Press.

Babcock, Glenn D. 1966. *History of the U.S. Rubber Co.: A Case Study in Corporate Management*. Bloomington: Foundation for the School of Business, Indiana University.

Baker, Wayne E. 1990. "Market Networks and Corporate Behavior." *American Journal of Sociology* 96:589–625.

Bateman, Warner M. 1895. "Private Corporations." *Ohio State Bar Association Reports, Proceedings of Annual Meeting*, 149–169.

Beach, Charles Fisk. 1891. *Commentaries on the Law of Private Corporations*. Chicago: T. H. Flood & Co.

Bell, Daniel. 1965. *The End of Ideology*. New York: Free Press.

Bennett, Smith W. 1901. "An Inquiry as to the Effect of the Double Stock Liability Incident to Ohio Corporations." *Ohio State Bar Association Proceedings* 22:149–170.

Berger, Peter L., and Thomas Luckmann. 1966. *The Social Construction of Reality*. New York: Anchor Books.

Berk, Gerald. 1990. "Constituting Corporations and Markets: Railroads in Gilded Age Politics." In *Studies in American Political Development*, vol. 3, edited by Karen Orren and Stephen Skowronek, 130–168. New Haven: Yale University Press.

————. 1994. *Alternative Tracks: The Constitution of American Industrial Order, 1865–1917*. Baltimore: Johns Hopkins University Press.

Berle, Adolf A., and Gardiner C. Means. 1932. *The Modern Corporation and Private Property*. New York: Macmillan.

Birkner, Michael J., and Herbert Ershkowitz. 1989. "Men and Measures: The Creation of the Second Party System in New Jersey." *New Jersey History* 107:41–60.

Blakey, Roy G. 1912. *The United States Beet-Sugar Industry and the Tariff*. New York: Columbia University Press.

Blau, Peter M. 1970. "A Formal Theory of Differentiation in Organizations." *American Sociological Review* 35:201–218.

Block, Fred. 1990. *Postindustrial Possibilities: A Critique of Economic Discourse*. Berkeley and Los Angeles: University of California Press.

Bogart, Ernest Ludlow. 1924. *Internal Improvements and State Debt in Ohio: An Essay in Economic History*. New York: Longmans, Green & Co.

Boisot, Louis. 1891. "The Legality of Trust Combinations." *American Law Register* 39:751–770.

Bonbright, James C., and Gardiner C. Means. 1932. *The Holding Company*. New York: McGraw-Hill Book Co.

Bosland, Chelcie C. 1949. *Corporate Finance and Regulation*. New York: Ronald.

Bostwick, Charles F. 1902. "Legislative Competition for Corporate Capital." Paper read before the annual meeting of the New York State Bar Association. January.

Boulding, Kenneth E. 1953. *The Organizational Revolution*. New York: Harper & Bros.

Braverman, Harry. 1974. *Labor and Monopoly Capital: The Degradation of Work in the Twentieth Century*. New York: Monthly Review.

Bringhurst, Bruce. 1979. *Antitrust and the Oil Monopoly: The Standard Oil Cases, 1890–1911*. Westport: Greenwood Press.

Bruchey, Stuart. 1968. "The Changing Economic Order." In *The Changing Economic Order*, edited by Alfred D. Chandler, Jr., Stuart Bruchey, and Louis Galambos, 140–148. New York: Harcourt, Brace & World.

———. 1990. *Enterprise: The Dynamic Economy of a Free People*. Cambridge: Harvard University Press.

Buckley, Peter J., and Brian R. Roberts. 1982. *European Direct Investment in the U.S.A. before World War I*. New York: St. Martin's Press.

Bunting, David. 1979. "Efficiency, Equity, and the Evolution of Big Business." Paper read at the annual meeting of the Western Economic Association, Las Vegas.

———. 1983. "The Origins of the American Corporate Network." *Social Science History* 7:129–142.

Bunting, David, and Jeffrey Barbour. 1971. "Interlocking Directorates in Large American Corporations, 1896–1964." *Business History Review* 65:315–335.

Burch, Philip H., Jr. 1972. *The Managerial Revolution Reassessed*. Lexington, Mass.: Heath.

Burgess, George H., and Miles C. Kennedy. 1949. *Centennial History of the Pennsylvania Railroad, 1846–1946*. Philadelphia: Pennsylvania Railroad Co.

Burns, Malcolm R. 1983. "Economics of Scale of Tobacco Manufacture, 1897–1910." *Journal of Economic History* 43:461–485.

Burton, Theodore E. 1911. *Corporations and the State*. New York: Appleton and Co.

Buxbaum, Richard M. 1979. "The Relation of the Large Corporation's Structure to the Role of Shareholders and Directors: Some American Historical Perspectives." In *Law and the Formation of the Big Enterprises in the 19th and Early 20th Centuries*, edited by Norbert Horn and Jürgen Kocka, 243–254. Göttingen: Vandenhoeck & Ruprecht.

Cadman, John W., Jr. 1949. *The Corporation in New Jersey: Business and Politics, 1791–1875*. Cambridge: Harvard University Press.

Calhoun, Craig. 1990. "Introduction: Toward a Sociology of Business." In *Comparative Social Research: A Research Annual*. Vol. 12, *Business Institutions*, edited by Craig Calhoun, 1–18. Greenwich, Conn.: JAI Press.

Callender, G. S. 1902. "The Early Transportation and Banking Enterprises of the State in Relation to the Growth of Corporations." *Quarterly Journal of Economics* 17:111–62.

Campbell, E. G. 1938. *The Reorganization of the American Railroad System, 1893–1900*. New York: Columbia University Press.

Campbell, John L., J. Rogers Hollingsworth, and Leon N. Lindberg, eds. 1991. *Governance of the American Economy*. New York: Cambridge University Press.

Campbell, John L., and Leon N. Lindberg. 1991. "The Evolution of Governance Regimes." In *Governance of the American Economy*, edited by John L. Campbell, J. Rogers Hollingsworth, and Leon N. Lindberg, 319–355. New York: Cambridge University Press.

Carlson, Waldemar. 1931. "Associations and Combinations in the American Paper Industry." Ph.D. dissertation, Harvard University.

Carosso, Vincent P. 1970. *Investment Banking in America: A History*. Cambridge: Harvard University Press.

———. 1987. *The Morgans: Private International Bankers, 1854–1913*. Cambridge: Harvard University Press.

Chamberlin, Emerson. 1969 [1905]. "The Loan Market." In *The New York Stock Exchange: Its History, Its Contribution to National Prosperity, and Its Relation to American Finance at the Outset of the Twentieth Century*, edited by Edmund C. Stedman, 443–454. New York: Greenwood Press.

Chandler, Alfred D. Jr., 1965. *The Railroads: The Nation's First Big Business*. New York: Harcourt, Brace & World.

———. 1969. "The Structure of American Industry in the Twentieth Century: A Historical Overview." *Business History Review* 43:255–281.

———. 1977. *The Visible Hand: The Managerial Revolution in American Business*. Cambridge: Harvard University Press.

———. 1979. "Administrative Coordination, Allocation, and Monitoring: Concepts and Comparisons." In *Law and the Formation of the Big Enterprises in the 19th and Early 20th Centuries*, edited by Norbert Horn and Jürgen Kocka, 28–52. Göttingen: Vanderhoeck & Ruprecht.

———. 1980. "The United States: Seedbed of Managerial Capitalism." In *Comparative Perspectives on the Rise of the Modern Industrial Enterprise*, edited by Alfred D. Chandler, Jr., and Herman Daems, 9–40. Cambridge: Harvard University Press.

———. 1990. *Scale and Scope: The Dynamics of Industrial Capitalism*. Cambridge: Harvard University Press.

Chicago Conference on Trusts. 1900. Chicago: Chicago Civic Federation.

Clark, John B. 1887. "The Limits of Competition." *Political Science Quarterly* 2:45–61.

Cleveland, Frederick A., and Fred W. Powell. 1909. *Railroad Promotion and Capitalization in the United States.* New York: Longmans, Green & Co.

Coase, Ronald H. 1937. "The Nature of the Firm." *Economica.* 4:386–405.

Cochran, Thomas C. 1948. *The Pabst Brewing Company: The History of an American Business.* New York: New York University Press.

———. 1953. *Railroad Leaders, 1845–1890: The Business Mind in Action.* Cambridge: Harvard University Press.

———. 1955. "The Entrepreneur in American Capital Formation." In *Capital Formation and Economic Growth,* by the National Bureau of Economic Research, 339. Princeton: Princeton University Press.

Coleman, James S. 1974. *Power and the Structure of Society.* New York: Norton.

———. 1990. *Foundations of Social Theory.* Cambridge: Harvard University Press.

Collins, B. W. 1980. "Economic Issues in Ohio's Politics during the Recession of 1857–1858." *Ohio History.* 89:46–64.

Cook, William W. 1891. *The Corporation Problem: The Public Phases of Corporations, Their Uses, Abuses.* New York: Putnam's.

———. 1903. *A Treatise on the Law of Corporations Having a Capital Stock.* Chicago: Callaghan and Co.

Creighton, Andrew L. 1990. "The Emergence of Incorporation as a Legal Form for Organizations." Ph.D. dissertation, Stanford University.

Cummings, Hubertis. 1950. "Some Notes on the State-Owned Columbia and Philadelphia Railroad." *Pennsylvania History* 17:39–49.

Daems, Herman, and H. van der Wee, eds. 1974. *The Rise of Managerial Capitalism.* The Hague: Nijhoff.

Dahl, Robert. 1961. *Who Governs?* New Haven: Yale University Press.

———. 1967. *Pluralist Democracy in the United States: Conflict and Consent.* Chicago: Rand McNally.

David, Paul. 1975. *Technical Choice, Innovation, and Economic Growth.* New York: Cambridge University Press.

———. 1986. "Understanding the Economics of QWERTY: The Necessity of History." In *Economic History and the Modern Economist,* edited by William N. Parker, 30–49. Oxford: Blackwell.

Davies, Joseph E. 1916. *Trust Laws and Unfair Competition.* Washington, D.C.: Government Printing Office.

Davis, John P. 1897. "The Nature of Corporations." *Political Science Quarterly* 12:273–294.

———. 1961 [1905]. *Corporations: A Study of the Origin and Development of Great Business Combinations and of Their Relation to the Authority of the State.* New York: Capricorn.

Davis, Joseph S. 1917. *Essays in the Earlier History of American Corporations.* Cambridge: Harvard University Press.

Davis, Lance E. 1965. "The Investment Market, 1870–1914: The Evolution of a National Market." *Journal of Economic History* 25:355–399.

Davis, Lance E., and Douglass C. North. 1971. *Institutional Change and American Economic Growth.* Cambridge: Cambridge University Press.

Diggens, John Patrick. 1984. "The Oyster and the Pearl: The Problem of Contextualism in Intellectual History." *History and Theory* 23:151–169.

DiMaggio, Paul J., and Walter W. Powell. 1983. "The Iron Cage Revisited: Institutional Isomorphism and Collective Rationality in Organizational Fields." *American Sociological Review* 48:147–60.

——. 1991. "Introduction." In *The New Institutionalism in Organizational Analysis*, edited by Walter W. Powell and Paul J. DiMaggio, 1–38. Chicago: University of Chicago Press.

Dixon, F. H. 1914. "The Economic Significance of Interlocking Directorates in Railway Finance." *Journal of Political Economy* 22:937–954.

Dobbin, Frank. 1994. *Forging Industrial Policy: The United States, Britain, and France in the Railway Age*. New York: Cambridge University Press.

Dodd, Edwin M., Jr. 1954. *American Business Corporations until 1860 with Special Reference to Massachusetts*. Cambridge: Harvard University Press.

Domhoff, G. William. 1967. *Who Rules America?* Englewood Cliffs, N.J.: Prentice-Hall.

Drucker, Peter F. 1946. *The Concept of the Corporation*. New York: John Day Co.

Duboff, Richard B., and Edward S. Herman. 1980. "Alfred Chandler's New Business History: A Review." *Politics and Society* 10:87–110.

Duguid, Charles. 1901. *The Story of the Stock Exchange: Its History and Position*. London: Grant Richards.

Dunning, John H. 1970. *Studies in International Investment*. London: Allen & Unwin.

Duval, George L. 1908. "Necessity and Purpose of Trust Legislation." *Annals of the American Academy of Political and Social Science* 32:63–68.

Dwight, Theodore W. 1888. "The Legality of Trusts." *Political Science Quarterly* 3:592–632.

Edwards, Richard C. 1979. *Contested Terrain: The Transformation of the Workplace in America*. New York: Basic Books.

Eichner, Alfred. 1969. *The Emergence of Oligopoly: Sugar Refining as a Case Study*. Baltimore: Johns Hopkins Press.

Elliott, Charles B. 1900. *A Treatise on the Law of Private Corporations*. Indianapolis and Kansas City: Bowen-Merrill Co.

Etzioni, Amitai. 1988. *The Moral Dimension: Toward New Economics*. New York: Free Press.

Evans, George H. 1948. *Business Incorporations in the United States, 1800–1943*. Princeton, N.J.: National Bureau of Economic Research.

Evans, Peter , Dietrich Rueschemeyer, and Theda Skocpol, eds. 1985. *Bringing the State Back In*. New York: Cambridge University Press.

Farrell, Richard T. 1971. "Internal-Improvement Projects in Southwestern Ohio, 1815–1834." *Ohio History* 80:4–23.

Fischer, Wolfram, and Peter Lundgreen. 1975. "The Recruitment and Training of Administrative and Technical Personnel." In *The Formation of National States in Western Europe,* edited by Charles Tilly, 456–561. Princeton: Princeton University Press.

Fishlow, Albert. 1966. "Productivity and Technological Change in the Railroad Sector, 1840–1910." In *Output, Employment, and Productivity in the United States after 1800*. New York: National Bureau of Economic Research.

Fligstein, Neil. 1990. *The Transformation of Corporate Control*. Cambridge: Harvard University Press.

Fogel, Robert W. 1964. *Railroads as an Economic Force*. Baltimore: Johns Hopkins Press.

Freedland, Fred. 1955. "History of Holding Company Legislation in New York State: Some Doubts as to the 'New Jersey First' Tradition." *Fordham Law Review* 24:369–411.

Frey, Robert L. 1985. "Introduction." In *Railroads in the Nineteenth Century*, edited by Robert L. Frey, xiii–xxxiii. Encyclopedia of American Business History and Biography. New York: Facts on File.

Freyer, Tony Allan. 1979. *Forums of Order: The Federal Courts and Business in American History*. Greenwich, Conn.: JAI Press.

Friedland, Roger, and Robert R. Alford. 1991. "Bringing Society Back In: Symbols, Practices, and Institutional Contradictions." In *The New Institutionalism in Organizational Analysis*, edited by Walter W. Powell and Paul J. DiMaggio, 232–263. Chicago: University of Chicago Press.

Friedland, Roger, and A. F. Robertson, eds. 1990. *Beyond the Marketplace: Rethinking Economy and Society*. New York: Aldine de Gruyter.

Galambos, Louis. 1970. "The Emerging Organizational Synthesis in American History." *Business History Review* 44:279–290.

Galbraith, John Kenneth. 1967. *The New Industrial State*. New York: Signet.

Glasberg, Davita Silfen. 1989. *The Power of Collective Purse Strings: The Effects of Bank Hegemony on Corporations and the State*. Berkeley: University of California Press.

Goodrich, Carter. 1960. *Government Promotion of American Canals and Railroads, 1800–1890*. New York: Columbia University Press.

Gordon, David M., Richard Edwards, and Michael Reich. 1982. *Segmented Work, Divided Workers: The Historical Transformation of Labor in the United States*. New York: Cambridge University Press.

Gordon, Robert W. 1983. "Legal Thought and Legal Practice in the Age of American Enterprise." In *Professions and Professional Ideologies in America*, edited by Gerald L. Geison, 70–110. Chapel Hill and London: University of North Carolina Press.

Grandy, Christopher. 1989a. "Can Government Be Trusted to Keep Its Part of a Social Contract?: New Jersey and the Railroads, 1825–1888." *Journal of Law, Economics, and Organization* 5:249–269.

———. 1989b. "New Jersey Corporate Chartermongering, 1875–1929." *Journal of Economic History* 49:677–692.

Granovetter, Mark. 1985. "Economic Action and Social Structure: The Problem of Embeddedness." *American Journal of Sociology* 91:481–511.

Greenberg, Stanley B. 1980. *Race and State in Capitalist Development: Comparative Perspectives*. New Haven: Yale University Press.

Grossman, Isador. 1920. "Corporate Organizations." *Ohio Law Reporter* 18: 269–289.

Hamilton, Gary G., and Nicole Woolsley Biggart. 1988. "Market, Culture, and Authority: A Comparative Analysis of Management and Organization in the Far East." *American Journal of Sociology* 94 Supplement:S52–S94.

Handlin, Oscar, and Mary F. Handlin. 1945. "The Origins of the American Business Corporation." *Journal of Economic History* 5:1–23.

Haney, Lewis H. 1917. *Business Organization and Combination*. New York: Macmillan.

Hannah, Leslie. 1979. "Mergers, Cartels, and Concentration: Legal Factors in the U.S. and European Experience." In *Law and the Formation of Big Enterprises in the 19th and Early 20th Centuries,* edited by Norbert Horn and Jürgen Kocka, 306–316. Göttingen: Verderhoeck & Ruprecht.

Hannan, Michael T., and John Freeman. 1987. "The Ecology of Organizational Founding: American Labor Unions, 1836–1985." *American Journal of Sociology* 92:910–943.

Hartz, Louis. 1968. *Economic Policy and Democratic Thought, 1776–1860.* Chicago: Quadrangle Books.

Heinsheimer, Norbert. 1888. "The Legal Status of Trusts." *Columbia Law Times* 2:51–58.

Herrmann, Frederick M. 1983. "The Constitution of 1844 and Political Change in Antebellum New Jersey." *New Jersey History* 101:29–52.

Hidy, Ralph W. 1949. *The House of Baring in American Trade and Finance: English Merchant Bankers at Work, 1763–1861.* Cambridge: Harvard University Press.

Hilferding, Rudolf. 1981. *Finance Capitalism.* Boston: Routledge and Kegan Paul.

Hindle, Brooke, and Steven Lubar. 1986. *Engines of Change: The American Industrial Revolution.* Washington, D.C.: Smithsonian Institution Press.

Hirsch, Susan. 1980. "From Artisan to Manufacturer: Industrialization and the Small Producer in Newark, 1830–1860." In *Small Business in American Life,* edited by Stuart W. Bruchey, 80–99. New York: Columbia University Press.

Hitchman, James H. 1970. "U.S. Control over Cuban Sugar Production, 1898–1902." *Journal of Inter-American Studies and World Affairs* 12:90–106.

Hodgson, Geoffrey M. 1988. *Economics and Institutions: A Manifesto for a Modern Institutional Economics.* Philadelphia: University of Pennsylvania Press.

Hogsett, Thomas H. 1905. "Regulation of Corporations." *Ohio State Bar Association, Proceedings of 26th Annual Session* 26:118–183.

Hollingsworth, J. Rogers. 1991. "The Logic of Coordinating American Manufacturing Sectors." In *Governance of the American Economy*, edited by John L. Campbell, J. Rogers Hollingsworth, and Leon N. Lindberg, 35–73. New York: Cambridge University Press.

Horn, Norbert and Jürgen Kocka, eds. 1979. *Law and the Formation of the Big Enterprises in the 19th and Early 20th Centuries: Studies in the History of Industrialization in Germany, France, Great Britain and the United States.* Göttingen: Vanderhoeck & Ruprecht.

Horwitz, Morton J. 1977. *The Transformation of American Law, 1780–1960.* Cambridge: Harvard University Press.

———. 1992. *The Transformation of American Law, 1870–1960.* New York: Oxford University Press.

Hounshell, David A. 1984. *From the American System to Mass Production, 1900–1932: The Development of Manufacturing Technology in the United States.* Baltimore: Johns Hopkins University Press.

Hovenkamp, Herbert. 1991. *Enterprise and American Law, 1836–1937.* Cambridge: Harvard University Press.

Hurst, J. Willard. 1956. *Law and the Conditions of Freedom in the Nineteenth-Century United States.* Madison: University of Wisconsin Press.

———. 1970. *The Legitimacy of the Business Corporation in the Law of the United States, 1780–1970.* Charlottesville: University of Virginia Press.

Hurst, J. Willard. 1978. "The Release of Energy." In *American Law and the Constitutional Order*, edited by Lawrence M. Friedman and Harry N. Schieber, 109–120. Cambridge: Harvard University Press.

Jacobstein, Meyer. 1907. *The Tobacco Industry in the United States*. New York: Columbia University Press.

Jacoby, Sanford M. 1990. "The New Institutionalism: What Can It Learn from the Old?" *Industrial Relations* 29:316–359.

James, John A. 1978. *Money and Capital Markets in Postbellum America*. Princeton: Princeton University Press.

———. 1983. "Structural Change in American Manufacturing, 1850–1890." *Journal of Economic History* 43:433–459.

Jenks, Jeremiah W. 1888. "The Michigan Salt Association." *Political Science Quarterly* 3:78–98.

Jenks, Leland H. 1927. *The Migration of British Capital to 1875*. New York: Knopf.

———. 1944. "Railroads as an Economic Force in American Development." *Journal of Economic History* 4:1–20.

Jepperson, Ronald L., and John W. Meyer. 1991. "The Public Order and the Construction of Formal Organizations." In *The New Institutionalism in Organizational Analysis*, edited by Walter W. Powell and Paul DiMaggio, 204–231. Chicago: University of Chicago Press.

Johnson, Chalmers A. 1968. *Revolutionary Change*. London: University of London.

Jones, Eliot. 1929. *The Trust Problem in the United States*. New York: Macmillan.

Jones, Richmond L. 1902. "Business Corporations in Pennsylvania." *Report of the Eighth Annual Meeting of the Pennsylvania Bar Association*, 345–352.

Jones, W. Clyde. 1895. "Trusts and Trade Monopolies." *National Corporation Reporter* 10:417–419.

Katznelson, Ira. 1981. *City Trenches: Urban Planning and Patterning of Class in the United States*. New York: Pantheon.

Keasbey, Edward Q. 1898. "Jurisdiction over Foreign Corporations." *Harvard Law Review* 12:1–23.

Keasbey, Edward Q. 1899a. "New Jersey and the Trusts." *New Jersey Law Journal* 22:357–368.

———. 1899b. "New Jersey and the Great Corporations." *Harvard Law Review* 13:198–278.

Keller, Morton. 1979. "Business History and Legal History." *Business History Review* 53:295–303.

Kertzer, David I. and Dennis P. Hogan. 1989. *Family, Political Economy, and Demographic Change: The Transformation of Life in Casalecchio, Italy, 1861–1921*. Madison: University of Wisconsin Press.

Kirkland, Edward C. 1961. *Industry Comes of Age: Business, Labor, and Public Policy, 1860–1897*. New York: Holt, Rinehart & Winston.

Lamoreaux, Naomi. 1985. *The Great Merger Movement in American Business, 1899–1904*. New York: Cambridge University Press.

Larcom, Russell Carpenter. 1937. *The Delaware Corporation*. Baltimore: Johns Hopkins Press.

Larson, Henrietta M. 1936. *Jay Cooke: Private Banker*. Cambridge: Harvard University Press.

Lash, Scott, and John Urry. 1987. *The End of Organized Capitalism*. Madison: University of Wisconsin Press.

Lazonick, William. 1993. *Business Organization and the Myth of the Market Economy*. New York: Cambridge University Press.

Lehman, Edward W. 1988. "The Theory of the State versus the State of Theory." *American Sociological Review* 53:807–823.

Lenin, V. I. 1971. "Imperialism, the Highest Stage of Capitalism." In *Selected Works: One Volume Edition*, 169–263. New York: International Publishers.

Leppert, Richard. 1988. *Music and Image: Domesticity, Ideology, and Sociocultural Formation in Eighteenth-Century England*. Cambridge: Cambridge University Press.

Lie, John. 1993. "Visualizing the Invisible Hand: The Social Origins of 'Market Society' in England, 1550–1750." *Politics and Society* 21:275–305.

Lightner, David L. 1983. "Railroads and the American Economy: The Fogel Thesis in Retrospect." *Journal of Transport History* 4:20–34.

Lindberg, Leon N., and John L. Campbell. 1991. "The State and the Organization of Economic Activity." In *Governance of the American Economy*, edited by John L. Campbell, J. Rogers Hollingsworth, and Leon N. Lindberg, 356–395. New York: Cambridge University Press.

Littlefield, Douglas R. 1984. "The Potomac Company: A Misadventure in Financing an Early American Internal Improvement Project." *Business History Review* 58:562–585.

Lively, Robert A. 1968. "The American System: A Review Article." In *The Changing Economic Order*, edited by Alfred D. Chandler, Jr., Stuart Bruchey, and Louis Galambos, 148–166. New York: Harcourt, Brace & World.

Livermore, Shaw. 1939. *Early American Land Companies: Their Influence on Corporate Development*. New York: Commonwealth Fund.

Livesay, Harold C., and Glenn Porter. 1971. "The Financial Role of Merchants in the Development of U.S. Manufacturing, 1815–1860." *Explorations in Economic History* 9:63–87.

Livingston, James. 1987. "The Social Analysis of Economic History and Theory: Conjectures on Late Nineteenth-Century American Development." *American Historical Review* 92:69–95.

Lockwood Trade Journal Co. 1940. *1690–1940, 250 Years of Papermaking in America*. New York: Lockwood Trade Journal Co.

Logan, John R., and Harvey L. Molotch. 1988. *Urban Fortunes: The Political Economy of Place*. Berkeley: University of California Press.

Lowi, Theodore J. 1984. "Why Is There No Socialism in the United States? A Federal Analysis." In *The Costs of Federalism*, edited by Robert T. Golembiewski and Aaron Wildavsky, 37–53. New Brunswick, N.J.: Transaction Books.

MacGill, Caroline E. 1948. *History of Transportation in the United States before 1860*. New York: Peter Smith (reprinted with the permission of the Carnegie Institution of Washington).

Maddala, G. S. 1977. *Econometrics*. New York: McGraw-Hill.

Maier, Charles S. 1987. *In Search of Stability: Explorations in Historical Political Economy*. Cambridge: Cambridge University Press.

Manchester, Herbert. 1935. *The Diamond Match Company: A Century of Service, of Progress, and of Growth, 1835–1935*. New York: Diamond Match Co.

Mann, Michael. 1984. "The Autonomous Power of the State: Its Origins, Mechanisms, and Results." *European Journal of Sociology* 25:185–213.

Manual of Statistics. Various years, 1890–1913. New York: Manual of Statistics Co.

Markham, Jesse W. 1955. "Survey of Evidence and Findings on Mergers." In *Business Concentration and Price Policy*, 141–182. Princeton: Princeton University Press.

Marshall, Edwin John. 1903. *The Law Governing Private Corporations in Ohio.* Cincinnati: W. H. Anderson Co.

Martin, Albro. 1971. *Enterprise Denied: Origins of the Decline of American Railroads, 1897–1917.* New York: Columbia University Press.

McClelland, P. D. 1968. "Railroads, American Growth, and the New Economic History: A Critique." *Journal of Economic History* 28: 105–123

McCraw, Thomas K. 1981. "Rethinking the Trust Question." In *Regulation in Perspective*, edited by Thomas K. McCraw, 1–55. Cambridge: Harvard University Press.

McCurdy, Charles W. 1978a. "American Law and the Marketing Structure of the Large Corporation, 1875–1890." *Journal of Economic History* 38: 631–649.

———. 1978b. "Justice Field and the Jurisprudence of Government-Business Relations: Some Parameters of Laissez Faire Constitutionalism, 1863–1897," in *American Law and the Constitutional Order*, edited by Lawrence M. Friedman and Harry N. Schieber, 246–265. Cambridge: Harvard University Press.

———. 1979. "The Knight Sugar Decision of 1895 and the Modernization of American Corporation Law: 1869–1903." *Business History Review* 53: 304–342.

McGuire, Patrick. 1989. "Instrumental Class Power and the Origin of Class-Based State Regulation in the U.S. Electric Utility Industry." *Critical Sociology* 16: 181–203.

———. 1990. "Money and Power: Financiers and the Electric Manufacturing Industry, 1878–1896." *Social Science Quarterly* 71:510–530.

McGuire, Patrick, Mark Granovetter, and Michael Schwartz. Forthcoming. *The Social Construction of Industry: Human Agency in the Development, Diffusion, and Institutionalization of the Electric Utility Industry.* New York: Cambridge University Press.

Meade, Edward S. 1903. *Trust Finance.* New York: D. Appleton & Co.

Mercer, Lloyd J. 1982. *Railroads and Land Grant Policy: A Study in Government Intervention.* New York: Academic.

Meyer, John W., and Brian Rowan. 1977. "Institutionalized Organization: Formal Structure as Myth and Ceremony." *American Journal of Sociology* 83:340–363.

Meyer, John W., and W. Richard Scott, eds. 1983. *Organizational Environments: Ritual and Rationality.* Beverly Hills, Calif.: Sage.

Michie, Ranald C. 1986. "The London and New York Stock Exchanges, 1850–1914." *Journal of Economic History* 46:171–187.

Mills, C. Wright. 1956. *The Power Elite.* New York: Oxford University Press.

Mintz, Beth, and Michael Schwartz. 1985. *The Power Structure of American Business.* Chicago: University of Chicago Press.

Mizruchi, Mark S. 1982. *The American Corporate Network, 1904–1974.* Beverly Hills, Calif.: Sage.

———. 1983. "Who Controls Whom? An Examination of the Relation between Management and Boards of Directors in Large American Corporations." *Academy of Management Review* 8:426–435.

Montague, Gilbert Holland. 1910. "Trust Regulation To-day." *The Atlantic Monthly* 105:1–9.

Morgan, E. Victor, and W. A. Thomas. 1962. *The Stock Exchange.* London: Elek Books.

Mullins, Jack Simpson. 1964. "The Sugar Trust: Henry O. Havemeyer and the American Sugar Refining Company." Ph.D. dissertation, University of South Carolina.

Myers, Frank E. 1970. "Social Class and Political Change in Western Industrial Societies." *Comparative Politics* 2:410.

Navin, Thomas R., and Marian V. Sears. 1955. "The Rise of a Market for Industrial Securities, 1887–1902." *Business History Review* 29:105–138.

Nelson, Ralph L. 1959. *Merger Movements in American History.* Princeton: Princeton University Press.

New York Legislature. 1897. *Report and Proceedings of the Joint Committee of the Senate and Assembly Appointed to Investigate Trusts.* Albany, N.Y.: Wynkoop Hallenbeck Crawford Co.

Noble, David F. 1977. *America by Design: Science, Technology, and the Rise of Corporate Capitalism.* New York: Knopf.

———. 1984. *Forces of Production: A Social History of Industrial Automation.* New York: Knopf.

Norich, Samuel. 1980. "Interlocking Directorates, the Control of Large Corporations, and Patterns of Accumulation in the Capitalist Class." In *Classes, Class Conflict, and the State,* 83–104. Cambridge, Mass.: Winthrop.

North, Douglass C. 1981. *Structure and Change in Economic History.* New York: Norton.

Noyes, Alexander D. 1910. "The Future of High Finance." *Atlantic Monthly* 105:229–239.

O'Connor, James. 1973. *The Fiscal Crisis of the State.* New York: St. Martin's.

Offe, Claus. 1972. "Political Authority and Class Structures—An Analysis of Late Capitalist Societies." *International Journal of Sociology* 2:73–108.

Offe, Claus, and Volker Ronge. 1975. "Theses on the Theory of the State." *New German Critique* 6:139–47.

Olson, Mancur, Jr. 1971. *The Logic of Collective Action.* New York: Schocken.

Parker, John S. 1911. *The Law of New Jersey Corporations.* vol. 1. Chicago: Callaghan & Co.

Parker, Rachel Rudmose. 1993. "The Subnational State and Economic Organization: State-level Variation in Corporation Law in the United States, 1880–1904." Ph.D. dissertation, University of California, Los Angeles.

Paul, Arnold M. 1978. "Legal Progressivism, the Courts, and the Crisis of the 1890s." In *American Law and the Constitutional Order,* edited by Lawrence M. Friedman and Harry N. Schieber, 283–289. Cambridge: Harvard University Press.

Peck, Sidney. 1975. "Current Trends in the American Labor Movement." *Insurgent Sociologist* 5:23–40.

Pennings, Johannes M. 1980. *Interlocking Directorates: Origins and Consequences of Connections among Boards of Directors.* San Francisco: Jossey-Bass.

Perlo, Victor. 1957. *The Empire of High Finance.* New York: International Publishers.

Perrow, Charles. 1981. "Postscript." In *Perspectives on Organization Design and Behavior,* edited by Andrew H. Van de Ven and William F. Joyce, 403–404. New York: Wiley.

———. 1986. "Economic Theories of Organization." *Theory and Society* 15: 11–45.

———. 1990. "Economic Theories of Organization." In *Structures of Capital: The Social Organization of the Economy,* edited by Sharon Zukin and Paul DiMaggio, 121–152. Cambridge: Cambridge University Press.

———. 1991. "A Society of Organizations." *Theory and Society* 20: 725–762.

Piore, Michael, and Charles Sabel. 1984. *The Second Industrial Divide.* New York: Basic.

Platt, Hermann K. 1973. "Jersey City and the United Railroad Companies, 1868: A Case Study of Municipal Weakness." *New Jersey City* 91:249–266.

———. 1990. "Railroad Rights and Tideland Policy: A Tug of War in Nineteenth-Century New Jersey." *New Jersey History* 108:35–58.

Plavchan, Ronald Jan. 1976. *A History of Anheuser-Busch, 1852–1933.* New York: Arno Press.

Polanyi, Karl. 1957. *The Great Transformation.* Boston: Beacon.

Porter, Glenn. 1992. *The Rise of Big Business, 1860–1920.* 2nd ed. Arlington Heights, Ill.: Harlan Davison.

Powell, Walter W. 1990. "Neither Market nor Hierarchy: Network Forms of Organization." In *Research in Organizational Behavior,* vol. 12, edited by Barry M. Staw and Larry L. Cummings. Greenwich, Conn.: JAI Press.

Powell, Walter W., and Paul J. DiMaggio. 1991. *The New Institutionalism in Organizational Analysis.* Chicago: University of Chicago Press.

Procter and Gamble. 1954. *Ivory 75.* Cincinnati: Procter and Gamble.

Ragin, Charles C. 1987. *The Comparative Method: Moving beyond Qualitative and Quantitative Strategies.* Berkeley: University of California Press.

Ransom, Roger. 1981. *Coping with Capitalism: The Economic Transformation of the United States, 1776–1980.* Englewood Cliffs, N.J.: Prentice-Hall.

Renner, K. 1949. *The Institutions of Private Law and Their Social Function.* London: Routledge & Kegan Paul.

Ripley, William Z. 1905. *Trusts, Pools, and Corporations.* Boston: Ginn & Co.

Robertson, James Oliver. 1985. *America's Business.* New York: Hill and Wang.

Robinson, Robert V., and Carl M. Briggs. 1990. "The Rise of Factories in Nineteenth-Century Indianapolis." *American Journal of Sociology* 97:622–656.

Rochester, Anna. 1934. *Rulers of America: A Study of Finance Capitalism.* New York: International Publishers.

Rodgers, Daniel T. 1978. *The Work Ethic in Industrial America, 1850–1920.* Chicago: University of Chicago Press.

Rogers, William P. 1915. "Powers, Duties, and Liabilities of Corporate Directors." *Ohio Law Reporter* 12:619–638.

Roy, William G. 1981. "The Vesting of Interests and the Determinants of Political Power: Size, Network Structure, and Mobilization of American Industries, 1886–1905." *American Journal of Sociology* 86:1287–1310.

———. 1982. "The Politics of Bureaucratization and the U.S. Bureau of Corporations." *Journal of Political and Military Sociology* 10:183–199.

———. 1983a. "The Unfolding of the Interlocking Directorate Structure of the United States." *American Sociological Review* 48:248–256.

———. 1983b. "Interlocking Directorates and the Corporate Revolution." *Social Science History* 7:143–164.

———. 1990. "Functional and Historical Logics in Explaining the Rise of the American Industrial Corporation." *Comparative Social Research* 12:19–44. Edited by Craig Calhoun.

Roy, William G., and Philip Bonacich. 1988. "Interlocking Directorates and Communities of Interest among American Railroad Companies." *American Sociological Review* 53:368–379.

Rubin, Julius. 1961. *Canal or Railroad? Imitation and Innovation in the Response to the Erie Canal in Philadelphia, Baltimore, and Boston.* Philadelphia: American Philosophical Society.

Ryan, Alan. 1987. *Property.* Minneapolis: University of Minnesota Press.

Sabel, Charles, and Jonathan Zeitlin. 1985. "Historical Alternatives to Mass Production: Politics, Markets, and Technology in Nineteenth-Century Industrialization." *Past and Present* (August):133–176.

Sackett, William E. 1914. *Modern Battles of Trenton.* New York: Neale Publishing Co.

Salsbury, Stephen. 1967. *The State, the Investor, and the Railroad: The Boston and Albany, 1825–1867.* Cambridge: Harvard University Press.

Scheiber, Harry N. 1969. *The Ohio Canal Era: A Case Study of Government and the Economy.* Athens: Ohio University Press.

———. 1975. "Federalism and the American Economic Order, 1789–1910." *Law and Society Review* 10:51–111.

———. 1978. "Property Law, Expropriation, and Resource Allocation by Government, 1789–1910." In *American Law and the Constitutional Order*, edited by Lawrence M. Friedman and Harry N. Schieber, 132–141. Cambridge: Harvard University Press.

Schisgall, Oscar. 1981. *Eyes on Tomorrow: The Evolution of Procter and Gamble.* Chicago: J. G. Ferguson Publishers.

Schotter, Howard W. 1927. *The Growth and Development of the Pennsylvania Railroad Company: A Review of the Charter and Annual Reports of the Pennsylvania Railroad Company, 1846 to 1926.* Philadelphia: Press of Allen, Lane & Scott.

Schwartz, Michael, and Frank Romo. Forthcoming. *The Rise and Fall of Detroit: How the American Automobile Industry Destroyed Its Capacity to Compete.* Berkeley and Los Angeles: University of California Press.

Scott, John. 1986. *Capitalist Property and Financial Power: A Comparative Study of Britain, the United States, and Japan.* Brighton: Wheatsheaf Books.

Scott, W. Richard. 1983. "The Organization of Environments: Network, Cultural, and Historical Events." In *Organizational Environments: Ritual and Rationality*, edited by John W. Meyer, 155–175. Beverly Hills, Calif.: Sage.

Scranton, Philip. 1989. *Figured Tapestry: Production, Markets, and Power in Philadelphia Textiles, 1885–1941.* Cambridge: Cambridge University Press.

Seager, Henry R., and Charles A. Gulick, Jr. 1929. *Trust and Corporation Problems.* New York: Harper & Bros.

Seavoy, Ronald E. 1982. *The Origins of the American Business Corporation, 1784–1855: Broadening the Concept of Public Service during Industrialization.* Westport, Conn.: Greenwood.

Sewell, William H. 1992. "A Theory of Structure: Duality, Agency, and Transformation." *American Journal of Sociology* 98: 1–29.

Shaw, Ronald E. 1990. *Canals for a Nation: The Canal Era in the United States, 1790–1860.* Lexington: University of Kentucky Press.

Sitterson, J. Carlyle. 1953. *Sugar Country: The Cane Sugar Industry in the South, 1753–1950.* Lexington: University of Kentucky Press.

Sklar, Martin. 1988. *The Corporate Reconstruction of American Capitalism, 1890–1916: The Market, the Law, and Politics.* Cambridge: Cambridge University Press.

Skocpol, Theda. 1979. *States and Social Revolution: A Comparative Analysis of France, Russia, and China.* New York: Cambridge University Press.

———. 1980. "Political Response to Capitalist Crisis: Neo-Marxist Theories of the State and the Case of the New Deal." *Politics and Society* 10:155–202.

Skowronek, Stephen. 1982. *Building a New American State: The Expansion of the National Administrative Capacities, 1877–1920.* New York: Cambridge University Press.

Smiley, Gene. 1981. "The Expansion of the New York Securities Market at the Turn of the Century." *Business History Review* 55:75–85.

Smith, David C. 1971. *History of Papermaking in the U.S.* New York: Lockwood.

Smith, Herbert K. 1905. "Incorporation by the States." *Yale Law Journal* 14:385–397.

Smith, J.B.R. 1912. *Nature, Organization, and Management of Corporations under "An Act Concerning Corporations (Revision of 1896)" of the State of New Jersey.* Newark: Soney & Sage.

Sobel, Robert. 1965. *The Big Board: A History of the New York Stock Market.* New York: Free Press of Glencoe.

Soref, Michael, and Maurice Zeitlin. 1987. "Finance Capital and the Internal Structure of the Capitalist Class in the United States." In *Intercorporate Relations: The Structural Analysis of Business,* edited by Mark Mizruchi and Michael Schwartz, 56–84. New York: Cambridge University Press.

Starr, Paul. 1982. *The Social Transformation of American Medicine.* New York: Basic.

Stedman, Edmund C., and Alexander N. Easton. 1969 [1905]. "The History of the New York Stock Exchange." In *The New York Stock Exchange: Its History, Its Contribution to National Prosperity, and Its Relation to American Finance at the Outset of the Twentieth Century,* edited by Edmund C. Stedman, 17–407. New York: Greenwood Press. Reprint.

Stevens, William S. 1913. *Industrial Combinations and Trusts.* New York: Macmillan.

Stimson, Frederic Jesup. 1911. *Popular Law-making: A Study of the Origin, History, and Present Tendencies of Law-making by Statute.* London: Chapman & Hall.

Stinchcombe, Arthur L. 1965. "Social Structure and Organizations." In *Handbook of Organizations,* edited by James G. March, 142–191. Chicago: Rand McNally.

Stover, John L. 1987. *History of the B&O Railroad.* West Lafayette, Ind.: Purdue University Press.

Studenski, Paul, and Herman E. Krooss. 1963. *Financial History of the United States: Fiscal, Monetary, Banking, and Tariff, Including Financial Administration and State and Local Finance.* New York: Random House.

Surface, George. 1910. *The Story of Sugar.* New York: Appleton & Co.

Tennant, Richard B. 1950. *The American Cigarette Industry: A Study in Economic Analysis and Public Policy.* New Haven: Yale University Press.

Thacher, Thomas. 1902. "Corporations at Home and Abroad." *Columbia Law Review* 2:350–363.

Tilly, Charles, ed. 1975. *The Formation of National States in Western Europe.* Princeton: Princeton University Press.

Tilly, Charles. 1978. *From Mobilization to Revolution.* Reading, Mass.: Addison-Wesley.

Tobin, James. 1958. "Estimation of Relationships for Limited Dependent Variables." *Econometrica* 26:24–36.

Tolbert, Pamela S., and Lynne G. Zucker. 1983. "Institutional Sources of Change in the Formal Structure of Organizations: The Diffusion of Civil Service Reform, 1880–1935." *Administrative Science Quarterly* 28:22–39.

U.S. Bureau of the Census. 1914. *Abstract of the Census of Manufactures.* Washington, D.C.: Government Printing Office.

———. 1975. *Historical Statistics of the United States: Colonial Times to 1970.* Washington, D.C.: Government Printing Office.

U.S. Bureau of Corporations. 1906. *Report of the Commissioner of Corporations on the Transporation of Petroleum,* vol. 1. Washington, D.C.: Government Printing Office.

———. 1907. *Report of the Commissioner of Corporations on the Transporation of Petroleum,* vol. 2. Washington, D.C.: Government Printing Office.

———. 1909. *Report of the Commissioner of Corporations on the Tobacco Industry.* Part 1, *Position of the Tobacco Combination in the Industry.* Washington, D.C.: Government Printing Office.

———. 1911. *Report of the Commissioner of Corporations on the Tobacco Industry.* Part 2, *Capitalization, Investment, and Earnings.* Washington, D.C.: Government Printing Office.

———. 1915. *Report of the Commissioner of Corporations on the Tobacco Industry.* Part 3, *Prices, Costs, and Profits.* Washington, D.C.: Government Printing Office.

U.S. Department of Commerce. 1975. *Historical Statistics of the United States: Colonial Times to 1970, Bicentennial Edition,* Part 1. Washington, D.C.: Government Printing Office.

U.S. House of Representatives. 1909. *Pulp and Paper Investigation Hearings.* 60th Cong., 2d Sess., Doc. 1502.

———. 1911. *Hearings Held before the Special Committee on the Investigation of the American Sugar Refining Co.* Washington, D.C.: Government Printing Office.

———. 1913. *Money Trust Investigation: Investigation of Financial and Monetary Conditions in the United States.* Washington, D.C.: Government Printing Office.

U.S. Industrial Commission. 1900a. *Preliminary Report on Trusts and Industrial Combinations,* vol. 1. Washington, D.C.: Government Printing Office.

———. 1900b. *Trusts and Industrial Combinations,* vol. 2. Washington, D.C.: Government Printing Office.

U.S. Industrial Commission. 1902. *Report of the Industrial Commission on Trusts and Industrial Combinations*; vol. 13. Washington, D.C.: Government Printing Office.

U.S. Interstate Commerce Commission. 1905. *Statistics of Railways of the United States, 1905*. Washington, D.C.: Government Printing Office.

Useem, Michael. 1984. *The Inner Circle*. New York: Oxford University Press.

Vandercook, John W. 1939. *King Cane: The Story of Sugar in Hawaii*. New York: Harper.

Wall, Joseph Frazier. 1989. *Andrew Carnegie*. Pittsburgh: University of Pittsburgh Press.

Ward, James A. 1975. "Power and Accountability on the Pennsylvania Railroad, 1846–1878." *Business History Review* 49:37–59.

———. 1980. J. Edgar Thomson: *Master of the Pennsylvania*. Westport, Conn.: Greenwood Press.

———. 1981. "Image and Reality: The Railway Corporate-State Metaphor." *Business History Review* 55:491–516.

Weber, Max. 1978. *Economy and Society*. Edited by Guenther Roth and Claus Wittich. Berkeley: University of California Press.

Weiss, Linda. 1988. *Creating Capitalism: The State and Small Business since 1945*. New York: Basil Blackwell.

Werner, Walter, and Steven T. Smith. 1991. *Wall Street*. New York: Columbia University Press.

White, Harrison C. 1981. "Where Do Markets Come From?" *American Journal of Sociology* 87:517–547.

Wickersham, George W. 1909. "State Control of Foreign Corporations." *Yale Law Journal* 19:1–16.

Wilkins, Mira. 1989. *The History of Foreign Investment in the United States to 1914*. Berkeley: University of California Press.

Williams, Benjamin H. 1929. *Economic Foreign Policy of the United States*. New York: McGraw-Hill.

Williamson, Jeffrey G. 1974. *Late Nineteenth Century Economic Development: A General Equilibrium History*. New York: Cambridge University Press.

Williamson, Oliver E. 1975. *Markets and Hierarchies: Analysis and Antitrust Implications*. New York: Free Press.

———. 1981. "The Modern Corporation: Origins, Evolution, Attributes." *Journal of Economic Literature* 19:1537–1568.

———. 1985. *The Economic Institutions of Capitalism: Firms, Markets, Relational Contracting*. New York: Free Press.

Zald, Mayer N. 1978. "On the Social Control of Industries." *Social Forces* 57: 79–102.

———. 1987. "History, Sociology, and Theories of Organization." University of Michigan Center for Advanced Studies in the Behavioral Sciences, Ann Arbor.

Zeitlin, Maurice. 1974. "Corporate Ownership and Control: The Large Corporation and the Capitalist Class." *American Journal of Sociology* 79:1073–1119.

———. 1980. "On Classes, Class Conflict, and the State: An Introductory Note." In *Classes, Class Conflict, and the State*, edited by Maurice Zeitlin, 1–37. Cambridge, Mass.: Winthrop.

———. 1989. *The Large Corporation and Contemporary Classes*. Cambridge: Polity.

Zerbe, Richard D. 1969. "The American Sugar Refinery Company, 1887–1914: The Story of a Monopoly." *Journal of Law and Economics* 12:339–376.

———. 1970. "Monopoly, the Emergence of Oligopoly, and the Case of Sugar Refining." *Journal of Law and Economics* 13:501–513.

Zucker, Lynne G. 1977. "The Role of Institutionalization in Cultural Persistence." *American Sociological Review* 42:726–742.

———. 1983. "Organizations as Institutions." In *Perspectives in Organizational Sociology: Theory and Research*, edited by Samuel B. Bacharach, 1–47. Greenwich, Conn.: JAI Press.

———. 1987. "Institutional Theories of Organizations." *Annual Review of Sociology* 13:443–464.

———. ed. 1988. *Institutional Patterns and Organizations: Culture and Environment*. Cambridge, Mass.: Ballinger.

Zukin, Sharon, and Paul DiMaggio, eds. 1990. *Structures of Capital: The Social Organization of the Economy*. Cambridge: Cambridge University Press.

INDEX

About the Author

WILLIAM G. ROY is Professor of Sociology
at the University of California, Los Angeles.